MULTIETHNIC EDUCATION
Theory and Practice

JAMES A. BANKS
University of Washington, Seattle

ALLYN AND BACON, INC.
Boston / London / Sydney / Toronto

To Lula, Cherry Ann, Rosie Mae, and Tessie Mae,
important women in my life,

and to Angela and Patricia

with the hope that this book
will help to make their adult world
better than ours.

Library of Congress Cataloging in Publication Data

Banks, James A
  Multiethnic education.

  Bibliography: p.
  Includes index.
  1. Minorities—Education—United States. I. Title.
LC3731.B365   371.97   80-20608
ISBN 0-205-07293-3 (Longwood)
ISBN 0-205-07300-X (College : pbk.)

Printing number and year (last digits):
10 9 8 7 6 5 4 3 2 1   85 84 83 82 81

Printed in the United States of America.

301 087

Contents

Preface

In response to the ethnic revitalization movements that emerged in the 1960s, educators in various parts of North America and the rest of the world have implemented programs and practices designed to respond more adequately to the needs of ethnic and immigrant groups, and to help these groups become more structurally integrated into their societies. These various programs and practices are characterized by myriad goals and strategies and are undergirded by diverse and often conflicting philosophical positions. Programs related to ethnic education are often conceptualized differently and are known by a variety of names, including multiracial education, multiethnic education, and multicultural education. Multicultural education is becoming the most widely used term in the United States, Canada, and Australia while multiethnic education is a popular term in Great Britain.

Despite the attempts by educators to implement sound programs in multiethnic education, there is, as in any emerging field, conceptual confusion, philosophical conflicts, and widespread disagreement about what should be the proper role of the public schools and universities in the ethnic education of students. Educators and social scientists with diverse and conflicting ideological positions are proposing a wide range of educational reforms and programs related to ethnic diversity.

This book is designed to help preservice and inservice educators to clarify the philosophical and definitional issues related to pluralistic education, to derive a clarified philosophical position, to design and implement effective teaching strategies that reflect ethnic diversity, and to derive sound guidelines for multiethnic programs and practices. This book describes actions educators can take to institutionalize educational programs and practices related to ethnic and cultural diversity.

This book is divided into six parts. Part I discusses the historical development of multiethnic education and its goals, problems, and promises. The philosophical and conceptual issues related to multiethnic education are discussed in Part II. Chapter 3 presents a typology for classifying ethnic groups which focuses on the complex nature of ethnic groups in modern American society. Chapters 4, 5, and 6 explore the conceptual and philosophical issues in multiethnic education. Part III focuses on the nature of ethnic studies, suggests needed reforms in the teaching of ethnic content, and presents a unit that constitutes a model for teaching ethnic content, decision making, and social action skills.

The unique learning styles, behavioral characteristics, and needs of ethnic students are discussed in Part IV. Many ethnic students come to school with learning characteristics and behaviors that conflict with those of the school. Consequently, they experience cultural conflict in the classroom. The chapters in Part IV present descriptions and guidelines designed to help educators work with ethnic students more successfully. Many ethnic students enter school speaking dialects and languages that differ from the Anglo-English favored by the school and the wider society. The number of such students within the nation's schools has increased dramatically in recent years as immigrants from a number of nations have come to the United States to improve their social, economic, and political plights. The special needs of these students are discussed in chapter 11, a chapter contributed by Professor Ricardo L. Garcia.

Part V discusses some of the important and continuing issues in multiethnic education. The policy and research implications of divergent concepts, teacher characteristics, the problems and promises of linking multiethnic and global education, and ethnicity and citizenship education are the enduring issues and problems considered in Part V. Part VI, the final section of this book, presents a rationale for ethnic pluralism and related guidelines that educators can use to design and implement curricula and programs related to cultural and ethnic diversity.

This book contains three appendices. Appendix A consists of an annotated bibliography of books educators can use to increase their knowledge and insights on issues related to ethnicity, race, culture, and education. A course inventory constitutes Appendix B. This inventory can help teachers at all levels to assess and improve the multiethnic components of their courses. Evaluation guidelines for multicultural–multiracial education are presented in Appendix C.

This book is designed for use as a text in courses in multiethnic education, ethnic studies, and multicultural education. It can also be successfully used as a supplementary text in general and specialized methods, curriculum, and foundations courses.

J. A. B.

Acknowledgements

I wish to thank Cherry A. Banks for stimulating and supporting my intellectual growth during the last decade, for thoughtful and helpful reactions to the chapters in this book, and for ably preparing the index. My daughters, Angela and Patricia, have taught me a great deal about how young children learn concepts in race relations and have consequently influenced my teaching, research, and writing.

I wish to thank my colleagues in the Area of Curriculum and Instruction, College of Education, University of Washington, for creating an atmosphere which fosters intellectual growth and dialogue. I am particularly grateful to the following colleagues for the stimulating conversations I have had with them over the years about issues related to race, ethnicity, and schooling: Willard Bill, Phillip C. Gonzales, Nancy Hansen-Krening, John Jarolimek, Juan Juarez, Samuel E. Kelly, James K. Morishima, and James A. Vasquez. I also wish to thank the present and former students at the University of Washington who have taken my graduate seminar on ethnicity and schooling. They have stimulated and fostered my intellectual growth. Many of the ideas and conceptualizations in this book were first presented to students in my graduate seminar. I would also like to thank Phillip C. Gonzales, Juan Juarez, and Christine C. Schaefer, colleagues at the University of Washington, for helping me compile the bibliography which constitutes Appendix A. I am especially grateful to Ricardo L. Garcia for preparing chapter 11.

I would like to thank the individals who prepared prepublication reviews of the manuscript. Phillip C. Gonzales reviewed chapter 11 and Eleanor Blumenberg, Carlos E. Cortés, and Geneva Gay prepared comments on chapter 15. The following individuals reviewed large parts of the manuscript at various stages of manuscript development: Terry W. Blue, Philip T. K. Daniels, Kopple C. Friedman, Ricardo L. Garcia, Albert Grande, Francis P. Hunkins, and Terrence N. Tice. While these reviews were insightful and helpful, I assume total responsibility for the contents of this book.

In writing this book, I incorporated some of my previously published papers. I am grateful to the National Academy of Education for a Spencer Fellowship which helped support my research from 1973 to 1976, and to the Univeristy of Washington for granting me a sabbatical leave during the 1976–77 academic year which enabled me to pursue my research full-time.

I would like to thank the following organizations, publishers, and individuals for permitting me to draw freely from the publications noted that I authored: Phi Delta Kappa, Inc., for *Multiethnic Education: Practices and Promises.* Bloomington, Indiana: Phi Delta Kappa Educational Foundation, 1977; and "A Response to Philip Freedman," *Phi Delta Kappan,* Vol. 58 (May, 1977), pp. 695–697. The National Council for the Social Studies for "Should Integration Be A Societal Goal in A Pluralistic Nation?" in Raymond H. Muessig, editor, *Controversial Issues in the Social Studies.* Washington, D.C.: National Council for the Social Studies, 1975, pp. 197–228; "Ethnic Studies as a Process of Curriculum Reform," *Social Education,* Vol. 40 (February, 1976), pp. 76–80; (with Carlos E. Cortés, Geneva Gay, Ricardo L. Garcia, and Anna S. Ochoa), *Curriculum Guidelines for Multiethnic Education.* Washington, D.C.: National Council for the Social Studies, 1976. *Integrated Education* for "Cultural Pluralism: Implications for Contemporary Schools," *Integrated Education* (January–February, 1976), Vol. 15, pp. 32–36. Academic Press, Inc., and Geneva Gay for (with Geneva Gay), "Ethnicity in Contemporary American Society," *Ethnicity,* Vol. 5 (September, 1978), pp. 238–251. Howard University Press for "Shaping the Future of Multicultural Education," *Journal of Negro Education,* Vol. 48 (Summer, 1979), pp. 237–252. College of Education, University of Georgia, for "Developing Cross-Cultural Competency in the Social Studies," *Journal of Research and Development in Education,* Vol. 13 (Winter, 1980), pp. 113–122. Heldref Publications for "Pluralism, Ideology and Curriculum Reform," *The Social Studies,* Vol. 67 (May–June, 1976), pp. 99–106; and "Ethnicity: Implications for Curriculum Reform," *The Social Studies,* Vol. 70 (January–February, 1979), pp. 3–10. The Association for Supervision and Curriculum Development for "Curricular Models for an Open Society," in Delmo Della-Dora and James E. House, eds., *Education for An Open Society.* Washington, D.C.: Association for Supervision and Curriculum Development, 1974, pp. 43–63; and "The Emerging Stages of Ethnicity: Implications for Staff Development," *Educational Leadership,* Vol. 34 (December, 1976), pp. 190–193. The American Association of Colleges For Teacher Education for "The Implications of Multicultural Education for Teacher Education," in Frank H. Klassen and Donna M. Gollnick, eds., *Pluralism and the American Teacher.* Washington, D.C.: American Association of Colleges for Teacher Education, 1977, pp. 1–30. Addison-Wesley Publishing Company for a figure from my book (with contributions by Ambrose A. Clegg, Jr.), *Teaching Strategies for the Social Studies,* Second Edition. Reading, Mass.: Addison-Wesley, 1977, pages 29 and 32.

I am grateful to the United States Office of Education, Department of Health, Education and Welfare, for a grant (made to the National Council for the Social Studies) which supported the development of chapters 16 and 17. However, the opinions expressed in these chapters do not necessarily reflect the position of the United States Office of Education, and no official endorsement by the United States Office of Education should be inferred. I wish to thank the Mershon Center, Ohio State University, for supporting the development of chapter 15, an earlier version of which was presented at the Center's Conference, "A Symposium on Citizenship and Education in Modern Society."

PART I

Multiethnic Education: Historical Development, Goals, and Practices

Introduction

Chapter 1 is a review of some of the major historical events related to ethnicity in American society since the turn of the century. It describes the development of educational reform movements related to pluralism within an historical context. The intergroup education movement of the 1940s and 1950s is also described and examined, and hypotheses that attempt to explain why the reforms related to this movement failed to become institutionalized on a significant scale are presented.

In chapter 1, the emergence of multiethnic-multicultural education is placed within an historical context. In chapter 2 the development of multiethnic-multicultural education in the 1960s and 1970s is described. The nature of multiethnic education, its goals, problems, and current practices are also discussed, as are the promises of multiethnic education. Multiethnic education is viewed as a process of curriculum reform that has the potential for spearheading change in the total educational environment.

1

The Historical Development of Multiethnic Education

The Rise of Nativism

Most of the European immigrants that came to North America before 1890 were from nations in Northern and Western Europe, such as Great Britain, Germany, Scandinavia, and Switzerland. Although conflicts developed between these various immigrant groups, the English were dominating social, economic, and political life in North America by the 1700s. As the twentieth century approached and new waves of immigrants began to arrive in the United States from Southern, Central, and Eastern Europe, the immigrants from Northern and Western Europe began to perceive themselves as the "old" immigrants and rightful inhabitants of America. They saw the new immigrants as a threat to American civilization and to the American democratic tradition. Sharp and often inaccurate distinctions were made between the "new" and "old" immigrants. A movement called nativism rose to stop the flood of "new" immigrants that was arriving in America.[1] The nativists pointed out that the new immigrants were primarily Catholics while the old immigrants were mainly Protestants. A strong element of anti-Catholicism became an integral part of the nativistic movement.

Because of their Catholicism, cultural differences, and competition for jobs with the "old" immigrants and native-born Americans, the new immigrants became the victims of blatant nativism. A suspicion and distrust of all foreigners became widespread near the turn of the century. The outbreak of the Great War in Europe in 1914 greatly increased the suspicion and distrust of immigrant groups in the United States and further stimulated nativistic feelings and groups. Nativism swept through the United States during the Great War. Nativists argued for one hundred percent Americanism and said that America should be for "Americans." The new immigrant groups tried desperately but unsuccessfully to prove their national loyalty to the nativists.

Nativism and Education

The public schools, colleges, and universities usually perpetuate the dominant ideologies and values that are promoted and embraced by the powerful groups within society.[2] Reflecting the prevailing goals of the nation as articulated by its powerful political and economic leaders, the schools and colleges promoted and embraced Americanization, blind loyalty to the nation, and showed a distrust of "foreigners" and immigrant groups during the turn of the century and World War I periods. The teaching of German and other foreign languages was prohibited in many schools. German books in school libraries were sometimes burned. Some schools prohibited the playing of music by German composers in music classes and in school assemblies.[3] In this atmosphere of virulent nativism, government sponsored propaganda, and emphasis on blind patriotism and Americanization, the idea of cultural pluralism in eduction would have been alien and perhaps viewed as seditious and un-American.

The Melting Pot

The assimilationist ideology that was pervasive near the turn of the century and during World War I was embodied and expressed in the play, *The Melting Pot.* This play, written by the English–Jewish author Israel Zangwill, opened in New York City in 1908. It became a tremendous success. The great ambition of the play's composer-protagonist, David Quixano, was to create an American symphony that would personify his deep conviction that his adopted land was a nation in which all ethnic differences would mix and from this a new person, superior to all, would emerge. What in fact happened, however, was that most of the immigrant and ethnic cultures stuck to the bottom of the mythical melting pot. Anglo-Saxon culture became dominant; other ethnic groups had to give up many of their cultural characteristics in order to fully participate in the nation's social, economic, and political institutions.[4]

However, as will be pointed out in chapter 6, cultural influence was not in one direction. Although the Anglo-Saxon Protestant culture became and remained dominant in the United States, other ethnic groups, such as the Germans, the Irish, Indians and Blacks, influenced the Anglo-Saxon culture as the Anglo-Saxon culture influenced the culture of these groups. However, the Anglo-Saxon Protestant culture has had the most cogent influence on American culture.[5] This influence has been in many cases positive. The American ideals of human rights, participatory democracy, and separation of church and state are largely Anglo-Saxon contributions to American civilization.

The American school, like other American institutions, embraced Anglo-conformity goals. One of its major goals was to rid ethnic groups of their ethnic traits and to force them to acquire Anglo-Saxon values and behavior. In 1909 Ellwood Patterson Cubberley, the famed educational leader, clearly stated a major goal of the common schools:

Everywhere these people [immigrants] tend to settle in groups or settlements, and to set up here their national manners, customs, and observances. Our task is to break up these groups or settlements, to assimilate
and amalgamate these people as part of our American race, and to implant
in their children, as far as can be done, the Anglo-Saxon conception of
righteousness, law and order, and popular government, and to awaken in
them a reverence for our democratic institutions and for those things in our
national life which we as a people hold to be of abiding worth.[6]

The Call for Cultural Pluralism

In the early years of the twentieth century, a few philosophers and writers,
such as Horace Kallen, Randolph Bourne, and Julius Drachsler, strongly
defended the rights of the immigrants living in the United States.[7] They
rejected the assimilationist argument made by leaders such as Cubberley.
They argued that a political democracy must also be a cultural democracy
and that the thousands of Southern, Eastern, and Central European immigrant groups had a right to maintain their ethnic cultures and institutions
in American society. They used a "salad bowl" argument, maintaining
that each ethnic culture would play a unique role in American society but
would also contribute to the total society. They argued that ethnic cultures
would enrich American civilization. They called their position *cultural pluralism,* and said that it should be used to guide public and educational policies.

The arguments of the cultural pluralists were a cry in the wilderness.
They fell largely on deaf ears. Most of America's political, business, and
educational leaders continued to push for the assimilation of the immigrant and indigenous racial and ethnic groups. They felt that only in this
way could they make a unified nation out of so many different ethnic
groups with histories of wars and hostilities in Europe. The triumph of the
assimilationist forces in American life were symbolized by the Immigration
Acts of 1917 and 1924.

The Immigration Act of 1917, designed to halt the immigration of
Southern, Central, and Eastern European groups, such as Poles, Greeks,
and Italians, required immigrants to pass a reading test to enter the United
States. When this act passed but failed to reduce the number of immigrants
from these nations enough to please the nativists, they pushed for and suc-
ceeded in getting another act passed, the Immigration Act of 1924. This act
drastically limited the number of immigrants that could enter the United
States from all European nations except those in Northern and Western
Europe. It ended the era of massive European immigration to the United
States and closed a significant chapter in American history.

Ethnic Education between the Two World Wars

Mainstream American leaders and educators generally ignored the voices advocating pluralistic policies in the early years of the twentieth century. However, because of the tremendous value and cultural diversity within the United States, rarely is there concensus within our society on any important social or educational issue. Consequently, while those who dominated educational policy usually embraced the assimilationist ideology and devoted little time and energy to the education of the nation's ethnic minority groups, other American leaders, researchers, and educators engaged in important discussions about the education of the nation's ethnic minorities, formulated educational policy related to ethnic groups, and did important research on American ethnic communities.[8] Ironically, however, often the policy formulated by those deeply concerned about the education of ethnic minorities was assimilationist oriented. This indicated the extent to which the assimilationist ideology had permeated American life and thought. However, there were always a few educational leaders who advocated pluralism.

Policies and programs in ethnic education did not suddenly arise during the ethnic revitalization movements of the 1960s and 1970s. These developments have gradually evolved over a long period. It is true, however, that they have intensified in various historical periods, usually because of heightened racial consciousness and concern stimulated by events such as racial conflicts and tensions. The evolutionary character of ethnic education in the United States will be illustrated by a brief discussion of the educational policies related to American Indians, Black Americans, and Mexican Americans between the two great world wars. The education of other ethnic groups, such as Jewish Americans, Italian Americans, and Puerto Rican Americans, could also be used to illustrate the evolutionary nature of ethnic education. However, the choice of these three ethnic groups can in part be justified by the fact that educational policy and programs related to them have stimulated enduring and controversial discussions and programs for most of the present century.

American-Indian Education

The ways in which American Indians should be educated has evoked a continuing debate since the late 1800s.[9] Since the 1920s, educational policy for American Indians has vacillated between strong assimilationism to self-determination and cultural pluralism. The landmark Meriam Report, issued in 1928, recommended massive reforms in American Indian education.[10] The Report recommended that Indian education be tied more closely to the community, the building of day schools in the community, the reformation of boarding schools, and that the curriculum in Indian schools be changed to reflect Indian cultures and the needs of local Indian communities.[11] The 1969 Senate Report on Indian Education, called the Kennedy Report, stated that many of the reforms recommended by the Meriam Report had not been attained.[12]

Black-American Education

Developments in the education of Black Americans were both active and controversial in the decades between the war years. Carter G. Woodson, a Black historian who received a doctorate from Harvard in 1912, did seminal research and work on Black histsory and Black education. Woodson founded the Association for the Study of Negro Life and History in 1915.[13] This organization was founded to sponsor and encourage research in Black history and to disseminate this research to scholars and teachers in Black schools and colleges. The Association started two important publications that are still published: the *Journal of Negro History* and *The Negro History Bulletin*. Woodson began Negro History Week in 1926 to commemorate milestones in Black history.

Black educational policy became very controversial within the Black community. Booker T. Washington and William E. B. DuBois set forth sharply contrastsing views about directions for Black education. Washington, a former slave and the most influential Black leader of his times, believed that Black students needed a practical, industrial education.[14] He implemented his ideas at the Tuskegee Institute in Tuskegee, Alabama. DuBois, the noted Black scholar and educational philosopher, felt that a "talented tenth" should be educated for leadership in the Black community. The "talented tenth," he argued, should study the classics, political philosophy, and other academic subjects.[15]

Mexican-American Education

During the 1930s and 1940s, considerable attention was focused on the education of Mexican-Americans by scholars and educators concerned with their educational plight. Most educators during this period, according to Carter and Segura, saw the school as an agency for the acculturation of Mexican-American students.[16] Betty Gould, for example, recommended what she considered effective methods for the acculturation of Mexican-American students in her 1932 thesis, "Methods of Teaching Mexicans."[17] Carter and Segura described Mexican-American education during the 1930s:

School programs for Chicano children during the 1930s emphasized vocational training and manual-arts training; learning of English; health and hygiene; and adoption of American core values such as cleanliness, thrift and punctuality. Segregation, especially in the early grades, was regularly recommended and commonly established. It was inexplicably argued that Americanization could best be accomplished by keeping foreigners out of contact with Americans.[18]

The voices speaking for the education of Mexican-Americans during the 1930s and 1940s, however, were not unanimous. George I. Sánchez, a pioneer Mexican-American educator and scholar, urged educators to consider the unique cultural and linguistic characteristics of Mexican-American students when planning and implementing educational programs for them.[19]

The Intergroup-Education Movement

Social, political, and economic changes caused by World War II stimulated a curriculum movement related to cultural and ethnic diversity which became known as intercultural education or intergroup education. World War II created many job opportunities in northern cities. Many Blacks and Whites left the South during the war years in search of jobs. More than 150,000 Blacks left the South each year in the decade between 1940 and 1950 and settled in northern cities. In northern cities such as Chicago and Detroit conflict developed between Blacks and Whites as they competed for jobs and housing. Racial conflict also occurred in the Far West. Mexican Americans and Anglos clashed in serious "zoot-suit" riots in Los Angeles during the summer of 1943. These racial conflicts and tensions severely strained race relations in the nation.

Racial tension and conflict were pervasive in northern cities during the war years. In 1943, race riots took place in Los Angeles, Detroit, and in the Harlem district of New York City. The most destructive riot during the war broke out in Detroit on a Sunday morning in June, 1943. More southern migrants had settled in Detroit during this period than in any other American city. The Detroit riot raged for more than thirty hours. When it finally ended, thirty-four persons were dead and property worth millions of dollars had been destroyed.[20] The Detroit riot stunned the nation and stimulated national action by concerned Black and White citizens. As written by Taba et al:

Dramatic riots in Detroit, Beaumont, Texas, and other places aroused nervous apprehensions about unity, and caused many American communities to act. There was a mushroom growth of organizations aimed at improving intergroup relations, such as civic unity councils, and mayors' and governors' committees for human relations. By the end of 1944, more than four hundred such councils and committees were reported, of which about three hundred had been organized after the Detroit riot.[21]

A major goal of intergroup education was to reduce racial and ethnic prejudice and misunderstandings.[22] Activities designed to reduce prejudice and to increase interracial understanding included the teaching of isolated instructional units on various minority groups, exhortations against prejudice, organizing assemblies and cultural get-togethers, disseminating information on racial, ethnic, and religious backgrounds, and banning books considered stereotypic and demeaning to ethnic groups. A major assumption of the intergroup-education movement was that factual knowledge would develop respect and acceptance of various ethnic and racial groups. Unlike the ethnic-studies movement of the late 1960s, however, the emphasis in the intercultural-education movement of the 1940s and 1950s was not on strong cultural pluralism or on maintaining or perpetuating strong ethnic loyalties. Nathan Glazer writes:

> One suspects that to advocates of intercultural education the picture of a decent America consisted of one in which Americans of whatever origin were really very much alike, and were not discriminated against for their origins, religion, or vestigial cultural differences. Certainly there was no notion that it was the task of the public schools to present or preserve a full-bodied version of ethnic cultures. It was enough to teach tolerance of whatever existed.[23]

An ambitious project during the period of intercultural education was the "Intergroup Education in Cooperating Schools" project supported by grants from the Educational Commission of the National Conference of Christians and Jews and sponsored by the American Council on Education.[24] Hilda Taba was the project's director. The project began in January, 1945 and continued through August, 1948.

The Teacher-Education Project

The "Intergroup Education in Cooperating Schools" project was designed to effect changes in elementary and secondary schools. The American Council on Education also sponsored a project to implement intergroup education in teacher education institutions. This project, called the "College Study in Intergroup Relations," was directed by Professor Lloyd Allen Cook of Wayne State University. The College Study was one of the "first cooperative efforts in the United States to improve teacher education in respect to intergroup relations."[25] One of the sponsors of the College Study was the Council on Cooperation in Teacher Education. Among the members of this Council were the American Association of Colleges for Teacher Education, the Association for Supervision and Curriculum Development, and the Department of Classroom Teachers of the National Education Association. The College Study had the endorsement of the leading professional educational associations.

Colleges and universities with teacher-education programs were eligible to apply for participation in the College Study Intergroup Relations Program. Twenty-four colleges were chosen to participate in the program during its four year duration (from 1945 to 1949). In selecting colleges for participation in the project, the project staff tried to select a representative sample of all teacher-training institutions, based on such criteria as geographical location, size, type of affiliation, and ethnic composition. Table 1.1 shows the colleges and universities that participated in the project and the years in which they participated.

Each of the twenty-four colleges that participated in the College Study developed a program in intergroup education in cooperation with the College Study staff. These projects varied greatly in focus, groups emphasized, and in the kinds of experiences undertaken. Adapting a required course, using folklore in intergroup education, attitude testing, intercollege exchanges and visits, planned experiences in community work, developing a philosophy of intergroup education, and independent faculty research are examples of the myriad projects and activities implemented within the twenty-four colleges that participated in the College Study.[26] Cook classified the diverse projects into six major categories, which he called "approaches to behavioral change":

1. *The intellectual approach.* Assumptions that facts alter values, ideas shape perceptions and lead to conduct changes. Example, the academic lecture and text-oriented course.

2. *The vicarious-experience approach.* An indirect approach, as in the use of movies, plays, and current fiction, where a prejudiced individual presumably takes the role of the out-group member, living his life, experiencing his world.

3. *The community study-action approach.* Participant-observer experiences in concrete life processes, for example, case studies of children, home visitation, field trips, social agency work, community-action groups, area studies.

4. *Exhibits, festivals, and pageants.* Campus or community display of Old World or other heritages, minority-group customs and contributions. Aim is to create in-group self-respect and out-group acceptance, that is, intergroup unity.

5. *Small-group process approach.* Use of the group as an instrument for the education of its members. Example, classroom-activity program, sociodrama, group-decision technique, community audit, any form of action research.

6. *Individual-conference approach.* Advice on personal problems, especially on value conflicts. Directive and nondirective therapy, individual case work, and referral.[27]

Table 1.1. Colleges in the College Study, 1945-49.*

College or University	Year of Participation*				Total Years of Participation*			
	1945	1946	1947	1948	1 Yr.	2 Yrs.	3 Yrs.	4 Yrs.
Atlanta University				✓	✓			
Arizona State College, Tempe		✓			✓			
Central Michigan College of Education, Mt. Pleasant		✓			✓			
Central Missouri State College, Warrensburg				✓	✓			
City College, New York City		✓	✓	✓			✓	
Colorado State College of Education, Greeley		✓	✓	✓			✓	
University of Denver				✓	✓			
Lynchburg College, Virginia		✓	✓	✓			✓	
Marshall College, Huntington, W.Va.	✓	✓				✓		
New Jersey State Teachers College, Trenton	✓	✓	✓	✓				✓
New York State College for Teachers, Albany	✓	✓				✓		
Ohio State University, Columbus	✓	✓				✓		
Roosevelt College, Chicago		✓	✓			✓		
San Francisco State Teachers College		✓		✓		✓		
Southwest Texas State Teachers College, San Marcos		✓			✓			
Springfield College, Massachusetts		✓			✓			
State Teachers College, Eau Claire, Wis.	✓	✓				✓		
State Teachers College, Milwaukee, Wis.		✓			✓			
Moorhead State Teachers College, Minnesota		✓	✓			✓		
Talladega College, Alabama		✓	✓			✓		
University of Florida, Gainesville		✓	✓			✓		
University of Pittsburgh	✓	✓				✓		
Wayne University, Detroit, Mich.	✓	✓	✓	✓				✓
West Virginia State College, Institute	✓	✓	✓	✓				✓
Total	8	21	10	10	8	10	3	3

Source: Reprinted with permission from Lloyd Allen Cook, Editor, *College Programs in Intergroup Relations* Washington, D.C.: The American Council on Education, 1950, p. 7.

* Does not include the eight colleges continuing in the Study, after one or more years of active participation, on a "limited service" basis.

The Intergroup-Education Movement Ends

The intergroup-education movement and its related reforms failed to become institutionalized within most American schools, colleges, and teacher-training institutions. This statement should not be interpreted to mean that the movement did not benefit our society and educational institutions. Cook has noted the tremendous impact that the College Study projects had on the individuals who participated in them. The action and research projects that were undertaken in the College Study contributed to our practical and theoretical knowledge about race relations and about intervention efforts that are designed to influence attitudes and behavior.[28] The basic idea of the College Study was a sound one that merits replication: teacher-training institutions formed a consortium to develop action and research projects to effect change.

It is also true that many individual teachers and professors, and probably many individual schools and teacher training institutions, continued some elements of the reforms related to intergroup education after the national movement faded. However, by the 1960s when racial tension intensified in the nation and race riots sprang up again, few American schools and teacher-education institutions had programs and curricula that dealt adequately with the study of racial and ethnic relations. However, most all-Black schools and colleges were teaching Black Studies and were in other ways responding to many of the unique cultural characteristics of Black students.

As we consider ways to institutionalize reforms related to multiethnic education, it is instructive to consider why the reforms related to intergroup education failed to become institutionalized in most American schools and colleges. The reforms related to the movement failed to become institutionalized, in part, for the following reasons:

1. The ideology and major assumptions on which intergroup education was based were never internalized by mainstream American educators.
2. Mainstream educators never understood how the intergroup education movement contributed to the major goals of the American common schools.
3. Most American educators saw intergroup education as a reform project for schools that had open racial conflict and tension and not for what they considered their smoothly functioning and nonproblematic schools.
4. Racial tension in the cities took more subtle forms in the 1950s. Consequently, most American educators no longer saw the need for action designed to reduce racial conflict and problems.
5. Intergroup education remained on the periphery of mainstream edu-

cational thought and developments and was funded primarily by special funds. Consequently, when the special funds and projects ended, the movement largely faded.

6. The leaders of the intergroup-education movement never developed a well articulated and coherent philosophical position that revealed how the intergroup-education movement was consistent with the major goals of the American common schools and with American Creed values.

Assimilationism Continues and Helps to Shape a Nation

Despite the intergroup-education reforms of the 1940s and 1950s, assimilationist forces and policies dominated American life from about the turn of the century to the beginning of the 1960s. The assimilationist ideology was not seriously challenged during this long period, even though there were a few individuals, such as Marcus Garvey in the 1920s, who championed separatism and ethnic pluralism.[29] These lone voices were successfully ignored or silenced.

Most minority as well as dominant group leaders saw the assimilation of America's ethnic groups as the proper societal goal. Social scientists and reformers during this period were heavily influenced by the writings of Robert E. Park, the eminent American sociologist who had once worked as an informal secretary for Booker T. Washington.[30] Park believed that race relations proceeded through four inevitable stages: *contact, conflict, accommodation,* and *assimilation.*[31] The most reform-oriented social scientists and social activists embraced assimilation as both desirable and inevitable within a democratic pluralistic nation such as the United States.

The American assimilationist policy shaped a nation from millions of immigrants and from diverse American Indian groups. The United States did not become an ethnically balkanized nation. This could have happened. The assimilationist idea also worked reasonably well for ethnic peoples who are White. However, it did force many of them to become *marginal* individuals and to deny family and heritage. This should not be taken lightly, for denying one's basic group identity is a very painful and psychologically unsettling process. However, most, but not all, White ethnic groups have been able, in time, to climb up the economic and social ladders.

The New Pluralism

The assimilationist idea has not worked nearly as well for ethnic peoples of color. This is what Blacks realized by the early 1960s. The unfulfilled promises and dreams of the assimilationist idea was a major cause of the Black civil rights movement of the 1960s. By the late 1950s and early 1960s, the combined forces of discrimination in such areas as employment, housing and education, and rising expectations, caused Afro-Americans to lead an unprecedented fight for their rights which became known as the Black civil rights revolution.

Many Blacks who had become highly assimilated Afro-Saxons were still unable to fully participate in many mainstream American institutions. Blacks were still denied many opportunities because of their skin color. They searched for a new ideal; many endorsed some form of "cultural pluralism." An idea born during the turn of the century was refashioned to fit the hopes, aspirations, and dreams of disillusioned ethnic peoples in the 1960s.

Blacks demanded more control over the institutions in their communities and that all institutions, including the schools, more accurately reflect their ethnic cultures. They demanded more Black teachers and administrators for their youths, textbooks that reflected Black culture, and cafeteria foods more like those their children ate at home.[32]

Educational institutions, at all levels, began to respond to the Black revolt. The apparent success of the Black revolt caused other alienated ethnic groups of color, such as Mexican Americans, Asian Americans, and Puerto Ricans to make similar demands for political, economic, and educational change.

Mexican-American studies and Asian-American studies courses that paralleled Black studies courses emerged.[33] The reform movements initiated by the ethnic peoples of color caused many White ethnic groups that had denied their ethnic cultures in the past to proclaim ethnic pride and to push for the inclusion of more information about White ethnic groups in the curriculum. This movement became known as the "new pluralism." Judith Herman writes,

> [It] has been described as reactive, as "me to," and essentially opportunistic and false. For some, it may have been. But for many, especially the new generation of ethnic leaders, it was a real response. It was in part a sense that the requirement for success in America seemed to be an estrangement from family and history; that for all its rhetoric about pluralism, America didn't mean for ethnicity to go beyond the boundaries of food, a few statues or parades honoring heroes, of colorful costumes and dances.[34]

In a sense, the Black civil rights movement legitimized ethnicity and other alienated ethnic groups began to search for their ethnic roots and to demand more group and human rights.

Summary

A large wave of immigrants from Southern, Central, and Eastern Europe entered the United States between 1890 and 1917. The Europeans that already lived in the United States during this period were primarily from Northern and Western Europe. Because of their cultural differences, Catholicism, and competition for jobs with native-born Americans, a nativistic movement arose to halt the immigration of the "new" immigrants. Nativism became widespread throughout the United States and influenced the nation's institutions, including the schools. The outbreak of World War I in Europe greatly increased nativistic expressions within the larger society and the schools. The schools tried to make the immigrants one-hundred percent Americans and to exclude all elements of "foreignness" from the curriculum.

A few philosophers and writers, such as Horace Kallen, Randolph Bourne, and Julius Drachsler, defended the rights of the immigrants and stated that cultural democracy should exist in a democratic nation such as the United States. The arguments of these writers, however, influenced few American leaders.

Most institutions within American society, including the schools, remained assimilationist oriented between World Wars I and II, and devoted little serious attention to the educational needs and problems of ethnic minority groups. However, a number of American educational and scholarly leaders formulated policy and programs for educating ethnic minorities during this period. The educational developments in Amercian-Indian, Afro-American, and Mexican-American education between the two wars illustrate the evolutionary nature of ethnic education in the United States.

The intergroup-education movement grew out of the social developments that emerged in response to World War II. Conflict and riots developed in American cities as Blacks and Whites and Anglos and Chicanos competed for housing and jobs. The intergroup-education movement tried to reduce interracial tensions and to further intercultural understandings. Developments in intergroup education took place at the elementary, secondary, and college level. The intergroup-education movement, itself only mildly pluralistic, did not seriously challenge the assimilationist ideology in American life. When the ethnic revitalization movements of the 1960s and 1970s and related educational-reform movements emerged, the intergroup-education movement had largely faded.

Notes

1. John Higham, *Strangers in the Land: Patterns of American Nativism 1860–1925* (New York: Atheneum, 1972).
2. Michael B. Katz, *Class, Bureaucracy, and Schools: The Illusion of Educational*

Change in America, expanded edition (New York: Praeger Publishers, 1975).

3. Wayne Moquin, ed., *Makers of America: Hypenated Americans, 1914–1924,* volume 7, (Chicago: Encyclopaedia Britannica Educational Corporation, 1971), p. 107.

4. Maldwyn Allen Jones, *American Immigration* (Chicago: University of Chicago Press, 1960).

5. Edward C. Stewart, *American Cultural Patterns: A Cross-Cultural Perspective* (LaGrange Park, Ill.: Intercultural Network, Inc., 1972).

6. Ellwood P. Cubberley, *Changing Conceptions of Education* (Boston: Houghton Mifflin, 1909), pp. 15–16.

7. Horace M. Kallen, *Culture and Democracy in the United States* (New York: Boni and Liveright, 1924); Randolph S. Bourne, "Trans-National America," *The Atlantic Monthly* 118 (July 1916); Julius Drachsler, *Democracy and Assimilation* (New York: Macmillan, 1920).

8. See Meyer Weinberg, *A Chance To Learn: A History of Race and Education in the United States* (New York: Cambridge University Press, 1977).

9. Estelle Fuchs and Robert J. Havighurst, *To Live on This Earth: American Indian Education* (Garden City, N.Y.: Doubleday, 1973).

10. Lewis Meriam, ed., *The Problem of Indian Administration* (Baltimore: Johns Hopkins University Press, 1928).

11. Margaret Szasz, *Education and The American Indian: The Road to Self-Determination, 1928–1973* (Albuquerque: University of New Mexico Press, 1974).

12. *Indian Education: A National Tragedy-A National Challenge.* 91st Congress, 1st Session, Report of the Committee on Labor and Public Welfare, Special Subcommittee on Indian Education, U.S. Senate. (Washington, D.C.: U.S. Government Printing Office, 1969).

13. See, for example, Carter G. Woodson and Charles H. Wesley, *The Negro in Our History* (Washington, D.C.: The Associated Publishers 1922); and Carter G. Woodson, *Mis-Education of the Negro* (Washington, D.C.: The Associated Publishers, 1933).

14. See Booker T. Washington, *Up From Slavery: An Autobiography* (New York: Doubleday and Company, 1901); and Louis R. Harlan, *Booker T. Washington: The Making of A Black Leader, 1856–1901* (New York: Oxford University Press, 1972).

15. W.E.B. DuBois, *The Souls of Black Folk* (New York: Fawcett Publications, Inc., 1961). (Published originally in 1903.)

16. Thomas P. Carter and Roberto D. Segura, *Mexican Americans in School: A Decade of Change* (New York: College Entrance Examination Board, 1979).

17. Betty Gould, "Methods of Teaching Mexicans" (Master's thesis, University of Southern California, 1932).

18. Carter and Segura, *Mexican Americans in School,* p. 17.

19. George I. Sánchez, *Forgotten People* (Albuquerque: The University of

New Mexico Press, 1940); George I. Sánchez, ed., *First Regional Conference on the Education of Spanish-Speaking People in the Southwest. Inter-American Education Occasional Papers,* no 1 (Austin: The University of Texas Press, March, 1946).

20. James A. Banks and Cherry A. Banks, *March Toward Freedom: A History of Black Americans,* rev. 2nd ed. (Belmont, Cal.: Fearon-Pitman Publishers, Inc., 1978), p. 103.
21. Hilda Taba, Elizabeth Hall Brady, and John T. Robinson, *Intergroup Education in Public Schools* (Washington, D.C.: American Council on Education, 1952), p. 15.
22. In my description of intergroup education, I have relied heavily on Taba et al. *Intergroup Education in Public Schools.*
23. Nathan Glazer, "Public Education and American Pluralism" in James S. Coleman et al, *Parents, Teachers and Children: Prospects for Choice in American Education* (San Francisco: Institute for Contemporary Studies, 1977), p. 89.
24. In addition to the book by Taba et al. cited above, other books in the intergroup education series include: Lloyd Allen Cook, *Intergroup Relations in Teacher Education* (Washington, D.C.: American Council on Education, 1951); and Hilda Taba et al., *Elementary Curriculum in Intergroup Relations* (Washington, D.C.: American Council on Education, 1950).
25. Lloyd Allen Cook, ed. *College Programs in Intergroup Relations* (Washington, D.C.: American Council on Education, 1950), p. viii.
26. Ibid.
27. Ibid, p. 15. Used with the publisher's permission.
28. Lloyd Allen Cook, "Intergroup Education," *Review of Educational Research* 17 (1947):266–278.
29. John Henrik Clarke, ed., with the assistance of Amy Jacques Garvey, *Marcus Garvey and the Vision of Africa* (New York: Vintage Books, 1974).
30. "Robert Ezra Park 1864–1944," in Lewis A. Coser, *Masters of Sociological Thought,* 2nd ed. (New York: Harcourt Brace, 1977), pp. 357–384.
31. Stanford M. Lyman, *The Black American in Sociological Thought: A Failure of Perspective* (New York: Capricorn Books, 1972), p. 27.
32. Stokely Carmichael and Charles V. Hamilton, *Black Power: The Politics of Liberation in America* (New York: Vintage, 1967).
33. John H. Burma, ed., *Mexican-Americans in the United States: A Reader* (Cambridge, Mass.: Schenkman Publishing Company, 1970); Emma Gee et al, ed., *Counterpoint: Perspective on Asian America* (Los Angeles: Asian American Studies Center, University of California,1976).
34. Judith Herman, *The Schools and Group Identity: Educating for a New Pluralism* (New York: American Jewish Committee, Institute on Pluralism and Group Identity, 1974), p. 15.

2

Multiethnic Education:
Nature, Goals, and Practices

The Emergence of Multiethnic/Multicultural Education

The emergence of multiethnic and multicultural education (chapter 4 discusses how these concepts differ) is a gradual and evolutionary process. When the Black protest movement began in the mid-1960s (signaled by the riot in the Watts district of Los Angeles in 1965), Blacks demanded that the schools and other institutions respond more adequately to their needs and aspirations. They called for more Black teachers for Black youths, community control of Black schools, and the rewriting of textbooks to make them more accurately reflect their history and culture in the United States. They also demanded Black studies courses.

Phase I: Monoethnic Courses

In time, other ethnic groups, such as Mexican Americans and American Indians, made demands on schools and colleges similar to those made by Blacks. These institutions responded by establishing courses on specific ethnic groups such as Black history, Black literature, Chicano history, and Chicano literature. This phase in the development of multiethnic/multicultural education may be considered Phase I. It was characterized by monoethnic courses, the assumption that only a member of an ethnic group should teach a course on that group, and a focus on White racism and how Whites have oppressed non-White minorities. A pervasive assumption made during Phase I ethnic studies courses was that Black studies were needed only by Black students and that Asian-American studies were needed only by Asian-American students.

Phase II: Multiethnic Studies Courses

As more and more ethnic groups, including White ethnic groups such as Jewish Americans and Polish Americans, began to demand separate courses and the inclusion of their histories and cultures in the curriculum, schools and colleges began to offer multiethnic studies courses which focus on several ethnic cultures and which view the experiences of ethnic groups from comparative perspectives. Courses such as "Ethnic Minority Music" and "The History and Culture of Minorities in the United States" are taught from comparative perspectives.

We may call the multiethnic studies phase of the development of multi-ethnic/multicultural education Phase II. Ethnic studies courses became more global, conceptual, and scholarly during this period. They also became less politically oriented and began to explore diverse points of view and interpretations of the experiences of ethnic groups in the United States. The recognition emerged and grew that ethnic studies should be designed for all students, and not just for students who were members of particular ethnic groups. A basic assumption of multiethnic studies courses is that ethnic groups have had both similar and different experiences in the United States and that a comparative study of ethnic cultures can result in useful concepts, generalizations, and theories.

Phase III: Multiethnic Education

As ethnic studies became more global and widespread, more and more educators began to recognize that reforming the course of study in schools and colleges was necessary but not sufficient to result in effective educational reform. The negative attitudes of many teachers made their use of new ethnic materials and teaching strategies ineffective and in some cases harmful. Educators also began to recognize that ethnic studies courses alone could not enable students such as Afro-Americans, Chicanos, and American Indians to achieve at levels comparable with the achievement levels of most Anglo-American students.

Research emerged that indicated how minority students are often placed in low academic tracts because of middle-class and Anglo-biased I.Q. tests,[1] and how students who speak a first language other than standard Anglo-American English often fail to achieve in school, in part, because of their language differences.[2] Studies that documented the affects of teacher attitudes on student achievement, attitudes, and behavior were published.[3] Research also revealed the negative attitudes and interactions that teachers often have with minority and low-income students.[4]

These recognitions and studies convinced many educators involved in minority education that ethnic studies courses and materials, no matter how soundly conceptualized and taught, could not by themselves bring about the kind of substantial educational reform that is needed to enable students from diverse racial and ethnic groups to experience educational equality. In other words, educators began to realize that ethnic studies were necessary but not sufficient to bring about effective educational reform and equity. Educators began to call for a more broadly conceptualized kind of educational reform, with a focus on the total school environment. Multiethnic education specialists view the total school as the unit of change, and not any one variable within the educational environment, such as materials or teaching strategies. This more broadly conceptualized reform movement became known as multiethnic education, which emerged as Phase III in the development of pluralistic education.

Phase IV: Multicultural Education

Some educators, such as Gwendolyn C. Baker, Carl A. Grant, and H. Prentice Baptiste, became interested in an educational reform movement that would deal not only with the educational problems of ethnic minority groups but with the educational problems of cultural groups such as women, handicapped persons, religious groups, and regional groups such as Appalachian Whites.[5] This broader reform movement is known as multicultural education, which is Stage IV of the development of pluralistic education.

Multicultural education is becoming increasingly popular within educational institutions, in part because the concept enables school districts and universities to pool limited resources to focus on a wide range of groups rather than limit their focus to racial and ethnic minorities. The *Standards* published by the National Council for Accreditation of Teacher Education require teacher education institutions to implement components, courses, and programs in multicultural education.[6]

Many educators support the multicultural education concept but are concerned that the focus of the movement may become so broad and global that the issues of *racism* and *racial discrimination,* important concerns of pluralistic education in the 1960s when it emerged, might become lost or deemphasized. Another problem with multicultural education is that the boundaries of the field are so broad that it is often difficult to determine which cultural groups are the primary focus or concern of multicultural educators.

Although multicultural education is becoming increasingly popular, a number of educators, such as Barbara A. Sizemore, Ricardo L. Garcia, Geneva Gay, and Wilma Longstreet, focus their research and curriculum work on ethnic minority groups.[7] The work of these educators is, of course, an integral part of multicultural education. An ethnic group is one important kind of cultural group in the United States (see chapter 4). Most specialists in multicultural education include ethnic minority groups within their defined boundaries.

A Caveat

Because of the historical and evolutionary way in which Phases I through IV of multiethnic-multicultural education is discussed above, the reader may understandably conclude that when Phase II emerged Phase I disappeared. This is not what in fact has happened or is happening. As illustrated in Figure 2.1, when Phase II emerged, Phase I continued, although perhaps in modified form and on a more limited scale. The earlier phases also begin to take on some of the characteristics of the newly emerging phases. Phase I types of ethnic studies courses became more conceptual and scholarly when Phase II of multiethnic-multicultural education began to emerge. The assumption also grew that an academically qualified individual, regardless of his or her ethnic group membership, could effectively teach an ethnic studies course on any ethnic group.

Phase V: Institutionalization

I am conceptualizing Phase V of the development of multiethnic-multicultural education as the institutionalization of the key and most effective components of Phases I through IV. Phase V is a *process* that is slowly occurring. Elements of multiethnic-multicultural education are beginning to permeate the curriculum and the total educational environment. However, this process is far too slow and limited. Strategies need to be designed that will increase the pace and scope of the institutionalization of multiethnic-multicultural education within the nation's schools and colleges. Figure 2.2 summarizes the historical development of multiethnic-multicultural education as discussed in this and the previous chapter.

The Goals of Multiethnic Education

Multiethnic education is a reform movement designed to make some major changes in the education of children and youths. Advocates of multiethnic education believe that many school practices related to race and ethnicity are harmful to students and reinforce many of the ethnic stereotypes and discriminatory practices in American society.

Multiethnic education assumes that ethnicity is a salient part of American life and culture. It also assumes that ethnic diversity is a positive element in a society because it enriches a nation and increases the ways in which its citizens can perceive and solve personal and public problems. Ethnic diversity also enriches a society because it provides individuals with more opportunities to experience other cultures and thus to become more fulfilled as human beings. When individuals are able to participate in a va-

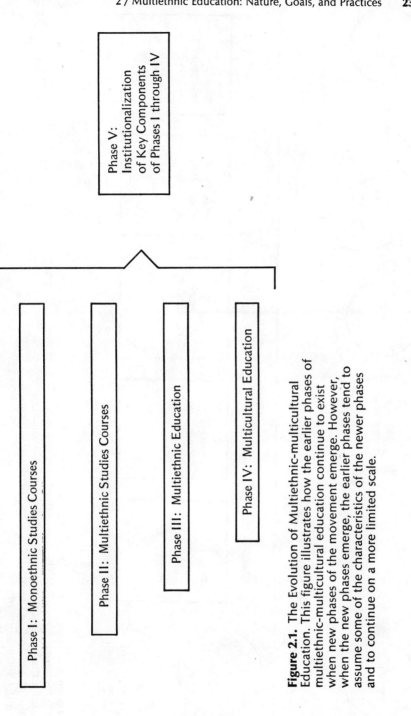

Figure 2.1. The Evolution of Multiethnic–multicultural Education. This figure illustrates how the earlier phases of multiethnic–multicultural education continue to exist when new phases of the movement emerge. However, when the new phases emerge, the earlier phases tend to assume some of the characteristics of the newer phases and to continue on a more limited scale.

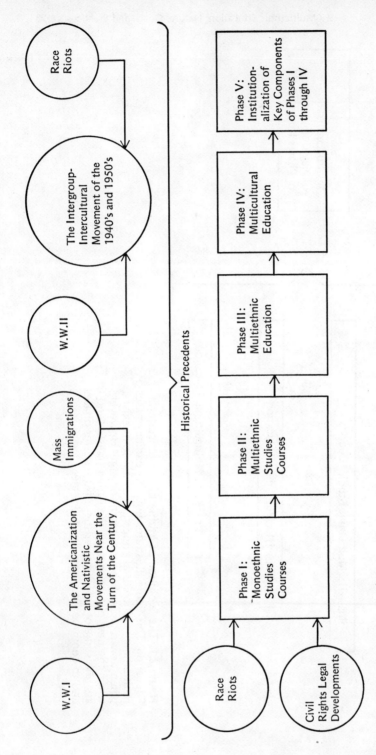

Figure 2.2. The Historical Development of Multiethnic-Multicultural Education. This figure illustrates the societal and historical forces that resulted in the development of the reforms related to multiethnic-multicultural education in the 1960s and 1970s.

riety of ethnic cultures, they are more able to benefit from the total human experience.

Individuals who only know, participate in, and see the world from their unique cultural and ethnic perspectives are denied important parts of the human experience and are culturally and ethnically encapsulated. Edwin Kiester, Jr., in *The Shortchanged Children of Suburbia*, tells an anecdote about an economically and culturally encapsulated child:

> The story is told about a little girl in a school near Hollywood who was asked to write a composition about a poor family. The essay began: "This family was very poor. The Mommy was poor. The Daddy was poor. The brothers and sisters were poor. The maid was poor. The nurse was poor. The butler was poor. The cook was poor. And the chauffeur was poor. . . ."[8]

Culturally and ethnically encapsulated individuals are also unable to fully know and to see their own cultures because of their cultural and ethnic blinders. We can get a full view of our own cultures and behaviors only by viewing them from the perspectives of other racial and ethnic cultures. Just as a fish is unable to appreciate the uniqueness of his aquatic environment, so are many Anglo-American children unable to fully see and appreciate the uniqueness of their cultural characteristics. A key goal of multiethnic education is to help individuals gain greater self-understanding by viewing themselves from the perspectives of other cultures.

Multiethnic education attempts to acquaint each ethnic group with the unique cultures of other ethnic groups. It also tries to help ethnic group members to see that other ethnic cultures are just as meaningful and valid as their own. Multiethnic education assumes that with acquaintance and understanding, respect may follow.

Another major goal of multiethnic education is to provide students with cultural and ethnic alternatives. Both the Anglo-American child and the Filipino-American child should be provided with cultural and ethnic options in the school. Historically, the school curriculum has focused primarily on the culture of the Anglo-American child. The school was, and often is, primarily an extension of the Anglo-American child's home and community culture and did not present the child with cultural and ethnic alternatives.

The Anglo-Centric curriculum, which still exists to varying degrees in most of the nation's schools, has harmful consequences for both Anglo-American children and ethnic minorities such as Afro-Americans and Mexican Americans. By teaching the Anglo-American child only about his or her own culture, the school is denying him or her the richness of the music, literature, values, life styles, and perspectives that exist among ethnic groups such as Blacks, Puerto Ricans in the United States, and Asian Americans. Anglo-American children should know that Black literature is uniquely enriching, and that groups such as American Indians and Mexican Americans have values which they may freely embrace. Many of the behaviors and values within these ethnic groups may help Anglo-American students to enrich their personal and public lives.

The Anglo-Centric curriculum negatively affects the ethnic child of color because he or she may find the school culture alien, hostile, and self-defeating. Most ethnic minority communities are characterized by some values, institutions, behavior patterns, and linguistic traits that differ in significant ways from those within the dominant society and in the schools.[9] Because of the negative ways in which ethnic students and their cultures are often viewed by educators, many of them do not attain the skills they need to function successfully within the wider society.

One of the major goals of multiethnic education is to provide all students with the skills, attitudes, and knowledge they need to function within their ethnic culture, the mainstream culture, as well as within and across other ethnic cultures. The Anglo-American child should be familiar with Black English; the Afro-American child should be able to speak and write standard English and to function successfully within Anglo-American institutions.

Another major goal of multiethnic education is to reduce the pain and discrimination members of some ethnic and racial groups experience in the schools and in the wider society because of their unique racial, physical, and cultural characteristics. Groups such as Filipino Americans, Mexican Americans, Puerto Ricans, and Chinese Americans often deny their ethnic identity, ethnic heritage, and family in order to assimilate and to participate more fully in America's social, economic, and political institutions. Individuals who are Jewish Americans, Polish Americans, and Italian Americans also frequently reject parts of their ethnic cultures when trying to succeed in school and in society. As Mildred Dickeman has insightfully pointed out, schools often force members of these groups to experience "self-alienation" in order to succeed.[10] This is a high price to pay for educational, social, and economic mobility.

When individuals are forced to reject parts of their racial and ethnic cultures in order to experience success, problems are created for both individuals and society. Ethnic peoples of color, such as Afro-Americans and Mexican Americans, experience special problems because no matter how hard they try to become like Anglo-Americans (the idealized ethnic group in the United States) most of them cannot totally succeed because of their skin color.

Some Blacks become very Anglo-Saxon in speech, ways of viewing the world, and in their values and behavior. These individuals become so Anglicized that we might call them "Afro-Saxons." However, such individuals may still be denied jobs or the opportunities to buy homes in all-White neighborhoods because of their skin color. They may also become alienated from their own ethnic communities and families in their attempts to act and be like White Anglo-Americans. These individuals may thus become alienated from both their ethnic cultures and the mainstream Anglo culture. Social scientists call such individuals "marginal" persons.

Individuals who belong to such groups as Jewish Americans and Italian Americans may also experience "marginality" when they attempt to deny their ethnic heritages and to become Anglo-Americans. Although they can usually succeed in looking and in acting like Anglo-Americans, they are likely to experience a great deal of psychological stress and identity conflict when they deny and reject family and their ethnic languages, symbols, behaviors, and beliefs. Ethnicity plays a cogent role in the socialization of ethnic group members; ethnic characteristics are a part of the basic identity of many individuals. When such individuals deny their ethnic cultures, they are rejecting an important part of self.

Marginal ethnic group members are likely to be alienated citizens who feel that they don't have a stake in society. Individuals who deny and/or reject their basic group identity, for whatever reasons, are not capable of becoming fully functioning and self-actualized persons. Such individuals are more likely than other citizens to experience political and social alienation. It is in the best interest of a political democracy to protect the rights of all citizens to maintain allegiances to their ethnic groups.[11] Research has demonstrated that individuals are quite capable of maintaining allegiance both to their ethnic group and to the nation state. Emerging social science research also indicates that individuals have a need for basic group identities, even in highly modernized societies.[12]

Another important goal of multiethnic education is to help students master essential reading, writing, and computational skills. Multiethnic education assumes that multiethnic content can help students to master important skills in these areas. Multiethnic readings and data, if taught effectively, can be highly motivating and meaningful. Students are more likely to master skills when the teacher uses content that deals with significant human problems, such as ethnicity within our society. Students are also more likely to master skills when they study content and problems related to the world in which they live. All American children live in a society where ethnic problems are real and salient. Many students live within highly ethnic communities. Content related to ethnicity in American society and to the ethnic communities in which many students live is significant and meaningful to students, especially to those who are socialized within ethnic communities. Advocates of multiethnic education believe that skill goals are extremely important.

Cross-cultural Competency

A key goal of multiethnic-multicultural education is to help students develop cross-cultural competency.[13] However, those of us working in the areas of multiethnic/multicultural education have not clarified, in any adequate way, the minimal level of cross cultural competency we consider appropriate and/or satisfactory for teacher education students or for students in the common schools. Nor have we developed valid and reliable ways to assess levels of cross-cultural competency. I think we know what questions to raise about cross-cultural functioning. However, we need to devote considerable time and intellectual energy to resolving these questions.

Is the Anglo-American student, for example, who eats a weekly meal at an authentic Mexican-American restaurant, and who has no other cross-ethnic contacts during the week, functioning cross-culturally? Most of us would probably agree that the act of eating at an ethnic restaurant, in and of itself, is not an instance of meaningful cross-cultural behavior. However, if the Anglo-American student, while eating at the Mexican-American restaurant, understands and shares the ethnic symbols in the restaurant, speaks Spanish while in the restaurant, and communicates and interacts positively and comfortably with individuals within the restaurant who are culturally Mexican-American, then he or she would be functioning cross-culturally at a meaningful level.

Levels of Cross-Cultural Functioning

We need to develop a typology that conceptualizes levels of cross-cultural functioning. We also need to determine which of these levels are desirable and practical for most of our teacher education and common school students to attain. In this chapter, I will present the skeletal outline of such a typology (see Figure 2.3).

Level I of cross-cultural functioning consists primarily of superficial and brief cross-cultural encounters, such as eating occasionally at a Chinese-American restaurant or speaking to the Jewish neighbor who lives across the street when you meet her in the street. Level II of cross-cultural functioning occurs when the individual begins to have more meaningful cross-cultural contacts and communications with members of other ethnic and cultural groups. He or she begins to assimilate some of the symbols, linguistic traits, communication styles, values, and attitudes that are normative within the "outside" cultural group. Level III of cross-cultural functioning occurs when the individual is thoroughly bicultural and is as comfortable within the adopted culture as he or she is within his or her primordial or first culture. Each of the two cultures is equally meaningful to the bicultural individual. The bicultural individual is bilingual and is adept at cultural-switching behavior. Level IV of cross-cultural functioning occurs when the primordial individual has been almost completely resocialized and assimilated into the "foreign" or host culture. This process occurs, for example, when the Afro-American individual becomes so highly culturally assimilated (in terms of behavior, attitudes and perceptions) into

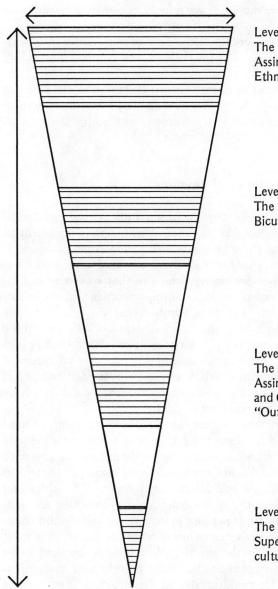

Level IV:
The Individual Is Completely
Assimilated into the New
Ethnic Culture

Level III:
The Individual Is Thoroughly
Bicultural

Level II:
The Individual Begins to
Assimilate Some of the Symbols
and Characteristics of the
"Outside" Ethnic Group

Level I:
The Individual Experiences
Superficial and Brief Cross-
cultural Interactions

Figure 2.3. Levels of Cross-cultural Functioning. This figure presents a conceptualization of levels of cross-cultural
competency. Cross-cultural functioning can range from
Level I (brief and superficial contacts with another ethnic
culture) to Level IV (in which the individual totally culturally assimilates into a new ethnic culture and consequently becomes alienated from his or her own ethnic
culture).

the Anglo-American culture that he or she is for all sociological purposes an "Afro-Saxon."

I think that most of us working in the field of multiethnic/multicultural education do not see Level I or Level IV of cross-cultural functioning as desirable goals of multiethnic education. Most of us would probably opt for Level II or Level III or some point between these two levels. I should quickly point out that this typology of levels is an ideal-type conceptualization in the Weberian sense and that continua exist both between and within the levels.

Multiethnic Education: Nature and Promises

Multiethnic education reaches far beyond ethnic studies or the social studies. It is concerned with modifying the total educational environment so that it is more reflective of the ethnic diversity within American society. This includes not only the study of ethnic cultures and experiences but making institutional changes within the school so that students from diverse ethnic groups have equal educational opportunities and the school promotes and encourages the concept of ethnic diversity.

Multiethnic education is designed for all students, of all races, ethnic groups, and social classes, and not just for schools that have racially and ethnically mixed populations. A major assumption made by advocates of multiethnic education is that multiethnic education is needed as much if not more by the Anglo-American, middle-class, suburban child as it is by the Mexican-American child who lives in the barrio.

Since multiethnic education is a very broad concept that implies total school reform, educators who want their schools to become multiethnic must examine their total school environment to determine the extent to which it is monoethnic and Anglo-Centric, and take appropriate steps to create and sustain a multiethnic educational environment. The ethnic and racial composition of the school staff, its attitudes, the formalized and hidden curricula, the teaching strategies and materials, the testing and counseling program, and the school's norms are some of the factors that must reflect ethnic diversity within the multiethnic school. These and other variables of the school environment that must be reformed in order to make the school multiethnic are illustrated in Figure 2.4.

The reform must be system-wide to be effective. While any one of the factors in Figure 2.4 may be the initial focus for school reform, changes must take place in all of the major school variables in order for multiethnic education to be successfully implemented. We learned from the ethnic studies movement of the 1960s that few substantial changes take place when you simply give teachers multiethnic materials but do not train them to use them or help them to acquire new conceptual frameworks for viewing American society and culture.

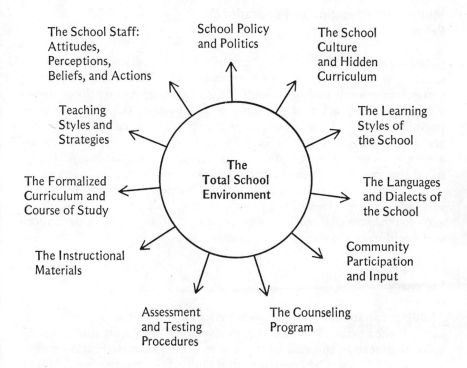

The School Staff: Attitudes, Perceptions, Beliefs, and Actions

School Policy and Politics

The School Culture and Hidden Curriculum

Teaching Styles and Strategies

The Learning Styles of the School

The Total School Environment

The Formalized Curriculum and Course of Study

The Languages and Dialects of the School

The Instructional Materials

Community Participation and Input

Assessment and Testing Procedures

The Counseling Program

Figure 2.4. The Total School Environment. In this figure, the total school environment is conceptualized as a system that consists of a number of major identifiable variables and factors, such as the school culture, school policy and politics, and the formalized curriculum and course of study. In the idealized multiethnic school, each of these variables reflects ethnic pluralism. While any one factor may be the focus of initial school reform, changes must take place in each factor to create and sustain an effective multiethnic educational environment.

The total school environment must be the unit of change, and not any one element, such as materials, teaching strategies, the testing program, or teacher training. While teacher training is very important, other changes must take place in the school environment in order to reform the school. Many teachers attain new insights, materials, and multiethnic teaching strategies during summer workshops. They are eager to try them in their schools. However, they become very discouraged when they return to their schools in the fall where traditional norms toward ethnic diversity often exist and where they frequently get no support from their administrators or peers. Without such support, teachers with new skills and insights give up and revert back to their old behaviors and attitudes.

Multiethnic Education and Educational Reform

Changing the school so that it reflects the ethnic diversity within American society provides a tremendous opportunity to implement the substantial curriculum reforms that are essential, such as conceptual teaching, interdisciplinary approaches to the study of social issues, value inquiry, and providing students with opportunities to become involved in social action and social participation activities. Thus, multiethnic education can serve as a vehicle for general and significant educational reform. This is probably its greatest promise. We can best view multiethnic education as a process as well as a reform movement that will result in a new type of schooling that will present novel views of the American experience and help students to acquire the knowledge, skills, and commitments needed to make our nation and world more responsive to the human condition.

Summary

Multiethnic-multicultural education has had an evolutionary development in the United States. The most recent developments in multiethnic/multicultural education emerged in response to the ethnic revitalization movements of the 1960s. The development of multiethnic/multicultural education since the 1960s can be conceptualized in five phases: (I) *monoethnic courses*—which emerged in response to the demands made by specific ethnic groups for inclusion of their cultures and histories in the curriculum; (II) *multiethnic courses*—which resulted when schools and colleges tried to integrate and relate the teaching of the histories and cultures of diverse ethnic groups; (III) *multiethnic education*—which emerged when educators working in ethnic studies realized that the total school environment, and not just the curriculum, needed to be reformed in order to increase educational opportunities for ethnic youths; (IV) *multicultural education*—an educational reform movement that is concerned with increasing educational equity for a range of cultural and ethnic groups; and (V) the *institutionalization of key components of Phases I through IV* of the development of multiethnic/multicultural education. Institutionalization of these reforms is very slowly taking place within the nation's schools, colleges, and universities.

Major goals of multiethnic education include: (1) helping students gain a greater self-understanding by viewing their cultures from the perspectives of other ethnic groups; (2) providing students with cultural and ethnic alternatives; (3) helping students attain cross-cultural competency, which consists of the skills, attitudes, and knowledge needed to function within their own ethnic culture, the mainstream American culture, as well as within and across other ethnic cultures; (4) helping to reduce the pain and discrimination that members of some ethnic groups experience in the schools and the wider society because of their unique racial and ethnic characteristics; and (5) helping students master essential reading, writing, and computational skills.

Helping students to develop cross-cultural competency is one of the most important goals of multiethnic education. However, we need new conceptualizations of cross-cultural functioning in order to identify objectives and to measure outcomes in cross-cultural education. The typology of cross-cultural functioning presented in this chapter conceptualizes four levels of cross-cultural behavior: *Level I*—The individual participates in superficial and brief cross-cultural interactions; *Level II*—The individual begins to assimilate some of the symbols of the "outside" ethnic group; *Level III*—The individual is thoroughly bicultural; and *Level IV*—The individual is completely assimilated into the new ethnic culture. The curriculum should help students to develop the attitudes, skills, and abilities needed to function between Levels II and III. Neither Level I nor Level IV is a desirable goal for cross-cultural education within a democratic pluralistic nation such as the United States.

Multiethnic education includes but is much more comprehensive than ethnic studies or curriculum reform related to ethnicity (see Part III). Multiethnic education is concerned with modifying the total school environment so that students from all ethnic groups will experience equal educational opportunities. Because it is a very global concept, educators must reform their total educational environments in order to implement multiethnic education.

Notes

1. Jane R. Mercer, "Latent Functions of Intelligence Testing in the Public Schools," in Lamar P. Miller, ed., *The Testing of Black Students* (Englewood Cliffs, N.J.: Prentice-Hall, 1974), pp. 77–94.
2. United States Commission on Civil Rights, *A Better Chance to Learn: Bilingual-Bicultural Education* (Washington, D.C.: The Commission, 1975).
3. Ray C. Rist, "Student Social Class and Teacher Expectations: The Self-Fulfilling Prophecy in Ghetto Education," *Harvard Educational Review* 40 (August 1970), pp. 411–451; Judith Kleinfeld, "Effective Teachers of Eskimo and Indian Students," *School Review* 83 (February 1975), pp. 301–344; United States Commission on Civil Rights, *Teachers and Students: Differences in Teacher Interaction with Mexican American and Anglo-Students; Report V: Mexican American Study* (Washington, D.C.: The Commission, 1973).
4. Ibid.
5. Gwendolyn C. Baker, "The Role of the School in Transmitting the Culture of All Learners in A Free and Democratic Society," *Educational Leadership* 36 (November 1978), p. 135; Carl A. Grant, Editor, *Multicul-*

tural Education: Commitments, Issues, and Applications (Washington, D.C.: Association for Supervision and Curriculum Development, 1977); H. Prentice Baptiste, Jr., *Multicultural Education: A Synopsis* (Houston, Tex.: University of Houston, College of Education, 1976).

6. *Standards for the Accreditation of Teacher Education* (Washington, D.C: National Council for the Accreditation of Teacher Education, 1977).

7. Barbara A. Sizemore, "PUSH Politics and the Education of American's Youth," *Phi Delta Kappan* 61 (January 1979), pp. 364–369; Ricardo L. Garcia, *Learning in Two Languages* (Bloomington, Ind.: Phi Delta Kappa Educational Foundation, 1976); Geneva Gay, "Curriculum for Multicultural Teacher Education," in Frank H. Klassen and Donna M. Gollnick, eds., *Pluralism and the American Teacher: Issues and Case Studies* (Washington, D.C.: American Association of Colleges for Teacher Education, 1977), pp. 31–62; Wilma S. Longstreet, *Aspects of Ethnicity: Understanding Differences in Pluralistic Classrooms* (New York: Teachers College Press, 1978).

8. Alice Miel with Edwin Kiester,Jr., *The Shortchanged Children of Suburbia* (New York: American Jewish Committee, 1967), p. 5.

9. Geneva Gay, "Viewing the Pluralistic Classroom as a Cultural Microcosm," *Educational Reasearch Quarterly* 2 (Winter 1978), pp. 45–49; Manuel Ramirez III and Alfredo Castañeda, *Cultural Democracy, Bicognitive Development and Education* (New York: Academic Press, 1974); John U. Ogbu, *Minority Education and Caste: The American System in Cross-Cultural Perspective* (New York: Academic Press, 1978).

10. Mildred Dickeman, "Teaching Cultural Pluralism," in James A. Banks, ed., *Teaching Ethnic Studies: Concepts and Strategies* (Washington, D.C.: National Council for the Social Studies, 1973), pp. 5–25.

11. David E. Apter, "Political Life and Cultural Pluralism," in Melvin M. Tumin and Walter Plotch, eds., *Pluralism in a Democratic Society* (New York: Praeger Publishers, 1977), pp. 58–91.

12. Harold R. Isaacs, "Basic Group Identity: The Idols of the Tribe," in Nathan Glazer and Daniel P. Moynihan, eds., *Ethnicity: Theory and Experience* (Cambridge, Mass.: Harvard University Press, 1975), pp. 29–52.

13. For a typology of cross-cultural awareness in international settings see Robert G. Hanvey, *An Attainable Global Perspective* (New York: Center for War/Peace Studies, undated), pp. 10–11.

PART II
Conceptual and Philosophical Issues in Multiethnic Education

Introduction

Multiethnic and multicultural education are characterized by much conceptual confusion and a wide range of competing ideologies regarding the role educational institutions should play in the ethnic education of students. Concepts such as ethnic group, ethnicity, multiethnic education, and multicultural education are often used by educators to convey diverse and often conflicting meanings and policies. Ideologies endorsed by educators range from strong assimilationism to ethnic separatism. The chapters in Part II are designed to identify and clarify the major conceptual and ideological issues related to ethnicity , assimilation, and pluralism in American society.

In chapter 3, there is a discussion of the nature of ethnicity in contemporary American society. Earlier conceptualizations about the nature of ethnic groups in American life are inadequate to explain many of the characteristics of ethnic groups that have emerged since the ethnic revitalization movements of the 1960s and 1970s. A typology for the study of ethnic groups is presented that emphasizes their multidimensional and complex nature in modern American society. In chapter 4, the boundaries for the major concepts related to multiethnic and multicultural education are discussed and delineated. Chapter 5 presents a typology for classifying ideologies related to ethnicity and schooling and proposes a new ideology to guide curriculum reform in the nation's schools, colleges, and universities.

In chapter 6 the reasons why Anglo-conformity, the melting pot, and cultural pluralism are misleading and/or incomplete concepts when used to analyze and study the nature of ethnicity in contemporary American society are examined. Structural pluralism and multiple acculturation are described as the most adequate concepts to describe ethnic group life in the United States today. The multiethnic ideology, which is introduced in chapter 5, is derived from these two concepts.

3

The Nature of Ethnicity
in American Society

The civil rights movement of the 1960s and the rise of the "new ethnicity" among White ethnic groups in more recent years have stimulated a great deal of interest and discussion in the nature of ethnicity and pluralism in contemporary American life. Most of the concepts, generalizations, and theories related to race and ethnicity that are currently in use were formulated prior to the Black protest movement of the 1960s and the rise of the "new ethnicity ."[1] Consequently, many of these concepts, generalizations and theories are inadequate for understanding ethnicity in contemporary American society. The characteristics of ethnic groups in the United States have changed substantially since the seminal theories of assimilation were developed by sociologists such as Louis Wirth and Robert E. Park.[2] In this chapter, we attempt to delineate some of the basic characteristics of ethnic groups in contemporary American society and to formulate a typology for defining and classifying ethnic groups that is more consistent with the current characteristics of ethnic groups than many existing definitions of ethnicity.

Ethnicity in American Society

Ethnicity is a cogent factor in American history, life, and culture. The expressions and manifestations of ethnicity vary with the characteristics of the ethnic group, the nature of its societal experiences, and the sociopolitical climate. Expressions of ethnicity are also related to the ways in which the dominant group responds to various immigrant and immigrant descendent groups, to the objectives that ethnic groups wish to achieve, and to the new events that serve as the catalysts for revitalization movements.[3]

Individuals and groups in the United States have often been denied cultural, political, and economic opportunities because of their ethnic group characteristics and their expressions of them. By the beginning of the 1800s, Anglo-Saxon immigrants and their descendents were the most powerful and influential ethnic group in America. English cultural traits,

I co-authored this chapter with Geneva Gay, Associate Professor of Education, Purdue University.

values, and behavioral patterns were widespread in colonial America. The English were also strongly committed to "Americanizing" (Anglicizing) all other immigrant groups, as well as to "civilizing" (according to the Anglo-Saxon definition of civilization) Blacks and various groups of American Indians.

Through the control of the major social, economic, and political institutions, the English denied to ethnic groups who differed from themselves opportunities to fully participate in the decision-making processes. Only those peoples who were culturally and racially like Anglo-Saxons received unqualified rights to total societal participation and social acceptance. Thus groups such as the French Huguenots, the Germans, the Irish, and the Scotch Irish were victims of much discrimination in colonial America. Southern and Eastern European immigrants, such as the Greeks, the Italians, the Slavs, and the Poles, who came to the United States in massive numbers in the late nineteenth century and the first decades of the twentieth century, were denied total societal participation.[4] Both the original English and the converted Anglo-Saxons saw these new arrivals as ethnically different from themselves, and thus undeserving of social acceptance and access to the social, economic, and political systems.[5]

The Assimilation and Inclusion of White Ethnic Groups

Early in America's history assimilation, or adherence to Anglo-Saxon sociocultural traditions and values, became a prerequisite to social acceptability and access to the political structure. Although in the beginning European immigrants tried desperately to establish and maintain European life-styles and institutions on American soil,[6] their efforts were largely doomed from the beginning because the English controlled the economic and political systems. The English used their power to perpetuate Anglo-Saxon institutions and culture, and to discourage the continuation of life-styles and value systems that were non-Anglo-Saxon. Non-English European immigrants were faced with the decision of either assimilation and inclusion into mainstream society or nonassimilation and exclusion from total participation in the social, economic, and political systems. They chose assimilation for a variety of reasons.[7] The immigrants who came from Northern and Western Europe came closest to a complete realization of the goal of total cultural assimilation because they were most like Anglo-Saxons physically and culturally.

The first generation of Southern, Central, and Eastern European immigrants also tried desperately to conform to society's demands for assimilation and integration. However, the process was not as easy or as successful to them as it had been for their Northern and Western predecessors. Undoubtedly, the degree to which they were physically, culturally, and psychologically unlike Anglo-Saxons partially accounted for their lower level of cultural and structural assimilation.[8] These factors may also partially explain the current resurgence of ethnicity among second and third generation White ethnics in the United States, such as the Poles, Czechs, Slovaks, and Greeks, and their push for the inclusion of their cultural heritages in school ethnic studies programs. This interest has become so widespread that many advocates of ethnicity, in the last several years, have begun to use that concept almost exclusively to refer to White ethnic groups.[9] Novak writes, "the new ethnicity . . . is a movement of self-knowledge on the part of members of third and fourth generations of Southern and Eastern European immigrants to the United States."[10]

The Assimilation and Exclusion of Non-White Ethnic Groups

Non-European, non-White ethnic groups, such as Afro-Americans, Chinese Americans, and Mexican Americans, faced a much more serious problem than Southern and Eastern European immigrants. While society demanded that they assimilate culturally in order to integrate socially, politically, and economically, it was very difficult for them to assimilate because of their skin color. Even when Blacks, Mexican Americans and American Indians succeeded in becoming culturally assimilated, they were still structurally isolated, and were denied full, unqualified entry into the organizations and institutions sanctioned by the larger society. They became, in effect, marginal persons, for they were not accepted totally either by their own ethnic group or by the mainstream culture. Their denial of their ethnic cultures made them unacceptable to members of their ethnic communities, while the majority culture denied them full membership because they were non-White. While the societal goal for European immigrants, especially those from Northern and Western Europe, was cultural assimilation and structural inclusion, the goal for non-Whites and non-European immigrants was cultural assimilation and structural exclusion.[11]

Thus, early in America's historical development Anglo-Saxon values and cultural norms were institutionalized as "American norms" and as "acceptable standards of behavior." They were perpetuated and transmitted through the socialization and enculturation of subsequent generations of Anglo-Saxon European immigrants. Anglo-Saxon customs and values were also perpetuated through the acculturation, but structural exclusion of nonwhite, non-European immigrant groups.

The latter goal was achieved through institutionalizing Anglo-Saxon customs and laws that demanded conformity by non-Whites to Anglo-Saxon behavioral patterns, but denied them entry into the social, political, and economic systems. The result, for many of these "colored peoples," such as Blacks and American Indians, was the loss of important aspects of their primordial cultures. The Anglo-Saxons sought to insure their dominance and power over these groups by stigmatizing their primordial cultures and institutions. Thus, when Africans arrived in America, the dominant group ridiculed their languages and punished them for practicing their African customs. Mexican Americans were not allowed to speak Spanish in the schools, even though the Treaty of Guadalupe Hidalgo guaranteed them the right to maintain and to perpetuate their language and culture.[12] Texas even passed laws that declared Mexican Americans to be Whites. In the 1800s, after most American Indians had been forced from their lands, subjugated to federal controls, and relegated to living on reservations, American policy makers began an aggressive campaign to "Americanize" the Indians.[13]

Distinctive Ethnic Traits in American Society

Undoubtedly, many immigrant groups lost much of the flavor of their original ethnic heritages through the evolutionary processes of assimilation, acculturation, adaptation, and cultural borrowing. Some groups (principally Northern and Western European immigrants, and to a lesser extent Southern, Central, and Eastern European immigrants) voluntarily gave up large portions of their ethnic cultures and became Anglo-Saxonized in return for the privilege of societal participation. Others were forced to abandon their original cultural heritages. The structural exclusion to which non-White, non-European immigrants and American Indian groups were subjected resulted in the perpetuation of distinctive ethnic traits and the development of unique cultural institutions and traditions.[14] The cultures of these ethnic minorities differed in degrees from the dominant culture because these groups created values, languages, life-styles, and symbols that they needed in order to survive the oppression, exclusion, and dehumanization to which they were subjected. These cultural traits were institutionalized and transmitted through the generations.

To some extent these cultural components are legacies from the original homelands of non-White ethnic groups, modified to accommodate the circumstances of living in America; to some extent they are new creations designed to meet the needs of particular ethnic groups. The cultural institutions and processes that were created clearly reflect the interactions between original cultural perspectives and the realities of American society. The various ethnic groups developed somewaht different cultural values because their ancestral homes, cultural perspectives, and experiences in America were different. The new cultures that emerged undoubtedly have some remnants from the original motherlands, but not necessarily in their original forms. Rather, the need to adapt to new surroundings and the effects of cultural sharing gave rise to new cultural forms.

The Black church, Black survival strategies, Black language, and Black civil rights organizations have some African cultural components, although these institutions, without question, were created by Africans in the Americas. They represent aspects of Black cultural life that were created to meet the unique social, economic, and political needs of Blacks. Black modes of communication emerged in response to the need to find viable means of surviving in a hostile environment without jeopardizing physical safety. Words, in addition to being communication devices, became power devices and helped Afro-Americans to survive. Black music has its primordial roots in the African heritage, but it is both an expression of the hopes, fears, aspirations, and frustrations of Blacks, and a reflection of their experiences in American society. The forces that gave rise to much of its lyrical content and rhythmic tempo were the prototype life experiences, both physical and psychological, of Blacks as a group.

The ethnic cultures of most European immigrants were largely amalgamated in the United States. America became a culturally diffused and a socially and politically stratified society. Northern and Eastern European immigrants were almost totally culturally assimilated and structurally integrated into the dominant Anglo-Saxon society. Eastern, Central, and Southern European immigrants were assimilated to a lesser extent, and the political and economic privileges which they experienced reflected their lower levels of assimilation. Non-White, non-European immigrants and American Indian groups (i.e., colored, highly visible peoples) were culturally diffused and largely structurally excluded.

The Nature of Ethnic Groups in Contemporary American Life

Our discussion of cultural and structural assimilation leads us to more complex questions concerning the nature of ethnic groups in contemporary American society, the functions they serve, and the extent to which they exist in the United States today. An ethnic group may be defined as an involuntary collectivity of people with a shared feeling of common identity, a sense of peoplehood, and a shared sense of interdependence of fate. These feelings derive, in part, from a common ancestral origin, a common set of values, and a common set of experiences.[15] Isajiw defines an ethnic group as "an involuntary group of people who share the same culture or descendents of such people who identify themselves and/or are identified by others as belonging to the same involuntary group."[16]

Identification with and membership in an ethnic group serves many useful functions. The ethnic group provides a network of preferred individual and institutional associations through which primary group relationships are established and personalities are developed. It serves psychologically as a source of self-identification for individuals. It provides a cultural screen through which national cultural patterns of behavior and the value systems of other groups are screened, assessed, and assigned meaning.[17] Isajiw suggests that ethnicity is a matter of double boundary building; boundaries from within that are maintained by the socialization process, and boundaries from without, which are established by the process of intergroup relations. The most important question to be considered in analyzing ethnicity in contemporary American society is related less to the extent to which cultural assimilation has occurred and more to how ethnic groups are perceived and identified by others in the larger society, especially those who exercise political and economic power.[18]

Ethnicity or ethnic group membership becomes important in relationships with other groups of people when one group discovers that it has great actual or potential political and economic power. Such is the case with the Japanese Americans in Hawaii and the Poles in Chicago. Ethnicity also becomes important when one is a member of a highly visible minority group, such as Afro-Americans, Asian Americans and Mexican Americans. It also becomes important when one ethnic group becomes conscious of being surrounded by another ethnic group,[19] such as Anglo-Saxon Protestants in Spanish Harlem and Whites who live in predominantly Black urban areas. Individuals who find themselves in these kinds of situations tend to turn to their own ethnic group for their intimate relationships, for reaffirmation of their identity, and for psychological and emotional support. Attempts to satisfy these kinds of needs often lead to ethnic alliances formed to influence social and political institutions. The individual feels that he or she benefits through the progress of his or her primary group (i.e., a sense of interdependence of fate). Therefore, as Greeley suggests:

> Many ethnic groups have emerged in this country because members of the various immigrant groups have tried to preserve something of the intimacy and familiarity of the peasant village during the transition into urban industrial living. These groups have persisted after the immigrant experience ... because of an apparently very powerful drive in many toward associating with those who, he believes, possess the same blood and the same beliefs he does. The inclination toward such homogeneous groupings simultaneously enriches the culture, provides for diversity within the social structure and considerably increases the potential for conflict.[20]

Greeley adds, "Visibility, sudden recognition of minority status, or being a large group in an environment where ethnic affiliation is deemed important—these three variables may considerably enhance social-psychological and social-organizational influence of ethnic groups."[21]

Toward the Development of a Typology for Classifying Ethnic Groups

The functions served by ethnic group affiliation suggests that there are several different ways of classifying ethnic groups in contemporary American society. While existing definitions of an ethnic group are useful, they are inadequate for studying the complex characteristics of contemporary ethnic groups in the United States.[22] Most of these definitions were formulated when ethnic group characteristics in American society were considerably different and prior to the civil rights movement of the 1960s and the rise of the "new ethnicity." New conceptualizations of ethnicity are needed to better reflect the emerging characteristics of ethnic groups in the United States.

It is impossible for a single definition of an ethnic group to adequately describe the multiple and complex dimensions of ethnic groups in contemporary American society. We need to develop a typology that will enable us to identify and to classify different types of ethnic groups and to determine the degrees to which various racial and ethnic groups manifest these identified characteristics. We attempt to formulate the basic elements of such a typology in this chapter. It is important for the reader to realize that our typology is an ideal type construct in the Weberian sense, and that no actual ethnic group will represent a "pure" type of any of our categories. Rather, various ethnic groups will exhibit the characteristics we identify to a greater or lesser degree. It is also unlikely that any particular ethnic group will completely lack any of the characteristics that we will describe. The reader should think of each of our ethnic group categories as a continuum.

Each type of ethnic group is an involuntary group whose members share a sense of peoplehood and an interdependence of fate. A *cultural* ethnic group is an ethnic group that shares a common set of values, experiences, behavioral characteristics, and linguistic traits that differ substantially from other ethnic groups within society. Individuals usually gain membership in such a group not by choice but through birth and early socialization. Individuals who are members of cultural ethnic groups are likely to take collective and organized actions to support public policies that will enhance the survival of the group's culture and ethnic institutions. Members of cultural ethnic groups also pass on the symbols, language, and other components of the cultural heritage to the next generation. The individual's ethnic cultural heritage is a source of pride and group identification.

An *economic* ethnic group is an ethnic group that shares a sense of group identity and sees its economic fate tied together. Individual members of the group feel that their economic fate is intimately tied to the economic future of other members of the group. The members of an economic ethnic group respond collectively to societal issues they perceive as critical to determining their economic status and work together to influence policies and programs that will benefit the economic status of the group. The individual within an economic ethnic group tends to feel that taking individual actions to improve his or her economic status is likely to be ineffective as long as the economic status of his or her ethnic group is not substantially improved.

A *political* ethnic group is an ethnic group that has a sense of shared political interests and a feeling of political interdependence. The group responds to political issues collectively and tries to promote those public policies and programs that will enhance the interests of its members as a group. Groups that are political ethnic groups are usually economic ethnic groups also since economics and politics are highly interwoven in American society. Thus, we can refer to those ethnic groups that work to influence political and economic policies that will benefit their collectivities as *ecopolitical ethnic groups.*

A *holistic* ethnic group is an ethnic group that has all of the characteristics of the various types of ethnic groups that we have described in their purest forms. Thus, a holistic ethnic group is an involuntary group of individuals who share a sense of peoplehood and an interdependence of fate, a common sense of identity, and common behavioral characteristics. Its members respond collectively to economic and political issues, and try to promote public programs and policies that will further the interests of the group as a whole. Afro-Americans and Mexican Americans closely approach the holisic ethnic group. American Indians, Puerto Ricans in the United States, and Asian Americans are acquiring more characteristics of a holistic ethnic group as the political maturity and collective political action of these groups increase.

Several questions proceed from our discussion: What is the structural relationship between ethnic groups and the larger American society? In a pluralistic society such as ours, is everyone a member of an ethnic group? Our analysis suggests that every American is a member of an ethnic group, that ethnicity exists on a continuum in contemporary American life, and that some individuals and groups are much more "ethnic" than others (see chapter 4). Thus it is more useful to attempt to describe the degree to which an individual or group is "ethnic," rather than to try to determine whether a particular individual or group is "ethnic." The lower-class, Black individual who lives in an all-Black community, speaks Black English, and who is active in Black political and economic activities is clearly more "ethnic" than the highly acculturated Black who tries desperately to avoid any contact with other Blacks.

Third generation Italian-Americans who are highly assimilated into the Anglo-Saxon culture may be ethnic only in a cultural sense, i.e., they share the values, life-styles, and sense of peoplehood with Anglo-Americans. They may do very little, however, to advance the political and economic interests of Anglo-Americans over the interests of non-Anglo-American ethnic groups. Afro-Americans, Puerto Ricans in the United States and Japanese Americans are all ethnic groups. However, they are structurally different kinds of ethnic groups and unless we keep the significant differences between these groups in mind when we are deriving generalizations, our conclusions are likely to be misleading.

Of the three groups, Afro-Americans, especially in the mid-1960s, more closely approach what we have described as a holistic ethnic group. Puerto Ricans in the United States, until recent years, have been primarily a cultural and economic ethnic group, but have not been very politically active in a collective sense. However, recently Puerto Ricans have been becoming more of a political ethnic group. Japanese Americans are probably the least ethnic of the three groups. This is true not only because Japanese Americans are highly culturally assimilated but because they are not very politically active in an "ethnic" sense. They are also very economically successful and consequently feel little need to take collective action to influence their economic condition.[23] In recent years, however, Japanese Americans have taken more collective political and economic actions, especially in Hawaii where they are increasingly becoming a powerful group. *The degree to which a particular cultural, nationality, or racial group is ethnic varies over time, in different regions, with social class mobility, and with the pervasive sociopolitical conditions within the society.*

Frequently, third and fourth generation descendants of immigrants who came from Northern and Western Europe (e.g., French, Germans, Irish, Dutch, etc.) are thought to have become Anglo-Saxon politically, socially, culturally, and ethnically. The contention is often made that these groups, through the processes of acculturation and assimilation, have lost all traces of their ethnic distinctiveness, internalized Anglo-Saxon values and behaviors, and consider their political and economic interests to be the same as those Americans whose origins are Anglo-Saxon. The preservation of the original ethnicity of these descendents has been determined on the basis of the presence or absence of classic overt behaviors attributable to the original ethnic group. When many of these are not found, conclusions are drawn to the effect that any ethnicity, aside from Anglo-Saxonism, is insignificant in defining the self-identity of descendants of Northern and Western European stock, in determining their primary group relationships, and in governing their social, political, and psychological behaviors. Their ethnic origins have been dismissed as meaningless and dysfunctional, except perhaps on rare occasions when families get together for reunions and to reminisce about "great grandma, the old country and the old days," fix an ethnic dish, hold an ethnic marriage ceremony, or observe ethnic holidays.

However, the resurgence or rediscovery of ethnicity and the recent and emerging research on White ethnic groups challenge the validity of these contentions. Data emanating from the research of such notable students of the "new ethnicity" as Novak and Greeley suggest that ethnicity among Whites is a complex variable that defies such simple explanations and/or dismissals, and that it is a persistent, salient factor in the lives of different groups of White Americans, even though they may be fourth generation immigrants.[24] Greeley explains that White "ethnicity is not a residual social factor that is slowly and gradually disappearing; it is, rather, a dynamic flexible social mechanism and can be called into being rather quickly and transformed and transmuted to meet changing situations and circumstances."[25]

Since the 1970s many White ethnic group members have become as concerned as ethnic minority groups with self-identity, with reestablishing contact with their ethnic and cultural histories, with developing a sense of ethnic unity, and with preserving their cultural heritages. This search for more gratifying responses to the question of "Who am I?" has rekindled an interest in ethnic heritage, and a growing awareness of the saliency of ethnicity in their lives. Whites from all sociocultural backgrounds (e.g., Irish, Italian, Polish, German, Czech, Slovak, Greek, etc.) have joined Blacks, Latinos, and American Indians in this search for identity. Therefore, it now seems more appropriate to talk about what Greeley calls the process of "ethnicization," or "ethnogenesis," instead of acculturation and assimilation, or "Americanization," if we are to understand the cultural diversity and ethnic dynamism in American society.[26] According to Greeley the so-called "new ethnicity" among White Americans is not new at all. Rather, it is a rebirth or revival of interest in a persistent force in the history and lives of *all* Americans. And, its resurgence in the 1970s was symbolic of the cyclical nature of the ethnicization process.

Unquestionably, a great deal of sociocultural exchange has taken place between the various immigrant groups and the American host society. But, this does not mean that either one is any less ethnic. The process of ethnicization leads to the creation of a broader "common culture," shared by both the host and immigrant groups. The immigrant groups take on certain attitudes, beliefs, values, and behaviors attributable to Anglo-Saxons, and English Americans adopt some of the immigrants' values, beliefs, customs, and symbols (see chapter 6). Other immigrant characteristics persist and become more distinctive in response to the challenge of American life. The result for third and fourth generation immigrants, such as Italian Americans, Polish Americans, or Irish Americans, is a cultural system that is a combination of commonly shared "American" traits and distinctive traits preserved from their original ethnic heritages.

To fully understand ethnicity when studying America's diverse populations attention needs to be given to the interrelationships between *ethnic identification, ethnic heritage,* and *ethnic culture.* This is especially important when studying White ethnic groups since ethnic differences within and between them are often subtle and complex. If identification, heritage, and culture are viewed as discrete dimensions or components of ethnicity, each with different behavioral manifestations, then one can proclaim his or her ethnicity by ascribing to any one or combination of these. *Ethnic identifica-*

tion refers to where one places himself or herself on the ethnic chart (e.g., "I am Irish, German, French, Norwegian, Slovak, Greek, or Black). *Ethnic heritage* is the specific study and conscious recollection of one's past history, both in America and the country of origin. *Ethnic culture* refers to the attitudes, values, personality styles, norms, and behaviors that correlate with ethnic identification.[27] Even though fourth generation Irish Americans, Polish Americans, or Italian Americans may identify neither physically, nor psychosocially with their original ethnic groups, and have little or no consciousness of their ethnic heritage, their "Irishness," "Polishness," or "Italianness," is still very much a part of their lives. Their values, behaviors, perceptions and expectations, that are considerably different from other Americans, are determined, to a great extent, by the cultural conditioning that persists from the original ethnic experience. These cultural traits are transmitted across generations through family structures and socializational processes, and are often so deeply embedded in the subconscious fiber of individuals that they are unaware of their existence. This is why we frequently assume that White ethnic groups, especially those who emigrated from Northern and Western Europe, lose their ethnic identity after three or four generations in America.

Undoubtedly, ethnicity is even stronger and more conscious among European descendants who came from Eastern, Southern, and Central Europe than those from Northern and Western Europe. Such groups as the Poles, Greeks, Italians, Slovaks, Czechs, and Hungarians are more recent arrivals in America; their ties with their original heritages, customs, values, and traditions are stronger, and they share less of a common culture with English Americans than do groups like the French and Germans. Their senses of ethnic identification, heritage, and culture are much more apparent in their daily lives because of the more distinct origins. They are less assimilated culturally and structurally than other White Americans, and the ethnicization process is less developed. Therefore, their original ethnicity is more highly accentuated, and they are more likely to behave in clearly discernible ways from Anglo-Saxons than are other European immigrants. These groups are likely to support ethnic candidates for public office, live in tightly formed ethnic communities, continue to speak their native languages, marry within their own ethnic groups, conform more rigidly to ethnic values, and perpetuate their ethnic heritages through family structures and socialization. The forces of differentiation acting on them are much stronger and function on more conscious, all inclusive levels than do the forces of homogenization.[28]

The ethnic groups in the United States that are the less assimilated culturally and structurally, and the most visible physically, such as Afro-Americans, Filipino Americans, Mexican Americans, and American Indians, as groups, have maintained even stronger senses of cultural identities. To a greater degree than Americans of either Western and Northern, or Southern and Eastern European descent, they feel that their life-styles and political interests conflict with those of the dominant society. They, therefore, consider themselves to be more "ethnic" than these other groups. They have created and maintained distinct cultural institutions, values, norms, and languages. Excluded ethnic groups are much more likely than structurally assimilated ethnic groups to emphasize their feelings of kinship, to promote their cultural identities, and to try to influence economic and political institutions so that public policies will be more responsive to their unique group needs. Thus, in the 1970s Blacks tried to gain control of schools located in predominantly Black communities and Chinese Americans in San Francisco united to oppose efforts to bus their children to schools outside of Chinatown. Mexican Americns are more likely to vote for a Chicano for public office than an Anglo-American because they usually feel that a Chicano will make decisions more consistent with their ethnic group interests than an Anglo-American.[29]

Both White and minority ethnic groups' preoccupation with their own ethnicity is situational and periodic. It surfaces and assumes a position of prominence in group activities at different times in history, and as different aspects of the psychosocial and ecopolitical identification processes demand attention. The nature of the particular identity need determines the way ethnicity is articulated, and the activities ethnic groups choose to accentuate their ethnicity. Whether that need is defined as the clarification or reaffirmation of cultural identity, the recollection and reevaluation of historical experiences, the manipulation of social forces to benefit the ethnic group's membership, or gaining political and economic power to advance the social positions of particular ethnic collectivities, it determines the "ethnic posture" of the group at any given time. Ethnic needs influence whether an ethnic collectivity functions as an *economic, political,* or *cultural ethnic group.* All ethnic groups assume these various identities at different stages in their developmental processes within the context of American society.

While our generalizations are basically valid, they are not applicable to the same degree to all members of all ethnic groups. This is why it is imperative, when studying ethnicity, to distinguish ethnic *group* behavior from the behavior of *individual* members of ethnic groups, to consider ethnicity from the perspective of functionality instead of merely as a descriptive trait, and to analyze behavior of ethnic groups in terms of ethnic identification, heritage, and culture. Some members of ethnic groups have little or no sense of ethnic kinship or interdependence of fate. They feel little or no sense of distinction or difference between themselves and the larger society. Some members do not identify with their ethnic group, even though they share its physical and/or cultural characteristics, and the larger society considers them to belong to it. For example, some descendents of Mexican-American parentage consider themselves White. They do not speak Spanish, have Anglicized their names, and conform to Anglo-Saxon cultural norms. Some Blacks believe that they are both culturally and structurally assimilated into the larger society. They have inculcated the values and life-styles of the dominant culture, consider themselves totally accepted by the majority society, feel a sense of alienation from Blacks as a group, and find it almost impossible to identify with the cultural and political goals of Blacks.

Summary

The characteristics of ethnic groups in the United States and the relationship between them have changed substantially since the major concepts and theories related to ethnic groups and ethnicity were formulated. The civil rights movement of the 1960s and the rise of the "new ethnicity " are social forces that profoundly influenced the nature of ethnicity in American society. New concepts and generalizations are needed to adequately describe the characteristics of ethnicity in contemporary American society.

In this chapter, we attempt to describe some of the major characteristics of ethnic groups in the United States and to develop a typology for classifying ethnic groups that is more consistent with the current characteristics of ethnic groups than many existing definitions and typologies. We identified several types of ethnic groups—cultural, economic, political, ecopolitical, and holistic—and concluded that while every American is a member of an ethnic group, ethnicity manifests itself in diverse forms in modern American life, and that Americans belong to many different kinds of ethnic groups. We also concluded that the degree to which a particular cultural, nationality, or racial group is "ethnic" varies with a number of social, economic, and political conditions within society.

Notes

1. Robert Blauner, *Racial Oppression in America* (New York: Harper and Row, 1972).
2. See Louis Wirth, "The Problem of Minority Groups," in Ralph Linton, ed., *The Science of Man in the World Crisis* (New York: Columbia University Press, 1945), pp. 347–372; and Robert E. Park, *Race and Culture* (New York: The Free Press, 1950).
3. Nathan Glazer and Daniel P. Moynihan, *Beyond the Melting Pot* 2nd ed. (Cambridge, Mass.: The M.I.T. Press, 1970).
4. John Higham, *Strangers in the Land: Patterns of American Nativism 1860–1925* (New York: Atheneum, 1972).
5. Maldwyn Allen Jones, *American Immigration* (Chicago: University of Chicago Press, 1960).
6. Nathan Glazer, "Ethnic Groups in America: From National Culture to Ideology," in Morroe Berger, Theodore Abel, and Charles H. Page,

eds., *Freedom and Control in Modern Society* (New York: Van Nostrand, 1954), pp. 158–173.

7. Nathan Glazer, "Cultural Pluralism: The Social Aspect," in Melvin M. Tumin and Walter Plotch, eds., *Pluralism in A Democratic Society* (New York: Praeger Publishers, 1977), pp. 3–24.

8. Milton M. Gordon, *Assimilation in American Life: The Role of Race, Religion and National Origins* (New York: Oxford University Press, 1964).

9. Michael Novak, *The Rise of the Unmeltable Ethnics: Politics and Culture in The Seventies* (New York: Macmillan, 1972).

10. Michael Novak, "The New Ethnicity," *Center Magazine.* Vol. 3 (July/August, 1974), p. 18.

11. Gordon, *Assimilation in American Life.*

12. Wayne Moquin and Charles Van Doren, eds., *A Documentary History of Mexican Americans* (New York: Bantam Books, 1971).

13. Alvin M. Josephy, Jr., *The Indian Heritage of America* (New York: Bantam Books, 1968).

14. Melville Herskovits, *The Myth of the Negro Past* (New York: Harper and Row, 1941).

15. Wsevolod W. Isajiw, "Definitions of Ethnicity," *Ethnicity* 1 (July 1974), pp. 111–124.

16. Ibid., p. 122.

17. Gordon, *Assimilation in American Life.*

18. Isajiw, "Definitions of Ethnicity" p. 122.

19. Andrew M. Greeley, *Why Can't They Be Like Us? America's White Ethnic Groups* (New York: E. P. Dutton and Company, 1971).

20. Ibid., p. 44.

21. Ibid., p. 46.

22. Isajiw, "Definitions of Ethnicity."

23. Harry H. L. Kitano, *Japanese Americans: The Evolution of A Subculture,* 2nd ed. (Englewood Cliffs, N.J.: Prentice-Hall, 1976).

24. See Michael Novak, *The Rise of the Unmeltable Ethnics*; "How American Are You if Your Grandparents Came from Serbia in 1888?", in Sallie TeSelle, ed., *The Rediscovery of Ethnicity* (New York: Harper and Row, 1973), pp. 1–20; "Cultural Pluralism for Individuals: A Social Vision," in Tumin and Plotch, pp. 25–57; and Andrew M. Greeley, *Ethnicity in the United States: A Preliminary Reconnaissance* (New York: Wiley Publishing Co., 1974); *and Why Can't They Be Like Us?*

25. Greeley, *Ethnicity in the United States,* p. 205.

26. Ibid., pp. 291–317.

27. Ibid.

28. Novak, in *The Rediscovery of Ethnicity*

29. Edgar Litt, *Ethnic Politics in America* (Glenview, Ill.: Scott, Foresman, 1970).

4

Concepts in Multiethnic Education

The wide range of educational concepts that have emerged in recent years to describe the diverse programs and practices related to ethnic pluralism reflect the widespread confusion over goals and strategies. Concepts such as multicultural education, multiculturalism, multiethnic education, ethnic education, ethnic studies, cultural pluralism, and ethnic pluralism are often used interchangeably or to convey different but highly ambiguous meanings. The study of ethnicity and pluralism is gaining increasing legitimization within the social science community and within the nation's schools and universities. Scholars such as Talcott Parsons and Daniel Bell have provided fresh perspectives on ethnicity within American society.[1] Increasingly, school districts are viewing the study of ethnicity as an integral part of the school curriculum.

However, the major concepts within the field of multiethnic education, and related practices, are confused and ambiguous. Concept clarification within this area is sorely needed so that objectives can be more clearly delineated and strategies for attaining them more appropriately designed. Concepts are exceedingly important. They influence our questions, research methods, findings, programs, and evaluation strategies. Multicultural education and multiethnic education, for example, have different programmatic and policy implications.

In this chapter, I define and delineate the boundaries of some of the major concepts related to education and ethnic diversity and suggest their different programmatic and policy implications. This conceptual analysis will hopefully help educators, at all levels, to better clarify, specify, and evaluate their goals that are related to ethnicity and racial diversity in the United States. A further discussion of concepts and their policy implications is found in chapter 12.

Multicultural Education

Of the concepts that are currently in vogue, multicultural education, or multiculturalism, is one of the most frequently used. Its usage varies widely in school districts and in the educational literature.[2] Sometimes it is used synonymously with ethnic studies; at other times it is used to describe mul-

51

tiethnic education. It is necessary to discuss the meaning of culture in order to describe what multicultural education theoretically suggests since culture is the root of multicultural.

Anthropological literature is replete with definitions of culture. In a comprehensive study of culture, Kroeber and Kluckhohn report over 160 definitions of the concept. However, culture does have some agreed on meanings. Wallis offers a useful definition:

> Culture is the life of a people as typified in contacts, institutions, and equipment.... [It] ... means all those things, institutions, material objects, typical reactions to situations, which characterize a people and distinguish them from other people.[3]

Thus, culture consists of the behavior patterns, symbols, institutions, values, and other human made components of society. It is the unique achievement of a human group that distinguishes it from other human groups. While cultures are in many ways similar, a particular culture constitutes a unique whole.

Culture is a generic concept with wide boundaries. Thus, we can describe the culture of the United States (the macroculture) as well as the various microcultures that constitute it, such as the southern culture, the bohemian culture, the youth culture, the culture of the intellectual community, and the female culture. These microcultures share many elements with the general American culture, but are in many ways unique. An individual may be a legitimate member of several microcultures at the same time. Thus, an individual may be southern, a bohemian, and a member of the intellectual community.

Multicultural education suggests a type of education that is concerned with creating educational environments in which students from all cultural groups will experience educational equity. Thus, within a global and inclusive multicultural education program, attention would necessarily focus on a wide range of cultural groups, such as the culture of females, the Black culture, the Amish culture, and the cultures of regional groups such as White southerners and Appalachian Whites. The problems these groups experience would be highlighted and compared. The total school environment would be reformed so that it would promote respect and equity for a wide range of cultural groups. Mulitcultural education, conceptualized in this way, would be based on the assumption that concepts such as prejudice, discrimination, identity conflicts, and alienation are common to diverse cultural groups.

A generic focus within a school reform effort, such as multicultural education, can make a substantial contribution to the liberal education of students. However, school reform efforts should go beyond the level of generic multicultural education and focus on the unique problems that women, Blacks, youths and other cultural groups experience in American society. Many of the problems these groups have are unique and require specialized analyses and strategies.

Multicultural education is a politically popular concept because it is often interpreted to mean lumping the problems of ethnic minorities, women, and other groups together. Public and school policies that are based primarily on lumping the problems of diverse groups together will prove ineffective and perhaps detrimental to all of the groups concerned. Because of the unique problems some ethnic and racial groups have in American society, school districts should implement *multiethnic* education to complement and strengthen *multicultural* education. These concepts are complimentary but not interchangeable.

The Nature of An Ethnic Group

An ethnic group is a cultural group with several distinguishing characteristics. There are many definitions of an ethnic group but none on which there is a complete agreement by social scientists. However, we may define an ethnic group as a group that shares a common ancestry, culture, history, tradition, sense of peoplehood, and that is a political and economic interest group. An ethnic group is primarily an involuntary group, although individual identification with the group may be optional.[4]

This definition suggests that groups such as Polish Americans, Irish Americans, and Anglo-Americans are ethnic groups. Afro-Americans and Mexican Americans are ethnic minority groups, a specific type of ethnic group. Members of an ethnic minority group have unique physical and/or cultural characteristics which enable members of other groups to easily identify its members, usually for the purposes of discrimination.[5]

Ethnic Group: A Multidimensional Concept

The definition of an ethnic group stated above suggests that all Americans are members of ethnic groups. However, within a modernized society, almost no individuals are totally "ethnic," since ethnic characteristics within a modern society are mediated by technology, acculturation, the physical amalgamation of ethnic groups, and other aspects of modernization. Thus, the appropriate question to ask about ethnic group membership within a modernized society is not whether or not an individual is "ethnic," but to what extent is he or she ethnic. Ethnic group membership is a multidimensional concept. It's separate variables can be identified, even though these variables are highly interrelated. An individual's level of ethnic behavior and characteristics can be determined by ascertaining the extent to which he or she has behavior and characteristics that reflect these ethnic variables.

The Relationship between Physical
Characteristics and Ethnic Behavior

It is very important to realize that ethnic behavior and characteristics should not be confused with an individual's biological characteristics and physical traits. It is true that there is often a close relationship between an individual's biological traits and his or her ethnic or cultural characteristics. In premodern societies, there was usually a one-hundred percent correlation between an individual's biological "ethnic" group and his or her cultural characteristics. This relationship exists to some extent today. Most Black Americans, for example, possess some degree of "Black" cultural characteristics.

However, some Black Americans have so few cultural traits that are "Black" and so little identification with Afro-Americans as an ethnic group that we might call them "Afro-Saxons." The same situation exists for many highly assimilated and upward mobile members of ethnic groups such as Mexican Americans, Asian Americans, and American Indians. Americans with an Italian surname may be so totaly culturally assimilated in terms of their values, behaviors, and perceptions that they are culturally not Italian Americans but are Anglo-Americans. An individual American who is one-eighth each of German, Australian, Romanian, Algerian, Chilean, Scotch, Italian, and Korean ancestry, and whose parents did not provide any conscious ethnic influence, is not necessarily without an ethnic identification or ethnic behavior.* He or she is most likely *culturally* an Anglo-American who has an identification with Anglo-Americans as an ethnic group. This identification with Anglo-Americans maybe conscious or unconscious. Most frequently, this type of individual will have an unconscious identification with Anglo-Americans as an ethnic group and will describe himself or herself as "merely an American."

The Variables of Ethnic Group Behavior

In my work on ethnic behavior, I have isolated eight major variables that can be used to conceptualize, measure, and determine the level of ethnic behavior of individuals or groups and the levels of cross-cultural competency of individuals (see Table 4.1). These variables are:

- languages and dialects
- nonverbal communications
- culture elements (such as foods, art forms, dances and literature)

* I took this hypothetical American from a private letter written to me by Professor Carlos E. Cortés of the University of California, Riverside. However, Professor Cortes and I interpret this individual's ethnic behavior and ethnicity differently.

- perspectives and world views
- behavioral styles and nuances
- ethnic values
- methods of reasoning and validating knowledge
- ethnic identification

Each of these variables can be conceptualized as existing on a continuum. Measurement techniques can be structured to determine the level of ethnic behavior and traits possessed by individual members of ethnic groups. This multidimensional conceptualization of ethnic behavior can help students to understand that an individual may be highly ethnic linguistically but highly assimilated in terms of his or her ethnic values and perspectives. This multidimensional conceptualization of ethnic group can also help students to better understand the complex nature of ethnic group life in the United States and to mitigate some of the serious and damaging misconceptions about ethnic groups that are pervasive within the schools and the larger society.

The last variable of ethnic group behavior identified above is the individual's psychological identification with his or her ethnic group. This variable is called *ethnicity*. It is one of the most important variables of ethnic group behavior within a modernized society. In some cases, it maybe the only significant variable of ethnic group behavior possessed by highly assimilated and upper-status members of ethnic groups within a modernized democratic society.

Multiethnic Education

Since an ethnic group is a unique kind of cultural group, multiethnic education is a specific form of multicultural education. Multiethnic education is concerned with modifying the total school environment so that it is more reflective of the ethnic diversity within American society. This includes not only the study of ethnic cultures and experiences but making institutional changes within the school setting so that students from diverse ethnic groups have equal educational opportunities and the school promotes and encourages the concept of ethnic diversity.

Multiethnic education is a generic concept that implies systematic school reform. Schools that wish to become multiethnic must undertake an institutional analysis to determine the degree to which they are assimilationist oriented and take effective actions to create and sustain a pluralistic school environment. The staff's attitudes, the testing program, counseling, power relationships, and grouping practices are some of the variables that reflect ethnic diversity within multiethnic schools. (See Figure 2.4 on page 31.)

Table 4.1. Matrix for Conceptualizing and Assessing Cross-cultural Behavior.

Variables	Understandings and Behaviors	Levels of Competency
Languages and dialects	The ability to understand and interpret the dialect and/or languages within the ethnic culture.	1 2 3 4 5 6 7 ←——————→
	The ability to speak the dialects and/or languages within the ethnic culture.	←——————→
Nonverbal communications	The ability to understand and accurately interpret the nonverbal communications within the ethnic group.	←——————→
	The ability to accurately communicate nonverbally within the ethnic group.	←——————→
Cultural elements	A knowledge and appreciation of culture elements within the ethnic cultures, such as food, art forms, music, dances, and literature.	←——————→
	The ability to share culture elements of the ethnic group, such as foods, art forms, music, literature, and dances.	←——————→
Perspectives and world views	The ability to understand and interpret the perspectives and world views normative within the ethnic group.	←——————→
	The ability to view events and situations from the perspectives normative within the ethnic group.	←——————→
Behavioral styles and nuances	The ability to understand and interpret behavioral styles and nuances that are normative within the ethnic group.	←——————→
	The ability to express behavioral styles and nuances that are normative within the ethnic group.	←——————→
Ethnic values	The ability to understand and interpret the values that are normative within the ethnic group.	←——————→
	The ability to behaviorally express values that are normative within the ethnic group.	←——————→
Methods of reasoning and validating knowledge	The ability to understand the methods of reasoning and validating knowledge that are normative within the ethnic group.	←——————→

Table 4.1 (Continued)

Variables	Understandings and Behaviors	Levels of Competency
	The ability to use methods of reasoning and validating knowledge that are normative within the ethnic group.	⟵——————⟶
Ethnic identification	Identification with ethnic group that is subtle and/or unconscious	⟵——————⟶
	Overt actions that show conscious identification with ethnic group.	⟵——————⟶

Ethnic Studies

Of the concepts I have discussed, ethnic studies, under various labels, has probably experienced the most vigorous and sustained development in the nation's schools.[6] Ethnic studies may be defined as the scientific and humanistic study of the histories, cultures, and experiences of the ethnic groups within a society. It includes but is not limited to a study of ethnic minority groups, such as Afro-Americans, Asian Americans, and Puerto Ricans in the United States. Ethnic studies refers primarily to the objectives, methods, and materials that make up the courses of study within schools. Thus the boundaries of ethnic studies are more limited than either multicultural or multiethnic education. It constitutes only one essential component of multiethnic education.

The concept of ethnic studies suggests that a wide variety of ethnic groups are studied within a comparative framework.[7] Students are helped to develop concepts, generalizations, and theories that they can use to better understand a wide range of human behavior. Modernized ethnic studies programs are not only comparative and conceptual but are interdisciplinary and cut across subject matter lines. Thus, within a globally conceptualized ethnic studies program, teachers of the humanities, the communication arts, and the sciences incorporate ethnic content into the curriculum when it is appropriate and feasible to do so. In this type of ethnic studies program, ethnic content is not reserved for special days, occasions, or courses.

Courses such as Black studies and Chicano studies, because they are highly specialized, are more appropriately referred to as such rather than as ethnic studies. Such specialized courses often serve important needs within particular schools. *However, a major goal of curriculum reform should be to incorporate ethnic content into the mainstream curriculum which is experienced by all students.*

Table 4.2 summarizes the focuses, objectives, and strategies of multicultural education, multiethnic education, and ethnic studies. Figure 4.1

Table 4.2. Programs and Practices Related to Pluralism in American Schools.

Program and Practice	Focus	Objectives	Strategies
Multicultural education	Cultural groups in the United States	To help reduce discrimination against diverse cultural groups and provide them with equal educational opportunities To present all students with cultural alternatives	Creating a school atmosphere that has positive institutional norms toward diverse cultural groups in the United States
Multiethnic education	Ethnic groups within the United States	To help reduce discrimination against victimized ethnic groups and to provide all students equal educational opportunities To help reduce ethnic isolation and encapsulation	Modifying the total school environment to make it more reflective of the ethnic diversity within American society
Ethnic studies	Ethnic groups within the United States	To help students develop valid concepts, generalizations, and theories about ethnic groups in the United States, to clarify their attitudes toward them, and to learn how to take action to eliminate racial and ethnic problems within American society To help students develop ethnic literacy	Modifying course objectives, teaching strategies, materials, and evaluation strategies so that they include content and information about ethnic groups in the United States

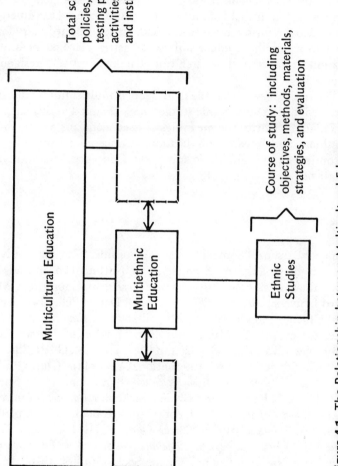

Total school environment, including policies, interactions, curriculum, testing program, extracurricular activities, lunch program, counseling, and institutional norms

Multicultural Education

Multiethnic Education

Ethnic Studies

Course of study: including objectives, methods, materials, strategies, and evaluation

Figure 4.1. The Relationship between Multicultural Education, Multiethnic Education, and Ethnic Studies.

illustrates how these concepts are related. Efforts to implement each of these ideas should be a major part of reform in the nation's schools, colleges, and universities.

Summary

A wide range of concepts are being used to describe programs and practices related to the ethnic, cultural, and racial diversity in the United States. The proliferation of concepts in part reflects the ideological confusions and disagreements in the field of multiethnic education and the emergent status of educational reform related to ethnic diversity. It is necessary for concepts related to multiethnic education to be better clarified before puralistic educational reforms and research can be more effectively designed and implemented.

The major concepts in the field, such as multicultural education, multiethnic education, and ethnic studies, are examined in this chapter. An effort is made to clarify the meanings of these concepts and to discuss their educational and research implications. Conceptual issues are important and continuing in multiethnic education. Conceptual questions and issues are returned to in chapter 12.

Notes

1. Talcott Parsons, "Some Theoretical Considerations on the Nature and Trends of Change of Ethnicity," in Nathan Glazer and Daniel P. Moynihan, eds., *Ethnicity: Theory and Experience* (Cambridge, Mass.: Harvard University Press, 1975), pp. 53–83; Daniel Bell, "Ethnicity and Social Change," in Glazer and Moynihan, eds., *Ethnicity*, pp. 141–174.
2. See, for example, "Multiculturalism," *Journal of Teacher Education* 26 (Summer 1975), pp. 119–132; and Carl A. Grant, Guest Editor, "Multicultural Education in the International Year of the Child: Problems and Possibilities," *Journal of Negro Education* 48 (Summer 1979), Special Issue.
3. Cited in A. L. Kroeber and Clyde Kluckhohn, *Culture: A Critical Review of Concepts and Definitions* (New York: Vintage Books, 1952), p. 161.
4. James A. Banks, Carlos E. Cortés, Geneva Gay, Ricardo L. Garcia, and Anna S. Ochoa, *Curriculum Guidelines for Multiethnic Education* (Washington, D.C.: National Council for the Social Studies, 1976), pp. 9–10.
5. James A. Banks, *Teaching Strategies for Ethnic Studies*, 2nd ed. (Boston: Allyn and Bacon, 1979), pp. 10–11.
6. David E. Washburn, "Ethnic Studies in the United States," *Educational Leadership* 32 (March 1975), pp. 409–412
7. I have developed these ideas in considerable detail in *Teaching Strategies for Ethnic Studies*.

5

Pluralism, Ideology, and Curriculum Reform

Since the 1960s school districts throughout the United States have implemented some reforms related to multiethnic education.[1] Many of these educational programs and practices lack clear goals, definitions, and effective staff development components. Some of the problems in multiethnic education result from conceptual and ideological confusion and conflicts. A number of crucial questions concerning the relationship between the school and ethnicity have not been satisfactorily clarified or resolved. These questions must be better clarified and resolved before we can design and implement more effective and justifiable programs related to ethnic diversity in America.

One of these key questions relates to the proper role of public institutions like the common school in the area of ethnicity. Should the common schools promote, remain neutral to, or ignore the ethnic characteristics of its students and the ethnic diversity within American life? Many educational leaders believe that the school should not ignore ethnicity and should implement curricular reforms related to pluralism. However, there is little agreement about what kinds of reforms should be initiated and how they can best be implemented.

Contemporary views on ethnicity and the schools range from those of Michael Novak, who believes that ethnicity should be an integral and salient part of the school curriculum,[2] to those of Nathan Glazer, who cautions that too much emphasis on ethnicity in the schools might be inimical to the common culture and promote the Balkanization of American society.[3] Mari-Luci Jaramillo argues that the school should promote ethnic identity and attachments but should be primarily concerned with the "visible minorities" because of their urgent needs and unique problems.[4] Contemporary views on ethnicity and the schools reflect divergent ideologies and have conflicting policy implications. These ideologies and their implications for school policy merit careful examination and discussion.

I will identify two major ideological positions related to ethnicity and cultural pluralism that are evident in most theoretical discussions on ethnicity and pluralism in the United States. The major assumptions and arguments of these positions will be discussed and their limitations as guides to curricular reform will be identified. I will then describe an eclectic ideological position that reflects both major ideologies and argue that it can best guide educational policy and curriculum reform.

It is very important for the reader to realize that the ideological positions that I will identify and describe are ideal types in the Weberian sense. The views of no particular writer or theorist can be accurately described by either of the two major positions in their ideal forms. However, various views on ethnicity and pluralism can be roughly classified using a continuum that has the two ideologies, in their ideal forms, at the extreme ends.

The two major positions are the cultural pluralist ideology and the assimilationist ideology. I am not the first observer to structure a typology related to ideologies and theories of pluralism in the United States. Gordon classifies theories of assimilation into three major categories: Anglo-conformity, the melting pot, and cultural pluralism.[5] Higham also identifies three ideologies: integrationist, pluralist, and pluralistic integrationist.[6] These two typologies as well as the one that I am presenting are in some ways similar but are different conceptualizations.

The Cultural Pluralist Ideology

The cultural pluralist ideology, in varying forms, is being widely articulated by writers today. Some writers, such as Charles V. Hamilton and Stokely Carmichael, endorse a "strong" version of pluralism,[7] while writers such as Michael Novak and Robert L. Williams endorse a much "weaker" form of cultural pluralism.[8] The pluralist makes various assumptions about the nature of American society, the function of the ethnic group in socializing the individual, and the responsibility that the individual member of a presumed oppressed ethnic group has to the "liberation struggle" of that group. The pluralist also makes certain assumptions about research, learning, teacher training, and the proper goals of the school curriculum.

The pluralist argues that ethnicity and ethnic identities are very important in American society. The United States, according to the pluralist, is made up of competing ethnic groups, each of which champions its economic and political interests. It is extremely important, argues the pluralist, for the individual to develop a commitment to his or her ethnic group, especially if that ethnic group is "oppressed" by more powerful ethnic groups within American society. The energies and skills of each member of an ethnic group are needed to help in that group's liberation struggle. Each individual member of an ethnic group has a moral obligation to join the liberation struggle. Thus the pluralist stresses the rights of the ethnic group over the rights of the individual. The pluralist also assumes that an ethnic group can attain inclusion and full participation within a society only when it can bargain from a powerful position and when it has "closed ranks" within.[9]

The pluralist views the ethnic group as extremely important in the socialization of the individual within a highly modernized society. It is within their own particular ethnic groups that individuals develop their languages, life-styles, and values, and experience important primary group relationships and attachments. The ethnic community also serves as a supportive environment for the individual and helps to protect him or her from the harshness and discrimination that he or she might experience in the wider society. The ethnic group thus provides the individual with a sense of identity and psychological support, both of which are extremely important within a highly modernized and technological society that is controlled primarily by one dominant ethnic group. The pluralist views the ethnic group as exceedingly important and believes that public institutions like the school should actively promote the interests of the various ethnic groups in its policies and in the curriculum.

The pluralist makes assumptions about research that differs from those made by the assimilationist. The pluralist assumes that ethnic minority cultures in the United States are not disadvantaged, deviant, or deficient but are well ordered and highly structured but *different* from each other and from the dominant Anglo-American culture. Thus the pluralist uses a "culture difference" model when researching ethnic groups while the assimilationist researcher uses a deficit model or a genetic model.[10] Because of their different research assumptions, the cultural pluralist researcher and the assimilationist researcher frequently derive different and often conflicting research conclusions. Researchers such as Stephan and Joan Baratz, Jane R. Mercer, and Robert L. Williams have used the cultural difference model extensively in their research studies on ethnic groups and have done a great deal to legitimize it within the social science and educational communities.[11]

The cultural pluralist also assumes that ethnic minorities have unique learning styles and that the school curriculum and teaching strategies should be revised so that they are more consistent with the cognitive and life-styles of ethnic group students. Ramirez and Castañeda have written insightfully about the unique learning styles of Mexican-American youths.[12] A recent study by Stodolsky and Lesser also supports the notion that the cognitive styles among ethnic groups sometimes differ.[13]

Pluralists, because of their assumptions about the importance of the ethnic group in the lives of students, believe that the curriculum should be drastically revised so that it will reflect the cognitive styles, cultural history, and present experiences and aspirations of ethnic groups, especially the "visible" minorities. The cultural pluralist believes that if the school curriculum were more consistent with the experiences of ethnic groups the learning and adjustment problems that minority students experience in the schools would be greatly reduced. Thus the cultural pluralist argues that learning materials should be culture-specific and that the major goal of the curriculum should be to help the child to function more successfully within his or her own ethnic culture. The curriculum should be structured so that it stresses events from the points of view of the specific ethnic groups. The curriculum should promote ethnic attachments and allegiances and help students to gain the skills and commitments that will enable them to help their ethnic group to gain power and to exercise it within the larger civic culture.

The Assimilationist Ideology

The assimilationist feels that the pluralist greatly exaggerates the extent of the cultural differences within American society. However, the assimilationist does not deny that ethnic differences exist within American society or that ethnicity is very important to some groups. However, the assimilationist and the pluralist interpret ethnicity in the United States quite differently. The assimilationist tends to see ethnicity and ethnic attachments as fleeting and temporary within an increasingly modernized world. Ethnicity, argues the assimilationist, wanes or disappears under the impact of modernization and industrialization. The assimilationist believes that ethnicity is more important in developing societies than in highly modernized societies and that it crumbles under the forces of modernization and democratization. The assimilationist sees the modernized state as being universalistic rather than characterized by strong ethnic allegiances and attachments.[14]

Not only do the assimilationists view ethnicity as somewhat noncharacteristic of modernized societies, they believe that strong ethnic attachments are rather dysfunctional within a modernized state. Assimilationists believe that the ethnic group promotes group rights over the rights of the individual, and that the individual must be freed of ethnic attachments in order to have choices within society. The assimilationist also views ethnicity as a force that is inimical to the goals of a democratic society. Ethnicity, argues the assimilationist, promotes divisions, exhumes ethnic conflicts, and leads to the Balkanization of society. The assimilationist sees integration as a societal goal in a modernized state and not ethnic segregation and separatism.

The assimilationist believes that the best way to promote the goals of American society and to develop commitments to the ideals of American democracy is to promote the full socialization of all individuals and groups into the common culture. Every society, argues the assimilationist, has values, ideologies, and norms that each member of that society must develop commitments to if it is to function successfully and smoothly. In the United States, these values are embodied in the American Creed and in such documents as the United States Constitution and the Declaration of Independence. In each society there is also a set of common skills and abilities that every successful member of society should master. In our nation these include speaking and writing the English language.

The primary goal of the common school, like other publicly supported institutions, should be to socialize individuals into the common culture and enable them to function more successfully within it. At best, the school should take a position of "benign neutrality" in matters related to the ethnic attachments of its students.[15] If ethnicity and ethnic attachments are to be promoted, this should be done by private institutions like the church, the community club, and the private school.

Like the cultural pluralist, the assimilationist makes assumptions about research related to minorities. Their conclusions reflect their assumptions. Assimilationists usually assume that subcultural groups that have characteristics that cause its members to function unsuccessfully in the common culture are deficient, deprived, and pathological, and lack needed functional characteristics. Researchers who embrace an assimilationist ideology usually use the genetic or the social pathology research model when studying ethnic minorities.[16]

The assimilationist learning theorist assumes that learning styles are rather universal across cultures (such as the stages of cognitive development identified by Piaget) and that certain socialization practices, such as those exemplified among middle-class Anglo-Americans, enhance learning while other early socialization practices, such as those found within most lower-class ethnic groups, retard the child's ability to conceptualize and to develop his or her verbal and cognitive abilities. Consequently, assimilationist learning theorists often recommend that ethnic minority youths from lower-class homes enter compensatory educational programs at increasingly early ages. Some have suggested that these youths should be placed in a middle-class educational environment shortly after birth.[17]

The assimilationist believes that curriculum materials and teaching styles should relate primarily to the common culture. Emphasis should be on our common civilization since all American citizens must learn to participate in a common culture that requires universal skills and competencies. Emphasis on cultural and ethnic differences might promote the Balkanization of our society and fail to promote socialization into the common civic culture. The school's primary mission within a democratic society should be to socialize youths into the civic culture of the United States.

The curriculum should stress the commonality of the heritage that all people share in this nation. This includes the great documents in American history such as the Declaration of Independence and events such as the American Revolution and the two great world wars. The curriculum should also help the child to develop a commitment to the common culture and the skills to participate in social action designed to make the practices in this nation more consistent with our professed ideologies. The school should develop within youths a "critical acceptance" of the goals, assumptions, and possibilities of this nation.

Attacks on the Assimilationist Ideology

In chapter 1 we discussed how the assimilationist ideology has historically dominated American intellectual and social thought.[18] Social and public policy in American society has also been most heavily influenced by the assimilationist ideology. Historically, the schools and other American institutions have viewed the acculturation of the immigrants and their descendents as one of their major goals. The nativists and the Americanizers wanted to make the immigrants "good, law-abiding Americans."[19]

Writers such as Horace Kallen, Randolph Bourne, and Julius Drachsler set forth the concepts of cultural pluralism and cultural democracy near the turn of the century, thereby challenging assimilationist policies and practices.[20] When the ethnic revitalization movements of the 1960s emerged the assimilationist ideology experienced perhaps its most serious challenge in American history.

The assimilationist ideology and the practices associated with it were strongly attacked by Third World* intellectuals, researchers, and social activists. The rejection of the assimilationist ideology by nonwhite intellectuals and leaders is historically very significant. This rejection represents a major break from tradition within ethnic groups, as Glazer observes.[21] Traditionally, most intellectuals and social activists among American minorities have supported assimilationist policies and regarded acculturation as a requisite for full societal participation. There have been a few staunch separatists among Afro-Americans and other ethnic groups throughout American history. However, these leaders have represented a cry in the wilderness. Significant, too, is the fact that many White liberal writers and researchers also began to attack the assimilationist ideology and the practices associated with it in the 1960s. This represented a major break from White liberal tradition. Some White liberal writers and researchers attacked the assimilationist ideology much more vigorously than did many Black intellectuals and writers. Some of the most passionate and perceptive advocates of the teaching and acceptance of Black English in the schools, for example, are liberal White researchers such as Joan Baratz, Roger Shuy, and William Labov.[22]

Third World writers and reseachers attacked the assimilationist ideology for many reasons. They saw it as a weapon of the oppressor that was designed to destroy the cultures of ethnic groups and to make their members personally ineffective and politically powerless. These writers also saw it as a racist ideology that justified damaging school and societal practices that victimized minority group children. Many minorities also lost faith in the assimilationist ideology because they had become very disillusioned

---

* "Third World is used here to refer to members of ethnic minority groups, such as Afro-Americans, Puerto Ricans, and Mexican Americans.

with what they perceived as its unfulfilled promises. The rise of ethnic awareness and ethnic pride also contributed to the rejection of the assimilationist ideology by many ethnic minorities in the 1960s. Many minority spokespersons and writers searched for an alternative ideology and endorsed some version of cultural pluralism. They viewed the pluralist ideology as much more consistent with the liberation of oppressed and stigmatized ethnic groups than the assimilationist ideology.

In recent years, "cultural pluralism" has come into vogue among curriculum specialist and is widely discussed and written about by educators. The pluralist ideology is verbally endorsed by many curriculum specialists in the schools, although many school people who verbally endorse cultural pluralism have not seriously examined all of the ramifications of the pluralist ideology and its full policy and curricular implications. The December, 1975, issue of *Educational Leadership*, a leading curriculum journal, was devoted to the implications of cultural pluralism for the curriculum. This special issue of the journal suggests the wide popularity of the concept among school people and curriculum specialists.

A Critique of the Pluralist and Assimilationist Ideologies

Although both the pluralist and assimilationist positions make some useful assumptions and set forth arguments that curriculum specialists need to seriously ponder as they attempt to revise the school curriculum, neither ideology, in its ideal form, is sufficient to guide the revision of the curriculum in the common schools. The pluralist ideology is useful because it informs us about the importance of ethnicity within our nation and the extent to which an individual's ethnic group determines his or her life chances in American society. The assumptions the pluralist makes about the nature of minority cultures, the learning styles of minority youths, and the importance of ethnic identity to many American children are also useful to the curriculum builder.

However, the pluralist exaggerates the extent of cultural pluralism within American society and fails to give adequate attention to the fact that gross cultural (if not structural) assimilation has taken place in American society. Gordon, who seriously questions the extent of cultural pluralism in American society writes, "Structural pluralism . . . is the major key to the understanding of the ethnic makeup of American society, while cultural pluralism is the minor one. . . ."[23] Exaggerating the extent of cultural differences between and among ethnic groups might be as detrimental for school policy as ignoring those which are real.

The pluralist also fails to give adequate attention to the fact that most members of ethnic groups participate in a wider and more universalistic culture than the ones in which they have their primary group attachments.

Thus the pluralist appears unwilling to prepare youths to cope adequately with the "real world" beyond the ethnic community. The cultural pluralist has also not clarified, in any meaningful way, the kind of relationship that should exist between antagonistic and competing ethnic groups that have different allegiances and conflicting goals and commitments. In other words, the pluralist has not adequately conceptualized how a strongly pluralistic nation will maintain an essential degree of societal cohesion.

The assimilationist argues that the school within a common culture should socialize youths so that they will be effective participants within that culture and will develop commitments to its basic values, goals, and ideologies. The assimilationist also argues that the schools should help youths to attain the skills that will enable them to become effective and contributing members of the nation state in which they live. It is important for curriculum developers to realize that most societies expect the common schools to help socialize youths so that they will become productive members of the nation state and develop strong commitments to the idealized societal values. Curriculum developers should keep the broad societal goals in mind when they reform the curriculum for the common schools.

However, the assimilationist makes a number of highly questionable assumptions and promotes educational practices that often hinder the success of youths who are socialized within ethnic communities that have cultural characteristics quite different from those of the school. The assimilationist's assumption that learning styles are universalistic rather than to some extent culture-specific is questionable. The assumption that all children can learn equally well from teaching materials that only reflect the cultural experiences of the majority group is also questionable and possibly detrimental to those minority group children who have strong ethnic identities and attachments.

When assimilationists talk about the "common culture," most often they mean the Anglo-American culture and are ignoring the reality that the United States is made up of many different ethnic groups, each of which has some unique cultural characteristics that are a part of America. The curriculum builder should seriously examine the "common culture" concept and make sure that the view of the common American culture that is promoted in the school is not racist, ethnocentric, or exclusive, but is multiethnic and reflects the ethnic and cultural diversity within American society. *We need to redefine what the common culture actually is and make sure that our new conceptualization reflects the social realities within this nation, and that it is not a mythical and idealized view of American life and culture.*

The Multiethnic Ideology

Since neither the cultural pluralist nor the assimilationist ideology can adequately guide curriculum reform within the common schools, we need a different ideology that reflects both of these positions and yet avoids their extremes. We also need an ideology that is more consistent with the realities in American society. We might call this position the multiethnic ideology and imagine that it is found near the center of our continuum, which has the cultural pluralist and the assimilationist ideologies at the extreme ends (see Table 5.1).

The multiethnic ideology has not historically been a dominant ideology in American society. However, the experiences of some ethnic groups in America, the Jews being the most salient example, are highly consistent

Table 5.1. Ideologies Related to Ethnicity and Pluralism in the United States.

The Cultural Pluralist Ideology ←	The Multiethnic Ideology →	The Assimilationist Ideology
Separatism	Open society Multiculturalism	Total integration
Primordial Particularistic	Universalized-primordialism	Universalistic
Minority emphasis	Minorities and majorities have rights	Majoritarian emphasis
Groups rights are primary	Limited rights for the group and the individual	Individual rights are primary
Common ancestry and heritage unifies	Ethnic attachments and ideology of common civic culture compete for allegiances of individuals	Ideology of the common culture unifies
Research Assumption Ethnic minority cultures in the United States are well ordered, highly structured, but different (language, values, behavior, etc.)	*Research Assumption* Ethnic minority cultures in the United States have some unique cultural characteristics; however, minority and majority groups share many cultural traits, values, and behavior styles	*Research Assumption* Subcultural groups which have characteristics which makes its members function unsuccessfully in the common culture are deprived, pathological, and lack needed functional characteristics
Culture difference research model	Bicultural research model	Social pathology research model and/or genetic research model

Table 5.1. (Continued)

The Cultural Pluralist Ideology ⟵	The Multiethnic Ideology ⟶	The Assimilationist Ideology
Minorities have unique learning styles	Minorities have some unique learning styles, but share many learning characteristics with other groups	Human learning styles and characteristics are universal
Curriculum Use materials and teaching styles that are culture specific. The goal of the curriculum should be to help the child to function more successfully within his or her own ethnic culture and help to liberate his or her ethnic group from oppression	*Curriculum* The curriculum should respect the ethnicity of the child and make use of it in positive ways; the goal of the curriculum should be to help the child to learn how to function effectively within the common culture, his or her ethnic culture, and other ethnic cultures	*Curriculum* Use materials and teaching styles that are related to the common culture; the curriculum should help the child to develop a commitment to the common civic culture and its idealized ideologies, e.g., the American Creed
Teachers Minority students need skilled teachers of their same race and ethnicity for role models, to learn more effectively, and to develop more positive self-concepts and identities	*Teachers* Students need skilled teachers who are very knowledgeable about and sensitive to their ethnic cultures and cognitive styles	*Teachers* A skilled teacher who is familiar with learning theories and is able to implement those theories effectively is a good teacher for any group of students, regardless of their ethnicity, race, or social class. The goal should be to train good teachers of children

with the multiethnic vision of society. Although the multiethnic ideology is less theoretically developed than the other two positions, it, like the other ideologies, makes a number of assumptions about the nature of American society, what the goals of our nation should be, and about research, learning, teacher training, and the school curriculum.

The multiethnic theorist feels that the cultural pluralist exaggerates the importance of the ethnic group in the socialization of the individual and that the assimilationist greatly understates the role of ethnic groups in American life and in the lives of individuals. Thus the multiethnic theorist believes that both the pluralist and the assimilationist have distorted views of the realities in American society. He or she assumes that while the ethnic group and the ethnic community are very important in the socialization of individuals, individuals are strongly influenced by the common culture during their early socialization, even if they never leave the ethnic community or enclave. The common American culture influences every member of society through such institutions as the school, the mass media, the courts, and the technology that most Americans share. Thus, concludes the multiethnic theorist, while ethnic groups have some unique cultural characteristics, all groups in America share many cultural traits. As more and more members of ethnic groups become upward mobile, ethnic group characteristics become less important but do not disappear. Many ethnic group members that are highly culturally assimilated still maintain separate ethnic institutions and symbols.[24]

The multiethnic theorist sees neither separatism (as the pluralist does) nor total integration (as the assimilationist does) as ideal societal goals, but rather envisions an "open society" in which individuals from diverse ethnic, cultural, and social class groups have equal opportunities to function and participate. In an "open society," individuals can take full advantage of the opportunities and rewards within all social, economic, and political institutions without regard to their ancestry or ethnic identity. They can also participate fully in the society while preserving their distinct ethnic and cultural traits, and are able to "make the maximum number of voluntary contacts with others without regard to qualifications of ancestry, sex, or class."[25]

In the multiethnic, open society envisioned by the multiethnic theorist, individuals would be free to maintain their ethnic identities. They would also be able and willing to function effectively within the common culture and within and across other ethnic cultures. Individuals would be free to act in ways consistent with the norms and values of their ethnic groups as long as they did not conflict with dominant American idealized values, such as justice, equality, and human dignity. All members of society would be required to conform to the American Creed values. *These values would be the unifying elements of the culture that would maintain and promote societal cohesion.*

Because of their perceptions of the nature of American society and their vision of the ideal society, multiethnic theorists believe that the primary goal of the curriculum should be to help students learn how to function more effectively within their own ethnic culture, within the mainstream American culture, and within other ethnic communities. However, multiethnic theorists feel strongly that during the process of education the school should not alienate students from their ethnic attachments but help them to clarify their ethnic identities and make them aware of other ethnic and cultural alternatives.

The multiethnic theorist believes that the curriculum should reflect the culture of various ethnic groups *and* the shared American culture. Students need to study all of these cultures in order to become effective participants and decision makers in a democratic pluralistic nation. The school curriculum should respect the ethnicity of students and make use of it in positive ways. However, the students should be given options regarding their political choices and the actions they take regarding their ethnic attachments. The school should not "force" students to be and feel ethnic if they choose to free themselves of ethnic attachments and allegiances.

The multiethnic theorist also assumes that ethnic minorities do have some unique learning styles, although they share many learning characteristics with other students. Educators should be knowledgeable about the aspects of their learning styles that are unique so that they can better help minorities to attain more success within the school and in the larger society.

While the multiethnic ideology can best guide curriculum reform and school policy, difficult questions regarding the relationship between the school and the child's ethnic culture are inherent within this position The multiethnic theorist argues, for example, that the school should reflect both the child's ethnic culture and the common societal culture. These questions emerge: How does the individual function within two cultures that sometimes have contradictory and conflicting norms, values, and expectations? What happens when the ethnic cultures of the students seriously conflict with the goals and norms of public institutions like the school? Do the institutions change their goals? If so, what goals do they embrace? The assimilationist solves this problem by arguing that the child should change to conform to the expectations and norms of public institutions.

Although I support the multiethnic ideology and have presented my proposals for curriculum reform within that ideological framework,[26] it is very difficult to satisfactorily resolve all of the difficult questions inherent within this ideology. However, public institutions like the school can and should "allow" ethnic group members to practice their culture specific behaviors as long as they do not conflict with the major goals of the school. One of the school's major goals is to teach students how to read, to write, to compute, and to think. The school obviously cannot encourage "ethnic" behavior if it prohibits students from reading. On the other hand, some students might be able to learn to read more easily from culturally sensitive readers than from Anglo-Centric reading materials like *Dick and Jane*. The multiethnic ideology is further examined and discussed in chapter 6.

Summary

School districts throughout the nation, stimulated by social forces and supported by private and public agencies, are implementing a wide variety of curriculum reforms related to pluralism and enthnicity in American society. However, there is widespread disagreement and confusion about what these reforms should be designed to attain and about the proper relationship that should exist between the school and the ethnic identities and attachments of students. Educators and social scientists who embrace divergent ideologies are recommending conflicting school and curricular policies.

We can think of these varying ideologies as existing on a continuum, with the cultural pluralist postion at one extreme end and the assimilationist position at the other. I have argued that neither of these ideologies, in their ideal forms, can effectively guide school policy and curriculum reform. Rather, school policy and curriculum reform can be best guided by an eclectic ideology that reflects both the cultural pluralist position and the assimilationist position, but that avoids their extremes. I have called this the multiethnic ideology .

Notes

1. David E. Washburn, "Ethnic Studies in the United States," *Educational Leadership* 32 (March 1975), pp. 409–412.
2. Michael Novak, "Cultural Pluralism for Individuals: A Social Vision," in Melvin M. Tumin and Walter Plotch, eds., *Pluralism in a Democratic Society* (New York: Praeger, 1977), pp. 25–57.
3. Nathan Glazer, "Ethnicity and the Schools," *Commentary* (September 1974), p. 59.
4. Mari-Luci Jaramillo, "Cultural Pluralism: Implications for Curriculum," in Tumin and Plotch, *Pluralism in a Democratic Society,* pp. 209–223.
5. Milton M. Gordon, *Assimilation in American Life: The Role of Race, Religion, and National Origins* (New York: Oxford University Press, 1964), p. 84.
6. John Higham, "Integration vs. Pluralism: Another American Dilemma," *The Center Magazine* 7 (July/August 1974), pp. 67–73.
7. Stokely Carmichael and Charles V. Hamilton, *Black Power: The Politics of Liberation in America* (New York: Vintage Books, 1967).
8. Michael Novak, "Cultural Pluralism for Individuals: A Social Vision"; Robert L. Williams, "Moderator Variables as Bias in Testing Black Children," *The Journal of Afro-American Issues* 3 (Winter 1975), pp. 77–90.
9. Carmichael and Hamilton, *Black Power;* Barbara A. Sizemore, "Separatism: A Reality Approach to Inclusion?" in Robert L. Green, ed., *Racial Crisis in American Education* (Chicago: Follett Educational Corporation, 1969), pp. 249–279.
10. Stephen S. Baratz and Joan C. Baratz, "Early Childhood Intervention: The Social Science Base of Institutional Racism," *Harvard Educational Review* 40 (Winter 1970), pp. 29–50; Gary Simpkins, Robert L. Williams, and Thomas S. Gunnings, "What a Culture a Difference Makes:

A Rejoinder to Valentine," *Harvard Educational Review* 41 (November 1971), pp. 535–541.

11. Baratz and Baratz, "Early Child Intervention"; Jane R. Mercer, "Latent Functions of Intelligence Testing in the Public Schools," in Lamar P. Miller, ed., *The Testing of Black Students* (Englewood Cliffs, N.J.: Prentice-Hall, 1974), pp. 77–94; Robert L. Williams, "Moderator Variables."

12. Manuel Ramirez III and Alfredo Castañeda, *Cultural Democracy, Bicognitive Development and Education* (New York: Academic Preess, 1974).

13. Susan S. Stodolsky and Gerald Lesser, "Learning Patterns in the Disadvantaged," *Harvard Educational Review* 37 (Fall 1967), pp. 546–593.

14. David Apter, "Political Life and Pluralism," in Tumin and Plotch, *Pluralism in a Democratic Society* pp. 58–91.

15. Nathan Glazer, "Cultural Pluralism: The Social Aspect," in Tumin and Plotch, *Pluralism in a Democratic Society,* pp. 3–24.

16. Arthur R. Jensen, "How Much Can We Boost IQ and Scholastic Achievement?" *Harvard Educational Review* 39 (Winter 1969), pp. 1–123; William Shockley, "Dysgenics, Geneticity, Raceology: Challenges to the Intellectual Reponsibility of Educators," *Phi Delta Kappan* 53 (January 1972), pp. 297–307.

17. Betty Caldwell, "What is the Optimal Learning Environment for the Young Child?" *American Journal of Orthopsychiatry* 37 (1967), pp. 9–21.

18. Nathan Glazer, "Cultural Pluralism."

19. John Higham, *Strangers in the Land: Patterns of American Nativism 1860–1925* (New York: Atheneum, 1972).

20. Horace M. Kallen, *Culture and Democracy in the United States* (New York: Boni and Liveright, 1924); Randolph S. Bourne, "Trans-National America," *The Atlantic Monthly* 118 (July 1916), p. 95; Julius Drachsler, *Democracy and Assimilation* (New York: Macmillan, 1920).

21. Nathan Glazer, "Cultural Pluralism."

22. Joan C. Baratz and Roger Shuy, eds., *Teaching Black Children to Read* (Washington, D.C.: Center for Applied Linguistics, 1969); William Labov, "The Logic of Nonstandard English," in Frederick Williams, ed., *Language and Poverty: Perspectives on a Theme* (Chicago: Markham Publishing Company, 1970), pp. 153–189.

23. Gordon, *Assimilation in American Life,* p. 159.

24. Ibid.

25. Barbara A. Sizemore, "Is There A Case for Separate Schools?" *Phi Delta Kappan* 53 (January 1972), p. 281.

26. James A. Banks, *Teaching Strategies for Ethnic Studies,* 2nd ed. (Boston: Allyn and Bacon, Inc., 1979).

6

The Multiethnic Ideology
and Education

The multiethnic educational reform movement emerged in response to the ethnic revitalization movements of the 1960s and related social and political events.[1] This reform movement has had, at best, very limited success. Pluralistic practices and materials remain primarily on the periphery of mainstream American education.

Practices such as ethnic studies, bilingual-bicultural education, and multiethnic education have not permeated the mainstream of American educational thought and practice. An important question that concerns multiethnic educators is how to begin this permeation process and the process of institutionalization. *A philosophy of ethnic pluralism must permeate educational institutions before ethnic studies curricula and materials can be effectively integrated into the curriculum.* It is important to focus on ways to institutionalize a philosophy of ethnic education while discussing strategies and tactics for implementing change.

We cannot assume that most educators have accepted the idea of multiethnic education and are waiting for appropriate strategies and materials to be developed before participating in educational reforms related to multiethnic education. I hypothesize that just the opposite is true: that educators are not using many available multiethnic strategies and materials because they believe that multiethnic strategies and materials will not contribute to their major educational goals and objectives.

Multiethnic education has not acquired legitimacy within mainstream educational thought and practice in the United States nor in other nations where I have studied multiethnic educational programs and practices, such as Mexico, France, Great Britain, and Canada.[2] An important question is: How can we legitimize multiethnic education within the nation's educational institutions? Once the concept of multiethnic education has become legitimized and most educators have internalized a philosophy of ethnic pluralism, the implementation of multiethnic education will become a logistical and technical problem.

The Root of the Problem: Ideological Resistance

Educators set forth a myriad of reasons to explain their basic indifference and limited response to educational reforms related to ethnic pluralism. These responses include the following:

1. Our children are unaware of racial differences; we will merely create problems that don't exist if we teach ethnic content. All of our children, whether they are Black or White, are happy and like one another. They don't see colors or ethnic differences.
2. We don't have any racial problems in our school and consequently don't need to teach about ethnic groups.
3. We don't teach about ethnic groups because we don't have any ethnic minorities attending our schools.
4. Ethnic studies will negatively affect societal unity and the common national culture.
5. We don't have time to add more content to what we are already teaching. We can't finish the books and units that we already have. Ethnic content will overload our curriculum.
6. We don't teach much about ethnic groups because we don't have the necessary materials. Our textbooks are inadequate.
7. We can't teach ethnic studies in our schools and colleges because most of our teachers are inadequately trained in this area of study. Many of them also have negative attitudes toward ethnic groups. They would probably do more harm than good if they tried to teach about ethnic and racial groups.
8. The local community will strongly object if we teach about race and ethnicity in our schools.
9. We don't teach much about ethnic groups in our schools because there is a lack of scholarship in this area. The research in ethnic studies is largely political and polemical.

Some of the above explanations, *but not most of them,* have a degree of validity and partially expain why multiethnic education has not become institutionalized within American schools and colleges. I will not discuss these claims in this chapter since I discuss them in considerable detail in chapter 7 and elsewhere.[3]

Most of these explanations do not reveal the root of the problem. *Ideological and philosophical conflicts between pluralistic and mainstream educators (who are basically assimilationists) is the major reason that educational reforms related to ethnic diversity have not become institutionalized within the American educational system.* In other words, the resistance to pluralistic education is basically ideological.

The Ideological Clash

In chapter 5, I used a Weberian type, ideal-type conceptualization to identify two major positions related to race and ethnicity in the nation's schools: the *cultural pluralist ideology* and the *assimilationist ideology*. These two ideologies, of course, exist on a continuum. Mainstream American educators, who are primarily assimilationists, make most of the major decisions that are implemented and institutionalized within the American schools and colleges. They are the gatekeepers of the status quo. Pluralistic educators are those small group of educators who advocate reforms to make American education more ethnically pluralistic. Mainstream and pluralistic educators embrace conflicting and oftentimes contradictory ideological positions about the nature of society, the nature of schooling, and about the purposes of schooling in a democratic nation such as the United States. The assumptions and ideological positions of mainstream and pluralistic educators are discussed in detail in chapter 5.

The Quest for a New Ideology

Neither the *assimilationist* nor the *cultural pluralistic ideology,* in their ideal or pure forms, can effectively guide curriculum reform in a democratic nation that has a universal culture that is both heavily influenced by and shared by all ethnic groups. Programs based primarily on assimilationist assumptions perpetuate misconceptions about the nature of American society and violate the ethnic identities of many students. Curricular practices that reflect an extreme notion of cultural pluralism also distort American realities and give inadequate attention to the universal American culture that strongly influences the behavior of all American citizens.

Both the assimilationist and cultural pluralist ideologies emanate from misleading and/or incomplete analyses of the nature of ethnicity in contemporary American society. The assimilationist ideology derives primarily from two conceptualizations of ethnicity in American society: *Anglo-conformity* and the *melting pot.* The cultural pluralist ideology emanates from a conceptualization of ethnicity in American society called *cultural pluralism.* I will summarize these conceptualizations of ethnicity in the United States and indicate why each is inadequate and/or misleading conceptualizations.[4] I will then present my own analysis of ethnicity in American society and derive a new ideology, called the *multiethnic ideology,* from my analysis. The multiethnic ideology I will present is one possible way to reduce the ideological resistance to pluralistic education.

Anglo-conformity suggests that ethnic groups gave up their cultural attributes and acquired those of Anglo Saxon Protestants. This concept describes a type of unidirectional assimilation. The *melting pot,* long embraced as an ideal in American society and culture, suggests that the various ethnic cultures within America were mixed and synthesized into a new culture, different from any of the original ethnic cultures. *Cultural pluralism* suggests, at least in its extreme form, that the nation is made up of various ethnic subsocieties, each of which has a set of largely independent norms, institutions, values, and beliefs.

Each of these conceptualizations presents major problems when one views the reality of ethnicity and race in America.[5] The Anglo-conformity conceptualization suggests that Anglo Saxons were changed very little in America and that other ethnic groups did all of the changing. This conceptualization is incomplete, unidirectional and static. The melting pot conceptualization is inaccurate and misleading because human cultures are complex and dynamic and don't melt like iron. Consequently, the melting pot is a false and misleading metaphor.

The strong cultural pluralist conceptualization denies the reality that we have a universal American culture that every American, regardless of his or her ethnic group, shares to a great extent This culture includes American Creed values as *ideals,* American English, a highly technological and industrialized civilization, a capitalistic economy, and a veneration of materialism and consumption. Richard Hofstadter has brilliantly argued that antiintellectualism is another key component in the universal American culture.[6] This is not to deny that there are important subcultural variants within the different ethnic subsocieties in America or that there are many nonuniversalized ethnic characteristics in American ethnic communities. These nonuniversalized ethnic subvariants will be discussed later.

Gordon believes that *structural pluralism* best describes the ethnic reality in American society.[7] According to Gordon, the ethnic groups in the United States have experienced gross levels of cultural assimilation but the nation is characterized by structural pluralism. In other words, ethnic groups are highy assimilated culturally (into the Anglo-American culture) but have separate ethnic subsocieties, such as Black fraternities, Jewish social clubs, and Chicano theaters.

Multiple Acculturation

While Gordon's notion of structural pluralism is helpful and deals more adequately with the complexity of ethnic diversity in modern American society than the other three concepts, I believe that multiple acculturation more accurately describes how the universal American culture was and is forming than the concept of cultural assimilation. The White Anglo-Saxon Protestant culture was changed in America as were the cultures of Africans and of Asian immigrants. African cultures and Asian cultures influenced and changed the WASP culture as the WASP culture influenced and modified African and Asian cultures. What we experienced in America, and what we are still experiencing, is multiple acculturation and not a kind of unidirectional type of cultural assimilation whereby the Black culture was influenced by the WASP culture and not the other way around.

The general or universal culture in the United States resulted from this series of multiple acculturations. This culture is still in the process of formation and change (see Figure 6.1). The universal American culture is not just a WASP culture, but contains important elements of the wide variety of ethnic cultures that are and/or were part of American society. Those ethnic cultural elements that became universalized and part of the general American culture have been reinterpreted and mediated by the unique social, economic, and political experience in the United States. *It is inaccurate and misleading to refer to the universal American culture as a WASP culture.*

This notion of American culture has been and is often perpetuated in the school and university curricula. It is, of course, true that the White

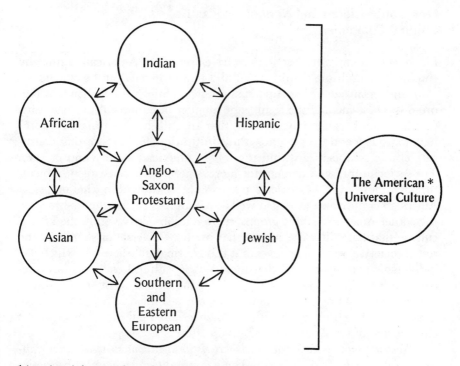

*American is here used to refer only to the United States.

Figure 6.1. The Development of American Culture. This figure illustrates how the American universal culture developed through a process conceptualized as *multiple acculturation*. While the Anglo-Saxon Protestant culture had the greatest influence on the development of the American culture, each of the various ethnic cultures influenced the Anglo culture and were influenced by it. Each of these cultures was also influenced by and influenced each other. These complex series of acculturations, which were mediated by the American experience and the American socio-cultural environment, resulted in the universal American culture. This process is still taking place today.

Anglo-Saxon Protestants have had a more profound impact on the universal American culture than any other single ethnic group. However, we can easily exaggerate the WASP influence on the general American culture. European cultures were greatly influenced by African and Asian cultures before the European explorers started coming to the Americas in the fifteenth century. The earliest British immigrants borrowed heavily from the American Indians on the East coast and probably would not have survived if they had not assimilated Indian cultural components and used some of their farming methods and tools.

Ethnic Subsocieties and Nonuniversalized Cultural Components

Figure 6.1 attempts to describe the development of American culture by emphasizing multiple acculturation and how ethnic cultural elements became universalized. Other American ethnic realities are not shown in Figure 6.1. These include the significant number of ethnic cultural elements that have not become universalized (that are still shared primarily by ethnic subgroups) and the separate ethnic institutions and groups that constitute ethnic subsocieties within the larger American society and culture. The sociocultural environment for most Americans is consequently bicultural. Almost every American participates both within the universal American culture and society as well as within his or her ethnic subsociety. Like other American ethnic groups, there is a subsociety within the WASP culture that has cultural elements that are not universal or shared by the rest of society. Patterson believes that this is a small subsociety in which few individuals participate and that most WASP cultural elements have become universalized. He writes, ". . . with the exception of small pockets such as the New England Brahmin elite, the vast majority of WASPs have abandoned the ethnic specificities of their original culture in favor of the elite version of the American universal culture."[8]

Nonuniversalized ethnic cultural characteristics and ethnic subsocieties are realities in contemporary American society. These cultural elements and subsocieties play an important role in the socialization of many Americans and help individual members of ethnic groups to satisfy important needs. Figure 6.2 illustrates the relationship between the universal American culture and ethnic subsocieties.

The Multiethnic Ideology

My analysis of ethnicity in American society leads to a philosophical position that may be called the *multiethnic ideology* since one of its key assertions is that Americans function within several cultures, including the main-

Ethnic Subsociety A

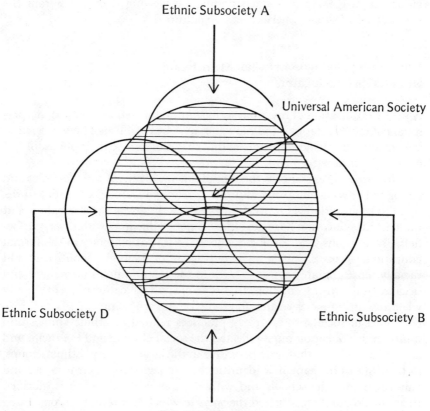

Universal American Society

Ethnic Subsociety D

Ethnic Subsociety B

Ethnic Subsociety C

Figure 6.2. Ethnic Subsocieties and the Universal American Society. In this figure, the universal American society is represented by the ruled area. This culture is shared by all ethnic groups within the United States. A, B, C, and D represent ethnic subsocieties that consist of unique ethnic institutions, values, and cultural elements that are non-universalized and shared primarily by members of specific ethnic groups.

stream culture and various ethnic subcultures. This multiethnic ideology suggests specific goals for curriculum reform related to ethnicity. A major goal of multiethnic education, derived from my analysis of the nature of ethnicity in American life, is to help students develop cross-cultural competency (discussed in chapter 2). Edward T. Hall, in his insightful book, *Beyond Culture*, underscores the importance of helping students to develop the skills and understandings needed to function cross-culturally. He writes, "The future depends on man's transcending the limits of individual cultures."[9] Another important goal of multiethnic education is to help individuals gain greater self-understanding by viewing themselves from the perspectives of other American ethnic cultures.

Establishing Dialogue between Mainstream and Pluralistic Educators

A major implication of my analysis for multiethnic education is that "personal contact" situations and dialogue must be established between mainstream and pluralistic educators so that they can resolve their philosophical conflicts and disagreements.

Ideological resistance is the root of our problem. Personal contact and dialogue between pluralistic and mainstream educators is essential to derive a basic solution. However, little serious discussion and debate about multiethnic education has taken place among educators with divergent beliefs, assumptions, and ideologies about the role of ethnicity in the formal educational process.[10] This is partly because of the highly politicized and racially tense climate that gave birth to the ethnic studies movement and because of the strong emotions that scholars and educators often exemplify when discussing issues related to ethnicity and schooling.

Born in social protest, early practices related to ethnic studies and multiethnic education often reflected the social climate and the racial and ethnic polarization that were pervasive in the larger society. Ethnic groups, in their quests to shape new identities and to legitimize their histories and cultures within the schools and within the larger society, often glorified their cultures and emphasized the ways in which they had been oppressed by the dominant Anglo-American society.

This early phase of ethnic protest and ethnic studies programs must be viewed within a broad social and political context. Groups that perceive themselves as oppressed and who internalize the dominant society's negative stereotypes and myths about themselves are likely to express strong ingroup feelings during the early stages of an ethnic revitalization movement. There is also an attempt to shape a new ethnic consciousness and group identity. During this phase, the group is also likely to strongly reject outside ethnic and racial groups, to romanticize its past, and to view contemporary social and political conditions from a highly subjective perspective.

An ethnic group that is experiencing the early stages of an ethnic revitalization movement is also likely to demand that the school curriculum portray a romanticized version of its history and to emphasize the ways in which the group has been oppressed and victimized by other ethnic and racial groups within the society. Extremely negative sanctions are directed against members of the ethnic group who do not endorse a strong "ethnic position." Consequently, little fruitful dialogue is likely to take place among individuals who hold conflicting ideological positions regarding ethnicity and educational policy. Members of both the "oppressed" and of the "oppressive" groups are likely to be ardent in their positions during the early stages of an ethnic revitalization movement (see chapter 10).

We have entered a new phase in the development of multiethnic education—a phase in which scholars who have serious reservations about multiethnic education feel free to express their concerns in a public forum, thereby stimulating dialogue that can lead to a better clarification of the issues and to a reduction of ideological conflict.[11] Open discussions related to ethnicity and schooling can now take place because the ethnic revitalization movements in the United States have reached a new developmental phase: emotions have cooled, perspective has been gained, and ethnic minorities are now engaging in serious introspection, research, and policy formation.[12]

Sharing Power

Another important implication of my analysis is that powerful groups that now dominate educational policy and decisions must be willing to share power with currently excluded and powerless ethnic groups before a multiethnic ideology can be developed and educational policy can be shaped that reflects the interests and aspirations of American ethnic minority groups. Historically in the United States, educational policy for powerless and structurally excluded ethnic groups, such as Blacks and Mexican Americans, has been made by powerful Anglo-American groups that controlled the educational system.[13] As pointed out in chapter 1, an Anglocentric education alienates minority groups from their ethnic cultures and frequently fails to help them attain the attitudes, skills, and abilities needed to function effectively within the mainstream of American society and within other ethnic subsocieties.

Powerless and excluded ethnic groups, such as Mexican Americans and Puerto Rican Americans, must participate in shaping educational policy in order for educational reforms related to ethnic diversity to become institutionalized within the American educational system.[14] The groups that exercise power in the American educational establishment design and run the schools so that they reflect their ideology, assumptions, values, and perspectives. The assimilationists who control the schools often see pluralism as a threat to the survival of America as they envision it. Ways must be devised for currently excluded ethnic groups to gain power in American education and to participate in major educational decisions that affect the education of their youths. Only in this way will a philosophy of ethnic pluralism become institutionalized within the American educational system and the system will become legitimate from the perspectives of ethnic minorities.[15] Curricular models which can help to lead to a sharing of power by structurally included and excluded groups are conceptualized and discussed in chapter 10.

Summary

Reforms related to ethnic and cultural diversity, such as ethnic studies and bilingual-bicultural education, have not become institutionalized within the American educational establishment. These educational reforms remain primarily on the periphery of American education. Educators set forth a variety of reasons to explain their lack of interest in multiethnic educational reforms. However, many of these reasons do not reflect the basic cause of resistance. The resistance to pluralistic educational reforms is primarily ideological. Most of the educators who control the schools are assimilationist oriented and see forms of pluralistic education as inconsistent with their basic values, commitments, and beliefs.

The assimilationist ideology that most educators who control the schools embrace derives from two conceptions of the nature of ethnicity in American society that are misleading and incomplete: Anglo-conformity and the melting pot. An effective ideology that can guide educational reform within an ethnically pluralistic nation such as the United States must be based on a more accurate analysis of the nature of ethnicity and race in America. Structural pluralism and multiple acculturation accurately describe the nature of ethnic group life in the United States. The multiethnic ideology derives from these conceptions of ethnicity and race in America. This ideology can be used to help reduce the ideological resistence to pluralistic education and to establish a thoughtful dialogue between mainstream and pluralistic educators. However, in order for a multiethnic ideology to be developed and to influence educational policy, powerful Anglo ethnic groups must share power with structurally exluded ethnic groups such as American Indians, Blacks, and Puerto Ricans.

Notes

1. *Report of the National Advisory Commission on Civil Disorders* (New York: Bantam Books, 1968).
2. James A. Banks, "Multiethnic Education Across Cultures: United States, Mexico, Puerto Rico, France and Great Britian," *Social Education* 42 (March 1978), pp. 177–185. Also see Raymond Giles, *The West Indian Experience in British Schools: Multi-Racial Education and Social Disadvantage in London* (London: Heinemann Educational Books Ltd., 1977).
3. See especially James A. Banks, *Multiethnic Education: Practices and Promises* (Bloomington, Ind.: Phi Delta Kappa Educational Foundation, 1977).
4. These conceptualizations are discussed in considerable detail in Milton Gordon, *Assimilation in American Life* (New York: Oxford University Press, 1964).
5. I first presented my notion of multiple acculturation in James A.

Banks, "Ethnicity: Implications for Curriculum Reform," *The Social Studies* 70 (January/February 1979), pp. 3-10.

6. Richard Hofstadter, *Anti-Intellectualism in American Life* (New York: Vintage, 1963). Other cultural components of the general American culture are discussed in Edward C. Stewart, *American Cultural Patterns: A Cross-Cultural Perspective* (LaGrange Park, Ill.: Intercultural Network, Inc., 1972).

7. Gordon, *Assimilation in American Life.*

8. Orlando Patterson, *Ethnic Chauvinism: The Reactionary Impulse* (New York: Stein and Day, 1977), p. 151.

9. Edward T. Hall, *Beyond Culture* (Garden City, N.Y.: Doubleday, 1977), p. 2.

10. This section is adapted from my paper, "A Response to Philip Freedman," *Phi Delta Kappan* 58 (May 1977), pp. 695-697.

11. In these two publications, the authors raise serious questions about aspects of ethnic education: Philip I. Freedman, "Multi-Ethnic Studies: Proceed with Caution," *Phi Delta Kappan* 59 (January 1977), pp. 401-403; Noel Epstein, *Language, Ethnicity and the Schools: Policy Alternatives for Bilingual-Bicultural Education* (Washington, D.C.: Institute for Educational Leadership, The George Washington University, 1977).

12. See, for example, "The Education of Black Americans," *Change: The Magazine of Learning* 11 (October 1979). This special issue of *Change* includes articles by such Black scholars as Bernard C. Watson, Charles V. Willie, and Derrick Bell. Also see Bernard C. Watson, *In Spite of the System: The Individual and Educational Reform* (Cambridge, Mass: Ballinger Publishing Company, 1974); William E. Cross, ed., *Third Conference on Empirical Research in Black Psychology* (Washington D.C.: The National Institute of Education, 1977).

13. Samuel Bowles and Herbert Gintis, *Schooling in Capitalist America: Educational Reform and the Contradictions of Economic Life* (New York: Basic Books, 1976); Michael B. Katz, *Class, Bureaucracy, and Schools: The Illusion of Educational Change in America,* expanded edition (New York: Praeger, 1975).

14. Barbara A. Sizemore, "Separatism: A Reality Approach to Inclusion?" in Robert L. Green, ed., *Racial Crisis in American Education* (Chicago: Follett Educational Corporation, 1969), pp. 249-279.

15. Charles V. Hamilton, "Race and Education: A Search for Legitimacy," *Harvard Educational Review* 38 (Fall 1968), pp. 669-684.

PART III
Teaching Strategies
for Multiethnic Education

Introduction

This part discusses some of the key problems, issues, and current practices in the teaching of ethnic studies and presents a teaching unit. Some of the major assumptions and practices in ethnic studies instruction are reviewed and criticized in chapter 7. The characteristics of an effective ethnic studies curricula are described and illustrated. Models for teaching ethnic studies issues and problems from diverse ethnic perspectives are presented and justified. A model for teaching decision-making and social-action skills using content and issues related to ethnic issues is also presented.

Chapter 8 illustrates how the decision-making model presented in chapter 7 can be used to organize and teach a social issues unit related to racial and ethnic diversity. This chapter consists of a comprehensive unit plan.

7

Teaching Ethnic Studies: Issues and Models

There are several widespread assumptions about ethnic studies that have adversely affected the development of ethnic studies curricular in the nation's schools. We need to examine and to challenge these assumptions and related school practices and to formulate new assumptions and goals for ethnic studies if the ethnic studies movement is going to serve as a vehicle for general curriculum reform. If we merely add ethnic content to the traditional curriculum, which has many problems, our efforts to modify the curriculum with ethnic content are likely to lead to a dead end. We need to reform the total school curriculum.

Assumptions about Ethnic Studies

Ethnic Studies as Ethnic Minority Studies

One pervasive assumption embraced by many educators is that ethnic studies deal exclusively or primarily with non-White minority groups, such as Asian Americans, American Indians and Puerto Ricans in the United States. This assumption is widespread within the schools. School ethnic studies curricula are often based on and reflect it. In many school ethnic studies programs, for example, little or no attention is devoted to the experiences of European-American ethnic groups, such as Jewish Americans, Polish Americans, and Italian Americans. This narrow conceptualization of ethnic studies emerged out of the social forces that gave rise to the ethnic studies movement in the 1960s and 1970s.

As pointed out in chapter 1, Black Americans staged a fight for their civil rights during the 1960s that was unprecedented in their history. They demanded control of various social, economic, and political institutions within the Black community. They also demanded that the school curriculum be reformed so that it would more accurately reflect their historical and cultural experiences in the United States.[1] Other ethnic minority groups, such as Mexican Americans, Asian Americans, and Puerto Ricans, were made acutely aware of their ethnic identity and struggles by the Black civil rights movement. These groups also called for new versions of school and college history that would more accurately reflect their experiences in the Americas.[2]

The types of ethnic studies programs that have been formulated in most school districts and colleges reflect the political and social demands that have been made within local communities. Responding largely to crises and public pressures, curriculum specialists have devised ethnic studies programs without giving serious thought to the basic issues that should be considered when curriculum changes are made. The nature of learning, the social and psychological needs of students, and social science theory and research are the types of problems and issues that received little if any consideration in the hurriedly formulated ethnic studies programs that now exist in many schools. Rather, the overriding consideration was to create some kinds of programs so that ethnic demands would be met and militant ethnic students and faculty would be silenced. Consequently, ethnic studies became defined as the study of ethnic minority groups; and most of the programs that were formulated were parochial in scope, fragmented, and were structured without careful planning and clear rationales.

Ethnic Studies and Ethnic Minorities

A related assumption that school people often make about ethnic studies is that only students who are members of a particular ethnic minority group should study that group's history and culture. This assumption, too, grew out of the historical and social forces of the 1960s. Blacks argued that Black students needed Black history in order to augment their self-concepts and identities.[3] Mexican Americans, American Indians, Puerto Ricans, and other ethnic minority groups set forth similar arguments about why specialized ethnic studies courses, such as Puerto Rican studies and Chicano studies, were needed. Using these arguments, many school people conveniently concluded that only Blacks needed Black studies and only Mexican-American students needed Chicano studies.

School ethnic studies programs frequently focus on one specific ethnic group, such as Puerto-Ricans, Afro-Americans, or American Indians.[4] The ethnic group on which the program focuses is usually either present or dominant in the local school population. In schools that are predominantly Mexican-American, there are usually courses in Chicano studies but no courses or experiences that will help students to learn about the problems and heritages of other ethnic groups, such as Afro-Americans, Flilpino Americans, or Jewish Americans. Significantly, specialized ethnic studies courses are rarely found in predominantly White schools and are almost always electives in schools with a large minority group population. The popularity of these courses has waned tremendously since the early 1970s. In some schools, few Black students are now taking Black studies courses.

Ethnic Studies as an Addition to the Curriculum

Many school people assume that ethnic studies are essentially additive in nature and that we can create valid ethnic studies programs by leaving the present curriculum essentially intact; we can simply add a list of minority group heroes and events to the list of Anglo-American heroes and events that are already studied in most social studies courses. These educators believe that we should teach about the heroic deeds of Booker T. Washington and Geronimo just as we teach about the heroic deeds of Betsy Ross and Abraham Lincoln, and that pictures of Black and American Indian heroes should be added to those of eminent White Americans that are already hanging in the school corridors and classrooms. In additive types of ethnic studies programs, students are required to memorize isolated facts about White history and Black history.

Conceptualizing ethnic studies as essentially additive in nature is problematic for several reasons. A large body of educational literature has documented the traditional and nonstimulating nature of many school courses and has stated why reform in classroom teaching is sorely needed.[5] While much curriculum reform has taken place in the teaching of school subjects in the last decade, especially in textbooks, in many classrooms teachers still emphasize the mastery of low level facts and do not help students to master high level concepts, generalizations, and theories.

Modifying the school curriculum to include ethnic content provides a tremendous opportunity to reexamine the assumptions, purposes, and nature of the curriculum and to formulate a curriculum with new assumptions and goals. Merely adding low level facts about ethnic content to a curriculum that is already bulging with discrete and isolated facts about White history and heroes will result in an overkill. Isolated facts about Crispus Attucks don't stimulate the intellect any more than isolated facts about Betsy Ross and Abraham Lincoln. To meaningfully integrate content about ethnic groups into the total school curriculum we must undertake more substantial and innovative curriculum reform.

Ethnic Studies as the Study of Strange Customs

Other assumptions are made about ethnic studies and many current school practices reflect them. Some teachers, especially in the lower grades, believe that ethnic studies should deal primarily with those tangible elements of minority cultures which seem strange and different to themselves and to their students. Consequently, experiences in the primary grades often focus on the foods and "strange" customs and artifacts of minority cultures, such as soul food, teepees, igloos, and chow mein. Focusing on the customs within ethnic minority groups that seem strange to teachers and their students is likely to reinforce stereotypes and misconceptions rather than help students to develop cultural sensitivity and knowledge of other cultures, which is usually the goal stated by teachers when they plan these types of learning experiences.

Since many primary grade teachers are unlikely to approach the study of cultural differences from an anthropological and sensitive perspective, their students are likely to conclude that cultural characteristics that are different from their own are indeed strange and different and that minority peoples share few characteristics with them. Emphasis in ethnic studies should be on the human characteristics and values of ethnic groups, and not on strange customs or tangible cultural elements like teepees and sombreros. Ethnic content should be used to help students learn that all human beings have common needs and characteristics, although the ways in which these traits are manifested frequently differ cross-culturally.

Ethnic Studies as the Celebration of Ethnic Holidays

Some teachers, again usually in the elementary grades, see ethnic studies primarily as the celebration of ethnic holiday, such as Martin Luther King's birthday and *Cinco de Mayo*. In many schools, lessons about ethnic groups are limited primarily to these types of special days and holidays. Some schools set aside particular days or weeks of the year for Black history and culture, Mexican-American history and culture, and Indian history and culture. In a few cases, especially in schools with a significant Jewish population, a special day for Jewish history and culture is set aside. The long-range effects of these kinds of special "ethnic days" might be detrimental and serve to reinforce the notion that ethnic groups, such as Afro-Americans and Jewish Americans, are not integral parts of American society and culture. This is especially likely to happen if ethnic groups are studied only on special days or in special units and lessons. The students are likely to conclude that American history and Black history are distinctly separate and mutually exclusive entities.

The notion that Afro-American, Jewish-American, and Mexican-American culture are integral parts of American Society must be reflected in the way in which American Studies is organized and in all activities and teaching strategies. Special units and days might prevent the students from developing the notion that these groups are integral parts of American society and culture. However, if ethnic minority groups are integral parts of the school curriculum, highlighting the experiences of a particular ethnic group is less likely to result in negative learning by students. The danger of negative learnings occurring is greatly increased when these types of experiences are isolated and are not integral parts of the total school curriculum.

Expanding the Definition of Ethnic Studies

Each of the major assumptions reviewed and criticized above, while widespread and in some cases understandable, is intellectually indefensible and continues to have adverse effects on ethnic studies in the schools. The assumption that ethnic studies is equivalent to ethnic minority studies is one of the most wide-spread beliefs held by school people.

It is both inaccurate and educationally unsound to assume that ethnic studies should be limited to a study of ethnic minority groups. Ethnic studies shoud be, in part, the scientific and humanistic examination of those variables related to ethnicity that influence human behavior. Any individual or group whose behavior can be totally or partially explained by variables related to ethnicity is an appropriate subject in ethnic studies.

A definition of ethnic group can help us to determine the parameters of ethnic studies and the curricular implications of the concept. In chapter 4 I defined an ethnic group as a group that shares a common ancestry, culture, history, tradition, sense of peoplehood, and that is a political and economic interest group. These characteristics of an ethnic group suggest that every American can be considered a member of an ethnic group. *However, individual members of ethnic groups vary widely in their levels of ethnic identification and ethnic behavior* (see chapter 4).

Our definition of ethnic group indicates that Anglo-Americans, Italian Americans, Polish Americans, Jewish Americans, as well as Afro-Americans and Puerto Ricans, should be studied within a comparative ethnic studies curriculum. Members of all of these groups exhibit behavioral characteristics that can be partically explained by variables related to ethnicity.

Ethnic studies programs should include but not be limited to a study of ethnic minority groups. An *ethnic minority group* is a particular type of ethnic group with several distinguishing charcteristics. Like an ethnic group, an ethnic minority group shares values, behavioral characteristics, and a sense of peoplehood, and is an economic and political interest group.[6] However, an ethnic minority group has unique physical and/or cultural characteristics that enable members of other groups to easily identify its members, usually for purposes of discrimination. Jewish Americans are an ethnic minority group with unique cultural characteristics; Afro-Americans have unique physical and cultural characteristics. Ethnic minorities are frequently a numerical minority and are often politically and economically powerless within a society. However, this is not always the case. In the Republic of South Africa, the Blacks are politically and economically powerless but are a numerical majority. However, they are considered a sociological minority.

To conceptualize ethnic studies as the study of ethnic minorities is inconsistent with the ways in which ethnicity is defined by sociologists and prevents the development of broadly conceptualized ethnic studies programs that compare and contrast the experiences of all of the immigrants who came to America and that help students to fully understand the complex role of ethnicity in American life and culture. Conceptualizing ethnic studies exclusively as the study of nonWhite ethnic groups also promotes a kind of "we-they" attitude among White students and teachers. Many students believe that ethnic studies is the study of "them," while American history is the study of "us." Some teachers assume that because ethnic studies is the study of "them," it should be taught only when there is a non-White population within the school to take ethnic studies courses.

Ethnic Studies: A Process of Curriculum Reform

Ethnic studies should not be limited to the study of ethnic minority groups although it should definitely include them. It should not be an addition to or an appendage to the regular curriculum. *Rather, ethnic studies should be viewed as a process of curiculum reform that will result in the creation of a new curriculum that is based on new assumptions and new perspectives, and that will help students to gain novel views of the American experience and a new conception of what it means to be American.* Since the English immigrants gained control over most economic, social, and political institutions early in our national history, to *Americanize* has been interpreted to mean to *Anglicize.* Especially during the height of nativism in the late 1800s and early 1900s, the English-Americans defined Americanization as Anglicization.[7] This notion of Americanization is still widespread within our society and schools today. Thus when we think of American history and American literature we tend to think of Anglo-American history and Anglo-American literature.

Reconceptualizing American Society

Since the assumption that only that which is Anglo-American is American is so deeply ingrained in curriculum materials and in the hearts and minds of many students and teachers, we cannot significantly change the curriculum by merely adding a unit or a lesson here and there about Afro-American, Jewish-American, or Italian-American history. Rather, we need to seriously examine the conception of *American* that is perpetuated in the curriculum and its basic purposes and assumptions.

It is imperative that we reconceptualize the ways in which we view

American society and culture in the school curriculum. We should teach about American culture from diverse ethnic perspectives rather than primarily or exclusively from the points of view of Anglo-American historians, scientists, writers, and artists. Most of the courses in the school curriculum are currently taught primarily from Anglo-American perspectives. These types of courses and experiences are based on what I call the *Anglo-American Centric Model* or Model A (see Figure 7.1). Ethnic studies, as a process of curriculum reform, can and often does proceed from Model A to Model B, the *Ethnic Additive Model*. In courses and experiences based on Model B, ethnic content is an additive to the major curriculum thrust, which remains Anglo-American dominated. Many school districts that have attempted ethnic modification of the curriculum have implemented Model B types of curricular changes. Black studies courses, Chicano studies courses, and special units on ethnic groups in the elementary grades are examples of Model B types of curricular experiences.

However, I am suggesting that curriculum reform proceed directly from Model A to Model C, the *Multiethnic Model*. In courses and experiences based on Model C, the students study historical and social events from several ethnic points of view. Anglo-American perspectives are only one group of several and are in no way superior or inferior to other ethnic perspectives. I view Model D, the Ethonational Model, types of courses and programs as the ultimte goal of curriculum reform. In this curriculum model, students study historical and social events from multinational perspectives and points of view. Since we live in a global society, students need to learn how to become effective citizens of the world community. This is unlikely to happen if they study historical and contemporary social events primarily from the perspective of ethnic cultures within this nation.

Teaching Multiethnic Perspectives

When studying a historical period, such as the colonial period, in a course organized on the *Multiethnic Model* (Model C), the inquiry does not end when the students view the period from the perspectives of Anglo-American historians and writers. Rather, they ponder these kinds of questions: Why did Anglo-American historians name the English immigrants "colonists" and other nationality groups "immigrants?" How do American Indians historians view the colonial period? Do their views of the period differ in any substantial ways from the views of Anglo-American historians? Why or why not? What was life like for the Jews, Blacks, and other ethnic groups in America during the seventeenth and eighteenth centuries? How do we know? In other words, in courses and programs organized on Model C, students view historical and contemporary events from the perspectives of different ethnic and racial groups.

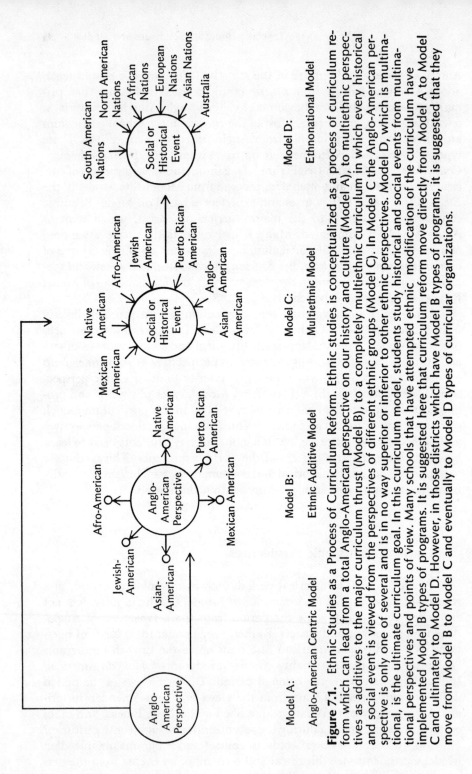

Figure 7.1. Ethnic Studies as a Process of Curriculum Reform. Ethnic studies is conceptualized as a process of curriculum reform which can lead from a total Anglo-American perspective on our history and culture (Model A), to multiethnic perspectives as additives to the major curriculum thrust (Model B), to a completely multiethnic curriculum in which every historical and social event is viewed from the perspectives of different ethnic groups (Model C). In Model C the Anglo-American perspective is only one of several and is in no way superior or inferior to other ethnic perspectives. Model D, which is multinational, is the ultimate curriculum goal. In this curriculum model, students study historical and social events from multinational perspectives and points of view. Many schools that have attempted ethnic modification of the curriculum have implemented Model B types of programs. It is suggested here that curriculum reform move directly from Model A to Model C and ultimately to Model D. However, in those districts which have Model B types of programs, it is suggested that they move from Model B to Model C and eventually to Model D types of curricular organizations.

Model A: Anglo-American Centric Model

Model B: Ethnic Additive Model

Model C: Multiethnic Model

Model D: Ethnonational Model

I am not suggesting that we eliminate or denigrate Anglo-American history or Anglo-American perspectives on historical events. I am merely suggesting that Anglo-American perspectives should be among many different ethnic perspectives taught in the school. Only by approaching the study of American society in this way will students get a global rather than an ethnocentric view of our nation's history and culture.

A historian's experience and culture, including his or her ethnic culture, cogently influences his or her views of the past and present.[8] However, it would be simplistic to argue that there is one Anglo-American view of history and contemporary events or one Black view. Wide differences in experiences and perceptions exist both within and across ethnic groups. However, those who have experienced a historical event or a social phenomenon, such as racial bigotry or internment, often view the event differently than those who have watched it from a distance.[9] There is no one Anglo-American perspective on the internment as there is no one Japanese-American view of it. However, accounts written by those who were interned, such as Takashima's powerful *Child in Prison Camp,* often provide insights and perspectives on the internment that cannot be provided by people who were not interned.[10] Individuals who viewed the internment from the outside can also provide us with unique and important perspectives and points of view. Both perspectives should be studied in a sound curriculum.

Only by looking at events, such as the internment, from many different perspectives can we fully understand the complex dimensions of American history and culture. Various ethnic groups within our society are often influenced by events differently and respond to and perceive them differently. One of the goals of ethnic studies should be to change the basic assumptions about what *American* means and to present students with new ways of viewing and interpreting American history and culture. Any goals that are less ambitious, while important, will not result in the substantial curricular reform which I consider imperative.

Ethnic Studies and Ethnic Conflict

Those of us in ethnic studies write and talk most frequently about the positive effects cultural diversity can have on American society. However, we rarely speak candidly about the conflict inherent within a society that is made up of diverse ethnic groups with conflicting goals, ideologies, and strong feelings of ethnocentrism. Some educators are deeply concerned that ethnic studies, by fostering ethnic pride, might lead to extreme ethnic conflict and the Balkanization of American society. In designing ethnic studies programs and experiences, we must give serious and thoughtful consideration to this complex question. Otherwise, this legitimate concern may become a rationalization for inaction and a justification for the status quo. Whether ethnic studies content and programs contribute to the development of dysfunctional ethnic polarization and social conflict or help to bring about democratic social change depends to some extent on the ways in which ethnic studies programs are conceptualized and taught. Ethnic studies programs that focus exclusively on the sins of Anglo-Americans and the virtues of oppressed minorities are less likely to help students to develop the kinds of skills and attitudes needed to function successfully within our pluralistic society than an ethnic studies program that focuses on helping students to develop humanistic attitudes and the skills to engage in reflective social action. There is little reason to believe that an ethnic studies program that fosters reflective social action is likely to promote dysfunctional ethnic conflict and polarization. However, this kind of ethnic studies program is designed to promote the development of social change that will make our society more open and just. Conflict is a necessary concomitant of any form of social change. *Consequently, ethnic studies should deal with systems and processes that will facilitate the resolution of ethnic conflict in a pluralistic society.*

The Objectives of Ethnic Studies

Developing Ethnic Literacy

To foster democratic social change and yet reduce dysfunctional ethnic and racial polarization, ethnic studies must have at least three major objectives: (1) to help individuals to clarify their ethnic identities and to function effectively within their own ethnic communities, (2) to help individuals to develop a sensitivity to and understanding of other ethnic cultures and to function effectively within them, and (3) to help individuals to develop the ability to make reflective decisions on social issues and to take actions to resolve social problems. Individuals who develop these characteristics and skills have what I call *ethnic literacy.*[11] The first two of these goals are discussed below. The final goal is examined in the next section.

An individual must clarify his or her own sense of ethnic and personal identity before he or she can positively relate to individuals who belong to other ethnic and racial groups. We need to foster the development of self-acceptance but discourage ethnic ethnocentrism. Although individuals within a pluralistic society must learn to accept their own identity and to become comfortable with it, they must also learn to function effectively within other ethnic cultures and to respond positively to individuals who belong to other ethnic groups. They must also learn how to interact with members of outside groups and how to resolve conflicts with them.

There is no inherent contradiction in teaching students how to understand and to function effectively within their own ethnic cultures and to understand and to function successfully within other ethnic cultures and communities, including the dominant culture. Both of these goals are equally significant within a pluralistic nation. The attainment of one is not likely to occur unless both are realized and fostered. It is extremely difficult for a Mexican-American child to accept his or her cultural heritage if it is demeaned by "significant others" in institutions like the school. It is also very difficult for Anglo-Americans to learn to respond to nonWhites positively and sensitively if they are unaware of the perceptions of their culture that are held by other ethnic groups and of the ways in which the dominant culture evolved and attained the power to shape the United States in its image.

We have never fully realized the positive effects that can accrue from the diverse nature of our society because the major goal of most social institutions, historically, has been to Anglicize ethnic groups, to disregard their ethnic cultures, and to foster a monocultural societal ideal. The result has been that almost every ethnic group has struggled to become culturally like Anglo-Americans. Those groups that have been the most successful have attained the highest levels of social and economic mobility. The ethnic groups in our society that are the most "ethnic" tend to be heavily concentrated in the lower and working classes. Because most of the institutions within our society tend to foster and to idealize Anglo-Saxon cultural characteristics and do not encourage Anglo-Americans to function in other ethnic cultures, Anglo-Americans are rarely required to function within other ethnic communities; members of other ethnic groups tend to reject their ethnic cultures and to strive to attain Anglo-American cultural traits. However, this is less true today than in the past. Ethnic diversity and cultural pluralism will not become ideals in our society until members of the dominant ethnic group and members of other ethnic groups better understand their own cultures and learn to function within and across cultures. With these goals, ethnic studies is more likely to foster constructive social change and to reduce, rather than to enhance, ethnic tension and conflict.

Developing Decision-making Skills

A third major objective of ethnic studies should be to help students develop the ability to make reflective decisions so that they can resolve personal problems, and through social action, influence public policy and develop a sense of political efficacy.[12] In many ethnic studies units and lessons, emphasis is on the memorization and testing of isolated historical facts about shadowy ethnic heroes and events of questionable historical significance. In these types of programs ethnic studies is merely an extension of the traditional curriculum.

Ethnic studies should have goals that are more consistent with the needs of a global society. Events within the last decade have dramatically indicated that we live in a world society that is beset with momentous so-

cial and human problems. Effective solutions to these tremendous problems can be found only by an active and informed citizenry capable of
making sound public decisions that will benefit the world community. It is
imperative that the total school curriculum play a decisive role in educating citizens capable of making intelligent decisions on social issues and
taking affirmative actions to help resolve them.

Elements of Reflective Decision Making

Decision making consists of several components, including the deriva-
tion of knowledge, prediction, value analysis and clarification, the synthesis
of knowledge and values, and the affirmation of a course of action (see Figure 7.2). While all decisions consist of knowledge, valuing, and prediction
components, reflective decisions must satisfy other requirements. To make
a reflective decision, the decision maker must use the scientific method to

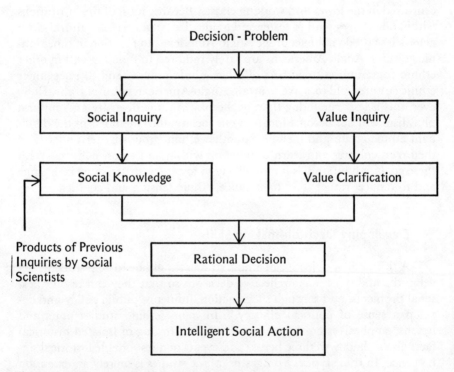

Figure 7.2. The Decision-making Process. (Reprinted with
permission from James A. Banks with Ambrose A. Clegg,
*Teaching Strategies for the Social Studies: Inquiry, Valuing
and Decision-Making,* Second Edition. Reading, Mass: Addison-Wesley, 1977, p. 29.)

attain knowledge. The knowledge must not only be scientific, it must be interdisciplinary and cut across disciplinary lines. Knowledge from any one discipline is insufficient to help us make intelligent decisions. To make reflective decisions about social issues, such as busing to achieve school desegregation and public welfare, the individual must view these problems from the perspectives of disciplines such as sociology, economics, political science, and anthropology. The perspectives of any one discipline is too limited to guide intelligent decision making and reflective social action.

Summary

Several widespread assumptions about the nature of ethnic studies are adversely affecting the development of ethnic studies curricula in the nation's schools, colleges, and universities. Many educators assume that ethnic studies: (a) is the study of ethnic minority groups; (b) should only be studied by ethnic minority students; (c) is an addition to the mainstream curriculum; (d) is the study of the strange and exotic characteristics of ethnic groups; and (e) is the celebration of ethnic holidays.

Each of these assumptions is examined and challenged in this chapter. The characteristics of an effective ethnic studies curriculum are also described. The ethnic studies curriculum should be based on a broad definition of ethnic group and include the study of both ethnic groups and ethnic minorities. Ethnic studies should also be viewed as a process of curriculum reform. By restructuring their curricula when integrating it with ethnic content, educators can create a new curricula based on fresh assumptions and perspectives. This new curricula will enable students to gain novel views of the American and human experience and new conceptions of what it means to be *American*. The ethnic studies curriculum should be based on Models C and D; curricular models that enable students to view events, concepts, and situations from diverse ethnic perspectives and points of view.

The multiethnic curriculum should help students to: (1) clarify their ethnic identities and to function effectively within their own ethnic communities; (2) develop a sensitivity to and understanding of other ethnic cultures and the ability to function effectively within them; and (3) develop the ability to make reflective decisions on social issues and to take actions to resolve personal and public problems. A model for teaching decision-making and social action skills is presented and described. The next chapter, chapter 8, consists of a teaching unit based on this model.

Notes

1. Nathan Hare, "The Teaching of Black History and Culture in the Secondary School," *Social Education* 33 (April 1969), pp. 385–388.

2. Jack D. Forbes, "Teaching Native American Values and Cultures," in James A. Banks, ed., *Teaching Ethnic Studies: Concepts and Strategies* (Washington, D.C.: National Council for the Social Studies, 1973), pp. 201–225; Rodolfo Acuña, *Occupied America: The Chicano's Struggle Toward Liberation* (San Francisco: Canfield Press, 1972). Strongly worded Asian-American perspectives on American history are in Amy Tachiki, Eddie Wong, Franklin Odo, with Buck Wong, eds., *Roots: An Asian American Reader* (Los Angeles: UCLA Asian American Studies Center, 1971). For a range of views by Puerto Ricans in the United States, see Francesco Cordasco and Eugene Bucchioni, eds., *The Puerto Rican Experience: A Sociological Sourcebook* (Totowa, N.J.: Littlefield Adams, 1973).

3. See essays in John W. Blassingame, eds., *New Perspectives on Black Studies* (Urbana, Ill.: University of Illinois Press, 1971).

4. Increasingly, school districts are formulating programs that deal with several ethnic groups. In most cases, however, the groups studied are represented in the local school population. Rarely, for example, are Puerto Ricans included in multiethnic units in cities such as Los Angeles and Seattle. A provincial regionalism still haunts school ethnic studies programs despite recent trends toward the development of more global and comparative approaches.

5. Arthur S. Bolster, Jr., "History, Historians, and the Secondary School Curriculum," *Harvard Educational Review* 32 (1962), pp. 39–65.

6. Nathan Glazer and Daniel P. Moynihan, *Beyond the Melting Pot: The Negroes, Puerto Ricans, Jews, Italians and Irish of New York City* (Cambridge, Mass.: M.I.T. Press, 1970), p. 17.

7. John Higham, *Strangers in the Land: Patterns of American Nativism 1860–1925* (New York: Atheneum, 1972).

8. Henry S. Commager, *The Nature and the Study of History* (Columbus, Ohio: Charles E. Merrill, 1966).

9. A perceptive and provocative discussion of "insider" and "outsider" views on historical and social events is presented in Robert K. Merton, "Insiders and Outsiders: A Chapter in the Sociology of Knowledge," *The American Journal of Sociology* 78 (July 1972), pp. 9–47.

10. See Shizuye Takashima, *A Child in Prison Camp* (Montreal, Canada: Tundra Books, 1971).

11. James A. Banks, "Teaching for Ethnic Literacy," *Social Education* 37 (December 1973), pp. 738–750.

12. James A. Banks (with Ambrose A. Clegg, Jr.), *Teaching Strategies for the Social Studies,* 2nd ed. (Reading, Mass.: Addison-Wesley, 1977).

8

Teaching Decision-making and Social-action Skills

A major objective of ethnic studies instruction is to help students develop the ability to make reflective decisions so they can resolve personal problems, and through social action, influence public policy and develop a sense of political efficacy. A model of reflective decision making, which consists of social science inquiry, value inquiry, the synthesis of knowledge and values, and social action is presented in chapter 7 (see Figure 7.2). The present chapter consists of a teaching unit that is based on the decision-making model described in chapter 7. The key question is this sample unit is: *Should integration be a societal goal in a pluralistic democratic nation?*

After discussing the nature and background of the public controversy and related subissues, steps the teacher and students can take to study the issue using the decision-making model presented in Figure 7.2 are illustrated.

Integration and Social Controversy

Controversy exists within an institution or a society when individuals and groups are unable to agree on basic goals or on the ways in which agreed on goals should be implemented. Controversy often results because of different values, beliefs, and attitudes held by various members of a society or community. Controversy has always existed in America regarding the treatment of ethnic groups who were excluded from full participation in the mainstream society. Controversy has arisen over questions regarding whether these groups should be forced to assimilate or maintain their ethnic cultures, and the extent to which they should be encouraged or permitted to participate in the institutions of the dominant society.

Since the late 1800s, much controversy has surrounded federal policy toward the American Indian. Federal policy has shifted from an emphasis on extreme assimilation to the encouragement of some degree of ethnic identity. When Native Americans were conquered and placed on reservations in the late 1800s, White authorities began efforts to civilize" them. The goal of federal policy was to quickly assimilate Indians into the dominant society.[1] In 1887 the Dawes Severality Act was passed to implement the new policy of assimilation. It was clear by the late 1920s that this policy had failed miserably. In 1934 Congress passed an act that sanctioned a new policy toward Indians that enabled and encouraged them to keep aspects of their cultures. Today, controversy still exists about the relationship the federal government should have with American Indians.

In the last several decades, much controversy has arisen about the integration of ethnic minorities into mainstream American society. These controversies are likely to continue until racism and discrimination are eliminated from American life. While integration was the major goal of most civil rights advocates in the 1950s, many of them emphasized pride in ethnic heritage, ethnic political and economic power, and ethnic self-determination in the 1960s and 1970s.[2] Many saw integration, at best, as a secondary goal. Some leaders considered integration antithetical to ethnic self-determination and cultural survival. Integration, they argued, demanded cultural assimilation, "cultural genocide" in the language of some, and geographical dispersion of the group, which destroys ethnic communities and thus their strong base for political power. These leaders pointed out that Black schools were often closed when desegregation plans were implemented, and that Black teachers and administrators often lost their jobs or were given inferior jobs when school integration occurred.

Other groups were opposing integration in the 1970s for different reasons. Many Whites in the North strongly opposed school integration plans that required the use of buses. Politicians took up their cause and became staunchly "anti-busing." Legislation designed to greatly reduce busing for school integration was enacted in the 1970s. Many individuals and groups also opposed affirmative action programs designed to achieve integration in public and private institutions for the reasons noted above.

Despite the articulate and aggressive groups that were opposing integration, integration had its strong advocates.[3] These individuals and groups argued that within a pluralistic society racial and ethnic integration is the only viable way for minorities to gain full participation in American life and for White Americans to acquire the attitudes they must have if we are ever going to have an open society. Traditional civil rights groups continued to fight segregation in the courts. Segregated northern schools became one of their key targets. They experienced a number of successes as district courts ordered northern school districts to desegregate.

Segregation in public accommodations, housing, and employment continued to be fought in the courts in the 1970s. The courts forced several major industrial firms to implement affirmative action programs to integrate their labor forces. By 1974 it was *illegal* to deliberately maintain segregation in most public and private institutions in the United States. *Yet, ironically, racial and ethnic segregation was a salient characteristic of American life in 1974.* Nearly 90 percent of the White students went to predominantly White schools; most Blacks attended Black schools. Blacks, as well as most other ethnic groups, were concentrated in segregated communities. Most Blacks, Whites, and other ethnic groups were married to members of their own groups. What was most ironic in 1974 was that many minority spokesmen as well as groups that they regarded as their oppressors were both advocating forms of segregation, but for different reasons.

Considering whether integration should be a major goal in a culturally pluralistic society will require students to seriously examine their values and racial attitudes, to gather data needed to state and test hypotheses, and to derive and formulate generalizations. They will also have the opportunity to make decisions that are consistent with their values and to act on them within the school and the larger community.

Some Subissues Related to the Major Problem

There is a large range of questions related to integration in a pluralistic society that students can state and research. Open housing, ethnic separatism, interracial marriage, and affirmative action are some of the key issues and problems that the class can explore when studying about ethnicity and race in American life. Specific problems related to the major question posed in this chapter follow.

Should Minorities Be Judged by Different Criteria Than Whites When Applying for Employment and Admission to Colleges and Universities?

Ethnic minority groups, such as Afro-Americans and Mexican Americans, often perform poorly on I.Q. and other standardized tests used by firms and educational institutions to select and screen employees and students. Consequently, the use of these tests and selection devices is *one factor* that has limited the number of minorities in predominantly White colleges and universities and in certain occupations. Many minorities believe that they are often required to have higher qualifications than Whites to get the same types of jobs and to achieve greater than Whites to earn the same promotions and recognition.

Some authorities maintain that these tests are discriminatory and that minorities perform poorly on them because they are standardized on White middle-class subjects and do not reflect the cultures and experiences of ethnic minorities.[4] Other authorities, such as Arthur R. Jensen and William Shockley, believe that minorities perform poorly on I.Q. and other tests because they are genetically inferior to Whites.[5]

The key issue in this complex problem is how employers and educational institutions can select competent minorities without using tests and selection devices that discriminate against specific groups.

Should Institutions Establish Quotas for Hiring and Admitting Ethnic Minorities?

To assure that a significant number of minorities will hold leadership roles within it, the National Education Association established minimum quotas for minority participation in 1974. The NEA constitution and by-laws require that there be a minimum of twenty percent ethnic minority representation on the board, executive committee, and on all other committees. The Anti-Defamation League of B'nai B'rith, a Jewish civil rights organization, hotly contested the NEA policies, calling them "unlawful, undemocratic and racist."[6] Jews were not included among the groups the NEA specified as minorities. The ADL argued that setting quotas was "reverse discrimination," and that individuals should be given positions solely on the basis of their qualifications and not on the basis of their ethnic group membership. NEA officials argued that both ethnicity and competency must be considered to assure minority participation since past policies had resulted in the virtual exclusion of ethnic minorities from key roles in the organization. NEA officials also maintained that it was important that ethnic minorities have key leadership roles because they provided the organization with unique kinds of points of view.

There are other dimensions to the problem of quotas. Quotas make some ethnic minorities uneasy because they feel that once a firm or an organization has filled its quota for a particular minority group, such as American Indians, other highly qualified Indians will not be hired.

Should Minorities Be Permitted to Establish Separate Facilities and Organizations in Publicly Supported Institutions?

In the 1960s, Black students at some colleges and universities demanded that separate dormitory facilities be provided, that only Blacks be allowed to teach and enroll in Black studies courses, and that Whites be prohibited from joining Black student organizations.[7] The students who made these demands were small minorities at predominantly White institutions that had, for a variety of reasons, historicaly admitted few or no Afro-American students. These students argued that they were alienated and frustrated on these campuses and experienced much discrimination. They felt that they needed separate dormitories and courses so that they could comfort each other and maintain a sense of ethnic identity. They maintained that Whites shouldn't teach or enroll in Black studies courses because their racism made it impossible for them to understand the Black experience. Further, they argued; Whites were part of the problem and

Black studies should focus on ways in which Afro-Americans can liberate themselves from the oppressor.

Many integrationists, Black and White, argued that the students were segregationists who were trying to establish apartheid on the campuses of tax-supported institutions.[8] They felt that such demands were illegal and unconstitutional and that college and university officials should staunchly resist them. Some schools, however, did grant Black students some of their demands. Integrationists also argued that if these demands were met, many of the legal gains made by civil rights groups in the 1950s against segregation would be greatly threatened. They felt that White segregationists would use concessions made to Afro-American students as part of their argument to reestablish segregation in predominantly White institutions and in public accommodation facilities.

Should Busing Be Used to Desegregate the Public Schools?

When district courts ordered northern school systems to desegregate, most of them had to bus Black and White children to integrated schools because most Americans live in tightly segregated communities. Strong resistance and violent reactions to busing designed to achieve racial integration erupted in many White communities when White students were bused to desegregated schools.[9] Most of the resisting White parents argued that they were not opposed to integrated schools, but wanted their children to go to school in their own neighborhoods and did not want them to take long bus rides across towns to attend desegregated schools.

Integration advocates argued that such parents were opposed to racially integrated schools and not to busing since 43 percent of all children were bused to school and only 3 percent were bused to achieve racial integration. Integration spokespersons maintained that the parents who were objecting to the busing that was done to achieve desegregated schools were not objecting to the much greater busing done to take children to segregated schools. Busing, they argued, was only opposed when it was used to bus children to desegregated schools.

Should Interracial and Interethnic Marriage Be Encouraged and Socially Accepted?

Although most ethnic minorities marry within their own ethnic groups, interracial marriage has increased greatly between some ethnic groups in recent years. In 1924 ony two percent of the Japanese Americans in Los Angeles county married outside of their ethnic group. Forty-nine percent of them married outside of their ethnic group in 1972.[10] Between 1966 and 1971, 31 percent of the Jewish Americans who married did not marry other Jews.[11] Although the number of Black-White marriages is still very low, there has probably been an increase in the number of Blacks dating Whites, especially on college and university campuses where the number of Black students increased substantially during the 1960s.

Some ethnic leaders are alarmed by the increase in the number of interracial and interfaith marriages and the increase in interracial dating. Some Orthodox Jewish Americans believe that interfaith marriages will undermind the Jews' sense of ethnic kinship and cultural identity. Some Japanese Americans perceive interracial marriages as a threat to Japanese-American values and institutions. Many Blacks, especially those who are nationalistic in their views, are strongly opposed to Black-White dating and marriages.[12]

Other people who oppose interracial dating and marriage argued that life is too difficult for interracial couples in American society, and that until the larger society can accept interracial marriage, people of different races should not marry. Such individuals also argue that people of different races should not marry because life is very difficult for their children, who are not fully accepted by either race.

People who defend interracial dating and marriage maintain that the United States is a free nation, and that every person has a right to date, love, and marry whomever he or she wishes as long as the relationship involves two mutually consenting adults.

Stages in Considering This Controversial Issue

Gathering Scientific Data

To make an intelligent decision on a social issue such as "Should integration be a societal goal in a puralistic nation?" the students will need to acquire knowledge. However, decisions can be no better than the knowledge on which they are based. To make reflective decisions, students must study high level concepts and master key generalizations. Generalizations can be taught in a variety of ways. However, it is necessary for students to use the *scientific method* to derive generalizations needed for decision making. When planning lessons to help students gain knowledge, the teacher should identify social science concepts and related generalizations that will help them to make intelligent decisions. Concepts should be selected from several disciplines, such as sociology, anthropology, history, and geography. *Discrimination, assimilation, ethnic group, culture, powerlessness,* and *separatism* are key concepts related to integration. After key concepts are identified, organizing (or key) generalizations related to the concepts are identified, and subideas related to the organizing generalizations and to the content chosen for study are stated. (A detailed example of this type of curriculum planning will not be presented here since I have discussed it at considerable length in my other writings.[13])

Value Inquiry

After the students have had an opportunity to derive social science generalizations related to a social issue, they should undertake lessons that will enable them to *identify, analyze,* and *clarify* their values related to them. Value lessons should be conducted in an open classroom atmosphere so that the students will be willing to freely express their beliefs and to openly examine them. If the teacher is authoritarian, the students will not express their actual feelings and attitudes. Beliefs that are unexpressed cannot be examined. Because of the way in which the teacher is viewed by most students, it is a good idea for the teacher to withhold his views on controversial issues until the students have had an opportunity to express their beliefs. When a teacher reveals his or her position on a social issue, many students will make statements they feel the teacher wants them to make rather than say things they actually believe. The teacher who opens a discussion on interracial marriage or open housing by saying that everybody should have the right to marry whomever they please or that open housing laws violate a seller's constitutional rights, cannot expect the students to state opposing beliefs. While some students will openly disagree with the teacher, most will not. I am not suggesting that the teacher should not state his or her positions on issues. However, experience suggests that when a teacher openly expresses his or her views early in class discussions the dialogue usually becomes stifled or slanted in one direction.

Decision Making and Social Action

After the students have derived social science generalizations and clarified their values regarding the social issue, the teacher should ask them to list all the possible actions they could take regarding integration in their school and community, and to predict the possible consequences of each alternative. It is imperative that the alternatives and consequences the students identify and state are realistic and are based on the knowledge they have mastered during the scientific phase of the unit. Alternatives and consequences should be intelligent predictive statements and not ignorant guesses or wishful thinking. After the students have discussed and weighed all of the alternative courses of action, they should decide on courses of action most consistent with their values and implement them within their school or community. For example, the students, or some of them, may decide that integration should be a major goal in a pluralistic society but that integration does not exist within their school. They might design a voluntary transfer plan with a local Black (or White, etc.) school and present it to the Board of Education for action. Figure 8.1 summarizes the major steps we have discussed for studying a social issue.

The Origin of the Issue

The teacher can begin a study of the key issues discussed in this chapter by asking the students to cut out items in the newspaper that deal with such issues as busing, open housing, affirmative action programs, and discrimination in employment. Examples of such cases in the 1970s were the violent reactions to busing that erupted in Pontiac, Michigan in 1971, the school desegregation order issued in Detroit by Judge Stephen J. Roth in 1972, the DeFunis case related to affirmative action at the University of Washington Law School in 1973, and the 1978 Bakke affirmative action case at the Medical School of the University of California at Davis.

The Definition of Key Concepts

When studying problems related to cultural pluralism and racial integration, the class should clarify the definitions of key terms and reach general agreement about what they mean. Terms such as *integration, race, desegregation, separatism, racism, discrimination,* and *cultural pluralism* are some of the key concepts that should be defined when racial integration is studied. Several of these terms are discussed below.

Some writers make a distinction between *integration* and *desegregation.* They define *desegregation* as the mere physical mixing of different racial and ethnic groups. *Integration,* for these writers, means much more. It occurs only when mutual respect and acceptance develops between different racial and ethnic groups who are members of the same institutions.

Separatism is sometimes said to exist when ethnic groups who are excluded from the dominant society establish ethnic organizations and institutions to meet their exclusive needs. Students can explore other definitions of separatism and identify instances of it within their communities. When discussing separatism, the class should try to distinguish *separatism* and *segregation.* These terms are highly related and are often confused. Separatist institutions are designed to help an ethnic group attain self-determination and political power and to enhance its ethnic culture. Segregated institutions in *minority communities* are usually created by the dominant society in order to keep minorities subjugated. These types of institutions are designed and controlled by the powerful groups in a society and not by the ethnic minority community. Thus, *separatist* and *segregated* institutions in

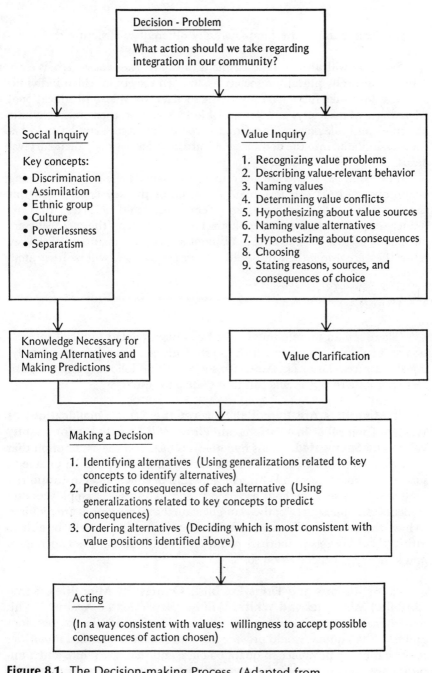

Figure 8.1. The Decision-making Process. (Adapted from James A. Banks with Ambrose A. Clegg, Jr., *Teaching Strategies for the Social Studies,* Second Edition. Reading, Mass: Addison-Wesley, 1977, p. 32. Copyright © 1977 by Addison-Wesley. Used with the publisher's permission.)

minority communities are fundamentally different in structure and function.

Students will also need to define a *culturally pluralistic society*. We *can* define a culturally pluralistic society as an open society in which individuals are able to take full advantage of the social, economic, and educational advantages of a society, and yet are able to maintain their unique ethnic identities and allegiances. Individuals would not necessarily have to become assimilated into the dominant culture in order to satisfy their survival needs.

The examples above are given merely to suggest the kinds of working definitions students can formulate for some of the key concepts in this chapter. Many other examples and definitions could be given. It is extremely important for students to know how the concepts they are using are defined by themselves and others. Without a clear understanding of the key terms they are using, their most diligent research efforts will be frustrated.

Hypotheses

There are an infinite number of hypotheses related to racial integration and cultural pluralism which the students can formulate when studying about race relations in American society. What follows is a list of *possible* hypotheses that students can formulate and test.

If Minorities Are Required to Meet the Same Qualifications as Whites, Then Most Institutions and Firms Will Remain Predominantly White and Segregated.   This hypothesis is based on the assumption that most ethnic minorities, perhaps for a variety of reasons, will be unable to successfully compete with Whites for jobs and in educational institutions if present criteria and methods are used to screen and select employees and students. An opposing hypothesis might state that if minorities are required to have the same qualifications as Whites, they would eventually be able to satisfy them because minorities could and would obtain the experiences and knowledge needed to do so.

If Institutions and Firms Establish Quotas for Minorities, Some Qualified Minorities and Whites Will Be Discriminated Against.   This hypothesis assumes that there are more qualified minorities for positions and slots than quotas would provide for, that some nonqualified minorities may be hired in peference to qualified ones, and that if a White and a minority are equally qualified, firms with quotas would hire the minorities until their quotas had been attained. It also assumes that qualified minorities would not be hired once such quotas were reached. A different hypothesis might suggest that firms and schools will recruit and hire minorities only if they are required to fulfill quotas.

If Open Housing Laws Are Enacted and Enforced, Then Whites Will Be Forced to Sell Their Homes at a Tremendous Loss. This hypothesis assumes that property values are greatly reduced when ethnic minorities move into predominantly White neighborhoods. A related hypothesis might state that if open housing laws are not enacted and enforced, housing segregation will increase.

If Busing Is Not Used to Desegregate the Public Schools, Most Blacks and Whites Will Continue to Attend Racially Segregated Schools. This hypothesis assumes that because of the housing patterns of Blacks and Whites, busing is necessary to desegregate the public schools. Another hypothesis might state that if open housing laws were enacted and enforced, neighborhood schools would become voluntarily integrated.

Testing the Hypotheses

The students will need to gather data to test the hypotheses they have formulated. Because of the nature of the hypotheses formulated above and the short history of most civil rights programs and legislation, little historical data are available about the effects of laws that prohibit segregation and discrimination. Also, like any other problems related to human behavior, problems in race relations are exceedingly complex. It is difficult to establish causal relationships with a high degree of certainty, such as if A then B, or if there is forced school integration (A), conflict (B) will develop between Blacks and Whites. There are too many other variables that may influence either A or B and thus affect the outcome of busing in a particular community. How forced integration affects the relationships between Blacks and Whites in a particular community may depend on who made the legal decision, whether a local or federal court, the extent of racial hostility within the community before the court order, the percentage of Blacks and Whites in the community that are involved in the busing program, the types of Black and White leaders in the community, and many other variables.

When students are gathering data to test hypotheses related to racial integration, they should be helped to see how difficult it is to establish relationships with a high degree of reliability. Another caveat is in order. Much of the information and data related to ethnic and racial problems is highly emotional and biased. It is often presented to support or invalidate a particular position or point of view. Examples of these types of studies abound in the literature on race relations. Rivlin has perceptively called this kind of research "forensic" social science.[14] Studies written in the forensic tradition include Jensen and Shockley's work on Black-White intelligence, Jencks et al's book on equality of educational opportunity, Banfield's *The Unheavenly City,* and Moynihan's *The Negro Family.*[15]

Pro-Black positions on issues are presented in most of the articles in the *Black Scholar*.[16] One way to partially solve this problem is to present the students with readings that support several positions of an issue, and that present data that support specific viewpoints.

Historical data on college admissions and employment of minorities will shed light on the first hypothesis stated above. Most minorities are poorly represented in the higher paying jobs in industry and government. However, even fewer held white-collar jobs before the civil rights legislation of the 1960s. Table 8.1 indicates that the percentage of Blacks in the labor force who were white-collar workers increased greater than the percentage of Whites who were white-collar workers between 1957 and 1970. When the Civil Rights Act of 1964 was enacted, many industries developed special incentive programs for the recruitment and hiring of ethnic minorities.

Since the 1800s, most Afro-American college students have attended predominantly Black colleges. In 1938, 97 percent of Black college students were attending Black colleges. When affirmative action programs were implemented in response to federal legislation, predominantly White colleges and universities aggressively recruited minority students, created special programs for them, and modified their admission requirements so that more promising minority youths could be admitted. The number of Black students attending predominantly White universities increased substantially in the 1960s. In 1970, 56 percent of all black students were attending predominantly white colleges and universities.[17] However, the number of Blacks in these colleges was still only a very small percentage of their total populations.

In studying the kind of information presented above, the students might conclude that their data lend some support to the notion that if minorities are required to meet the same qualifications as Whites, firms and institutions may remain predominantly White. However, the severe limitations of their data and the possibility that many other factors besides the modification of qualifications influenced the number of minorities that en-

Table 8.1. Black and White White-collar Workers.

	1957	*1970*	*Percent Increase*
Percent of Blacks in the labor force that were white-collar workers	12.8	27.9	15.1
Percent of Whites in the labor force that were white-collar workers	44.2	50.8	6.6

Adapted from *Statistical Abstract of the United States*. Washington, D.C.: U.S. Government Printing Office, 1971, p. 133.

tered institutions in the 1960s must be considered before they close their investigation. Such factors as more aggressive recruitment of minorities, more financial support for them, more extensive and improved counseling and supportive services, and the rising level of expectations among ethnic minorities, may have been the *major variables* that led to an increase of ethnic minorities within predominantly White universities and firms. Thus, the students would have to conclude that their hypothesis was at best only partially and weakly supported by their data.

Some Tentative Conclusions

Below are some tentative conclusions the students *might* reach after they have studied about racial integration and examined their values regarding racial mixing.

1. Ethnic minorities should be required to have the same qualifications for jobs and to enter college as any other persons. However, the ways in which these qualifications are determined should be modified so that they reflect ethnic diversity and so that minorities will not be victimized by discriminatory tests and other selective devices which are based exclusively on the dominant culture. Institutions and firms should aggressively recruit minorities to increase the pool from which they can select. This type of policy will, in the long run, result in the hiring of minorities who are as qualified as their White counterparts. In the short run, however, it might mean that industries and universities will not be able to increase the numbers of minorities in their populations at a very rapid rate.

2. Institutions should not establish quotas for minorities, but should implement affirmative action programs that will enable them to aggressively recruit minorities and give preference to them if minorities and Whites are equally qualified. The goal should be to have an integrated staff or student body that includes people who represent diverse ethnic and racial groups, and not to get a specific number from each ethnic group. This policy will result in the employment of minorities but will not restrict their number or encourage the hiring of minorities who are less qualified than White employees, or the admission of minority students who cannot succeed in college.

3. Open housing laws should be enacted in all communities to assure that every American will have the opportunity to buy the house which he or she wants and can afford regardless of his or her race or ethnic group. If effectively enforced, open housing laws are not likely to result in many interracial communities since Whites usually move out of neighborhoods when minorities move into them. No legal actions should be taken to prevent freedom of movement by Whites. However, planned interracial communities should be established since people who grow up in interracial

communities have more positive racial attitudes and are more likely to live in interracial neighborhoods and to send their children to interracial schools.

4. The establishment of interracial schools should be a major goal of American society. Any reasonable plans, including those which require busing, should be implemented if they are needed to establish and maintain desegregated schools. Parents who are opposed to interracial schools and/or busing should have the right to take their children out of the public schools. However, they should not be allowed to dictate or unduly influence school policy. Major societal goals and American Creed Values (such as equality and justice) should take precedence over the whims of special interest and pressure groups. If a school district takes a strong position vis-à-vis interracial schools and busing, hostile pressure groups, which are usually small but vocal minorities, will eventually accept the school's policy and lose both community support and wide public forums for their views.

Suggested Methods for Teaching about Integration and Public Controversy

Initiating the Unit

The teacher can begin a study of integration and public controversy by reading the class a current *case study* taken from the newspaper or a news magazine that deals with a controversial policy and/or issue related to integration. An example of such a case study taken from a newspaper and questions the class can discuss follow:

NEA Constitution, By-laws Are Racist, Illegal, Anti-defamation League says

Palm Beach, Fla. The Anti-Defamation League of B'nai B'rith has condemned as "unlawful, undemocratic and racist" the new constitution and bylaws of the National Educational Association. . . .

According to Peirez, the NEA Constitution specifically designates as ethnic minorities, blacks, Mexican-Americans, other Spanish-speaking groups, Asian-Americans and Indians. The NEA authorizes those minorities alone to nominate minority candidates for its board of directors and executive committees.

It further requires that there be a minimum of 20 percent ethnic minority representation on the NEA board, executive committee and all other committees and that delegates to its national representative assembly from state and local affiliates be allocated on the basis of the ethnic minority percentage of the population or be denied credentials.

The NEA Constitution also provides that nominations for NEA president be restricted to certain ethnic minority groups if, after 11 years, no member of such a group has been elected.[18]

Questions

1. Do the quotas established by the NEA Constitution constitute reverse discrimination? Why or why not?
2. Should institutions and organizations practice reverse discrimination when trying to compensate for past injustices? Why or why not?
3. Does the NEA Constitution violate the civil rights of Whites? Why or why not?
4. What effects do you think the NEA Constitution and bylaws will have on minorities in the organization? On Whites in the organization? Why?

Social Science Inquiry

When the teacher has launched the study of integration with a case study such as the one above, the students should study historical information that will enable them to understand the forces that have shaped public policy regarding racial integration. Attention should be given to the legalization of segregation that took place in the decades after the Civil War. Ask individual students to prepare and present reports on the following topics:

- the Black codes
- the poll tax
- the grandfather clause
- the Dred Scott Decision
- *Plessy* v. *Ferguson*

When these reports are presented to the class, the students should discuss these questions: Why did segregation become widespread in the post–Civil War period? Why was it legalized? How did these laws affect Black Americans? White Americans? Other Americans?

*Ask the students to pretend that they are the Supreme Court in 1896 and that they are hearing the case of Homer Plessy, a mulatto who complains that he has to sit in separate cars on trains that pass through his native state of Louisiana. Plessy argues that this type of segregation violates protection guaranteed to him by the Fourteenth Amendment to the Constitution. Ask individual students to role play the roles of the Supreme Court justices, Homer Plessy, and the prosecuting and defense attorneys. After the arguments on both sides have been presented to the Court, the judges should deliberate and then rule on the case. After the role-play situation, the class should discuss:

1. ways in which their simulated court was similar and different from the actual Supreme Court in 1896
2. whether the role-players were able to successfully assume the attitudes and viewpoints of people who lived in 1896
3. what the "separate but equal" doctrine meant in 1896 and what it means today

*At the turn of the century, two major civil rights organizations were formed to fight for the rights of Afro-Americans: the National Association for the Advancement of Colored People and the National Urban League. It was also during this period that two major civil rights leaders became nationally eminent, Booker T. Washington and W.E.B. DuBois. Washington and DuBois became staunch opponents because they held opposing views about racial equality and the ways in which the Afro-American should be educated. Ask the class to read Washington's biography, *Up From Slavery*, and selections from W.E.B. DuBois's *The Souls of Black Folks*. The class should discuss the views of these two men and determine which of their ideas were valid and which were not. After the class has discussed the views of DuBois and Washington, ask two students to role-play a debate between the two men regarding steps the Afro-American should take to achieve racial equality.

*Most of the national civil rights organizations in the early 1900s were interracial. Ask the students to do required readings on the history and development of the NAACP and the National Urban League. When they have completed the readings; they should compare and contrast these two organizations with the Niagara Movement and earlier Black protest movements, such as the Negro Convention Movement and the African Civilization Society. Particular attention should be paid to: (1) reasons why the organizations emerged, (2) who made policy and held key positions within them, (3) types of problems that arose within the organizations, (4) the major goals of the organizations, and (5) ways in which the organizations succeeded or failed and why.

*Black separatist movements developed early in American history. Some of the earliest were led by such Blacks as Martin R. Delany and Paul Cuffee. Ask the students to research the lives of these men and to present dramatizations that show ways in which they were advocates of Black nationalism. Marcus Garvey, another Black separatist, attained eminence in the 1930s. Ask the class to read his biography, *Black Moses*, by E. D. Cronon, and to list ways in which Garvey was similar to and different from earlier Black nationalist leaders.

*In the 1930s, 1940s, 1950s, and 1960s racial segregation received a number of severe blows that culminated in the *Brown* decision of 1954 and the Civil Rights Act of 1964. Ask the students to develop a chronology that lists the major civil rights legislation that was enacted between 1930 and 1964. After the chronology is developed, the students should discuss these questions:

1. What were the major social and political factors that led to the passage of each of these bills?
2. Why has racial segregation actually increased in American society in recent years even though so many civil rights bills have been enacted?

*The major goal of the civil rights movement in the 1950s was to desegregate public accommodation facilities and other institutions. Action tactics and court battles achieved much desegregation. However, by 1965, many Afro-Americans, especially young Black activists, were disillusioned with the attainments of the movement and realized that integration alone would not eliminate the Afro-Americans' major social, economic, and political problems. These young activists felt that both the goals and tactics of the movement should be changed. They issued a call for "Black Power!" The students can gain an understanding of the concept of Black power by reading *Black Power: The Politics of Liberation in America* by Stokely Carmichael and Charles V. Hamilton. Many Black integrationists rejected the views of Black power advocates. Ask the class to thoroughly research the views of the men and women listed below and to simulate a national convention of Black civil rights leaders in which they discuss the problem, "What should be the future course of Black Americans: Integration or Separatism?"

(a) Martin Luther King
(b) Roy Wilkins
(c) Roy Innis
(d) Angela Davis
(e) Stokely Carmichael
(f) H. Rap Brown
(g) Vernon Jordan
(h) Rev. Jesse Jackson
(i) Shirley Chisholm
(j) Bobby Seale
(k) Huey Newton
(l) Imamu Amiri Baraka
(m) Richard G. Hatcher
(n) Julian Bond
(o) Ronald V. Dellums
(p) Barbara Jordan

Individual students should be asked to research and play the roles of each leader in the convention. After the major question has been discussed, the convention participants should then develop an action agenda for Black Americans in the 1980s that they all can endorse.

Value Inquiry

After the students have had an opportunity to gather factual data related to integration, they should examine their values, attitudes, and beliefs regarding racial mixing. A wide variety of strategies and materials can be used to help students to examine and clarify their values. Some valuing exercises appropriate for studying about integration are given below. These strategies are adapted from techniques developed by Simon, Howe, and Kirschenbaum.[19]

Spread of Opinion

The teacher should divide the class into several small groups and give each of the groups a piece of paper with one of these issues written on it:

- forced busing
- interracial marriage
- open housing laws
- reverse discrimination
- separatism
- quotas
- interracial adoptions
- interracial dating
- segregated fraternities and sororities

Each of the groups should identify a number of positions that can be taken on the issue given to them. Each member of the group should write a statement defending one of these positions, whether he or she agrees with it or not. When the statements have been completed, the students should discuss each issue and state their own positions on it.

Unfinished Sentences

The teacher should ditto the following list of statements and give a copy to each of the students. The students should be asked to complete the statements with the words and phrases they first think of when they read each statement. After the students have completed the statements, the teacher should divide the class into small groups and ask the students to discuss, "What I learned about myself from this exercise."

1. If I were Black (or White, Mexican American, etc.) I would . . .
2. People who riot are . . .
3. Most Blacks are . . .
4. If a Black (or a Mexican American, etc.) famiy moved into my neighborhood, I would . . .
5. If I were forced to ride a bus to an integrated school each day, I would . . .
6. If my sister married a Black (or a White, etc.), I would . . .
7. People of other races make me feel . . .
8. A *racist* is a person who . . .
9. If I were called a *racist*, I would . . .
10. Most Whites are . . .
11. Special programs created for minorities are . . .
12. Minorities who participate in special programs are . . .
13. People who are opposed to interracial marriage are . . .
14. Minorities who score poorly on I.Q. tests are . . .

Strongly Agree/Strongly Disagree

The teacher should duplicate the following list of statements and give a copy to each of the students. Ask the students to indicate the extent to which they agree or disagree with the statements by writing one of the following letter combinations in front of each statement:

- SA = Strongly agree
- AS = Agree somewhat
- DS = Disagree somewhat
- SD = Strongly disagree

After the students have responded to each of the statements, divide the class into small groups and ask the students to discuss their responses in their groups.

_____ 1. I am prejudiced toward some racial and ethnic groups.
_____ 2. I would not live in a predominantly Black (or White, etc.) neighborhood.

_____ 3. People who riot should be put in jail.

_____ 4. Most Mexican Americans are poor because they are lazy.

_____ 5. Most Whites are racists.

_____ 6. I would encourage my sister to marry a Black (or a White, etc.) if she wanted to.

_____ 7. Minorities should meet the same college admission requirements as Whites.

_____ 8. I.Q. tests are unfair to minorities and should be abandoned.

_____ 9. Students should not be required to be bused to desegregate schools.

_____ 10. Only Blacks should teach Black Studies.

_____ 11. Universities and firms should establish quotas for minorities.

_____ 12. Black militants are racists.

_____ 13. White fraternities and sororities should be required to admit Blacks, Mexican Americans, Asian Americans, and other ethnic minorities.

Values Grid

An effective summary valuing activity for this unit is the valuing grid. Place Table 8.2 on a ditto stencil and make copies for each of the students.*

Ask the students to make brief notes about how they feel about each of the eleven issues listed in the table. Each issue will have been discussed during earlier parts of the unit. The following seven questions are taken from the valuing strategy developed by Simon et al.[20] List the following questions on the board and explain each of them to the students.

1. Are you *proud* of (do you prize or cherish) your position?
2. Have you *publicly affirmed* your position?
3. Have you chosen your position from *alternatives?*
4. Have you chosen your position after *thoughtful consideration* of the pros and cons and consequences?
5. Have you chosen your position *freely?*
6. Have you *acted* on or done anything about your beliefs?
7. Have you acted with *repetition*, pattern, or consistency on this issue?

Ask the students to write "Yes" or "No" in each of the squares in the chart to indicate their responses to each of the seven questions for each issue. When the students have individually completed the grid, they should break up into groups of three's and discuss as many of their responses that they would like to discuss.

Table 8.2.

Issue	1	2	3	4	5	6	7
1. forced busing							
2. interracial housing							
3. interracial marriage							
4. interracial dating							
5. racial quotas							
6. segregated schools							
7. Black separatism							
8. racial riots							
9. White racism							
10. affirmative-action programs							
11. Black English							

Decision Making and Social Action

When the students have gathered scientific data and clarified their values, they should identify *alternative courses of actions* they can take regarding integration in a pluralistic society, and the *possible consequences* of each course of action. Individual and/or groups should then formulate plans to implement courses of action that are most consistent with their values. Below are some possible action projects that some of the students may decide to implement.

Action Projects

1. If the school is segregated: Developing and implementing a volunteer transfer plan with a local school whose population is predominantly of another race.
2. Conducting a survey to determine the kinds of jobs which most minorities have in local hotels, restaurants, and firms, and if necessary, urging local businesses to hire more minorities in top level positions. Conducting boycotts of local businesses that refuse to hire minorities in top level positions.
3. Conducting a survey to determine the treatment of ethnic groups in all of the courses and textbooks in the school and recommending

ways in which the school curriculum can become more integrated, suggesting that a permanent review board be established to examine all teaching materials and determine how they treat ethnic groups. Presenting these recommendations to appropriate school officials and pressuring them to act on the recommendations.

4. Conducting a survey to determine what local ethnic organizations and leaders are within the community. Inviting some of them to participate in school programs and projects, such as assemblies and classes.

5. Conducting a survey to determine whether the school and public libraries have adequate collections of books and materials about American ethnic groups. If necessary, recommending books and materials which should be purchased and pressuring the libraries to buy them.

6. Conducting a survey to determine what local laws exist (and how they are enforced) regarding open housing, discrimination in public accommodations, etc., and if necessary, developing recommendations regarding changes which should be made in the laws or in the ways in which they should be implemented. Presenting these recommendations to appropriate public officials and pressuring them to act on the recommendations.

7. If the school is racially segregated: Developing plans for exchange activities and programs with a school whose population is predominantly of another race.

8. Conducting a survey to determine the racial and ethnic composition of the school staff (including secretaries, teachers, janitors, etc.) and if necessary, recommending appropriate action to take to make the school more integrated. Presenting these recommendations to appropriate school officials and pressuring them to act on the recommendations.

9. Conducting a survey to determine whether the posters, bulletin boards, photographs, and school holidays reflect the ethnic diversity of American life and, if necessary, implementing a plan to make the total school environment more integrated and multiethnic.

10. If the school is interracial: Conducting a survey to determine if there are examples of racial conflict and tension within the school. If there are, formulating and implementing plans to alleviate these problems.

Summary

This chapter illustrates how the teacher can help students develop decision-making and social action skills by studying a public controversy related to racial and ethnic pluralism in the United States. The decision-making model illustrated in this chapter consists of social science inquiry, value inquiry, the synthesis of knowledge and values, and reflective decision making and social action. The sample unit on integration presented in this chapter illustrates how each component of the decision-making model can be implemented in the classroom. Possible actions that the students might take that are related to racial integration are also suggested.

Notes

1. Alvin M. Josephy, Jr., *The Indian Heritage of America* (New York: Bantam, 1968), pp. 345–366.
2. Stokely Carmichael and Charles V. Hamilton, *Black Power: The Politics of Liberation in America* (New York: Vintage, 1967). Diverse views on integration are presented in "Which Way Black America? Separation? Integration? Liberation?" *Ebony* 25 (August 1970), a special issue.
3. M. Young Whitney, Jr., *Beyond Racism: Building An Open Society* (New York: McGraw-Hill, 1969); and Roy Wilkins, "Whither Black Power?" in Mortimer J. Adler, Charles Van Doren, and George Ducas, eds., *The Negro in American History*, vol. 1 (Chicago: Encyclopedia Britannica Educational Corporation, 1969), pp. 112–115.
4. See the essays in LaMar P. Miller, ed., *The Testing of Black Students* (Englewood Cliffs, N.J.: Prentice-Hall, 1974).
5. Arthur R. Jensen, "How Much Can We Boost IQ and Scholastic Achievement?" *Harvard Educational Review* 39 (Spring 1969), pp. 273–356; William Shockley, "Dysgenics, Geneticity, Raceology: Challenges to the Intellectual Responsibility of Educators," *Phi Delta Kappan* 53 (January 1972), pp. 297–307.
6. "NEW Constitution, By-laws Are Racist, Illegal, Anti-Defamation League Says," *New York Teacher* (February 3, 1974).
7. For an exploration of these issues, see John W. Blassingame, ed., *New Perspectives on Black Studies* (Urbana: University of Illinois Press, 1971).
8. See Kenneth B. Clark, "A Charade of Power: Black Students at White Colleges," in Blassingame, *New Perspectives on Black Studies,* pp. 116–122.
9. Robert L. Green, "Racism in American Education," in Robert L. Green, ed., *Racial Crisis in American Education* (Chicago: Follett Educational Corporation, 1969), p. 274.
10. Akemi Kikumura and Harry H. L. Kitano, "Interracial Marriage: A Picture of the Japanese Americans," *The Journal of Social Issues* 29, no. 2 (1973), p. 69.
11. Dorothy Rabinowitz, "The Trouble With Jewish-Gentile Marriages," *New York* 6 (August 20, 1973), p. 26.
12. Ponchitta Pierce, "Marriage and the Educated Black Woman," *Ebony* 28 (August 1973), pp. 160–166.

13. James A. Banks with Ambrose A. Clegg, *Teaching Strategies for the Social Studies: Inquiry, Valuing and Decision-Making*, 2nd ed., Reading, Mass.: Addison-Wesley, 1977; James A. Banks, *Teaching Strategies for Ethnic Studies*, 2nd ed. (Boston: Allyn and Bacon, 1979).

14. Alice M. Rivlin, "Forensic Social Science," *Harvard Educational Review* 43 (February 1973), pp. 61–75; see also Joyce A. Ladner, ed., *The Death of White Sociology* (New York: Vintage, 1973).

15. Jensen, "How Much Can We Boost IQ"; Shockley, "Dysgenics, Geneticity, Raceology"; Christopher Jencks et al., *Inequality: A Reassessment of the Effect of Family and Schooling in America* (New York: Basic Books, 1972); Edward C. Banfield, *The Unheavenly City* (Boston: Little, Brown, 1970); Daniel P. Moynihan, *The Negro Family: A Case for National Action* (Washington, D.C.: U.S. Government Printing Office, 1965).

16. A collection of articles reprinted from the *Black Scholar* are in Robert Chrisman and Nathan Hare, eds., *Contemporary Black Thought* (New York: The Bobbs-Merrill Co., 1973).

17. Alan Pifer, *The Higher Education of Blacks in the United States* (New York: Carnegie Corporation of New York, 1973), p. 37.

18. "NEW Constitution," *New York Teacher.*

19. Simon et al., *Values Clarification*, pp. 35–37, 241–257, 252–254. Reprinted by permission of A & W Publishers, Inc. from *Values Clarification: A Handbook of Practical Strategies for Teachers and Students*, by Sidney B. Simon, Leland W. Howe, and Howard Kirschenbaum. Copyright © 1972; copyright © 1978 by Hart Publishing Co., Inc.

20. Ibid, p. 36. Reprinted by permission of A & W Publishers, Inc. from *Values Clarification: A Handbook of Practical Strategies for Teachers and Students*, by Sidney B. Simon, Leland W. Howe, and Howard Kirschenbaum. Copyright © 1972; copyright © 1978 by Hart Publishing Co., Inc.

PART IV
Student Characteristics, Ethnicity, and Curriculum Reform

Introduction

A basic assumption of multiethnic education is that students have diverse ethnic, cultural, racial, and social class characteristics. These characteristics influence the learning process and teacher-student interactions. Problems for both students and teachers develop when the culture of the classroom conflicts with the values, behaviors, and learning styles of ethnic students. Learning is facilitated when the teacher is aware of and sensitive to the cultural, social class, and ethnic characteristics of his or her students. Skillful teachers in the multiethnic classroom are able to design and implement teaching strategies that reflect the social class, ethnic, and cultural characteristics of students and to help them attain the behaviors, attitudes, and skills needed to fucntion within the universalistic American society as well as within and across other ethnic cultures. They can do this without alienating students from their ethnic cultures and communities.

The chapters in this part discuss the student characteristics that influence the learning process and describe curricular experiences and guidelines for students with different social class, ethnic, and racial characteristics. Chapter 9 emphasizes the tremendous differences that exist within ethnic groups and discusses the curricular implications of these intraethnic differences. A typology of the stages of ethnicity is presented to help the reader conceptualize and observe differences within ethnic groups. Curricular goals, objectives, and models for both dominant and excluded ethnic groups are presented in chapter 10. In chapter 11 there is a discussion of the curricular policies and needs of students who come to school speaking a variety of dialects and languages that differ from standard Anglo-English.

9

The Stages of Ethnicity:
Implications for Curriculum Reform

Assumptions about Ethnic Students

When planning multiethnic experiences for students, we tend to assume that ethnic groups are monolithic and have rather homogeneous needs and characteristics. We often assume, for example, that individual members of ethnic minority groups, such as Jewish Americans and Afro-Americans, have intense feelings of ethnic identity and a strong interest in learning about the experiences and histories of their ethnic cultures. Educators also frequently assume that the self-images and academic achievement of ethnic minority youths will be enhanced if they are exposed to ethnic studies programs that focus on the heroic accomplishments and deeds of their ethnic groups and highlight the ways in which ethnic groups have been victimized by the dominant Anglo-American society.

Ethnic Groups Are Complex and Dynamic

These kinds of assumptions are highly questionable and have led to some disappointments and serious problems in ethnic studies programs and practices. In designing multiethnic experiences for students, we need to take the psychological needs and characteristics of ethnic group members and their emerging and changing ethnic identities into serious consideration. Ethnic groups, such as Afro-Americans, Jewish Americans, Italian Americans, and Anglo-Americans, are not monolithic but are dynamic and complex groups.

Many of our curriculum development and teacher education efforts are based on the assumption that ethnic groups are static and unchanging. However, ethnic groups are highly diverse, complex, and changing entities. Ethnic identity, like other ethnic characteristics, is also complex and changing among ethnic group members. Thus there is no one ethnic identity among Blacks that we can delineate, as social scientists have sometimes suggested, but many complex and changing identities among them.[1]

Effective educational programs should help students to explore and clarify their own ethnic identities. To do this, such programs must recognize and reflect the complex ethnic identities and characteristics of the individual students in the classroom. Teachers should learn how to facilitate the identity quests among ethnic youths and help them to become effective and able participants in the common civic and national culture.

The Stages of Ethnicity: A Typology

To reflect the myriad and emerging ethnic identities among teachers and ethnic youths, we must make some attempt to identify them and to describe their curricular and teaching implications. The description of a typology that attempts to outline the basic stages of the development of ethnicity among individual members of ethnic groups follows. The typology is a preliminary ideal type construct in the Weberian sense and constitutes a set of hypotheses that are based on the existing and emerging theory and research and on the author's study of ethnic behavior.

This typology is presented to stimulate research and the development of concepts and theory related to ethnicity and ethnic groups. Another purpose of the typology is to suggest preliminary guidelines for teaching about ethnicity in the schools and colleges and for helping students and teachers to function effectively at increasingly higher stages of ethnicity. In a 1979 study, Ford developed an instrument to measure the first five of these six stages of ethnicity and administered it to a sample of classroom teachers. She concluded that her study demonstrated that teachers are spread into the five stages that I had hypothesized.[2] The sixth stage of the typology was developed after the Ford study was completed.

Stage 1: Ethnic Psychological Captivity

During this stage the individual inculcates the negative ideologies and beliefs about his/her ethnic group that are institutionalized within the society. Consequently, he/she exemplifies ethnic self-rejection and low self-esteem. The individual is ashamed of his/her ethnic group and identity during this stage and may respond in a number of ways, including avoiding situations that bring him/her into contact with other ethnic groups or striving aggressively to become highly culturally assimilated. Conflict develops when the highly culturally assimilated psychologically captive ethnic is denied structural assimilation or total societal participation.

Individuals who are members of ethnic groups that have historically been victimized by cultural assaults, such as Polish Americans and Italian Americans, as well as members of highly visible and stigmatized ethnic groups, such as Afro-Americans and Chinese Americans, are likely to experience some form of ethnic psychological captivity. The more that an ethnic group is stigmatized and rejected by the dominant society, the more likely are its members to experience some form of ethnic psychological captivity. Thus, individuals who are Anglo-Americans are the least likely individuals in the United States to experience ethnic psychological captivity.

Stage 2: Ethnic Encapsulation

Stage Two is characterized by ethnic encapsulation and ethnic exclusiveness, including voluntary separatism. The individual participates primarily within his or her own ethnic community and believes that his or her ethnic group is superior to that of other groups. Many individuals within Stage 2, such as many Anglo-Americans, have internalized the dominant societal myths about the superiority of their ethnic or racial group and the innate inferiority of other ethnic groups and races. Many individuals who are socialized within all-White suburban communities and who live highly ethnocentric and encapsulated lives may be described as Stage 2 individuals. Alice Miel describes these kinds of individuals in *The Shortchanged Children of Suburbia.*[3]

The characteristics of Stage 2 are most extreme among individuals who suddenly begin to feel that their ethnic group and its way of life, especially its privileged and ascribed status, is being threatened by other racial and ethnic groups. This frequently happens when Blacks begin to move into all-White ethnic communities. Extreme forms of this stage are also manifested among individuals who have experienced ethnic psychological captivity (Stage 1) and who have recently discovered their ethnicity. This new ethnic consciousness is usually caused by an ethnic revitalization movement. This type of individual, like the individual who feels that the survival of his or her ethnic group is threatened, is likely to express intensely negative feelings toward outside ethnic and racial groups.

However, individuals who have experienced ethnic psychological captivity and who have newly discovered their ethnic consciousness tend to have highly ambivalent feelings toward their own ethnic group and try to confirm, for themselves, that they are proud of their ethnic heritage and culture. Consequently, strong and verbal rejection of outgroups usually takes place. Outgroups are regarded as enemies, racists, and in extreme manifestations of this stage, are viewed as planning genocidal efforts to destroy their ethnic group. The individual's sense of ethnic peoplehood is escalated and highly exaggerated. The ethnic individual within this stage of ethnicity tends to strongly reject members of his or her ethnic group who are regarded as assimilationist oriented, liberal, who do not endorse the rhetoric of separatism, or who openly socialize with members of outside ethnic groups, especially with members of a different racial group.

The Stage 2 individual expects members of the ethnic group to show strong overt commitments to the liberation struggle of the group or to the protection of the group from outside and "foreign" groups. The individual often endorses a separatist ideology. Members of outside ethnic groups are likely to regard Stage 2 individuals as racists, bigots, or extremists. As this type of individual begins to question some of the basic assumptions of his or her culture and to experience less ambivalence and conflict about his or her ethnic identity, and especially, as the rewards within the society become more fairly distributed among ethnic groups, he or she is likely to become less ethnocentric and ethnically encapsulated.

Stage 3: Ethnic Identity Clarification

At this stage the individual is able to clarify his or her attitudes and ethnic identity, to reduce intrapsychic conflict, and to develop clarified positive attitudes toward his or her ethnic group. The individual learns to accept himself or herself, thus developing the characteristics needed to accept and respond more positively to outside ethnic groups. Self-acceptance is a requisite to accepting and responding positively to others. During this stage, the individual is able to accept and understand both the positive and negative attributes of his or her ethnic group. The individual's pride of his or her ethnic group is not based on the hate or fear of outside groups. Ethnic pride is genuine rather than contrived. Individuals are more likely to experience this stage when they have attained a certain level of economic and psychological security and have been able to have positive experiences with members of other ethnic groups.

Stage 4: Biethnicity

Individuals within this stage have a healthy sense of ethnic identity and the psychological characteristics and skills needed to participate successfully in his or her own ethnic culture as well as in another ethnic culture. The individual also has a strong desire to function effectively in two ethnic cultures. We may describe such an individual as biethnic. Levels of biethnicity vary greatly. Many Afro-Americans, in order to attain social and economic mobility, learn to function effectively in Anglo-American culture during the formal working day. The private lives of these individuals, however, may be highly Black and monocultural.

Non-White minorities are forced to become biethnic to some extent in order to experience social and economic moiblity. However, members of dominant groups, such as Anglo-Americans, can and often do live almost exclusive monocultural and highly ethnocentric lives.

Stage 5: Multiethnicity and Reflective Nationalism

The Stage 5 individual has clarified, reflective, and positive personal, ethnic, and national identifications; positive attitudes toward other ethnic and racial groups; and is self-actualized. The individual is able to function, at least beyond superficial levels, within several ethnic cultures within his or her nation and to understand, appreciate, and share the values, symbols and institutions of several ethnic cultures within his or her nation. Such multiethnic perspectives and feelings, I hypothesize, help the individual to live a more enriched and fulfilling life and to formulate creative and novel solutions to personal and public problems.

Individuals within this stage have a commitment to their ethnic group, an empathy and concern for other ethnic groups, and a strong but *reflective* commitment and allegiance to the nation state and its idealized values, such as human dignity and justice. Thus, such individuals have reflective and clarified ethnic and national identifications and are effective citizens in a democratic pluralistic nation. Stage 5 individuals realistically view the United States as the multiethnic nation that it is. They have cross-cultural competency within their own nation and commitment to the national ideals, creeds, and values of the nation state.

The socialization that most individuals experience, especially within the United States, does not help them to attain the attitudes, skills, and perspectives needed to function effectively within a variety of ethnic cultures and communities. Although many Americans participate in several ethnic cultures at superficial levels, such as eating ethnic foods and listening to ethnic music (called Level I in chapter 2), few probably participate at more meaningful levels and learn to understand the values, symbols, and traditions of several ethnic cultures and are able to function within other American ethnic cultures at meaningful levels (Level II through III, see chapter 2).

Stage 6: Globalism and Global Competency

The individual within Stage 6 has clarified, reflective, and positive ethnic, national, and global identifications and the knowledge, skills, attitudes, and abilities needed to function within ethnic cultures within his or her own nation as well as within cultures outside his or her nation in other parts of the world. The Stage 6 individual has the ideal delicate balance of ethnic, national, and global identifications, commitments, literacy, and behaviors. This individual has internalized the universalistic ethical values and principles of humankind and has the skills, competencies, and commitment needed to take action within the world to actualize his or her values and commitments.

Characteristics of the Stages of Ethnicity Typology

This typology is an ideal type construct (see Figure 9.1) and should be viewed as dynamic and multidimensional rather than as static and linear. The characterisics within the stages exist on a continuum. Thus, within Stage 1, individuals are more or less ethnically psychologically captive; some individuals are more ethnically psychologically captive than others.

The division between the stages is blurred rather than sharp. Thus a continuum also exists between as well as within the stages. The ethnically encapsulated individual (Stage 2) does not suddenly attain clarification and acceptance of his or her ethnic identity (Stage 3). This is a gradual and developmental process. Also, the stages should not be viewed as strictly sequential and linear. I am hypothesizing that some individuals may never experience a particular stage. However, I hypothesize that once an individual experiences a particular stage, he or she is likely to experience the stages above it sequentially and developmentally. I hypothesize, however, that individuals may experience the stages upward, downward, or in a zigzag pattern. Under certain conditions, for example, the biethnic (Stage 4) individual may become multiethnic (Stage 5); under new conditions the same individual may become again biethnic (Stage 4), ethnically identified (Stage 3), and ethnically encapsulated (Stage 2). Note, for example, the extent to which Jewish Americans, who tend to express more positive attitudes toward non-Whites than other White ethnic groups, became increasingly in-group oriented as Israel became more threatened and as the expressions of anti-Semitism escalated in the 1970s.[4] Northern White ethnic groups became increasingly more ethnically encapsulated as busing for school desegregation gained momentum in northern cities in the 1970s.[5]

Figure 9.1 illustrates the dynamic and multidimensional characteristics of the development of ethnicity among individuals. Note especially the arrowed lines that indicate that continua exist both horizontally and vertically.

Preliminary Curricular Implications of the Stages of Ethnicity Typology

The discussion that follows on the curricular implications of the stages of ethnicity typology should be viewed as a set of tentative hypotheses that merit testing by educators and researchers interested in ethnicity and edu-

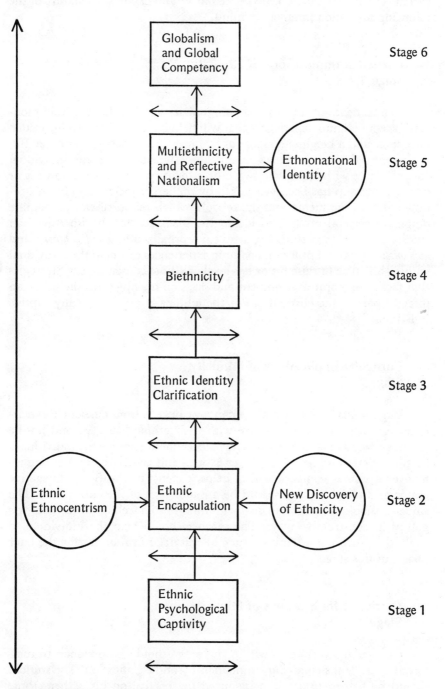

Figure 9.1. The Stages of Ethnicity: A Typology.

cation. The reader should keep the tentative and exploratory nature of the following discussion foremost in mind.

Curricular Implications of Ethnicity
Stage 1

The student within this stage of ethnicity can best benefit from monoethnic content and experiences that will help him or her to develop ethnic awareness and a heightened sense of ethnic consciousness (see chapter 10). Such monoethnic experiences should be designed to help the individual come to grips with his or her own ethnic identity and to learn how his or her ethnic group has been victimized by the larger society and by institutions, such as the media and the schools, which reinforce and perpetuate dominant societal myths and ideologies. Black studies, Jewish American studies, and Chicano studies courses conceptualized in *interdisciplinary* and *humanistic* ways, and other monoethnic experiences can help the individual within this stage to raise his or her level of ethnic consciousness. Strategies that facilitate moral development and decision-making skills should be an integral part of the curriculum for the ethnically psychologically captive individual.[6]

Curricular Implications of Ethnicity
Stage 2

Individuals within this stage can best benefit from curricular experiences that accept and empathize with their ethnic identities and hostile feelings toward outside groups. The teacher should accept the individual's hostile feelings and help him or her express and clarify them. A strong affective curricular component that helps students to clarify their negative ethnic and racial feelings should be a major part of the curriculum. The students should be helped to deal with their hostile feelings toward outside groups in constructive ways. The teacher should help the individual to begin the process of attaining ethnic identity clarification during the later phases of this stage.

Curricular Implications of Ethnicity
Stage 3

Curricular experiences within this stage should be designed to reinforce the student's emerging ethnic identity and clarification. The student should be helped to attain a balanced perspective on his or her ethnic group. A true acceptance of one's ethnic group involves accepting its glories as well as its shortcomings. The individual in this stage of ethnicity can accept an objective view and analysis of his or her ethnic group, whereas an objective analysis is often very difficult for Stage 1 and Stage 2 individuals to accept. Value clarification and moral development techniques should be used to enhance the individual's emerging ethnic identity clarification.

Curricular Implications of Ethnicity
Stage 4

Curricular experiences should be designed to help the student to master concepts and generalizations related to an ethnic group other than his or her own and to help him or her to view events and situations from the perspective of another ethnic group. The student should be helped to compare and contrast his or her own ethnic group with that of another ethnic group. Strategies should also be used to enhance the individual's moral development and his or her ability to relate positively to his or her own ethnic group and to another ethnic group.

Curricular Implications of Ethnicity
Stage 5

The curriculum at this stge of ethnicity should be designed to help the student develop a global sense of ethnic literacy and to mastery concepts and generalizations about a wide range of ethnic groups. The student should also be helped to view events and situations from the perspectives of different ethnic groups within the United States as well as within other nations. The student should explore the problems and promises of living within a multiethnic cultural environment and discuss ways in which a multiethnic society may be nurtured and improved. Strategies such as moral dilemmas and case studies should be used to enable the individual to explore moral and value alternatives and to embrace values, such as human dignity and justice, that are needed to live in a multiethnic community and global world society.

Curricular Implications of Stage 6

At this stage, the student has acquired three levels of identifications that are balanced: an ethnic, national and global identification and related cross-cultural competencies. Since the typology presented in this chapter constitutes a continuum, the process of acquiring an effective balance of ethnic, national, and global identifications and related cross-cultural competencies is a continuous and ongoing *process.* Thus, the individual never totally attains the ideal ethnic, national, and global identifications and related cross-cultural skills for functioning within his or her ethnic group, nation, and world. Consequently, a major goal of the curriculum for the Stage 6 individual is to help the student to function at Stage 6 more effectively.

Knowledge, skills, attitudes, and abilities that students need to function more effectively within their ethnic group, nation, and world should be emphasized when teaching students at Stage 6. This includes knowledge about the individual's own ethnic group, other ethnic groups, the national culture, and knowledge about other nations in the world. Valuing strategies, such as moral dilemmas and case studies that relate to the individual's ethnic group, nation, and world, should also be effectively used at this stage to enhance the student's developing sense of ethnic, national, and global identifications. A major goal of teaching students within this stage is to help them understand how to determine which particular allegiance—whether ethnic, national, or global—is most appropriate within a particular situation. Ethnic, national, and global attachments should be prioritized differently within different situations and events. The student within Stage 6 should learn how to determine which identification is most appropriate for particular situations, settings, and events.

Summary

When planning multiethnic experiences for students and teachers, we need to consider the ethnic characteristics of individuals. In designing curricula related to ethnicity, we often assume that ethnic groups are monolithic and have rather homogeneous needs and characteristics. However, students differ greatly in their ethnic identities and characteristics just as they differ in their general cognitive and affective development.[7] Consequently, some attempt should be made to individualize experiences for students within the multiethnic curriculum.

The description of a typology that attempts to outline the basic stages of the development of ethnicity among individual members of ethnic groups is presented in this chapter. This typology is a preliminary ideal type construct in the Weberian sense and constitutes a set of hypotheses that is based on the existing and emerging theory and research and the author's study of ethnic behavior. The six stages within the typology are: Stage 1: *Ethnic Psychological Captivity;* Stage 2: *Ethnic Encapsulation;* Stage 3: *Ethnic Identity Clarification;* Stage 4: *Biethnicity;* Stage 5: *Multiethnicity and Reflective Nationalism;* and Stage 6: *Globalism and Competency.* It is hypothesized that individuals within these different stages should be exposed to curricular experiences consistent with their levels of ethnic development. The curricular implications of each of the stages of ethnicity are discussed.

Notes

1. Social scientists frequently suggest, for example, that Afro-Americans have confused racial identities and ambivalent attitudes toward their ethnic group. The typology that I present, however, suggests that only a segment of Blacks can be so characterized and that those Blacks are functioning at Ethnicity Stage 1. For the classical social pathology interpretation of the Afro-American personality see Abram Kardiner and Lionel Ovesey, *The Mark of Oppression: A Psychosocial Study of the American Negro* (New York: Norton, 1951).
2. Margaret Ford, "The Development of An Instrument for Assessing Levels of Ethnicity In Public School Teachers," Ed.D. diss., University of Houston, 1979.
3. Alice Miel with Edwin Kiester, Jr., *The Shortchanged Children of Suburbia* (New York: Institute of Human Relations Press, The American Jewish Committee, 1967).
4. See especially Arnold Forster and Benjamin R. Epstein, *The New Anti-Semitism* (New York: McGraw-Hill, 1974).
5. For a sympathetic essay on White ethnics who find themselves in this situation see Nathan Glazer, "The Issue of Cultural Pluralism in America Today," in Joseph A. Ryan, *White Ethnics: Life in Working-Class America* (Englewood Cliffs, N.J.: Prentice-Hall, 1973), pp. 168–177.
6. James A. Banks with Ambrose A. Clegg, *Teaching Strategies for the Social Studies: Inquiry, Valuing and Decision-Making*, 2nd ed. (Reading, Mass.: Addison-Wesley, 1977).
7. Jean Piaget, *Six Psychological Studies* (New York: Random House, 1968); Lawrence Kohlberg and Rochelle Mayer, "Development as the Aim of Education," *Harvard Educational Review* 42 (November 1972), pp. 449–496.

10

Curricular Models
for an Open Society

The Characteristics of an Open Society

It is necessary to define an open society before we can design a curriculum that will enable students to develop a commitment to that kind of social system, and the strategies and skills needed to create and maintain it. This is essential because each curriculum is normative since it is designed to create and sustain a specific set of beliefs, attitudes, and institutions. In this chapter, an open society is defined as one in which individuals from diverse ethnic, cultural, and social class groups have equal opportunities to participate. Individuals can take full advantage of the opportunities and rewards within all social, economic, and political institutions without regard to their ancestry or ethnic identity. They can also participate in the society while preserving their distinct ethnic and cultural traits,[1] and are able to "make the maximum number of voluntary contacts with others without regard to qualifications of ancestry, sex or class."[2]

In an open society, rewards and opportunities are not necessarily evenly disributed, but they are distributed on the basis of the knowledge and skills that each person can contribute to the fulfillment of the needs of society. The societal needs referred to here consist of those systems and institutions that every society must have to function, such as a system of education, government, and the production and distribution of goods and services. The kind of society I am proposing has never existed in the human experience. History and contemporary social science teach us that in every past and present society, individuals have had and still have widely unequal opportunities to share fully in the reward systems and benefits of their society. The basis for the unequal distribution of rewards is determined by elitist groups in which power is centered.

Powerful and Excluded Ethnic Groups

Powerful groups decide which traits and characteristics are necessary for full societal participation. They determine necessary traits on the basis of the similarity of such traits to their own values, physical characteristics, life-styles, and behavior. At various points in history, celibacy, sex, ethnicity, race, religion, as well as many other variables have been used by

141

powerful groups to determine which individuals and groups would be given or denied opportunities for social mobility and full societal participation. In colonial America, White Anglo-Saxon male Protestants with property controlled most social, political, economic, and military institutions. They excluded from full participation in decision-making peoples, such as American Indians and Blacks, who were different from themselves. They invented and perpetuated stereotypes and myths about groups that were politically, economically, and socially excluded to justify their exclusion.[3]

Power Relationships in the United States

The United States, like most other nations, is dominated by a few powerful groups who admit or deny individuals opportunities to participate in society on the basis of how similar such individuals are to themselves.[4] White Anglo-Saxon male Protestants with money are the most valued persons in contemporary American Society; an individual who may be so classified has maximum opportunities to participate in America's social, economic, and political institutions.[5] As ethnic individuals become more similar to Anglo-Saxon Protestants in culture, values, beliefs, and behavior, their chances for attaining structural inclusion into American society increase. It is very difficult for ethnic individuals who do not acquire Anglo-Saxon cultural characteristics to attain social, economic, and political mobility in the United States.

In this chapter, I use *excluded, powerless,* and *oppressed* to describe those ethnic groups such as American Indians, Mexican Americans, and Afro-Americans who, *as groups,* do not fully participate in the nation's economic and social institutions and who exercise little political power. The concepts *dominant, majority,* and *powerful* ethnic groups are used to describe ethnic groups such as Anglo-Saxon and German American Protestants. These ethnic collectives, as groups, exercise considerable economic and political power in the United States and often determine the norms and standards by which other ethnic groups are judged.

Creating an Open Society

To create the kind of open society I have defined above, we will either have to redistribute power so that groups with different ethnic and cultural characteristics will control entry to various social, economic, and political institutions, or we will have to modify the attitudes and actions of individuals who will control future institutions so that they will become less ethnocentric and permit people who differ from themselves culturally and physically to share equally in society's reward system on the basis of the *real* contributions they can make to the functioning of society. We can conceptualize these two means to an open society as models.

Curricular Models

Model I may be called a *shared power model. The goal of this model would be to create a society in which currently excluded ethnic groups would share power with dominant ethnic groups.* They would control a number of social, economic, and political institutions, and would determine the criteria for admission to these institutions. The methods used to attain the major ends of this model would be an attempt to build group pride, cohesion, and identity among excluded ethnic groups, and help them to develop the ability to make reflective political decisions, to gain and exercise political power effectively, and to develop a belief in the humanness of their own groups.

The alternative means to an open society may be called Model II, *enlightening powerful groups model. The major goal of this model would be to modify the attitudes and perceptions of dominant ethnic groups so that they would be willing, as adults, to share power with excluded ethnic groups.* They would also be willing to regard excluded ethnic groups as humans, unwilling to participate in efforts to continue their oppression, willing to accept and understand the actions by excluded groups to liberate themselves and willing to take *action* to change the social system so that it would treat powerless ethnic groups more just. The major goals within this model focus on helping dominant ethnic groups to expand their conception of who is human, to develop more positive attitudes toward ethnic minorities, and a willingness to share power with excluded ethnic groups. Figures 10.1 and 10.2 summarize these two models.

The Characteristics and Goals of Model I

Most individuals who are acutely aware of the extent to which excluded ethnic groups are powerless in America will probably view the *shared power model* as more realistic than Model II. This model, if successfully implemented, would result in the redistribution of *power* so that ethnic groups that have been and still are systematically excluded from full participation in America would control such institutions as schools, courts, industries, health facilities, and the mass media. They would not necessarily control all institutions within America, but would control those in which they participated and which are needed to fulfill their individual and group needs. These groups would be able to distribute jobs and other rewards to persons, who, like themselves, are denied such opportunities by present powerful ethnic groups. During the 1960s, the Nation of Islam used this model to create employment and eductional opportunities for poor and excluded Blacks.[6] The community control movement was an unsuccessful attempt to implement this model.[7] Elements within this model have been used by such groups as Jews and Catholics to enable them to participate more fully in shaping public policy.[8]

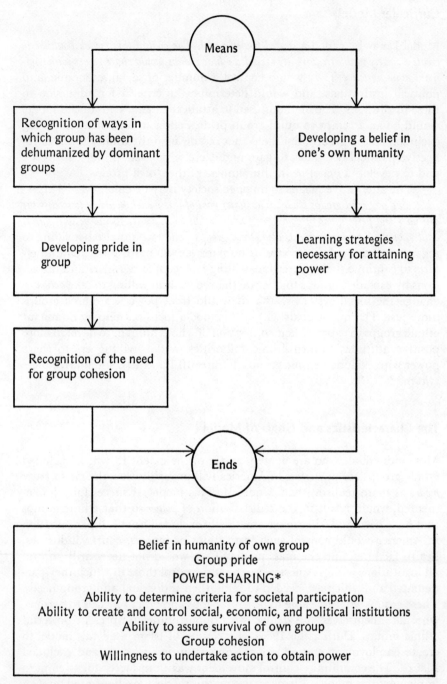

Means

Recognition of ways in which group has been dehumanized by dominant groups

Developing a belief in one's own humanity

Developing pride in group

Learning strategies necessary for attaining power

Recognition of the need for group cohesion

Ends

Belief in humanity of own group
Group pride
POWER SHARING*
Ability to determine criteria for societal participation
Ability to create and control social, economic, and political institutions
Ability to assure survival of own group
Group cohesion
Willingness to undertake action to obtain power

*Major end of model.

Figure 10.1. Model I — Shared Power Model.

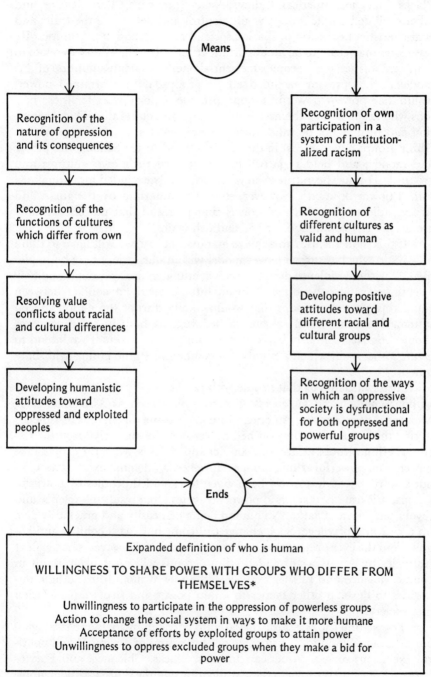

Means

Recognition of the nature of oppression and its consequences

Recognition of own participation in a system of institutionalized racism

Recognition of the functions of cultures which differ from own

Recognition of different cultures as valid and human

Resolving value conflicts about racial and cultural differences

Developing positive attitudes toward different racial and cultural groups

Developing humanistic attitudes toward oppressed and exploited peoples

Recognition of the ways in which an oppressive society is dysfunctional for both oppressed and powerful groups

Ends

Expanded definition of who is human

WILLINGNESS TO SHARE POWER WITH GROUPS WHO DIFFER FROM THEMSELVES*

Unwillingness to participate in the oppression of powerless groups
Action to change the social system in ways to make it more humane
Acceptance of efforts by exploited groups to attain power
Unwillingness to oppress excluded groups when they make a bid for power

*Major end of model.

Figure 10.2. Model II — Enlightening Powerful Groups Model.

In a society in which power is shared by different ethnic groups, Blacks, Chicanos, American Indians, Asian-Americans, Puerto Ricans, and other excluded ethnic groups would control and determine the traits and characteristics necessary for sharing societal rewards and opportunities. IQ test scores may cease to be an important criteria, but the ability to relate to ethnic minorities may become an essential one.[9] A major assumption of this model is that present excluded ethnic groups, if they attained power, would, like present powerful groups, provide opportunities for those persons who are most like themselves physically and culturally. This assumption may or may not be valid, since some evidence suggests that powerless ethnic groups have, at least in the past, idealized Anglo-Saxons with power and money, and held negative feelings toward their own cultures and groups.[10] This has been true even when previously excluded individuals assumed power positions. However, studies summarized by Baugman and Arnez indicate that this situation is changing and that powerless ethnic groups are developing more pride and cohesion.[11]

If this model is used to achieve an open society, we will have to think of ways in which a shared power model within our society may be implemented without violence directed against ethnic minority groups; and how essential societal cohesion may be maintained without conflict between competing powerful groups that would totally disrupt the nation's social system. There are valid reasons to believe that both of these concerns should be taken seriously by educators and policy makers if we intend to create a society in which a number of competing ethnic groups will share power.

History teaches us that people with power usually do not relinquish it without conflict and violence.[12] Ethnic groups such as Afro-Americans, Mexican Americans and American Indians became the victims of violence during the 1960s when they pushed aggressively for their civil rights.[13] Excluded ethnic groups clearly risk conflict and violence when they try to take power from powerful ethnic groups. However, a dilemma exists. Throughout history, power has rarely been given to excluded peoples by powerful groups; it is usually taken and power struggles often result in violence and revolution. Writes Clark, "No human being can easily and graciously give up power and privilege. Such change can come only with conflict and anguish and the ever present threat of retrogression."[14] However, since violent strategies by America's excluded ethnic groups will most likely result in counterviolence and further exclusion, the school should help ethnic minorities to develop other tactics to attain power and structural inclusion into society.

Translating the *shared power model* into curriculum goals and strategies, our attention would focus primarily on the victims of structural and political exclusion, such as American Indians, Blacks, Chicanos, and Puerto-Ricans. We woud try to help these students attain the skills, attitudes, abilities, and strategies needed to attain power while maintaining an essential degree of societal cohesion. We would help these students see, through valid content samples, how previously excluded and politically powerless groups in history have attained power, and how certain nonreflective actions and inactions can result in further exclusion and victimization. Case studies of groups such as unionized auto workers and public school teachers can serve as examples of groups that have successfully attained significant amount of power in the United States without widespread violence or further victimization.[15]

The Assumptions of Model II

Model II, whose primary goal is to help majority group students such as Anglo-Americans develop more positive attitudes toward structurally excluded ethnic groups such as Mexican Americans and Puerto Ricans, rests on a number of assumptions. We have little evidence to support the validity of these assumptions. If anything, current data gives us little hope in this model as an effective way to achieve an open society.[16] It assumes that most Anglo-Americans experience a moral dilemma created by the contradiction inherent in the ideals in America democratic values and the experiences of ethnic minorities in the United States. Myrdal, in his classic study of race relations in America, stated that most White Americans experience a moral dilemma because of the inconsistency between American democratic ideals and the treatment of Blacks in the United States.[17] It is possible that such a dilemma does not exist for many White Americans because they do not perceive ethnic minorities such as Chicanos and American Indians as groups who deserve equity and human rights.

Thus, it may be unrealistic to assume that teaching majority group students about the harsh experiences that ethnic minority groups have experienced in the United States will cause them to become more willing to regard ethnic minorities as fellow humans with certain entitlements in order to resolve their moral dilemmas related to race and democracy in the United States. Some writers argue that discriminatory policies toward ethnic minorities are deliberate.[18] If this argument is valid, then teaching majority group students about the brutalities of slavery, or the inhumanity of Indian reservations, cannot be expected to significantly affect the ways in which majority ethnic groups treat Blacks, American Indians, and other structurally excluded ethnic groups in the United States.

Purposes of Models

While these two models represent what I feel are the basic ways by which we can create an open society, they are ideal-type constructs. And like any ideal-type constructs or models, they are best used for conceptualization purposes. The laws of the land, the current organization of schools, and the types of student populations in many American schools make it difficult, in many cases, to implement either Model I or Model II in *pure* form. However, these models can help the curriculum specialist to determine the kind of *emphases* that are necessary for the curriculum for different student populations. *While the curriculum for excluded and dominant ethnic groups should have many elements in common, I believe that the central messages these groups receive in the curriculum should in some cases differ.*

In the following paragraphs, I will discuss, using the two models as departure points, the kinds of *emphases* that I feel should constitute the curricula for *excluded* and *powerful* ethnic groups in order to create and sustain an open society. I intend to take into account the limitations of each of the models in my recommendations, and to suggest ways in which they may be reduced. In those situations in which teachers have students from both powerful and excluded ethnic groups, it will be necessary for them to combine elements from both models in order to structure an effective curriculum.

The Curriculum for Excluded Groups: Curricular Implications of Model I

The curriculum I recommended for excluded ethnic groups will include most of the elements of Model I. However, it will also include elements from Model II because a pure, shared power model curriculum may result in a totally fragmented and dehumanized society.

Throughout history, excluded ethnic minority groups have been taught by the larger society that they were less than human, and that they deserve the low status in society in which they most often find themselves. Notes Baldwin, "The American triumph—in which the American tragedy has always been implicit—was to make Black people despise themselves. When I was little I despised myself; I did not know any better."[19] A large body of evidence collected by the Clarks in the 1940s, and by Morland in recent years, indicate that minority groups often accept the definitions of themselves that are perpetuated by dominant groups.[20] Studies reviewed by Arnez and conducted by Baughman and his students, suggest that the self-perceptions of minority groups may be changing, largely because of the positive influence of the ethnic movements of the 1960s.[21] However, Goldschmid's intensive review of the literature indicates that ethnic minority groups sometimes hold negative attitudes toward themselves and their race.[22]

The curriculum for ethnic minority groups should recognize their feelings toward self, help them to clarify their racial attitudes, liberate them from psychological captivity, and convince them of their humanness, since the dominant society often makes them believe that they are less than human. Writes Johnson: "The African descendants in America, having passed through three phases of education in America—de-Africanization, dehumanization, and, finally, an inferior caste status—through application of self-determination and the establishment of a voluntary self-separated school system, can educate themseles."[23]

Ethnic minorities will be able to liberate themselves from psychological and physical oppression only when they know how and why the myths about them emerged and were institutionalized and validated by the scholarly community and the mass media. A curriculum that has as one of its major goals the liberation of excluded ethnic groups must teach them the ways in which all social, political and economic institutions in this society, including the schools, the academic community and the mass media, have contributed to their feelings of inferiority and powerlessness.

They should be taught how social science knowledge often reflects the norms, values, and goals of the powerful ethnic groups in society, and how it often validates those belief systems that are functional for groups in power and dysfunctional for excluded and powerless ethnic groups.[24] When teaching students about the ways in which social knowledge has served to validate the stereotypes and myths about them, the teacher can use as examples Ulrich B. Phillips' racist descriptions of the nature of slavery, Moynihan's controversial study of the Black family, Jensen's work on Black-white intelligence, and Banfield's interpretations of the riots of the 1960s.[25] Textbook descriptions of Asian-Americans, American Indians, Puerto Ricans, and Chicanos can also be used to teach ethnic peoples about ways in which social knowledge has been used to perpetuate inaccurate and misleading views of their histories and cultures.[26]

While studying about the ways in which they have been psychologically and physically dehumanized is necessary to help excluded ethnic groups to liberate themselves, it is not sufficient. They must be helped to develop the ability to make reflective public decisions so that they can gain power and shape public policy that affects their lives. They must also develop a sense of political efficacy, and be given practices in social action strategies which teaches them how to get power without violence and further exclusion. *In other words, excluded groups must be taught the most effective ways to gain power.* The school must help them become effective and reflective *political activists.* I am defining *reflective* decision making and social action as those kinds of decisions and social action that will enable excluded ethnic groups to attain power, but will at the same time insure their existence as a group and essential societal cohesion. Opportunities for social action, in which students have experience in obtaining and exercising power, should be emphasized within a curriculum that is designed to help liberate excluded ethnic groups.[27] Since oppression and racism exists within the school as well as within most other American institutions, students can be provided practice in shaping public policy and in gaining power within their classroom, school, or school system.

The curriculum for excluded ethnic groups must not only help release them from psychological captivity, and focus on social action, it must also help them to develop humanistic attitudes toward members of their own group, as well as toward other excluded groups, since coalitions among ethnic peoples is necessary for them to gain and exercise political power. The fact that individuals are more likely to attain power when working in groups than when working alone is a highly important generalization that should be incorporated into a curriculum that has liberation as its goal.

The school should also make an effort, when teaching excluded ethnic groups how to attain power and to develop an appreciation of their cultural identification, to prevent them from becoming chauvinistic and ethnocentric, and from developing negative attitudes and perceptions about other cultural and ethnic groups, including powerful ethnic groups. Ethnic minority groups should also be taught that the means they use to attain power and political influence should not violate American democratic values such as human dignity and equality.

Presently excluded ethnic groups should learn to value their own cultures, try to attain power, and develop group solidarity and identity in order to participate fully in society. However, they should also learn to respect and value other ethnic cultures and institutions within American society and to develop a commitment to the nation state, to idealized American values, and to the common American culture that all Americans share. *Any efforts in multiethnic education should acknowledge and respect the common American culture and identity.* The humanistic emphasis, which is a Model II component, must be incorporated into a curriculum for excluded ethnic groups to help prevent them from developing ethnocentric attitudes, perceptions, and behaviors.

Curriculum for Dominant Ethnic Groups: Curricular Implications of Model II

Since we have no reliable ways of knowing that a Model I type curriculum would lead to an open society as I have defined it in this chapter, the curriculum builder should also implement elements of Model II in appropriate settings; i.e., in settings that contain dominant ethnic groups. What I am suggesting is that since both of these models have severe limitations, and since we know little about ways to create an open society because we have never made a serious effort to create one, we should take a multiple approach to the problem. Also, the two models are complementary and not contradictory. If we succeed in enlightening or changing the attitudes of dominant ethnic groups so that they become more willing to share power with excluded ethnic groups, then the struggle for power among powerless ethnic peoples would consequently be less intense, and thus less likely to lead to violence and societal chaos.

The elements that constitute Model II have been among the most widespread methods used by educators and policy makers to create a more humane society and better opportunities for Blacks, American Indians, Chicanos, Asian Americans, and other powerless ethnic groups in the United States. This approach is suggested by such terms as *intergroup education, intercultural education, human relations, race relations,* and *intercultural education.* Massive efforts were undertaken by such organizations as the American Council on Education and the Anti-Defamation League of B'nai B'rith in the 1940s and 1950s to implement workshops to change the attitudes of teachers and students toward ethnic minority groups (discussed in chapter 1).

Hilda Taba and her colleagues developed a theoretical rationale for intergroup education, conducted numerous workshops, and published a number of books for the American Council of Education. Taba identified four major goals of intergroup education: (1) to provide pupils with facts, ideas, and concepts basic to intelligent understanding of group relations; (2) to develop the ability to think objectively and rationally about people, their problems, relationships, and cultures; (3) to develop those feelings, values, attitudes, and sensitivities necessary for living in a pluralist society; and (4) to develop skills necessary for getting along with individuals and for working successfully in groups.[28]

Jean D. Grambs, another leader in intergroup education, states the assumption of the approach:

> *If a person can learn to hate and distrust others, he can learn to like and trust others.* . . . This is the basic assumption of intergroup education. . . . Intergroup education similarly assumes that, as a result of selected materials and methods, individuals will be changed, that their attitudes and behaviors toward persons of other groups, and toward members of whatever group they themselves belong to, will be changed. The change will result in *more* acceptance of persons who differ and *more* acceptance of one's own difference from others.[29]

Other leaders in the field also assume that we can teach people new attitudes toward excluded groups. Writes Trager and Yarrow, "Children learn what they live; in a culture which practices and condones prejudice, one behaves and thinks with prejudice. If children are to learn new ways of behaving, more democratic ways, they must be *taught* new behaviors and new values."[30] The seminal study by Trager and Yarrow supports the assumption that democratic attitudes can be taught to children if a deliberate program of instruction is designed for that purpose.[31]

The primary goal of intergroup education (Model II elements) is to "enlighten" dominant ethnic groups by changing their attitudes and perceptions of excluded ethnic minorities. Attempts are made to enlighten dominant ethnic group members by creating experiences for them in which they read or hear about prejudice, discrimination and institutionalized racism in America. Frequently the participants are also required or encouraged to examine their racial and ethnic attitudes, perceptions, and behaviors.[32]

It is difficult to determine how much potential Model II approaches have for changing the racial attitudes, beliefs, and behaviors of individuals. These methods have never been extensively implemented. Individuals are often not exposed to Model II type experiences until they are adults. Such adults usually attend a two- or three-week workshop, or a course in race relations for a quarter or a semester. Evidence suggests that these experiences usually have little permanent impact on adults' racial attitudes, although other kinds of experiences (used in conjunction with lectures and readings) seem to have some lasting influence on the racial attitudes of adults.[33] It is predictable that a short workshop would have limited affect on adults' racial attitudes since an experience of twenty hours or less cannot be expected to change attitudes and perceptions that an individual has acquired over a twenty-year period, especially when the basic institutions in which they live reinforce their preexperimental attitudes.

Because of the meager results that have been obtained from Model II approaches, some educators feel that this model should be abandoned, and that a shared power model is the only realistic way in which to achieve an open society. As an individual who has conducted many race relations workshops, I greatly respect individuals who endorse this point of view. However, I feel that Model II approaches should be continued, but the ways in which they are implemented should be greatly modified. They should be continued and expanded because: (1) We have no assurance that a shared power model will succeed in this period of our history (however, we also have no assurance that it will not); (2) Model II strategies have never been extensively implemented, rather they are usually used in experiments with students or with teachers when a racial crisis develops in a school district; (3) research suggests that the racial attitudes of children can be modified by curriculum intervention, especially in the earliest years; the younger children are, the greater the impact that curriculum intervention is likely to have on their racial feelings;[34] and (4) racism is a serious, dehumanizing pathology in this society that the school has a moral and professional responsibility to help eradicate.

Earlier I discussed the severe limitations of Model II, and the questionable assumptions on which it is based. Later I argued that elements of this model should be implemented in appropriate settings. I do not see these two positions as contradictory; rather, I feel that when curriculum builders are aware of the limitations of their strategies, they can better use, evaluate, and modify them. A knowledge of the limitations of a curriculum strategy will also prevent the curriculum builder from expecting unrealistic outcomes. For example, a knowledge of the limitations of Model II will help teachers to realize that a unit on race relations during "Black heritage month" will most likely have little influence on the racial attitudes of their students. They will know that only a modification of their total curriculum is likely to have any significant impact on their students' racial attitudes and beliefs, and that even with this kind of substantial curriculum modification, the chances for modification of racial attitudes will not be extremely high, especially if they are working with older students or adults. Curricular experiences are more likely to change students' racial *beliefs* than their racial *attitudes*.[35]

Increasing the Effectiveness of Model II Approaches

Despite the severe limitations of Model II as it is currently used in the schools and in teacher education, I believe that substantial modifications in the implementation of Model II components can significantly increase this model's impact on the racial attitudes and perceptions of dominant ethnic group individuals. The ultimate result of an effective implementation of the model may be that children of dominant ethnic groups, as adults, will be more likely to perceive excluded ethnic groups as humans, and thus more likely to share power with them, and allow them to participate more fully in America's social, economic, and political institutions. All of these statements are, at best, promising hypotheses, but I base them on experience, gleamings from research, and faith. In the next few paragraphs, I will suggest ways in which the implementation of a Model II type curriculum can have maximum opportunity to "enlighten" or modify the racial attitudes, beliefs, and perceptions of students.

By the time that the child enters school, he or she has already inculcated the negative attitudes toward ethnic minorities that are pervasive within the larger society. Although this fact has been documented since Lasker's pioneering research in 1929,[36] teachers are often surprised to learn in workshops that even kindergarten pupils are aware of racial differences and assign different values to Blacks and Whites. This fact alone gives us little hope for effective intervention. However, a related one does. The racial attitudes of kindergartners are not as negative or as crystallized as those of fifth graders.[37] As children grow older, and no systematic efforts are made to modify their racial feelings, they become more bigoted. The curriculum implications of this research are clear. To modify children's racial attitudes, a deliberate program of instruction must be structured for that purpose in the earliest grades. The longer we wait, the less our chances are for success. By the time the individual reaches adulthood, the chances for successful intervention become almost—but not quite—nil.

Effective intervention programs must not only begin in the earliest grades; but the efforts must be sustained over a long period of time, and material related to cultural differences must permeate the entire curriculum. Also, a variety of media and materials enhances chances for successful intervention. A unit on American Indians in the second grade, and a book on Mexican Americans in the third grade, will do little to help students understand or accept cultures that are different from their own. A "hit and miss" approach to the study of cultural differences may do more harm than good. While there may be times when a separate in-depth unit on an American ethnic minority culture is educationally justified in order to teach a concept such as acculturation or enculturation, most often when ethnic groups are studied in this way the students are likely to get the impression that ethnic minorities have not played an integral and significant role in the shaping of this society and its institutions, and that they are not "real" Americans. Frequently, Blacks, American Indians, Chicanos, Puerto Ricans, and Asian Americans are studied only when they are presented as "problems" by the textbook writer or curriculum builder.

Students should also be helped to come to grips with the pervasive value dilemmas within our society and their own interpersonal value conflicts. Many students verbally claim that they value equality and freedom for excluded ethnic minorities but harshly condemn aggressive efforts by these groups to attain human rights. Teachers should help students to see why these actions are contradictory and inconsistent. They have a professional responsibility to help students to see the contradictions and conflicts in their beliefs, and to reflectively analyze their values and express a willingness to accept their consequences.

Some beliefs are inherently contradictory. Education should help students to acquire clarified, consistent beliefs that can guide meaningful and purposeful action of which they can be proud. The contradictions between the values expressed in our national documents and the ways in which minority groups are treated in the United States should also constitute an important part of a curriculum that intends to enlighten dominant ethnic group individuals. A number of valuing inquiry models and strategies are available for use by teachers to help students to analyze personal and public value problems and conflicts.[38]

Summary

To create an open society, it is necessary to clearly define such a social system and design a curriculum specifically to achieve and perpetuate it. An open society is a social system in which individuals from diverse ethnic, cultural, and social class groups can freely participate, and have equal opportunities to gain the skills and knowledge the society needs in order to function. Rewards within an open society are based on the contributions each person, regardless of his or her ancestry or social class, can make to the fulfillment of the society's functional requirements.

Two models by which we may achieve and maintain an open society are presented in this chapter. Model I, or the *Shared Power Model*, focuses on helping excluded ethnic groups to attain power so they can control a number of social, economic, and political institutions, and determine who may participate in these institutions. These groups would also determine how rewards would be distributed. A second model, the *Enlightening Powerful Groups Model*, focuses on changing the attitudes, beliefs, perceptions, and behaviors of members of powerful ethnic groups so that they will share power with excluded ethnic groups, regard them as groups that deserve human rights, and take actions to eliminate institutionalized racism and discrimination in the United States.

The complexity of our society makes it impossible for either of these models to be implemented in pure form. Also, both models are ideal-type concepts that are based on a number of unverified assumptions. However, these models can help the curriculum builder to determine the kinds of emphases that would constitute an open society-curriculum for excluded, powerful, and mixed groups, for planning programs, and for ascertaining the effectiveness of various curriculum strategies.

Notes

1. Talcott Parsons, "Full Citizenship Rights for the Negro American," in Talcott Parsons and Kenneth B. Clark, eds., *The Negro American* (Boston: Houghton Mifflin, 1965), pp. 721–722.
2. Barbara A. Sizemore, "Is There a Case for Separate Schools?" *Phi Delta Kappan* 53 (January 1972), p. 281.
3. John Hope Franklin, *Racial Equality in America* (Chicago: University of Chicago Press, 1976).
4. C. Wright Mills, *The Power Elite* (New York: Oxford University Press, 1956); G. William Domhoff, *Who Rules America?* (Englewood Cliffs, N.J.: Prentice-Hall, 1967).
5. Barbara A. Sizemore, "Social Science and Education for a Black Identity," in James A. Banks and Jean D. Grambs, eds., *Black Self-Concept: Implications for Education and Social Science* (New York: McGraw-Hill, 1972).
6. C. Eric Lincoln, *The Black Muslims in America* (Boston: Beacon Press, 1961).
7. Barbara R. Hatton, "Community Control in Retrospect: A Review of Strategies for Community Participation in Education," in Carl A. Grant, ed., *Community Participation in Education* (Boston: Allyn and Bacon, 1979), pp. 2–20.
8. Andrew M. Greeley, *Why Can't They Be Like Us? America's White Ethnic Groups* (New York: Dutton, 1975); Leonard Dinnerstein, Roger L. Nichols, and David M. Reimers, *Natives and Strangers: Ethnic Groups and the Building of America* (New York: Oxford University Press, 1979).
9. Samuel Bowles and Herbert Gintis, *Schooling in Capitalist America: Educational Reform and the Contradictions of Economic Life* (New York: Basic Books, 1976).

10. See James A. Banks, "Racial Prejudice and the Black Self-Concept," in Banks and Grambs, *Black Self-Concept*, pp. 5–35.

11. See Nancy L. Arnez, "Enhancing the Black Self-Concept Through Literature," in Banks and Grambs, *Black Self-Concept*, pp. 93–116; and E. Earl Baugman, *Black Americans: A Psychological Analysis* (New York: Academic Press, 1971).

12. Crane Brinton, *The Anatomy of Revolution* (New York: Vintage Books, 1962).

13. Harry H. L. Kitano, *Race Relations* (Englewood Cliffs, N.J.: Prentice-Hall, 1974).

14. Kenneth B. Clark, "Introduction: The Dilemma of Power," in Parsons & Clark, *The Negro American*, p. xv.

15. Richard B. Morris, ed. *The U.S. Department of Labor Bicentennial History of the American Worker* (Washington, D.C.: U.S. Government Printing Office, 1976).

16. Gordon W. Allport, *The Nature of Prejudice*, 25th anniv. ed. (Reading, Mass.: Addison-Wesley, 1979), pp. 479–500.

17. Gunnar Myrdal, *An American Dilemma: The Negro Problem and Modern Democracy*, vols. 1 & 2 (New York: Harper and Row, 1962).

18. Martin Carnoy, *Education as Cultural Imperialism* (New York: David McKay, 1974); Bowles and Gintis, *Schooling in Capitalist America*.

19. James Baldwin, "An Open Letter to my Sister, Angela Y. Davis," in Angela Y. Davis et al, *If They Come in the Morning* (New York: Signet Books, 1971), p. 20.

20. Banks, "Racial Prejudice and the Black Self-Concept," in Banks and Grambs, *Black Self-Concept*.

21. Arnez and Baughman, "Enhancing the Black Self-Concept."

22. Marcel L. Goldschmid, ed., *Black Americans and White Racism: Theory and Research* (New York: Holt, 1970).

23. Edwina C. Johnson, "An Alternative to Miseducation for the Afro-American People," in Nathan Wright, Jr., *What Black Educators Are Saying* (New York: Hawthorn Books, Inc., 1970), p. 198.

24. Barbara A. Sizemore, "Social Science and Education for a Black Identity," in Banks and Grambs, *Black Self-Concept*.

25. Ulrich B. Phillips, *Life and Labor in the Old South* (Boston: Little, Brown, 1929); Daniel P. Moynihan, *The Negro Family: The Case for National Action* (Washington, D.C.: U.S. Government Printing Office, 1965); Arthur R. Jensen, "How Much Can We Boost IQ and Scholastic Achievement," *Harvard Educational Review* 39 (Winter 1969), pp. 1–123; Edward C. Banfield, *The Unheavenly City* (Boston: Little Brown, 1970).

26. Lloyd Marcus, *The Treatment of Minorities in American History Textbooks* (New York: Anti-Defamation League of B'nai B'rith, 1961); Irving A. Sloan, *The Negro in Modern History Textbooks* (Chicago: American Federation of Labor, 1966); James A. Banks, "A Content Analysis of the

Treatment of the Black American in Textbooks," *Social Education* 33 (December 1969), pp. 954–957, ff, p. 963.

27. For a discussion of decision-making and social-action programs see James A. Banks with Ambrose A. Clegg, *Teaching Strategies for the Social Studies: Inquiry, Valuing and Decision-Making*, 2nd ed. (Reading, Mass.: Addison-Wesley, 1977); and Fred M. Newmann, *Education for Citizen Action: Challenge for Secondary Curriculum* (Berkeley, Calif.: McCutchan, 1975).

28. Hilda Taba, Elizabeth H. Brady, and John T. Robinson, *Intergroup Education in Public Schools* (Washington, D.C.: American Council on Education, 1952), p. 36. This summary of Taba's theory is taken from June V. Gilliard, "Intergroup Education: How, For What, and For Whom?", paper, University of Washington, Seattle, 1971.

29. Jean Dresden Grambs, *Intergroup Education: Methods and Materials* (Englewood Cliffs, N.J.: Prentice-Hall, 1968), p. 1.

30. Helen G. Trager and Marian Radke Yarrow, *They Learn What They Live: Prejudice in Young Children* (New York: Harper and Brothers, 1952), p. 362.

31. Ibid.

32. Charlotte Epstein, *Intergroup Relations for the Classroom Teacher* (New York: Houghton Mifflin, 1968).

33. For a summary of this research, see James A. Banks, "Racial Prejudice and the Black Self-Concept."

34. Phyllis A. Katz and Sue Rosenberg, "Modification of Children's Racial Attitudes," *Developmental Psychology* 14 (1978), pp. 447–461.

35. Allport, *The Nature of Prejudice*.

36. Bruno Lasker, *Race Attitudes in Children* (New York: Henry Holt, 1929).

37. Charles Y. Glock et al, *Adolescent Prejudice* (New York: Harper and Row, 1975).

38. A number of such strategies are presented in James A. Banks with Ambrose A. Clegg, *Teaching Strategies for the Social Studies*.

11

Language, Ethnicity, and Education

If all students only spoke school-English, there would be little need for much of this chapter. The reality is we live in a multilingual society. Many students enter school speaking a non-English language or a dialect of American English. These students are described as "linguistically-different," "linguistic minorities," "bilingual" or "bidialectal." Being linguistically-different involves more than merely speaking a "foreign" language or a different English dialect. Speaking a certain language or dialect ties one to particular ethnic and cultural groups that hold values and attitudes that may conflict with the teachers' values and attitudes.

Some linguistic differences are innocuous. Whether students prefer "ain't" over "isn't" is inconsequential. No one is too concerned if a student speaks with a Hoosier twang. Or, if a student from Boston says "Cuba" as though it were pronounced "Cuber," no one seems to worry about the "mispronunciation." But, if a Black student prefers to say "I be sick" rather than "I am sick," or if a Chicano student pronounces "sit" as though it were "seat," then concern about the student's purported language deficiencies emerge. Some differences are not innocuous, especially if they cause communication breakdowns between teachers and students. Problems for both teachers and students arise when the classroom communication system—couched in the culture reflected by speakers of school-English—conflict with the student's communication system. Subtle but potent instances of miscommunication can lead to larger problems of student alienation, discontent, and academic failure. In effect, students who experience communicative conflict may retreat or withdraw from the school's society.

Teaching in a multilingual society poses difficult questions. Isn't it enough to teach students to communicate in the nation's main language? Doesn't every country need a national language for cohesion and international survival? Can I be expected to know every non-English language that my students speak? This chapter will attempt to answer troublesome questions like these by describing the myriad relationships between culture, ethnicity, and language, and the relationships between national educational

This chapter is contributed by Ricardo L. Garcia, Associate Professor, Graduate School of Education, University of Utah, Salt Lake City, Utah.

policy and language instruction. Benchmarks are provided to assist with the implementation of linguistic pluralism within the classroom.

The Relationship between Language and Culture

Language and culture are two characters on the same coin. If culture is "heads," language is "tails." In chapter 4 culture is defined as a generic way of life consisting of values, beliefs, behavior patterns, symbols, and institutions unique to a particular group or society. Language is a culture's primordial institution. Language establishes the bond between individuals and between individuals and groups, that makes group life possible. Without language, group life (as we currently know it) is inconceivable. Language, an organized social institution, serves at least three functions: (1) intergroup communications; (2) transmission of the group's ethnicity and culture; and (3) the systemic recording of the group's ethnicity, culture, and history, which serves to give a group identity.

A group's language provides the group with an organized medium of communication. Group members can tune into the group with little difficulty because they speak the "same" language, and in general, share the same meaning. Second, a group's language provides a medium for transmitting group values, beliefs, and attitudes. The language helps to set parameters for group living. Third, the language provides a medium to record a group's ethnicity, culture and history. Thus, language serves as a time-binding agent, tieing the past with the present. Part of group existence is knowing how the past percolates into the present. A group's folklore and myths are recorded in its language; thus, the group sustains itself by way of the oral tradition, i.e., teaching its youth orally about the past, or by way of the literacy tradition, i.e., teaching its youth about the past by having its youth read the written word.

Acquisition of Speech, Dialect, and Ethnicity

A primary parental function is to prepare youth to live in society. Parents use their dialect to describe, proscribe, and otherwise delineate the rules for group and social living. Social norms and mores are taught the youth *via* parental dialect. In this respect, speech acquisition is a socialization agent used by parents to prepare youth for social living. Children acquire ethnicity and speech through their parents and immediate family. Initially, children learn these attributes verbally and nonverbally, i.e., infants initially acquire ethnicity and speech by the ways parents and siblings speak, hold, and touch them. By six months of age, for example, an infant's sexual identity has been conveyed to it by parental and sibling contact.

The onset of ethnicity precedes speech acquisition. The onset of ethnicity begins at birth when children are first introduced to their immediate social environment, their parents and family. Yet, children are also introduced to their parents' dialect; the parental dialect organizes and categorizes the children's social environment. The primary vehicle for transmission of parental ethnicity is their dialect. Consequently, while the onset of ethnicity precedes speech acquisition, soon after birth ethnicity and speech acquisition become conterminous.[1]

Dialect and speech acquisition are a natural human phenomenon. All humans, irrespective of culture, nationality, race, social class, or caste acquire speech. Speech acquisition is universal for all humans. With minor exceptions, e.g., the severely handicapped or mentally retarded, speech is naturally acquired by humans. Speech serves as a tool for living within speech communities as well as a tool for categorizing and interpreting experiences.[2]

People acquire and develop speech along a format of progressive social development. At first, a person's speech is egocentric. As an infant learns to use words to satisfy biological needs, the infant's vocabulary revolves around words that satisfy these needs, e.g., "I hungy" (hungry). As the infant develops into more of a social being, a vocabulary and grammatical system to satisfy social needs is necessitated. By six months children begin babbling, uttering streams of sounds that resemble the inflections of natural sentences, and that communicate telegraphic messages. By age four, children exhibit control over the basic sentence patterns and most sounds of their parent's dialect. Thus, meaningful speech communication begins.

Linguistically speaking, children usually acquire a unique speech system termed an "idiolect." An idiolect is a person's unique manner of speaking that begins in early childhood, and to a large extent, remains throughout his or her life. Everyone develops unique ways of speaking, i.e., everyone develops a "personal dialect," by virtue of unique physical and emotional characteristics. For example, a person may develop a preference for certain consonants and thereby prefer to use words that contain these sounds; or, a person may develop a preference for certain idioms, inflections, or expressions. The ubiquitous satires of movie actors like James Cagney, "You dirty rats!" or John Wayne, "Ya gotta put muscle inta it!" exemplify exaggerated idiolects.

Language and Dialect

As children grow they develop a dialect spoken by their parents and immediate family. A dialect is a variation of an idealized language model, i.e., a dialect is a valid communication medium that contains its own rules of logic and grammar.[3] In the United States, most people speak a dialect of standard American English, which is the idealized version of the English language within the United States. (Of course, there are some citizens of the United States whose first dialect is not English). "Standard American English" is perceived to be the language's grammatical rules taught in the public schools of the United States and the usage used by journalists, television newscasters, and the educated populace. However, while teachers and journalists write in standard American English, they nonetheless speak in a dialect of English. This point is made clear by comparing the speaking and writing styles of former United States presidents. Presidents Kennedy, Johnson, and Nixon all wrote their speeches in standard American English. Yet when reading their speeches, their speech dialects became apparent. Kennedy with his Bostonian pronunciations, Johnson with his Texas drawl, and Nixon with his middle-western idioms, e.g., poppycock!, all spoke a different dialect of Standard English.

The point is that language and dialect are not the same. A "language" is an idealized model for communication; a "dialect" is a real speech and grammatical system used by a group for communication. The Swiss linguist, Ferdinand Saussure, called the former *langue* (language) and the latter *parole* (dialect). (Sometimes I may use "language" and "dialect" interchangeably. However, the distinction between language as an idealized model and dialect as an actual, real spoken communication medium is important to keep in mind.)

American English

The *langue* of United States society is the so-called standard English; its *parole* consists of at least four distinctively different dialects: Black English, eastern English, general American, and southern English. The dialects are mutually intelligible but they do differ in intonations and vocabulary. The latter three dialects are diverse; eastern English is divided into three sub-dialects as is the southern dialect; the general American dialect is a conglomeration of all remaining United States English dialects spoken in the Midwest, Southwest, Far West, and Northwest. The three dialects differ primarily in vocabulary, intonation, and idioms; while they are mutually intelligible, their grammatical systems do not differ significantly.[4]

Black English dialect, when compared to other United States dialects, does differ grammatically. One theory about the origin of Black English is that it is a Creole or "pidgin" English dialect which evolved during slavery in the South.[5] With emancipation and the gradual emigration of Blacks, the dialect spread to other parts of the country, in particular to large industrial cities in the Northeast and the Ohio Valley. Currently, it is still used in Black communities. Some of the dialect's characteristic which distinguish it from other dialects are:

1. The use of the third person singular verbs without adding the "s" or "z" sound, eg., "The man walk" instead of "The man walks."

2. Nonuse of "s" to indicate possessives, e.g., "The girl hat" instead of "The girl's hat."
3. The use of the "f" sound for the "th" sound at the end or middle of a word, e.g., "nuf'n" instead of "nothing."
4. Elimination of "l" or "r" sounds in words, e.g., "Tomorrow I bring the book" instead of "Tomorrow I'll bring the book;" and, "It is you book" instead of "It is your book."
5. The use of the verb "be" to indicate further time, e.g., "He be here in a few hours."
6. The use of "it" instead of "there," e.g., "It's a boy in my room named Bill" instead of "There's a boy in my room named Bill."[6]

An interesting aside is that some southern Whites (even those with enough status to escape the label of being nonstandard speakers) show characteristics that place their dialect close to Black English. Also, not all Blacks speak Black English, but often some Whites assume that all Blacks do speak the dialect.

United States Bidialectalism and Bilingualism

Within the United States, some ethnic groups develop dual or multiple dialects of English. Almost everyone in United States society is somewhat "bidialectal" in the sense that everyone speaks their individual idiolects as well as a group dialect. However, here "bidialectalism" is used to mean the ability to speak two distinctively different American English regional or cultural group dialects. For example, as a group, Blacks speak the Black English dialect as well as standard English. Not all Blacks speak Black English; rather, as an ethnic group, Blacks have developed skills in using two different dialects of English.

Some groups develop bilingual abilities. "Bilingualism" is used here to mean the ability to speak with two distinctively different language systems, e.g., Spanish and English, German, and English. At one time, German Americans were the most literate bilinguals in the United States. Bilingual German newspapers, periodicals, radio programs, and books attested to their high level of German-English bilingualism.[7] However, the anti-Germanic feelings sparked by World War I and inflamed by World War II with Germany substantially doused German-American bilingualism. Currently, Puerto Ricans, as a group, speak Spanish and English. In Puerto Rico, Spanish is considered the native language, but a speaking knowledge of American English is required for high school graduation.

Again, as with bidialectalism, not all members of a group need to be bilingual for the group to be considered bilingual. In the above illustration, Puerto Ricans as a group are Spanish-English bilingual, but not all Puerto Ricans are bilingual. Bilingually speaking, some groups are more active than others. Some groups are currently attempting to restore their native language, such as many American Indian tribes. Others are working diligently to teach their youth the native language, e.g., Greek Americans. Other groups use two languages for daily transactions, e.g., Chinese Americans and Cuban Americans.

More than twenty-five European languages are spoken in the U.S. Some of these languages are (1) Spanish, (2) Italian, (3) German, (4) Polish, (5) French, (6) Yiddish, (7) Russian, (8) Swedish, (9) Hungarian, and (10) Norwegian. Add these languages to the Asian (Vietnamese) and Middle Eastern (Persian) languages now spoken as well as the historically spoken American Indian languages, and the sum is apparent—the United States is multilingual.

Linking Ethnicity and Language

The fundamental role played by a language or a dialect is group communication. While people aren't restricted to language for communication, language is of overarching importance because it is the fundamental medium through which ethnicity is transmitted and shared. A language system in general, and a dialect in particular, serve as tools to categorize, interpret, and share experiences. Ethnicity and language thus intertwine, language being the medium and ethnicity the message.

Youngsters learn the content of their ethnic cultures through their parent's dialect. The dialect is used to convey ethnic meaning to the youngsters; later, as the youngsters master the dialect, they use it to convey ethnic content. The dialect serves the youngsters in the formation of their perceptions, attitudes, and values about their physical and human environment. Anthropologists Sapir and Whorf reported in their studies of language and perceptions that a person's dialect influences and informs one's view and perception of reality.[8] For example, in American English there exists only several conceptions of snow, e.g., "powder snow" or "wet snow." Within the Eskimo language, there exists a considerable number of conceptions of snow. The reason for the difference is simply that snow is of greater economic and social importance to the Eskimo than it is to most English-speaking peoples. The vocabulary of a group's language will reflect distinctions and categories that are important to the group. Conversely, relatively unimportant categories will be reflected minimally. Or, the category may be nonexistent within the group's vocabulary.

The grammatical system of a group's language reflects the group's attitude toward its physical environment. For example, the Navajo language emphasizes the reporting of events in motion. For example, when describing a large mountain, a Navajo may say in Navajo, "the mountain is busy being big and blue." In this case, the Navajo describes the physical environment as fluid. In American English, the mountain's description, "the mountain is big and blue" perforces the description of a static physical environment. Thus, the Navajo and English descriptions reflect differing ethnic interpretation of the natural environment.

These comments shouldn't be interpreted to mean that language determines ethnicity. Rather, language serves as a mirror to ethnicity, reflecting a person's values, beliefs, and attitudes. Actually, sociolinguistic rules, i.e., what, when, how, and how much language should be used, are governed by one's ethnicity.[9] Note what's being said regarding property in the following scenarios (based on my personal observations):

Scenario I:
   Ruth: Mom, where's my Barbie doll?
   Mother: I lent it to Sue.
   Ruth: Why'd you do that?
   Mother: She wanted to play with it.
   Ruth: But, it's my doll and . . .
   Mother: Okay! Okay! Go tell her I said she's to give it to you.
Scenario II:
   Rita: Mom, where's my Barbie doll?
   Mother: I let your sister use it.
   Rita: But I want to use it.
   Mother: You can use one of your other dolls.
   Rita: But Mom!
   Mother: Maybe your sister would trade it for one of the other dolls.
   Rita: Well, okay.

In scenario I there is an implicit assumption that the doll is Ruth's exclusive property. The mother violated Ruth's property rights by lending the doll without talking to Ruth. The mother acted outside the bounds of her role. In this scenario, the mother's role is to enforce property rights. In scenario II there is an implicit assumption that the dolls are the family's collective property. The mother acted within the bounds of her role as property rights coordinator. The language used in both scenarios serve as a microscopic reflection of the attitudes toward property ownership and the mother's role governing ownership.

At one time, language was feared. The belief existed that language acted as some kind of extra-terrestrial force to subconsciously tryannize people to think and feel in certain ways.[10] Of course, people can be influenced to behave in certain ways with propagandistic linguistic manipulation. But, people give meaning to language, and meaning is derived from within the context of a language community. My hunch is that ethnicity impacts language, in particular its vocabulary items, in significant ways. Consequently, ethnicity—as a broadly-based emotion and sense of group identity—is reflected in an ethnic group's dialect and lexicon. Because an ethnic group uses a dialect to embody and transmit its ethnic content, knowledge about the ethnic group presupposes knowledge of its dialect. To know an ethnic group one must know its dialect.

The Relationship between Language and National Policy

Our discussion of ethnicity, language, and dialectal development leads us to broader, more complex questions regarding the role of language in United States society. Does linguistic diversity impede national cohesion? Is it possible to have a nation when everyone speaks a different language, as in the *Old Testament's Tower of Babel?* What is the experience of other linguisiti-cally-diverse nations? How do these nations build cohesion and yet allow linguistic diversity? How are a nation's goals linked with language and ethnicity? Most of these questions will be answered explicitly. Some will be answered implicitly. What is important is that we approach these questions broadly, viewing them on an international scale. Once viewing them internationally, we can better analyze them nationally.

Nationalism and ethnicity are similar group phenomena. Both involve group identity, a sense of peoplehood and an interdependence of fates, requiring allegiance to some group. At times, the two phenomena conflict. Countries throughout the world have had to deal with the issue of how to build national unity while allowing ethnic group diversity. If ethnic groups are given too much autonomy, national unity is threatened; if ethnic groups are suppressed too much, then ethnic group dissent emerges, again threatening national cohesion. Some countries have dealt with ethnic group diversity by allowing minority groups to maintain their languages and cultures (pluralism). In India, for example, one can pledge allegiance to the national government, and without penalty or legal recrimination, identify with his or her ethnic group. Ethnic and national loyalty require bilingualism, i.e., a speaking knowledge of the national language, *Hindustani,* and one's ethnic group language.[11] Peru, Ecuador, and Paraguay are other examples of countries that accommodate indigenous linguistic groups.

Other countries (such as Chile, Brazil, Australia, Argentina) have dealt with ethnic group diversity by absorbing minority groups into their majority culture, imposing both their language and culture on the minority groups (assimilation). Some countries neither assimilate nor allow free pluralism. Rather, they impose forced separation of races (apartheid) such as the Republic of South Africa. These countries are the vestiges of White, racial colonialism. In heterogeneous societies, ethnic group identity and national group identity are not mutually exclusive, if the national group has at least one language in common. (See chapter 14 for a discussion of ethnic and national group identifications).

Central to a country's development of nationalism is the designation of an official language. An official language serves the functions of political and psychological integration on a national scope. A nation's official language(s) embodies, carries, and conveys the nation's symbols. National anthems, slogans, and oaths of allegiance in the national language(s) meld a nation's spirit. The national language(s) act as the political unification agent and communication medium among the nation's citizens. For national communications and political unification, the requirements for establishing an official language are simple:

1. A national language should be capable of serving as a medium of social, economic, legal, and political intercourse throughout the nation.
2. It should be the speech of the majority of the nation's citizens.
3. It should have a standardized writing system throughout the nation.

Not so simple are the politics of language standardization. For example, requirement one presumes that within any nation, whose boundaries many times cut across ethnic and tribal group lines, one language can be singled out as the language comprehendable to all the language groups in the nation. Requirement two presumes that the majority of the nation's citizens have the power to implement their language as the national language. In colonized nations, for example, the language of the colonizer (usually a numerical minority) was imposed on the colonized (the numerical majority group). In multilingual nations, the difficulties of language planning depends on the number of language groups vieing for their language as the national standard. The language competition and conflict emerge from the political ambitions of the various groups.

National Goals and Language Education Policy

All nations have one or more languages stipulated as their official language(s). Some countries, such as France, have an official language regulated by a language academy. Other countries have an official bilingual policy, such as Canada, allowing for English and French to coexist as official languages. Some countries, India and Russia for example, have one official language that is used nationally, but allow regional languages and dialects to be used and taught within their respective regions. Due to the centrality of language to nationalism, the selection as to which language or languages to use in a nation's school as the medium(s) of instruction is a critical national decision. The language(s) taught to the nation's future citizens become the embodiment of the national spirit and agent for national unification.

Eighteenth century powers, such as France, Spain, and England recognized the importance of languages for political domination and control.

Subsequently, they always imposed their languages on the people they wanted to colonize. In the United States during the late nineteenth and early twentieth centuries, feelings about American English ran so high that most states enacted laws that prohibited the use of any non-English languages in the public schools. It was during this time that the United States government was trying to form a strong national identity.

Educational language policies are inextricably bound with a nation's internal and external political goals. When a nation's national goal is to assimilate all citizens so that they speak a single language, its language education programs will foster monolingualism in the nation's single, standard language. When a nation's internal goal is to maintain its ethnic and linguistic plurality, then its language education programs will foster knowledge in a national language standard while concurrently fostering literacy in the differing languages or dialects spoken by its citizens. When a nation's external political goal is to develop communication ties with other countries, its language programs will foster literacy in the national standard as well as literacy in other languages generally not spoken by its citizens. When a nation's internal goal is to revive a lost national identity—lost as a consequence of conquest or colonialism—its language programs will foster restoration of the nation's preferred language.

On a global scale there exists at least four distinctively different forms of educational policy goals that pertain to language:

1. assimilation
2. pluralization
3. internationalization
4. vernacularization

What follows is a description of the policy goals and their consequent language programs.

Assimilation

This type of language policy promotes cultural assimilation. The intent is to assimilate foreign language speakers into the dominant linguistic and cultural group of the nation. Some bilingual programs in the United States are examples. They are called transitional programs; their intent is to assimilate some linguistic minority group. The linguistic majority group perceives the nation as a monolingual melting pot that has one standard language; other languages, or dialects of the standard, are perceived as substandard languages or dialects. The student's "substandard" language or dialect is used as the medium of instruction to compensate for his or her limited English-speaking abilities. Use of the "substandard" language-dialect is transitional. As soon as the student learns English well enough to receive instruction, then use of the student's language is discontinued and instruction is in English only. The nation's language standard is elitist. The national standard is held up as the only acceptable standard; divergent dialects or foreign languages are perceived as separate and unequal to the national standard.

Pluralization

This language policy promotes cultural pluralism. The intent is to allow different language/cultural groups to coexist within a nation and to equalize schooling by using the student's home language and culture for instruction. Some bilingual programs in the United States are examples. In these bilingual maintenance programs, the non-English language group is encouraged to maintain its bilingual-bicultural status. Under pluralization a nation's language standard is egalitarian, i.e., each language has its respective standard; the non-national languages and dialects are perceived as having separate and equal standards.

Internationalization

This type of language program is multilingual. Schools teach multiple languages. The intent is to create a multilingual nation. Switzerland is an example. In Switzerland, four languages are taught to students; the nation is landlocked and surrounded by European countries. To successfully communicate with these countries, the citizens need to speak the languages of neighboring countries. Under internationalization, a nation desires to communicate with other nations. It has a multiple language standard; the language standard of other languages is adopted by the country as well as its national standard.

Vernacularization

This type of language program restores the nation's indigenous language and establishes it as the national standard. The Republic of the Philippino (Philippines) Islands is an example. The country was colonized by the Spanish and United States governments. Each government imposed its language on the nation and prohibited the use of the indigenous languages, such as *Ilocano* and *Tagalog*, in all public institutions. Now the Philippine nation is free of colonial rule; it has declared the vernacular language, *Tagalog*, as its standard language. Under vernacularization, the desired national goal is pride in the nation's indigenous language(s) and culture. The new vernacular is established as the nation's language standard. Yet, because its citizens speak the language(s) of their former colonizers, bilingual programs are developed, using both the restored language and the colonizer's language(s).

Bilingual Instructional Methods in the United States

The purpose of bilingual instruction is to increase academic achievement by using the student's home language as the main communication medium. Bilingual instruction involves the use of two languages for instruction for part or all of the activities within the classroom. One language is English; the other language is the student's home language, i.e., the language spoken in the home. English is taught as a second language. Many times the student's first significant introduction to English is when he or she enters school. In other instances, the student may begin school with minimum English language skills.

Two methods of teaching the non-English speaking students are (1) the native language, and (2) English as a second language (ESL) methods. The native language method uses the student's home language in all subject areas. After mastery in listening, speaking, reading, and writing, the student is introduced to English as a second language (ESL). The method's supposition is that native language literacy should be achieved before the student is introduced to the English language arts. Having achieved native language literacy, the student should have no difficulty transferring to English. Rarely is reading of English taught until the student masters native language listening and speaking skills.

The second method, English as a second language (ESL), is sometimes called the direct method. ESL is a method that teaches the student immediate English language skills. The ESL pull-out system takes the student out of the classroom daily for instruction in the English language arts. The student returns to the class for instruction in other subjects. The ESL intensive system immerses the student in the English language arts for extensive time periods. When the student learns to speak the language, then reading in English is introduced. When the student reads English, he or she is returned to the monolingual English classroom.

Language Policy in the United States

The United States has no official *de jure* language policy; it has an informal *de facto* national standard, American English. Social customs and usages, rather than governmental agencies, tend to regulate languages in the United States. Non-English languages are allowed in public documents and institutions; their use is limited by varying state laws. To a great extent the United States is still an English-centric language nation. Non-English languages are considered "foreign" languages. Even the languages indigenous to the United States, the languages of American Indians, are viewed as "foreign" by some citizens of the United States.

Equal Educational Opportunity and Language Programs

The federal government of the United States has formulated equal educational opportunity policies that focus on language education programs. Particularly the *Bilingual Education Act* and the U.S. District Court decisions, *Lau* v. *Nichols* and *School Children* v. *Ann Arbor School Board,* explicitly established policies that impact public school language instruction.

In 1968, Public Law 90-247, *The Bilingual Education Act,* was enacted. *The Bilingual Education Act,* the seventh amendment to the Elementary and Secondary Education Act of 1965 (Title VII) declared that it was "to be the policy of the United States to provide financial assistance to local education agencies to develop and carry out new and imaginative elementary and secondary school programs designed to meet the special education needs . . . (of) children who come from environments where the dominant language is other than English."[12] The act stipulated it would be the policy of the U.S. government to financially assist in the development and implementation of bilingual education programs in U.S. public schools and trust territories.

In 1973, the act was changed to the *Comprehensive Bilingual Education Amendment Act of 1973.* The act was extended for training bilingual teachers and bilingual teacher trainers. The Act's policy recognized that: (1) large numbers of children have limited English-speaking ability, (2) many of these children have a cultural heritage that differs from that of English-speaking people, and (3) a primary means by which a child learns is through using his or her language and cultural heritage. The Act provided financial assistance for extending and improving existing bilingual-bicultural programs in public schools, for improving resource and dissemination centers, and for developing and publishing bilingual-bicultural curriculum materials. Assistance was also provided for stipends and fellowships so that teachers and teacher-educators could be trained in bilingual-bicultural methodology.

A major catalyst for bilingual instruction was the United States Supreme Court ruling of *Lau* v. *Nichols* that provisions for the same teachers, programs, and textbooks in the same language for all students in the San Francisco school district did not provide equal educational opportunity when a sizeable number of the student body's native language was not English. In part the ruling held:

There is no equality of treatment merely by providing students with the same facilities, textbooks, teachers, and curriculum; for students who do not understand English are effectively foreclosed from any meaningful education.... Where inability to speak and understand the English language excludes national origin-minority group children from effective participation in the education program offered by a school district, the district must take affirmative steps to rectify the language deficiency in order to open its instructional program to these students.[13]

While the ruling did not mandate bilingual instruction for non-English speaking students, it did stipulate that special educational programs were necessary if schools were to provide equal educational opportunity for such students.

Equal educational opportunity policy regarding speakers of Black English has been formulated. The policy was precipitated by the United States District Court ruling in *Martin Luther King Jr. Elementary School Children* v. *Ann Arbor School District* in 1979. A case was made for students who speak Black English, "Black vernacular," or "Black dialect" as a home and community language. The plaintiffs argued that language differences impeded the Black students' equal participation in the school's instructional program because the instructional program was conducted entirely in the standard school English dialect. Using linguistic and educational research evidence, the lawyers for the students established,

... that unless those instructing in reading recognize (1) the existence of a home language used by the children in their own community for much of their non-school communications, and (2) that this home language may be a cause of the superficial difficulties in speaking standard English, great harm will be done. The child may withdraw or may act out frustrations and may not learn to read. A language barrier develops when teachers, in helping the child to switch from the home ("Black English") language to standard English, refuse to admit the existence of a language that is the acceptable way of talking in his local community.[14]

Therefore, the Court ruled to require, "... the defendant Board to take steps to help its teachers to recognize the home language of the students and to use that knowledge in their attempts to teach reading skills in standard English."[15] *The ruling requires the recognition of the student's home and community dialect as a valid communication medium.* The ruling also requires use of the student's dialect as an educational resource rather than a linguistic liability.

Reflecting the spirit of the equal educational language policies, the National Council of Teachers of English (NCTE) issued a policy statment supporting a student's right to his or her dialect:

In November 1974, the National Council of Teachers of English passed a resolution emphasizing that students have a right to speak and learn in their own language, in the dialect that makes them comfortable and gives them a sense of their own identity and worth....[16]

The statement affirms the right of students to speak their own dialects and encourages English teachers to concentrate on teaching language as a tool for creative and critical thinking. The National Council for the Social Studies confirms the NCTE stance with its position statement, "Schools should foster the study of ethnic group languages as legitimate communication systems."[17] Equal educational opportunity policies are also supported by the President's Commission on Foreign Language and International Studies. The Commission states that United States citizens will profit from intensive language studies and from international education. The Commission recommends the internationalization of national goals.[18]

Toward a Policy for Multiethnic Linguistic Pluralism

 policy of linguistic pluralism is essential for multiethnic education. The policy should provide parameters so that teachers can accommodate linguistic differences as well as teach about linguistic diversity in the United States. The policy should contain two dimensions (see Figure 11.1). The two dimensions could be tied to a broader policy of ethnic pluralism, i.e., a policy setting parameters for accommodating ethnic differences and teaching about ethnic diversity in the United States (see Figure 11.2). To form

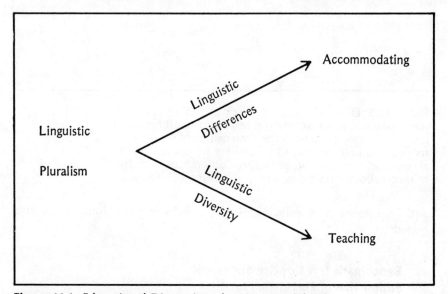

Figure 11.1. Educational Dimensions for Linguistic Pluralism. Linguistic pluralism operates within the dimensions of linguistic differences and linguistic diversity. Teachers are encouraged to accommodate their student's linguistic differences and also to teach about linguistic diversity in the United States.

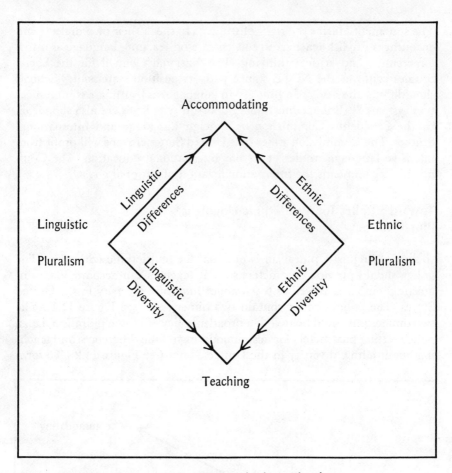

Figure 11.2. Dimensions of Linguistic and Ethnic Pluralism. Linguistic pluralism should be linked to ethnic pluralism which operates within the dimensions of ethnic differences and ethnic diversity. Teachers are encouraged to
accommodate their students' ethnic differences and also
to teach about ethnic diversity in the United States.

and implement a pluralistic policy the following benchmarks are suggested:

Benchmark 1: A Concise Statement
Supportive of Linguistic Pluralism
Should Be Made

School English ethnocentrism—the attitude that school English is superior to other dialects and languages—is the nexus of the problem. The
policy statement would stand for linguistic pluralism and against school

English ethnocentrism. The statement would have two major dimensions: (1) accommodating linguistic differences, and (2) teaching about linguistic diversity, both fostering a climate of respect for linguistic differences.

Benchmark 2: Teachers Should Be Cognizant of Their Linguistic Biases against the Dialects or Languages of Linguistically Different Students

Again, linguistic ethnocentrism lies at the nexus of the problem. Primarily, respect for the student's home dialect should be fostered. Rather than viewing the home dialect as defective, teachers should view the dialect as a source of strength. Students do not enter school speaking a substandard dialect; they may enter school speaking nonschool-standard English or a different language. The position that youngsters speak a substandard version of English is an imposition of school English as the only English dialect capable of use for learning.

Benchmark 3: Instructional Strategies Should Accommodate Linguistically Different Students

Linguistically-different students should not be placed in special language programs that segregate them from the regular classroom. In fact, positive intercultural experiences can be fostered in linguistically-diverse classrooms. When there are a large number of non-English speakers of the same language, a bilingual teacher is feasible. However, if possible, monolingual English-speaking students should be incorporated into this otherwise linguistically segregated arrangement. With students who speak Black English, or other nonschool English dialects, standard school-English should be taught as an alternate dialect necessary for broader social interactions. All students need to learn to understand, read, and write in standard English. Therefore, the linguistic resources of linguistically-different students should be maximized to teach basic English literacy.

Benchmark 4: Curriculum Materials Should Reflect the Linguistic Diversity in the United States

This benchmark requires multilingual permeation of curriculum materials. Teachers should use every opportunity to incorporate nonschool

English dialects and languages in all their curriculum materials. Examples I've seen work in the classroom are:

1. learning to count in Spanish, French, German, or some other language
2. learning that people call their neighborhoods by differing names, *ghetto* (Italian origin), *barrio* (Spanish for neighborhood)
3. learning to read the Chinese calendar.

The list is endless and the approach feasible. Incorporating linguistic diversity into curriculum materials does not require much language-learning for the teacher. The new language or dialect adds variety to otherwise routine learning activities.

Summary

Language and culture interweave. For students, language and culture are the heads and tails of the same coin. Rejection of the students' language is tantamount to cultural rejection. Because the United States needs a national language, literacy in standard English should be taught in schools; however, because of the linguistic diversity in the United States, the equal educational opportunity language policies that foster respect for linguistic differences should be sustained.

Language provides a bond between individuals and between individuals and groups. It serves these important group functions: (1) intergroup communication, (2) transmission of group's culture, and (3) group identity. In the United States, individuals speak some dialect of American English. Some also speak a non-English language in additional to an English dialect (bilingualism); some speak two dialects of American English, such as some Blacks (bidialectalism). All of these individuals reflect their ethnicity and cultural preferences through the language(s) or dialect(s) they speak.

All countries have a formal or informal language policy that fosters a national language standard. However, the world's nations treat the non-national languages of their societies differently. Some have a policy of assimilation that prohibits the use of any language in public institutions except the national standard. Some have a policy of pluralism that allows the use of nonofficial languages in public institutions. Others have a policy of vernacularization that attempts to restore an indigenous language as the national standard; and, some nations have a policy of internationalization that attempts to transform their citizens into a multilingual society.

The policy of the United States has evolved from assimilation to pluralism. Until the middle 1970s the use of non-English languages in public schools was prohibited in most states. Due to the bilingual education movement and the *Lau* v. *Nichols* decision, the United States now has a policy of linguistic pluralism. The policy provides non-English speaking students equal educational opportunities through bilingual and English as a second language programs. Linguistic pluralism, as a national policy goal, was further buttressed by the National Council of Teachers of English and the National Council for the Social Studies which issued supportive position statements. The Michigan U.S. District Court ruling involving the Ann Arbor School District supported linguistic pluralism for the education of Black English speaking students. Also, the President's Commission on Foreign Language and International Studies recommends a policy of internationalization for public and higher education in the United States.

A workable policy of linguistic pluralism involves teaching within two dimensions: (1) linguistic differences, and (2) linguistic diversity. The first dimension requires teachers to accommodate in both curriculum materials and teaching strategies their students' linguistic differences. The second dimension, linguistic diversity, requires teachers to teach about linguistic diversity in the United States to all their students, irrespective of their students' daily language usage. The first dimension provides linguistic minority and bidialectal students an equal opportunity to learn school subjects. The second dimension provides all students a broad, nonethnocentric understanding of the multilingual diversity of United States society.

Notes

1. Robbins Burling, *Man's Many Voices: Language in its Cultural Context* (New York: Holt, Rinehart, 1978), pp. 117–119; see also, George Miller, *Language and Communication* (New York: McGraw Hill, 1951), see especially chapter 7, "Verbal Behavior of Children."
2. Dell Hymes, "Functions of Speech," in F. Gruber, ed., *Anthropology and Education* (Philadelphia: University of Pennsylvania Press, 1961), pp. 55–83; see also, Dan Slobin I, *A Field Manual for Cross-Cultural Study of the Acquisition of Communicative Competence* (Berkeley: University of California Press, 1967).
3. William Labov, "The Logic of Nonstandard English," in F. Williams, ed., *Language and Poverty* (Chicago: Markham, 1970), pp. 153–189.
4. Albert H. Marckwardt, "Regional and Social Variations," in Robert B. Glenn, ed., *Language and Culture* (Marquette, Mich.: Northern Michigan Press), 1974, pp. 181–193; see also, A. D. Edwards, *Language in Culture and Class* (London: Heinemann Educational Books, 1976), p. 46.
5. Paul Stoller, *Black American English* (New York: Dell Publishing Company, 1975), pp. 17–48.
6. The list was culled from Joan Baratz and Roger W. Shuy, *Teaching Black Children to Read* (Washington, D.C.: Center for Applied Linguistics, 1969); Ralph W. Fasold and Roger Shuy, *Teaching Standard English in the Inner City* (Washington, D.C.: Center for Applied Linguistics, 1970); William Labov, *Language in the Inner City* (Philadelphia: Uni-

versity of Pennsylvania Press, 1972); Walter Wolfram, *A Sociolinguistic Description of Negro Speech* (Washington, D.C.: Center for Applied Linguistics, 1969). (The list here is meant to highlight Black dialect differences. An in-depth study of the dialect is encouraged to prevent sterotypes about it.)

7. Joshua Fishman, *Language Loyalty in the United States* (London: Mouton Press, 1966), pp. 206–252.
8. Edward Sapir, *Culture, Language, Personality* (Berkeley: University of California Press, 1958); see also, B. L. Whorf, *Language, Thought and Reality* (New York: Wiley, 1956), pp. 65–86.
9. Harry Hoijer, "Cultural Implications of Some Navajo Linguistic Categories," *Language* 27 (1951), pp. 111–120.
10. S. I. Hayakawa, *Language in Thought and Action* (New York: Harcourt, Brace, World, 1949), pp. 100–117; see also, Stuart Chase, *The Tyranny of Words* (New York: Harcourt, Brace, 1938).
11. M. K. Gandhi, *Evil Wrought By the English Language* (Ahmedabad: Navajivan Publishing House, 1958), p. 25.
12. Hannah N. Geffert, Robert J. Harper, Salvador Sarmiento, and Daniel Schember, *The Current Status of U.S. Bilingual Legislation* (Arlington, Va.: Center for Applied Linguistics, May 1975), pp. 121–123.
13. *Lau v. Nichols,* 414 U.S. 563, 39 L. Ed 2nd, 94 S. Ct 786, 1974.
14. *Martin Luther King Jr. Elementary School Children, et. al.* v. *Ann Arbor School District Board,* U.S. District Court, East District, Michigan, Civil Action No. 7-71861, 1979.
15. *Children* v. *Ann Arbor,* p. 41.
16. National Council of Teachers of English, *Students' Right to Their Own Language* (Urbana, Ill.: NCTE, 1974).
17. James A. Banks, Carlos E. Cortés, Geneva Gay, Ricardo Garcia, and Anna S. Ochoa, *Curriculum Guidelines for Multiethnic Education* (Arlington, Va.: National Council for the Social Studies, 1976), p. 39.
18. *Strength Through Wisdom: A Critique of U.S. Capability,* A Report to the President from the President's Commission on Foreign Language and International Studies. Washington, D.C.: U.S. Government Printing Office, 1979.

PART V

Continuing Issues
in Multiethnic Education

Introduction

This part discusses some of the continuing issues in multiethnic education. The issues discussed in this part are important problems in multiethnic education that have not been satisfactorily resolved and that frequently evoke divergent responses from educators with different ideologies and experiences, and who work in different settings.

The wide range of concepts used in multiethnic education is a continuing problem that is often muted in the literature. Diverse concepts are often used to convey similar meanings and practices. In chapter 12 there is a discussion of the relationship between culture, ethnicity, race, and education. The research and policy implications of each of these concepts are delineated.

In chapter 13, another continuing issue in multiethnic education—multiethnic teacher education—is discussed. Considerable discussion and dialogue occur about the kinds of experiences and training teachers need in order to function more effectively within culturally and ethnically diverse educational settings. Most teachers agree that their past and current teacher education programs have ill-equipped them for multiethnic classrooms. Chapter 13 discusses the characteristics needed by effective multiethnic teachers and steps teachers can take to increase their ability to function in multiethnic educational environments.

One of the problems that haunts most educational innovations is the fragmentation that characterize educational reform movements. Often little is done to help teachers relate curricular reform efforts such as women's studies, multiethnic education, and global education. Fragmentation must be reduced in educational reform efforts in order to increase the impact of educational innovations. Chapter 14 explores the problems and promises of linking multiethnic and global education and how these two reform movements relate to the expanding identifications of ethnic youths.

In recent years, educators have devoted considerable attention to questions related to citizenship education. Chapter 15 discusses the complex relationship between ethnic and national commitments and ways to help ethnic students become effective and reflective citizens within a modernized democratic nation state.

12

Race, Ethnicity, and Education

What are the concepts currently being used to guide educational policy and research related to culture, ethnicity, and race? What are the research and policy implications of these concepts? In this chapter I answer these questions by discussing the strengths and limitations of the most popular concepts being used in multiethnic education. After discussing the meanings and problems of multicultural education and cultural pluralism, I conclude that concepts related to *race* and *ethnicity* can best guide research and educational policy related to racial and ethnic minorities. This chapter concludes with a discussion of several imperatives in multiethnic education.

Multicultural Education: A Comprehensive but Inadequate Concept

Culture is the root of multicultural. In chapter 4, I define culture as the behavior patterns, symbols, institutions, values, and other human-made components of society. It is the unique achievement of a human group that distinguishes it from other human groups. While cultures are in many ways similar, a particular culture constitutes a unique whole. Although the Navajo Indians in the southwestern part of the United States share cultural traits with Anglo-Americans, such as clothing and modes of transportation, they have a distinctive culture.

If we are going to use concepts that are sociologically and anthropologically valid, and I feel that we should, then the concept of multicultural education should reflect sociological and anthropological usage. Anthropologically, multicultural education suggests a type of education that is, in some form or fashion, concerned with a wide range of cultural groups in society. Because multicultural is a very broad and inclusive concept, and because it focuses on *cultural* differences, it is not an *adequate* concept to guide research and policy decisions on problems related to racial and ethnic minorities. It is not clear from the literature on multicultural education, for example, which groups are meant to be the target populations in multicultural educational reform.[1]

The concept of multicultural education implies that cultural differences is the root problem that results in intergroup tensions and conflicts.

However, racial problems are often more significant in intergroup relations than cultural differences. Multicultural education is a useful concept in that it enables the educational reformer to focus on a range of excluded and oppressed groups within society. This is the strength of the concept and is probably why it has so many educational advocates. However, it is not an *adequate* concept. We need other concepts related to multicultural education, such as race and ethnicity, to guide educational policy that will focus more directly on the unique problems and characteristics of particular groups in society.

Multicultural education provides a useful umbrella for the study of excluded groups within society. However, we need more specific concepts related to multicultural education to guide theory, research, and educational policy on specific groups such as ethnic groups and women. The concept of sexism, for example, is very important when dealing with women's issues just as the concepts of race and racism are important for the individual who is researching or designing educational policy for ethnic minorities.

Cultural Pluralism and Its Problems

I have tried to indicate why the concept of multicultural education is not a sufficient concept when used to describe issues and problems related to race, ethnicity, and education. Cultural pluralism, another concept that educators often use in discussions about race and education, also poses problems.

As pointed out in chapter 1, the idea of cultural pluralism emerged near the turn of the century when nativists and patriotic groups were focusing widespread hostility on the masses of Southern and Eastern European immigrants that were entering the United States. Liberal philosophers and writers originated the concept of cultural pluralism to defend the cultural democracy of the "new" European immigrants.

Horace M. Kallen, who popularized the concept of cultural pluralism and eloquently articulated it, argued that a democracy does not exist unless groups are able to maintain their ethnic characteristics and identities. Kallen felt that cultural pluralism was possible only in a democratic society. Kallen argued cogently that the cultures of the various immigrant groups would greatly strengthen American civilization. He viewed a society made up of diverse ethnic cultures as "an orchestration of mankind."[2] Kallen wrote, "As in an orchestra every type of instrument has its specific *timbre* and *tonality*, founded in its substance and form; as every type has its appropriate theme and melody in the whole symphony, so in society, each ethnic group may be the natural instrument, its temper and culture may be its theme and melody and the harmony and dissonances and discords of them all make the symphony civilization."[3] Julius Drachsler, Kallen's contemporary, also argued for cultural diversity and maintained that "cultural democracy" should be a societal goal in the United States just as political and economic democracy are goals.[4]

Cultural pluralism, as envisioned by Kallen, Drachsler, and other writers in the 1920s, was destined to fail in the United States. Although many European Americans tried to establish European institutions on American soil and to maintain their ethnic cultures, the Americanizing influences were too overwhelming for them to survive. The public schools, the American press, and the federal government played key roles in paralyzing the efforts to establish and maintain European cultures in America. Anglo-American culture and its institutions dominated and were not seriously challenged by the waves of immigrants that entered the United States in the late nineteenth and early twentieth centuries. The immigrants and their children found it necessary to acquire Anglo-Saxon culture traits before they were allowed to fully participate in American society. Most European Americans chose inclusion rather than exclusion. Consequently, they eventually became Anglo-Americans. Although there are still significant ethnic differences among some European American groups, such as Italian Americans, Greek Americans, and Polish Americans, most European Americans are culturally and politically Anglo-Americans. They see their interest and destiny tied to that of Anglo-Americans. Race is one of the major factors that enables European Americans to maintain a sense of peoplehood and group identity.

The above discussion suggests several reasons why the concept of cultural pluralism presents difficulties when used to conceptualize the current problems ethnic minorities experience in the schools. Cultural pluralism, as envisioned by its author, largely failed in the United States. Most European Americans are culturally Anglo-Americans. Kallen used the concept to describe the experiences and to promote cultural democracy for European immigrants, and for nonWhite ethnic groups. The experiences of European immigrants and those of racial minorities in the United States are frequently compared in contemporary discussions of cultural pluralism.

Problems with the Immigrant Analogy

These kinds of comparisons are usually very misleading. While European immigrants and non-White immigrants had some similar kinds of experiences, the issue of institutional racism is often minimized or diverted in these kinds of comparisons. Using the "immigrant analogy" to explain the contemporary problems of Afro-Americans, Kristol argues that their major problems do not relate to race, but are caused by the fact that Blacks arrived rather late in highly urbanized northern areas.[5] This kind of argument completely ignores the fact that Afro-Americans have been settling in northern cities in significant numbers since the 1890s, the same period in which many Southern, Central and Eastern European immigrants arrived in American cities. Writes Osofsky:

> It has been customary . . . to begin discussions of northern Negro life with
> the Great Migration of World War I. Although this was certainly dramatic
> and important, significant Negro migration to northern cities began in the
> 1890s. Harlem was an important area of Negro settlement *prior* to the war.
> The Negro ghettos of Philadelphia and Chicago were also founded before
> World War I.[6]

The time of their arrival in northern cities does not explain the discrimination that Afro-Americans have experienced in the cities both before
and after the large migration during the World War I period. One of the
difficulties with the concept of cultural pluralism is that it tends, because it
focuses primarily on cultural rather than racial differences, to lead to the
kinds of inaccurate comparisons made by Kristol. The experiences of European immigrants and those of nonWhite peoples in the United States have
been essentially different because of the importance of race in American
society. Blauner has commented on this point,

> Though they faced great hardships and even prejudice and discrimination
> on a scale that must have been disillusioning, the Irish, Italians, Jews, and
> other groups had the advantage of European ancestry and white skins. . . .
> Sociologists interpreting race relations in the United States have rarely
> faced the full implications of these differences. The *immigrant model* became
> the main focus of analysis, and the experiences of all groups were viewed
> through its lens. It suited the cultural mythology to see everyone in
> America as an original immigrant, a later immigrant, a quasi-immigrant
> or a potential immigrant.[7]

Race as a Factor in Intergroup Problems

The phrase "education for cultural pluralism" assumes that the intergroup
problems in American society are primarily cultural rather than racial.
Widespread cultural assimilation has taken place among ethnic minorities
in the United States, especially among those who have attained upward
social mobility. Some research indicates that the values, goals and aspirations of lower-class Afro-American youths are strikingly similar to those of
middle-class Whites.[8] Thus, while there are significant cultural differences
between Anglo-Americans and most ethnic minorities, Anglo-Americans
and ethnic minorities share many cultural traits. When cultural differences
are minimized, conflict between non-White minorities and Whites still frequently occurs. The cause of most of this conflict seems to be racial rather
than cultural. Gordon seriously questions the extent of cultural pluralism
in American society, *"Structural pluralism . . . is the major key to the understanding
of the ethnic makeup of American society, while cultural pluralism is the minor one. . . .*
The most salient fact . . . is the mintenance of the structurally separate
subsocieties of the three major religious and the racial and quasi-racial

groups, and even vestiges of the nationality groups, along *with a massive trend toward acculturation of all groups . . . to American culture patterns."*[9] (Emphasis added.)

The cultural and ethnic differences that exist among racial groups must be reflected in educational programs designed to reduce intergroup tension and to foster interracial understanding. However, overemphasis on cultural differences and cultural pluralism may divert attention from racial differences and racial hostility. We seriously error when we try to understand ethnic conflict in the schools by focusing exclusively on cultural differences between Anglo-Americans and ethnic minorities. If we develop educational programs and policies that are designed to make students more accepting of cultural differences but fail to deal seriously with problems caused by racial differences, we will not solve our most basic intergroup problems. This is especially true in light of the fact that widespread cultural assimilation is taking place in American society and cultural differences between ethnic minorities and Anglo-Americans will probably be less significant in the future than they are today.

Complex Questions Raised by Cultural Pluralism

Cultural pluralism also causes the same kinds of conceptual difficulties that multicultural education poses. Education for cultural pluralism, in principle, is concerned, in some way, with all cultures within a society. The Ku Klux Klan is a cultural group that advocates White supremacy. Other cultures in our society promote ideologies that are inconsistent with a democratic nation. Does education for cultural pluralism imply tolerance and acceptance of these kinds of cultures? Do we really mean that we want to promote acceptance of all cultures in the schools? If not, which cultures are we talking about? Do we mean that we want to promote acceptance only for cultures that are, in our view, consistent with a democratic ideology? Who is to determine which cultures are to be promoted in the schools? Cultural pluralism raises these complex questions. If we are going to use the concept, we should be able to respond to them intelligently and be able to defend our answers. Racism, sexism, and dehumanization are aspects of human cultures that can be justified with the cultural pluralism argument.

New Concepts as Distractions

I am deeply concerned about concepts related to race and education that educators and social scientists have recently exhumed or invented. Scholars often invent concepts and terms that frequently divert attention from the real issues with which they should be dealing and/or invent terms that they find more emotionally palatable. When new terms are stipulated, valuable time must be spent trying to clarify their meanings and to determine their programmatic implications.

Many academicians are more comfortable discussing unexamined concepts they have stipulated than they are trying to determine whether institutional racism exists within their own institutions, whether they play a role in perpetuating it, and what steps they might be able to take to help reduce it.[10] In most current discussions about issues related to race and education, concepts such as institutional racism, power, race, and internal colonialism are conspicuously absent. Rather, new and more comfortable concepts, such as multicultural education, cultural pluralism, and multiculturalism are the fashionable phrases. We should not let unexamined ideas and emerging concepts divert attention from the serious problems our nation faces, such as institutional racism, poverty, powerlessness, and political alienation. The rise of neoconservatism in the late 1970s and the renaissance that the Ku Klux Klan was experiencing by the late 1970s indicate that while the concept of racism might be out of fashion in academia, it is institutionalized in American life and is frequently expressed in blatant forms. The publicity and legitimacy that the popular press gave to Arthur R. Jensen in 1980 for his new book arguing that Blacks are intellectually inferior indicated that racism was supported by many institutions in American life as late as the last part of this century.[11] We need to conceptualize our problems in ways that will bring the basic issues into sharp focus.

Education for Ethnic and Racial Diversity

Concepts and terms related to *ethnicity* are the most useful and appropriate for conceptualizing the problems we should be tackling because most definitions of ethnicity focus on the *culture* and *race* of immigrant and immigrant descendent groups. We must concentrate on both of these variables when designing programs to reduce intergroup conflict. In his study of definitions of ethnicity, Isajiw found that *culture* was the second most frequently mentioned attribute of ethnicity and that *race* (and physical characteristics) was the fourth. Other frequently occurring attributes included common national or geographic origin, religion, language, sense of peoplehood, common values, separate institutions, and minority or subordinate status.[12] Gordon's definition of ethnic group highlights the importance of race:

> When I use the term "ethnic," I shall mean by it any group which is defined or set off by race, religion, or national origin, or some combination of these categories ... these categories have a common social-psychological referent in that all of them serve to create, through historical circumstances, a sense of peoplehood.[13]

Both racial and cultural differences must be reflected in educational programs designed to reduce intergroup conflict and misunderstanding. Many of our efforts, however, must focus directly on reducing institutional, individual, and cultural racism,[14] since racial differences, and not more generalized cultural differences, is the cause of the most serious psychological problems which minority youths often experience in the schools,[15] and of racial conflict in the United States. Daniels and Kitano emphasize the latter point:

> ... Although the long range causes of the current crisis are many, the conclusion is almost inescapable that the root cause was the pervasive nature of American racism—a racism which, although it grew less and less oppressive as the twentieth century wore on, consistently refused admission into full membership in society to the vast majority of colored Americans.[16]

The relationship between racism and the rejection of the cultures of ethnic minorities by dominant groups must also be considered when formulating educational policy to reduce interethnic conflict. Racism is one of the major reasons why many Whites perceive and evaluate the cultures of ethnic minority groups negatively. Intergroup problems frequently arise not because of the nature of the cultural differences between Whites and nonWhites, but because of the race of the individual or group who exhibits the specific cultural characteristics. The language of poor Blacks is often ridiculed, while the speech of White Bostonians, which is as much a dialect as Black English, is frequently admired by Anglo-Americans. In the recent past, Mexican American children were often prohibited from speaking Spanish in many schools in the Southwest.[17] However, when Spanish was spoken by Whites it was usually viewed as a useful and esteemed language. Gay has called this phenomenon "cultural racism":

> [Another] form of racism is that which involves the elevation of the White Anglo-Saxon Protestant cultural heritage to a position of superiority over the cultural experiences of ethnic minority groups. It involves elements of both institutional and individual racism. The idea that "White is right" prevails in this expression of racism. Only those values, attitudes, beliefs, traditions, customs, and mores ascribed to by Whites are considered acceptable and normal prescriptions of behavior. Anything else is labeled deviant, abnormal, degenerate, and pathological. If this belief were to remain in the realm of attitudes, it would be merely ethnocentrism. It becomes racism when Whites use power to perpetuate their cultural heritage and impose it upon others, while at the same time destroying the culture of ethnic minorities.[18]

Because we need to focus our attention on variables related to both race and culture, and the complex interactions and relationships between these two major variables, *ethnic and racial diversity* is a much better concept than *cutural pluralism* or *multicultural education* to describe and guide research and policy efforts related to the education of ethnic minorities.

Educational Imperatives

There are a number of basic issues and problems related to race, ethnicity, and education, that warrant immediate and decisive action. Much discussion and debate about these problems has taken place in recent years, especially since the ethnic revitalization movements of the 1960s. However, programs to ameliorate these problems have most often been based on racial insensitivity, unexamined assumptions, educational cliques, and racist research.[19] We must act thoughtfully and decisively. The alternative is a nation torn by racial strife with a rigid social class system stratified along racial lines. I will now discuss several basic issues we need to examine in order to design effective programs to foster multiracial living and understanding.

Reducing Racial Conflict

A top priority must be to implement programs and practices designed to modify the negative racial attitudes of students. Research indicates that both Black and White children are aware of racial differences at an early age, and tend to express more negative attitudes toward Blacks than toward Whites.[20] Research further suggests that the racial attitudes of youths tend to become more negative and crystallized as they grow older if deliberate efforts are not made to influence them.[21]

To successfully modify the racial attitudes of students, experiences designed to influence the racial feelings and perceptions of teachers must be implemented. The attitudes, behavior, and the perceptions of classroom teachers have a profound impact on the social atmosphere of the school and the attitudes of students.[22] Teachers are even more important than the materials they use because the ways in which they present material highly influence how they are viewed by students. Teachers must be strongly committed to a racially tolerant school atmosphere before such a sitting can be created and maintained.

Unfortunately, available research indicates that many teachers display negative attitudes and behavior toward minority students, especially those who are poor. Studies by Leacock, Rist, and Gay indicate that teachers, in both subtle and overt ways, communicate negative feelings to their minority students and have a disproportionate number of negative verbal and nonverbal interactions with them.[23]

These types of studies suggest that teacher in-service training is absolutely imperative if we are going to reduce institutional racism in the school setting. In-service training for teachers and other school personnel must have at least two major objectives: (1) to help teachers to gain a new conceptualization of American history and culture and (2) to help them to confront their racial feelings, which can be a painful process, and if not handled competently, destructive, and unsettling. However, despite these risks, it is essential that teachers clarify their racial feelings before they can contribute positively to the reduction of racial prejudice in children and function effectively within a multiethnic setting.

The school can also help to reduce cultural racism and ethnocentrism by maximizing the cultural options of Anglo-American youths, and helping them to break out of their ethnic encapsulations. These youths need to learn that there are other ways of being, of feeling, and of perceiving. Most Americans, including Anglo-Americans, are socialized within ethnic enclaves where they learn one basic life-style. Consequently, they assume that their way is the only way, or that it is the only legitimate cultural style. Other life-styles seem strange, different, and exotic. Most ethnic minority individuals are forced to function within the dominant culture. However, many Anglo-Americans are never required to function within other ethnic cultures. The school should provide all students with opportunities to become familiar with other races, life styles and cultures, and help young people to develop *ethnic literacy* and become more sophisticated about other cultures. Most Americans are ignorant about ethnic cultures other than their own.

Anglo-American youths should be taught that they have cultural options. We severely limit the potentiality of students when we merely teach them aspects of their own cultures. Anglo-American students should realize that using Black English is one effective way to communicate; that American Indians have values, beliefs, and life-styles that may be functional for them; and that there are alternative ways of behaving and of viewing the universe that are practiced within the United States that they can freely embrace. By helping Anglo-American students to view the world beyond their limited racial and ethnic perspectives, we will enrich them as human beings and enable them to live more productive and fulfilling lives.[24]

Multiethnic Testing

To make the school a truly multiethnic institution, major changes must be made in the ways in which we test and ascertain student abilities. Most of the intelligence tests that are administered in the public schools are based on an "Anglo-conformity, monocultural model."[25] Many students who are socialized within other ethnic cultures find the tests and other aspects of the school setting alien and intimidating. Consequently, they perform poorly on such tests and are placed in low academic tracks, special education classes, and low reading groups. Research indicates that teachers who teach in these kinds of situations tend to have low expectations for their students and often fail to create the kinds of learning environments that will enable them to master the skills and abilities needed to function successfully in society.[26]

Standardized intelligence testing, in the final analysis, serves to legitimize the sta-
tus quo and to keep powerless ethnic groups at the lower rungs of the social ladder. The
results of such tests are used to justify the noneducation of minority youths
and to relieve those who are responsible for their learning from accountability. We need to devise novel approaches to assess the abilities of minority youths, and tests that will reflect the cultures in which they are socialized. However, it will do little good for us to create novel assessment
procedures that reflect their cultures unless, at the same time, we implement curricular and teaching practices that are also multiethnic and multiracial. Students who score well on an ethnically oriented intelligence test
are not likely to achieve well within an alien school culture that has a curriculum that is unrelated to their feelings, perceptions, and cultural experiences. Mercer has identified some changes which multicultural testing ne-
cessitates:

> ... A Mulicultural pespective would recognize the integrity and value of
> different cultural traditions. It would not assume that the Anglo-American
> culture is necessarily superior to other traditions, or that Anglo-conformity
> is imperative for social cohesion. It would accept the fact that there are
> multiple cultural mainstreams in modern America and that individual cit-
> izens have the right to participate in as many of these mainstreams as they
> wish. Differences in life styles, language, and values would be treated with
> respect, and persons from minority cultures would not be regarded as cul-
> turally disadvantaged, culturally deprived, or empty vessels.[27]

Summary

The issues and problems related to race and education are immensely
complex and exceedingly difficult to diagnose and solve. Many variables
influence the relationships between nonWhite ethnic minorities and White
Americans, such as socioeconomic status, ethnicity, values, language, and
behavioral patterns. Variables related to culture and ethnicity will remain
important in explaining interactions between racial groups as long as they
are socialized within different ethnic communities and have negative attitudes toward the cultural differences exhibited by other racial groups.

However, focus on ethnic and cultural variables must not divert attention from the role of individual and institutional racism in American
society. Racism is the basic cause of many of the serious psychological
problems that ethnic minorities experience in the schools and in the larger
society. The interaction of race and culture also explains many interracial
problems. Individuals and groups frequently respond negatively to specific
cultural behaviors because they are exhibited by racially stigmatized ethnic minorities.

Effective educational policy and programs must be based on research and theory
that focus on both race and culture and the complex interactions between these two major
variables and related variables, such as socioeconomic status. Programs that focus

exclusively on cultural differences are not likely to lead to positive interracial interactions and understandings. An exclusive "culture" approach is also limited by the extensive degree of cultural assimilation in American society. Race, however, cannot totally explain interethnic problems because there are significant cultural differences between some minority cultures and Anglo-American culture. Because of the immense complexity of the problem, we need to examine multiple variables when trying to determine causes and to devise effective change programs related to race and education. Further research and analyses need to better clarify the relationship between culture and race in explaining interracial problems and conflict. Concepts related to race and ethnicity can best guide research and programmatic efforts related to the education of ethnic minority students.

Notes

1. Jean D. Grambs, *Multicultural Teacher Education: Issues Without Answers,* The Illinois Association of Colleges for Teacher Education Monograph No. 1 (January 1979).
2. Horace M. Kallen, *Culture and Democracy in the United States: Studies in the Group Psychology of the American Peoples* (New York: Boni and Liveright Publishers, 1924), p. 124.
3. Ibid., pp. 124–125.
4. Julius Drachsler, *Democracy and Assimilation: The Blending of Immigrant Heritages in America* (New York: Macmillan, 1920).
5. Irving Kristol, "The Negro Today Is Like the Immigrant Yesterday," *New York Times Magazine* (September 11, 1966), p. 50.
6. Gilbert Osofsky, *Harlem: TheMaking of a Ghetto,* 2nd ed. (New York: Harper Torchbooks, 1971), p. x.
7. Robert Blauner, *Racial Oppression in America* (New York: Harper and Row, 1972), p. 56.
8. Charles A. Valentine, "Deficit, Difference, and Bicultural Models of Afro-American Behavior," *Harvard Educational Review* 41 (May 1971), pp. 137–157.
9. Milton M. Gordon, *Assimilation in American Life* (New York: Oxford University Press, 1964), p. 159.
10. In recent years, a number of writers have presented lucid discussions and definitions of racism. Gay's definition is helpful and perceptive, "Racism is ... any activity, individual or institutional, deliberate or not, predicated upon a belief in the superiority of Whites and the inferiority of ethnic minorities, which serves to maintain White supremacy through the oppression and subjugation of members of ethnic minority groups." Geneva Gay, "Racism in America: Imperatives for Teaching Ethnic Studies," in James A. Banks, ed., *Teaching Ethnic Studies: Concepts and Strategies* (Washington, D.C.: National Council for the Social Studies, 1973), p. 30.

11. Arthur R. Jensen, *Bias in Mental Testing* (New York: The Free Press, 1980).
12. Wsevolod W. Isajiw, "Definitions of Ethnicity," *Ethnicity* 1 (July 1974), p. 117.
13. Gordon, *Assimilation in American Life,* pp. 27–28.
14. Geneva Gay, "Racism in America," pp. 31–34.
15. Kenneth B. Clark, *Prejudice and Your Child,* 2nd ed. (Boston: Beacon Press, 1963).
16. Roger Daniels and Harry H. L. Kitano, *American Racism: Exploration of the Nature of Prejudice* (Englewood Cliffs, N.J.: Prentice-Hall, 1970), p. 118.
17. U.S. Commission on Civil Rights, *Toward Quality Education for Mexican Americans.* Report VI. (Washington, D.C.: The Commission, 1974).
18. Gay, "Racism in America," p. 33.
19. Kenneth B. Clark, "Social Policy, Power and Social Science Research," *Harvard Educational Review* 43 (February 1973), pp. 113–121; Stephen S. Baratz and Joan C. Baratz, "Early Childhood Intervention: The Social Science Base of Institutional Racism," *Harvard Educational Review* 40 (February 1970), pp. 29–50.
20. J. Kenneth Morland, "A Comparison of Race Awareness in Northern and Southern Children," *American Journal of Orthopsychiatry* 36 (January 1966), pp. 23–31.
21. Mary Ellen Goodman, *Race Awareness in Young Children* (New York: Collier Books, 1964).
22. Helen H. Davidson and Gerhard Lang, "Children's Perceptions of Their Teachers' Feelings Toward Them Related to Self-Perception, School Achievement, and Behavior," *Journal of Experimental Education* 29 (1960), pp. 107–118.
23. Eleanor B. Leacock, *Teaching and Learning in City Schools* (New York: Basic Books, 1969); Ray C. Rist, "Student Social Class and Teacher Expectations: The Self-Fulfilling Prophecy in Ghetto Education," *Harvard Educational Review* 40 (August 1970), pp. 411–451; Geneva Gay, "Differential Dyadic Interactions of Black and White Teachers With Black and White Pupils in Recently Desegregated Social Studies Classrooms: A Function of Teacher and Pupil Ethnicity" (Washington, D.C.: National Institute of Education, 1974).
24. James A. Banks, "Cultural Pluralism and the Schools," editorials, *Educational Leadership* 31 (December 1974), pp. 163–166.
25. Jane R. Mercer, "Latent Functions of Intelligence Testing in the Public Schools," in Lamar P. Miller, ed., *The Testing of Black Students* (Englewood Cliffs, N.J.: Prentice-Hall, 1974), p. 91.
26. Robert Rosenthal and Lenore F. Jacobson, *Pygmalion in the Classroom: Self-Fulfilling Prophecies and Teacher Expectations* (New York: Holt, 1968).
27. Mercer, "Latent Functions," p. 91.

13

Characteristics
of the Multiethnic Teacher

What are the attitudes, skills, behaviors, and other characteristics needed to become an effective teacher in an educational setting that reflects ethnic diversity? What steps can you take to attain these characteristics? What kind of education have most teachers received about ethnic groups in the United States? How can cross-cultural functioning help the teacher to become a more effective multiethnic educator? What are the problems and promises of cross-cultural behavior?

This chapter is designed to answer these questions. It identifies and describes the major components needed by teachers to function effectively within multiethnic educational environments. A multiethnic educational environment does not necessarily have students within it from diverse ethnic and racial groups. *It promotes norms, values, and behaviors that reflect the ethnic and racial diversity in American society.* Such an environment can exist within an all-White suburban school as well as within an inner-city school that has a multiethnic student population. However, many schools which have multiethnic student populations cannot be characterized as *multiethnic* because of their Anglo-centric norms, behaviors, and values.

To function effectively within multiethnic educational environments, teachers need to acquire: (1) more democratic attitudes and values; (2) a multiethnic philosophy; (3) the ability to view events and situations from diverse ethnic perspectives and points of view; (4) an understanding of the complex and multidimensional nature of ethnicity in American society; (5) knowledge of the stages of ethnicity and their curricular and teaching implications; and (6) the ability to function at increasingly higher stages of ethnicity. Figure 13.1 summarizes these characteristics.

Teacher Education in the United States

Most teachers in the nation's schools have not had the opportunity to acquire the knowledge, attitudes, skills, and behaviors summarized in Figure 13.1 because of the nature of teacher education in the United States. Teacher education in the United States, like the American common school curriculum, has historically been Anglo-centric and dominated by the assmilationist forces in American society.[1] A major goal of the common school was to help immigrant and ethnic group youths to acquire the cultural

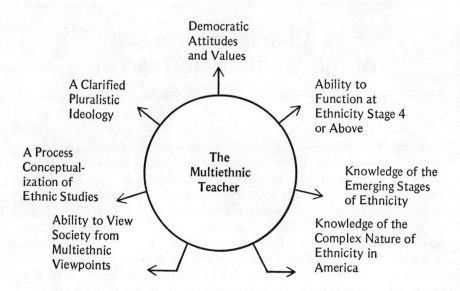

Figure 13.1. Characteristics of the Multiethnic Teacher. To function effectively in ethnically pluralistic environments, the teacher must have democratic attitudes and values, a clarified pluralistic ideology, a process conceptualization of ethnic studies, the ability to view society from diverse ethnic perspectives and points of view, knowledge of the emerging stages of ethnicity, knowledge of the complex nature of ethnicity in America, and the ability to function at Ethnicity Stage 4 or above. Reformed teacher-education programs should be designed to help teachers acquire these attitudes, conceptual frameworks, knowledge, and skills.

characteristics and values of Anglo-Americans. The goals of the common school reflected those of the larger society. Teacher education institutions reinforced dominant societal goals and ideologies and socialized teachers so that they would become effective agents of the assimilationist ideology.[2] This ideology maintains that ethnicity is "un-American" and that ethnic identifications are dysfunctional within a modernized democratic nation.[3]

The ethnic revitalization movements of the 1960s and 1970s caused many teacher educators to question their assimilationist policies and to examine alternative theories and ideologies related to ethnic pluralism in the United States.[4] Increasingly, teacher educators are beginning to realize the importance of ethnicity in the socialization of many individuals within American society and are becoming aware of the ways in which the ethnic characteristics of individuals and groups are often used to deny them equal educational opportunities.[5] The American Association of Colleges for Teacher Education (AACTE), through its publications and institutes, has encouraged its member institutions to include multiethnic and multicultural components in their teacher education programs.[6] In its "No One

Model American" statement published in 1973, AACTE endorsed cultural pluralism.

> To endorse cultural pluralism is to endorse the principal that there is no one model American. To endorse cultural pluralism is to understand and appreciate the differences that exist among the nation's citizens. It is to see these differences as a positive force in the continuing development of a society which professes a wholesome respect for the intrinsic worth of every individual. Cultural pluralism is more than a temporary accommodation to racial and ethnic minorities. It is a concept that aims toward a heightened sense of being and of wholeness of the entire society based on the unique strengths of its parts.
>   Cultural pluralism rejects both assimilation and separatism as ultimate goals.[7]

The AACTE publications and institutes have encouraged many of its member institutions to integrate components of multicultural education into their teacher education programs. *The Standards for Accreditation of Teacher Education,* issued by the National Council for Accreditation of Teacher Education (NCATE), require all of its member institutions to include multicultural components in their teacher education programs.[8] These *Standards* became effective on January 1, 1979. About 80 percent of the nation's teacher education institutions are members of NCATE. Consequently, this requirement has stimulated many actions to implement programs in multicultural education. However, these efforts have experienced many problems. They are often special programs, noncomprehensive in scope, noninstitutionalized, and not an integral part of the mainstream program in teacher education. These programs have also been hampered by a lack of consensus among educators about the meaning of multicultural education,[9] ambiguous goals, and by the declining resources that the nation's colleges of education were experiencing by the beginning of the 1980s. This is how the NCATE defines multicultural education:

> Multicultural education is preparation for the social, political, and economic realities that individuals experience in culturally diverse and complex human encounters. These realities have both national and international dimensions. This preparation provides a process by which an individual develops competencies for perceiving, believing, and behaving in differential cultural settings. Thus, multicultural education is viewed as an intervention and an on-going assessment process to help institutions and individuals become more responsive to the human condition, individual cultural integrity, and cultural pluralism in society.[10]

Democratic Attitudes and Values

The teacher is the most important variable in the student's educational environment. Teachers, therefore, need to have positive attitudes and high academic expectations for minority students. What does research say about how teacher attitudes and expectations influence student academic achievement, self-concepts, and behaviors? What does research say about the kinds of attitudes and perceptions teachers have toward ethnic minority youths?

Research suggests that teachers, next to parents, are the most significant others in students' lives, and that classroom teachers play an important role in the formation of students' attitudes and self-perceptions. A study by Davidson and Lang indicates that the assessment that students make of themselves is related to the assessment significant people make of them.[11] The study demonstrated that children's self-appraisals are significantly related to their perceptions of their teacher's feelings. In both subtle and overt ways, teachers influence their students' racial feelings and self-perceptions.

A number of researchers have investigated the attitudes and perceptions which teachers have of ethnic and racial groups and the effects of their attitudes on students' self-concepts, attitudes, perceptions, and behavior. This research suggests that many teachers have prejudicial attitudes and perceptions of racial and lower socioeconomic groups and that these prejudicial attitudes influence their verbal and nonverbal interactions with students as well as student behavior and attitudes.

Some researchers have suggested that the race of teachers is a significant variable in determining their relationship with students. Gottlieb found that the White teachers in his sample disliked teaching inner-city Black students more than the Black teachers.[12] The White teachers more frequently described Black children as talkative, lazy, fun-loving, high-strung, and rebellious. Black teachers more frequently described them as fun-loving, happy, cooperative, energetic, and ambitious. Half of the White teachers in a study conducted by Clark felt that Black students were innately inferior to Whites and were unable to learn in the school.[13] They believed that inner-city Black schools should become custodial institutions and not remain educational institutions.

Other research suggests that the race of teachers is not an important variable that affects their attitudes and patterns of interactions with racial minorities and low income students. This research indicates that teachers tend to have prejudicial attitudes toward poor and minority children regardless of their racial and ethnic group membership. After an extensive study of Mexican-American education, Carter concluded that:

> Spanish-surname teachers generally subscribe to the view of Anglo teachers. Even the racist position finds a few adherents who assume that the degree of Indian blood in an individual influences his intellectual capacity. Mexican American and Anglo teachers appear to be equally effective or ineffective with Mexican-American children.[14]

Kleinfeld, in a study of teachers of Athabascan Indian and Eskimo students, concluded that the teacher's instructional style rather than his or her ethnic-group membership distinguished effective from non-effective teachers of Indian and Eskimo youths.[15] She writes:

> Two central characteristics seem to distinguish effective teachers from ineffective teachers. The first and most important characteristic is the effective teacher's ability to create a climate of emotional warmth that dissipates students' fears in the classroom and fulfills their expectations of highly personalized relationships. The second characteristic is the teacher's ability to resolve his own ambivalent feelings about the legitimacy of his educational goals and express his concern for the village students, not by passive sympathy, but by demanding a high quality of academic work.[16]

Rist investigated the grouping practices and interaction patterns within an all-Black class during its kindergarten, first- and second-grade years.[17] All of the teachers and administrators in the school studied were Black. This study also suggests that the race of teachers is not an important variable in determining their attitudes and interactions with minority and lower class students. In this study, the kindergarten teacher "placed the children in reading groups which reflected the social class composition of the class. . . . [T]hese groups persisted throughout the first several years of elementary school."[18] Rist concluded that a caste system existed within the classroom which reinforced and perpetuated the class system of the larger society. The Black teachers in the Rist study had apparently internalized dominant societal attitudes toward lower socioeconomic individuals and reinforced them in the classroom.

A monograph in the Mexican-American Education Study series indicates that teacher interactions with Mexican-American and Anglo students exemplify an Anglo bias.[19] The six categories in which the disparities were statistically significant were praising or encouraging acceptance or use of student ideas, questioning, positive teacher response, all noncriticizing teacher talk, and all student speaking.[20] The monograph also indicates that Mexican-American students speak significantly less in class than Anglo students. The report states:

> The total picture of classroom interaction patterns . . . is that of a teaching process which is failing to involve the Mexican-American student to the same extent as the Anglo pupil, both in terms of quantity and quality of interaction. Teachers speak less often, and less favorably, to Mexican Americans than to Anglos. At the same time, Chicano pupils generally speak out less in class than do Anglo pupils. In view of the central importance of interaction to learning, it is evident that Chicano pupils are not receiving the same quality of education in the clasroom as Anglo pupils.[21]

Gay found that both Black and White teachers interact differently with Black and White students in desegregated social studies classrooms.[22] Teachers were more positive, encouraging, and reinforcing toward White students. White students also received more opportunities to participate in substantive academic interactions with teachers. Black pupils' verbal interactions with teachers were primarily nonacademic, procedural, critical, and nonencouraging.

Parsons, in an important study, found that a school he examined within a Mexican-American community reinforced the dominant societal attitudes and perceptions of Mexican Americans and perpetuated the social class stratifications that existed among Anglos and Mexican Americans.[23] Parsons concluded that the teachers were the primary socialization agents in the school which reinforced and perpetuated social class and ethnic stratification. He quotes one teacher who explains why she put an Anglo boy in charge of a small group of Mexican-Americn boys:

> ... I think Johnny needs to learn how to set a good example and how to lead others. His father owns one of the big farms in the area and Johnny has to learn how to lead the Mexicans. One day he will be helping his father and he will have to know how to handle Mexicans. I try to help him whenever I can.[24]

The studies reviewed above suggest that many teachers have internalized the dominant societal attitudes and values toward minority and lower socioeconomic groups and that they often reinforce these attitudes and values in the classroom. The extent to which the race of teachers is a significant variable in determining their relationship with students seems unclear. However, a number of careful studies, including those by Kleinfeld, Rist, and Gay, indicate that teachers, regardless of their racial or ethnic-group membership, tend to internalize and perpetuate dominant societal values and attitudes toward racial and social class groups. This research suggests that teachers must acquire more democratic attitudes and values before schools can practice social class and cultural democracy.[25]

Changing Teacher Attitudes and Behaviors

What can teachers do to change their racial attitudes, perceptions, and behaviors? While researchers have amply documented the nondemocratic attitudes and interactions that teachers frequently have with minority and low income students, a paucity of work has been done on effective techniques that can be used to change teachers' racial attitudes and behavior. Smith concluded that the racial attitudes of adults can be significantly modified in a positive direction by contact and involvement in minority group cultures.[26] Bogardus found that a five-week intergroup education workshop, which consisted of lectures on racial problems, research projects, and visits to community agencies, had a significantly positive effect on the participants' racial attitudes.[27]

An extensive review of the research suggests that changing the racial attitudes of adults is a cumbersome task.[28] To maximize the chances for successful intervention programs, experiences must be designed specifically to change attitudes. Courses with general or global objectives are not likely to be successful. Courses that consist primarily or exclusively of lecture presentations have little import. Diverse experiences, such as seminars, visitations, community involvement, committee work, guest speakers, films, multimedia materials, and workshops, combined with factual lectures, are more effective than any single approach. Community involvement and cross cultural interactions (with the appropriate norms in the social setting) are the most cogent techniques. Psychotherapy is also promising. Individuals who express moderate rather than extreme attitudes are the most likely to change. This is encouraging since most prejudiced individuals exemplify an average degree of prejudice.

A Multiethnic Philosophy

Teachers need to clarify their philosophical positions regarding the education of ethnic minorities and to endorse an ideology that is consistent with the multiple acculturation and structural pluralism that characterize American society. Teachers should be aware of the major ideologies related to ethnic pluralism in the United States, and able to examine their own philosophical positions and to explore the policy and teaching implications of alternative ideologies. Teachers with an assimilationist ideology will most likely teach a unit on the American Civil War differently than a teacher with a multiethnic ideology. Effective multiethnic teachers should embrace a philosophical position that will facilitate their effectiveness in culturally and racially diverse educational environments. Teachers who endorse a multiethnic ideology as defined in chapter 6 respect and value the ethnic characteristics of ethnic students but also believe these students need to acquire the values, skills, attitudes, and abilities needed to function successfully within the universalistic American culture.

Chapters 5 and 6 present and summarize the major philosophical positions related to race and ethnicity in the United States and delineates the limitations of ideologies and concepts such as *cultural assimilation, Anglo-conformity, the melting pot,* and *cultural pluralism.* Each of these ideologies and concepts are based on incomplete and/or inaccurate conceptualizations of the nature of ethnic group life in the United States.

Effective teachers in the multiethnic classroom must endorse what I described in chapter 6 as the multiethnic ideology. This ideology derives from the complex and multidimensional nature of ethnicity in modern

American society. However, since most classroom teachers were socialized within a society, schools, and teacher education institutions that had Anglo-centric norms and were assimilationist oriented, many teachers are therefore likely to embrace an assimilationist ideology and to view pluralistic ideologies (whether weak or strong) as un-American, radical, and unpatriotic. It is very difficult for individuals to change their philosophical orientations or even to question their currently held ideological beliefs. They have a great deal of affective and intellectual commitment to their ideological orientations and values. These ideologies are deeply held and result from years of informal and formal socialization.

Teachers should first examine their currently held ideological positions related to race and ethnicity in the United States. If they feel that they need to change their ideological orientations in order to become effective multiethnic teachers (The teacher who is a strong pluralist is probably as ineffective in a multiethnic classroom as the teacher who is a strong assimilationist), they should enroll in courses and seek other educational experiences related to race and ethnicity. Vicarious as well as direct experiences with other cultures, if they are open to these experiences, will help teachers to examine their philosophical beliefs. The caveats about cross-cultural functioning discussed later in this chapter should be studied by teachers who seek cross-cultural experiences as a way to help them examine their philosophical beliefs. With these kinds of cross-cultural experiences, teachers will have opportunities to interact with individuals with widely differing ideologies and value positions about pluralism and race in America.

Teachers should also examine the *possible consequences* of embracing various philosophical beliefs. They should discuss how different philosophical orientations toward race and ethnic group life in the United States may influence their behavior in the classroom and the academic achievement and emotional growth of ethnic students. A number of researchers have observed that Black students tend to be more action oriented and expressive in their learning styles than Anglo-American students.[29] Research by Ramírez and Castañeda indicates that Mexican-American youths tend to be more field sensitive than field independent in their learning styles than Anglo pupils.[30] They also tend to be less individually competitive than Anglo students.[31] The ideological positions and commitments of teachers, whether conscious or unconscious, influence how they respond to the different cultural learning styles and characteristics of Black and Mexican-American students. Teachers who are staunch assimilationists are likely to regard these different behaviors of Black and Mexican-American students as negative and pathological characteristics that should be eradicated. Teachers who are more multiethnic in their philosophical orientations are more likely to perceive these behaviors of Black and Chicano students as legitimate and functional cultural behaviors that they should build on and use when planning and teaching.

Assimilationism and Anglo-centricism: Problems for Teachers

I am often asked in workshops what is the greatest single problem teachers face when they try to plan and implement a multiethnic curriculum and school environment. Is it lack of sensitive and effective multiethnic teaching materials, lack of administrative support, student resistance, lack of adequate planning time, parental resistance, or some other problem? I have given this question much serious thought in the thirteen years that I have been training teachers in ethnic studies and multiethnic education. While the factors mentioned above are problems for many teachers who want to implement multiethnic education, I do not believe that they are the most difficult problems faced in multiethnic teaching. The two most serious problems faced when planning and implementing multiethnic education are the strong *assimilationist ideology* that many teachers have (discussed above) and their inability to view this society from diverse ethnic perspectives and points of view. These problems are no doubt related to other societal problems. Many teachers, for example, might hold tenaciously to an assimilationist ideology or be unable to view the United States from the perspectives of Indian and Black writers and social scientists because of racist attitudes[32] or the fear that new ideologies and new conceptualizations of American society will lead to a sharing of power by dominant and currently excluded ethnic groups (see chapter 10).

Whatever the root cause of these problems, and many reasonable hypotheses can be stated, the strong assimilationist ideology that many teachers embrace and their inability to view this nation from diverse ethnic perspectives are, in my view, the most difficult problems that must be overcome when multiethnic educational programs are designed and implemented.

Viewing Society from Diverse Ethnic Perspectives

Teachers need to acquire a conceptualization of the American experience that is based on novel assumptions and on accurate knowledge about the role and place of the United States in the world today. Textbooks, the mass media, and other parts of our culture continue to perpetuate many myths about American society and Americanism that are culturally encapsulating and ethnocentric.[33] Teachers need to acquire new perspectives about the nature and development of the United States and develop the ability to view this nation from the perspectives of ethnic groups that have historically been oppressed and excluded in this nation.

I do not mean to suggest that Anglo-American perspectives and views on history and contemporary American society should be excluded from

the school curriculum. However, students can gain a sophisticated understanding of the complex nature of our nation and society only by viewing
events, situations, and concepts from the perspectives of the diverse ethnic
groups that have shaped and are shaping our nation.

In a brilliant and illuminating essay on the sociology of knowledge,
Robert K. Merton introduces the concepts of the "insiders" and the "outsiders."[34] He discusses their varying views on social phenomena and their
various claims about the legitimacy of their perspectives and points of view.
The insider claims that only a member of his or her group can really know
and consequently validly describe the experiences of his or her group. The
outsider, who attempts to describe a group to which he or she does not belong, claims that he or she can give a more objective account of the social
experiences of other groups because he or she can observe with the least
subjectivity. Merton concludes that neither the insider nor the outsider has
an exclusive claim on valid knowledge and that the perspectives of both are
needed to give us a more total view of social reality. In order to gain a more
complete understanding of the events and the consequences of events in
America, teachers need to view them from the perspectives of the Anglo-
Americans, who have been and are the "insiders" because of their inclusion
within American society, as well as from the perspectives of ethnic groups
such as American Indians and Puerto Ricans, ethnic groups who have historically been and are largely excluded from full participation in American
life. These groups have largely been "outsiders."

Teachers should not only be able to view American society and culture
from diverse ethnic perspectives and points of view. They should also be
able to teach American history, science, literature, and other disciplines
from the perspectives of different ethnic groups. The school and the teacher
education curriculum should be organized on what I call Models C and D
(see chapter 7). In these models, students are helped to view events, concepts, and situations from the perspectives of different ethnic groups within
the United States as well as within other nations.

The Complex Nature of Ethnicity
in American Society

Classroom teachers need a better understanding of the complex nature of
ethnicity within modern American society. Misconceptions about the nature of ethnicity within the United States are widespread among the general population, teachers, and their students. When many teachers think of
an ethnic group, they think of non-White groups such as Black Americans
and Japanese Americans. They therefore confuse an *ethnic* group with a *racial* group. Teachers can better understand the complex nature of ethnicity
in the United States if they learn to distinguish several concepts that are
often confused such as ethnic group, ethnicity, ethnic minority group, race,

and culture. Ethnic group, ethnic minority group, ethnicity, and culture are defined in chapter 4.

Race is a problematic concept because physical anthropologists have been unable to structure racial categories that are consistent and widely accepted. The concept of race is used to differentiate and classify various human subgroups on the basis of their biological characteristics.

The definitions of ethnic group, ethnicity, ethnic minority group, race, and culture presented in this book enables us to make some useful statements about these concepts and their interrelationships. The definition of ethnic group presented in chapter 4 suggests that every American is to some degree ethnic. However, it is best to view ethnic group and ethnicity as continuous rather than as discrete concepts. In other words, it is more fruitful to ask the question, "To what extent is an individual or group ethnic?" than, "Is the individual or group ethnic?" The first question suggests that ethnic group and ethnicity are continuous rather than discrete concepts. The latter question implies that ethnic group behavior and ethnicity are "either or" discrete variables. The multidimensional conceptualization of ethnicity and ethnic group presented in this book enables the teacher to involve each student in the classroom in a discussion and analysis of his or her ethnic roots and characteristics. It allows the teacher to get away from the "we-they" notion of ethnic groups that is so pervasive within the schools and the larger society.

The Teacher and the Stages of Ethnicity

To successfully work with students from diverse ethnic backgrounds, teachers should be knowledgeable about the ethnic characteristics of their students. Students differ in their ethnic identities and characteristics just as they differ in their cognitive and affective development.[35] Consequently, the teacher should make some attempt to individualize multiethnic experiences for students.

These three hypothetical students might need somewhat different curricular experiences related to race and ethnicity. Juan was socialized within a rather conservative Mexican-American community in the Southwest. Jessie Mae, who is Black, spent Saturday afternoons during her early years in a Black awareness school. John is an Anglo-American student who has never had any firsthand experiences with non-White ethnics. These students are now in the same eighth-grade social studies class. The teacher is beginning a unit on race relations in the United States. Each of these students will need some unique experiences tailored to their complex and emerging ethnic identities. Chapter 9 presents a typology that outlines the basic stages of the development of ethnicity among individual members of ethnic groups that teachers can use as a guide when trying to identify the ethnic characteristics of students.

To become more effective multiethnic educators, teachers should try to determine their own stage of ethnicity and become sensitive to their ethnic behaviors and characteristics. The teacher should not only try to help students function at higher stages of ethnicity but should try to function at higher stages of ethnicity themselves. Teachers who are functioning primarily at Stages 1 and 2 cannot realistically be expected to help students develop positive racial attitudes toward different ethnic and racial groups or to help students to function at higher stages of ethnicity. Once teachers are aware of their own ethnic attitudes, behaviors, and perceptions, they can begin an action program designed to change their behavior if necessary. Such a program may consist of individual readings, taking courses at the local college or university, or participating in cross-cultural experiences either in this nation or in other nations.

Cross-cultural Experiences: Problems and Promises

Teachers who plan to have cross-cultural experiences in this or other nations should be aware of both the problems and promises of functioning in a different culture. Functioning cross-culturally, in the final analysis, is usually rewarding and personally revealing. Since enculturation into our own cultures is primarily a subconscious process, we can learn a great deal about our norms, values, behaviors, and perceptions by functioning in other cutural environments.

To acquire the maximum benefits from cross-cultural functioning, the individual must be able to interpret their experiences accurately and develop a sophisticated level of *cross-cultural awareness*. Hanvey has developed a typology of levels of cross-cultural awareness that is presented in Table 13.1. Individuals who are able to attain Level IV of cross-cultural awareness are likely to benefit most from cross-cultural experiences and to develop higher levels of cross-cultural behavior (discussed in chapter 2).

Despite its positive long-range outcomes, an individual functioning within another culture frequently experiences cultural shock, confusion, and makes embarassing cultural mistakes. All individuals are likely to experience cultural shock during their first experiences in another culture. The greater the differences between the new culture and their own ethnic and/or national culture, the greater the cultural shock individuals are likely to experience.

Americans can experience cultural shock within ethnic cultures in this nation as well as in other nations. Anglo-Americans who have had few experiences with Black American culture and have not traveled outside the United States are likely to experience cultural shock when they first visit a traditional Black Baptist Church as well as when they first visit a nation such as Mexico.

Table 13.1. Levels of Cross-cultural Awareness.

Level	Information	Mode	Interpretation
I.	awareness of superficial or very visible cultural traits: stereotypes	tourism, text-books, National Geographic	unbelievable, i.e. exotic, bizarre
II.	awareness of significant and subtle cultural traits that contrast markedly with one's own	culture conflict situations	unbelievable, i.e. frustrating, irra-tional
III.	awareness of significant and subtle cultural traits that contrast markedly with one's own	intellectual anal-ysis	believable, cogni-tively
IV.	awareness of how another feels from the standpoint of the insider	cultural immer-sion: living the culture	believable be-cause of subjec-tive familiarity

From Robert G. Hanvey, *At Attainable Global Perspective,* 1975. Reprinted with per-mission of the author and publisher, Center for Global Perspectives, New York (218 East 18th St., New York 10003).

Some preparation before experiencing another culture may help to re-duce cultural shock and enable the individual to function more successfully within it. Such preparation may consist of readings, (especially literary works because literature often conveys the nuances and subtleties of a cul-ture), viewing films, and interacting with individuals socialized within the culture. However, no amount of preparation will totally eliminate cultural shock and cultural mistakes during an individual's first experience with a culture. If teachers are knowledgeable about the rewarding as well as the problems of cross-cultural functioning, they will be better able to interpret their cross-cultural experiences accurately and will therefore benefit more from them in the long run.

Hypotheses Regarding Cross-cultural Behavior

I have developed some hypotheses regarding cross-cultural behavior that are based on my own functioning in other cultures (such as Guam, Mexico, the Virgin Islands, and different ethnic cultures within the United States), my observations of and conversations with other individuals who have functioned cross-culturally, and my reading of the literature related to cross-cultural functioning.[36] These hypotheses should be helpful to individ-uals who are planning cross-cultural experiences and to those who are trying to interpret their cross-cultural interactions and behavior or the cross-cultural behaviors of others.

- The weaker the ethnic boundaries are between ethnic cultures, the more likely cross-cultural functioning will occur between these cultures.
- The weaker the ethnic boundaries between ethnic cultures, the easier cross-cultural functioning will be for individuals in those cultures. Individuals who have weak ethnic cultural characteristics and ethnic identities are more likely to participate in cross-cultural behavior than individuals with strong ethnic characteristics and ethnic identities.
- Psychological discomforts and confusion is so potentially high in cross-cultural functioning that cross-cultural behavior will occur only when motivation is high for functioning cross-culturally and the potential rewards are substantial.
- Subethnic boundaries (within an ethnic group) are often distinct and tight. Consequently, individuals who are socialized within one subethnic culture may experience problems and conflicts when functioning within another subethnic culture within his or her ethnic group.
- As an individual becomes more competent in functioning within an outside ethnic culture, his or her personal ethnicity and ethnic behavior changes and/or reduces in intensity.
- The response to the individual who is functioning cross-culturally by the outside ethnic group influences the depth and nature of his or her cross-cultural behavior and his or her psychological interpretation of his or her cross-cultural behavior.

Summary

This chapter discusses the attitudes, knowledge, skills, behaviors, and other characteristics teachers need to function effectively within an educational setting that promotes respect for and literacy about racial and ethnic differences in American society. Such an educational setting does not have to contain students from diverse ethnic groups. However, it has norms and values that respect and value cultural and racial differences. Historically, because of their Anglo-centric and assimilationist orientation, teacher education institutions have not helped teachers to attain most of the attitudes, knowledge, skills, and behaviors that are discussed in this chapter.

To function effectively within a pluralistic educational environment, teachers need to acquire: (a) more democratic attitudes and values; (b) a multiethnic philosophy; (c) the ability to view events and situations from diverse ethnic perspectives; (d) an understanding of the complex and multidimensional nature of ethnicity in American society; (e) knowledge of the stages of ethnicity and their curricular and teaching implications; and (f) the ability to function at increasingly higher stages of ethnicity. Cross-cultural functioning can help teachers to acquire these skills, attitudes, and abilities. However, in order to accurately interpret their cross-cultural experiences, teachers should be aware of both the problems and promises of functioning within other cultures.

Notes

1. Mildred Dickeman, "Teaching Cultural Pluralism," In James A. Banks, ed., *Teaching Ethnic Studies: Concepts and Strategies* (Washington, D.C.: National Council for the Social Studies, 1973), pp. 5–25.
2. Michael B. Katz, *Class, Bureaucracy, and Schools: The Illusion of Educational Change in America,* expanded ed. (New York: Praeger, 1975).
3. John Porter discusses the problems of ethnicity within a modernized society in "Ethnic Pluralism in Canadian Perspective," in Nathan Glazer and Daniel P. Moynihan, eds. *Ethnicity: Theory and Experience* (Cambridge, Mass.: Harvard University Press, 1975), pp. 267–305.
4. "Case Studies in Multicultural Teacher Education," in Frank H. Klassen and Donna M. Gollnick, eds., *Pluralism and the American Teacher: Issues and Case Studies* (Washington, D.C.: American Association of Colleges for Teacher Education), pp. 163–238.
5. See for example, "Multicultural Education and the Disciplines," *Journal of Teacher Education* 28 (May–June 1977); and Carl A. Grant, ed., *Multicultural Education: Commitments, Issues and Applications* (Washington, D.C.: Association for Supervision and Curriculum Development, 1977).
6. Among the many publications that AACTE has issued related to multicultural education since 1970 are the following: William A. Hunter, ed., *Multicultural Education Through Competency-Based Teacher Education* (Washington, D.C.: AACTE, 1974); Thomas Thompson, ed., *The Schooling of Native America* (Washington, D.C.: AACTE, 1978); and Francis X. Sutman, Eleanor L. Sandstrom, and Francis Shoemaker, *Educating Personnel for Bilingual Settings: Present and Future* (Washington, D.C.: AACTE, 1979).
7. *No One Model American: A Statement on Multicultural Education* (Washington, D.C.: AACTE, November, 1973), unpaginated flyer.
8. *Standards for Accreditation of Teacher Education* (Washington, D.C.: National Council for Accreditation of Teacher Education, 1977).
9. Jean D. Grambs, *Multicultural Education: Issues Without Answers,* The Illinois Association of Colleges for Teacher Education Monograph No. 1 (January 1979).
10. *Standards for the Accreditation of Teacher Education,* p. 4.

11. Helen H. Davidson and Gerhard Lang, "Children's Perceptions of Their Teachers' Feelings Toward Them Related to Self-Perception, School Achievement, and Behavior," *Journal of Experimental Education* 29 (December 1960), pp. 107–118.
12. David Gottlieb, "Teaching and Students: The Views of Negro and White Teachers," *Sociology of Education* 27 (Summer 1964), pp. 345–353.
13. Kenneth B. Clark, "Clash of Cultures in the Classroom," in Meyer Weinberg, ed. *Learning Together* (Chicago: Integrated Education Associates, 1964).
14. Thomas P. Carter, *Mexican Americans in School: A History of Educational Neglect* (New York: College Entrance Examination Board, 1970), p. 118.
15. Judith Kleinfeld, "Effective Teachers of Eskimo and Indian Students," *School Review* 83 (February 1975), pp. 301–344.
16. Ibid., p. 318.
17. Ray C. Rist, "Student Social Class and Teacher Expectations: The Self-Fulfilling Prophecy in Ghetto Education," *Harvard Educational Review* 40 (August 1970), pp. 411–451.
18. Ibid., p. 70.
19. U.S. Commission on Civil Rights, *Teachers and Students: Differences in Teacher Interaction With Mexican American and Anglo Students, Report V: Mexican American Education Study* (Washington, D.C.: U.S. Government Printing Office, 1973).
20. Ibid., p. 17.
21. Ibid., pp. 18–19.
22. Geneva Gay, "Differential Dyadic Interactions of Black and White Teachers with Black and White Pupils in Recently Desegregated Social Studies Classrooms: A Function of Teacher and Pupil Ethnicity" (Washington, D.C.: National Institute of Education, January 1974), pp. vii–x.
23. Theodore W. Parsons, Jr., "Ethnic Cleavage in a California School," Ph.D. thesis, Stanford University, August 1965, quoted in Carter, *Mexican Americans in School,* pp. 82–84.
24. Ibid., p. 83.
25. Castañeda has written insightfully about cultural democracy and American public education. See Alfredo Castañeda, "The Educational Needs of Mexican-Americans," in Alfredo Castañeda, Richard L. James, and Webster Robbins, *The Educational Needs of Minority Groups* (Lincoln, Neb.: Professional Educators Publications, Inc., 1974).
26. F. T. Smith, "An Experiment in Modifying Attitudes Toward the Negro," summarized in Arnold M. Rose, *Studies in the Reduction of Prejudice* (Chicago: American Council on Race Relations, 1947), p. 9.
27. Emory S. Bogardus, "The Intercultural Workshop and Racial Distance," *Sociology and Social Research* 32 (1948), pp. 798–802.
28. Research on changing the racial attitudes of adults is reviewed in

James A. Banks, "Racial Prejudice and the Black Self-Concept," in James A. Banks and Jean D. Grambs, eds., *Black Self-Concept: Implications for Education and Social Science* (New York: McGraw-Hill, 1972), pp. 5–35.

29. Geneva Gay, "Viewing the Pluralistic Classroom as a Cultural Microcosm," *Educational Research Quarterly* 2 (Winter 1978), pp. 45–59; Roger D. Abrahams and Geneva Gay, "Black Culture in the Classroom," in Roger D. Abrahams and Rudolph C. Troike, eds., *Language and Cultural Diversity in American Education* (Englewood Cliffs, N.J.: Prentice-Hall, 1972), pp. 67–84.

30. Manuel Ramírez and Alfredo Castañeda, *Cultural Democracy, Bicognitive Development, and Education* (New York: Academic Press, 1974).

31. James A. Vasquez, "Bilingual Education's Needed Third Dimension," *Educational Leadership* 38 (November 1979), pp. 166–168.

32. Judy H. Katz, *White Awareness: Handbook for Anti-Racism Training* (Norman, Oklahoma: University of Oklahoma Press, 1978); Geneva Gay, "Racism in America: Imperatives for Teaching Ethnic Studies," in James A. Banks, ed., *Teaching Ethnic Studies: Concepts and Strategies*, pp. 27–49.

33. *Strength Through Wisdom: A Critique of U.S. Capability*, A Report to the President from the President's Commission on Foreign Language and International Studies (Washington, D.C.: U.S. Government Printing Office, November 1979).

34. Robert K. Merton, "Insiders and Outsiders: A Chapter in the Sociology of Knowledge," *The American Journal of Sociology* 78 (July 1972), pp. 9–47.

35. Jean Piaget, *Six Psychological Studies* (New York: Random House, 1968); Lawrence Kohlberg and Rochelle Mayer, "Development as the Aim of Education," *Harvard Educational Review* 42 (November 1972), pp. 449–496.

36. See especially Edward C. Stewart, *American Cultural Patterns: A Cross-Cultural Perspective* (LaGrange Park, Ill.: Intercultural Network, Inc., 1972).

14

Linking Multiethnic and Global Education: Problems and Promises

Multiethnic and Global Education:
Parallel Goals and Problems

The school curriculum should help students develop the knowledge, skills, attitudes, and abilities needed to function within various ethnic cultures within this nation. However, because we live in a highly interdependent global world society, the school should also help students develop the knowledge, attitudes, and competencies needed to function within cultures outside of the United States. Global educators point out, however, that global education in the United States is experiencing problems that in many ways parallel those of multiethnic education.[1]

Education abut ethnic groups in the United States can be characterized as Anglo-centric and culturally encapsulating. Education about other nations is often nonreflective, extremely nationalistic, and Eurocentric.[2] The study of other nations is often limited to a study of nations in the Western world with scant attention paid to nations in Asia, Africa, and the Middle East.[3] When other nations are studied, often little attempt is made to help students to view the events, situations and problems from the perspectives of the peoples who live in these nations.

Linking Multiethnic and Global Education:
Promises

Because of their interrelationships and shared goals, educators should try to better relate multiethnic and global education. A linkage would help reduce the tremendous fragmentation that now characterizes the school curriculum as well as contribute to important student learnings in cultural studies. If students develop the ability to view events and situations from the perspectives of ethnic groups in this nation, they will be better able to view events within other nations from the perspectives of the peoples who are the major participants in these events. Students who are able to relate positively to and function within a variety of ethnic cultures in the United States are more likely to function successfully in foreign cultures than individuals who view domestic ethnic cultures as alien and exotic enclaves. We can reduce nonreflective nationalism and ethnocentrism in students by

211

helping them to become more ethnically literate and competent citizens in their own nation.

Cortes writes insightfully about the relationship between multicultural and global education:

> Although they differ in emphasis, these two educational reform movements are linked by their common concerns. Both seek to improve human and intergroup relations. Both seek to increase awareness of the impact of global and national forces, trends, and institutions on different groups of people, including nations and ethnic groups. Both seek to reduce stereotyping and increase intergroup understanding. Both seek to help students comprehend the significance of human diversity, while at the same time recognizing underlying, globe-girdling commonalities. Both seek to improve intercultural communication. Both seek a better future for all, through helping to make today's students more constructive future actors on the changing state of the world.[4]

Linking Multiethnic and Global Education: Problems

While we should attempt to link and relate multiethnic and global education, each reform movement has unique characteristics that should be respected and maintained in any linkage efforts. We should not assume that multiethnic and global education are identical. This assumption would create new problems and further complicate existing ones. *Many educators often confuse studies about the countries of origin of ethnic groups with the study of these groups in the United States.* They assume, for example, that when they are teaching about Mexico they are teaching about Mexican Americans.

Some evidence suggests that publishers also confuse the study of the homelands of United States' ethnic groups with the study of these groups. While preparing a textbook in ethnic studies, I asked a national sample of major publishers of children's tradebooks to send me examination copies (for annotation) of their books that dealt with ethnic groups in the United States. Nearly a third of the books that the publishers sent to me for annotation dealt with foreign nations that are the homelands of ethnic groups in the United States, such as Africa, Mexico, Japan, China, and the Philippines. While information about their original homelands can often help students to better understand the values and behaviors of ethnic groups in the United States, members of American ethnic groups are distinctly *American* in their national identifications and overarching values and commitments. Most members of these groups also deeply resent being perceived or labeled as non-American or as non-United States citizens.

Another possible problem may arise when we try to link multiethnic and global education. It is possible that many teachers will totally ignore domestic ethnic groups and teach exclusively about the original homelands of American ethnic groups. Some teachers are much more comfortable teaching about Mexicans who live across the border or about Africans in Nigeria than they are when teaching about Mexican Americans or Afro-Americans who live in their own communities. They will therefore teach about Mexico and Nigeria but will rarely teach content related to Mexican Americans and Afro-Americans. Teaching about distant lands is apparently much less threatening to many teachers than teaching about ethnic cultures, problems, and conflicts within their own nation and community. *Special ways to mitigate this problem should be pursued in any attempt to link multiethnic and global education.*

While I am recommending that multiethnic and global education be joined and related, I am also stating that each of these reform movements have unique contributions to make to the general education of American students; *these uniqueness should be maintained and recognized in any linkage attempts.* United States ethnic cultures should not be confused with cultures that exist in nations such as Mexico, Africa, and China. Cultures that exist in these nations should not be confused with ethnic cultures in the United States.

Linking Multiethnic and Global Education by Helping Students Develop Interrelated Identifications

Despite some problems that may emerge, linking multiethnic and global education can result in important learning outcomes if proper precautions are taken. Multiethnic and global education are related because of the similarity in the skills, attitudes, and behaviors that both reform movements are trying to help students develop. Both multiethnic and global education have as major goals helping students to develop cross-cultural competency, (the knowledge, attitudes, skills, and abilities needed to function in diverse cultural settings) and helping students to develop the ability to view events, situations, and problems from the perspectives of different ethnic and nationality groups.

Multiethnic and global education are related in still another important way: students can develop clarified and reflective global identifications only after they have developed clarified and reflective *ethnic* and *national* identifications. The rest of this chapter discusses the need for the school curriculum to help students develop three interrelated identifications: *ethnic, national, and global.*

Ethnic, National, and Global Identifications

In this chapter, I am defining *identification* as "a social-psychological process involving the assimilation and internalization of the values, standards, expectations, or social roles of another person or persons . . . into one's behavior and self-conception.[5] When an individual develops an identification with a particular group he or she "internalizes the interests, standards, and role expectations of the group."[6] Identification is an evolving, dynamic, complex, and ongoing process and not a static or unidimensional conceptualization. All individuals belong to many different groups and consequently develop multiple group identifications. Students have a sexual identification, a family identification, a racial identification, as well as identifications with many other formal and informal groups.

A major assumption of this chapter is that all students come to school with ethnic identifications, whether they are conscious or unconscious. Many Anglo-American students are consciously aware of their national identifications as *Americans* but are not consciously aware of the fact that they have internalized the values, standards, norms, and behaviors of the Anglo-American ethnic group. Students who are Afro-Americans, Jewish Americans, Mexican Americans and Italian Americans are usually consciously aware of both their ethnic and national identifications. However, many students from all ethnic groups come to school with confused, unexamined and nonreflective ethnic and national identifications and with almost no global identification or consciousness.

Identity is a global concept that relates to all that we are. Our societal quest for a single, narrow definition of "American" has prevented many Americans from getting in touch with that dimension of their identity that relates to ethnicity. Ethnic identification for many Americans is a very important part of their personal identity. The individual who has a confused, nonreflective or negative ethnic identification lacks one of the essential ingredients for a healthy and positive personal identity.

The school should help students to develop three kinds of highly interrelated identifications that are of special concern to multiethnic educators: an *ethnic,* a *national* and a *global* identification. The school should help students to develop ethnic, national, and global identifications that are *clarified, reflective, and positive.* Individuals who have *clarified* and *reflective* ethnic, national, and global identifications understand how these identifications developed, are able to thoughtfully and objectively examine their ethnic group, nation, and world, and understand both the personal and public implications of these identifications.

Individuals who have *positive* ethnic, national, and global identifications evaluate their ethnic, national, and global communities highly and are proud of these identifications. They have both the desire and competencies needed to take actions that will support and reinforce the values and norms of their ethnic, national, and global communities. Consequently, the school should not only be concerned about helping students to develop reflective ethnic, national, and global identifications; it should also help them to acquire the cross-cultural competencies (which consist of knowledge, skills, attitudes, and abilities) needed to function effectively within their ethnic, national, and world communities.

Ethnic Identification

The school within a pluralistic democratic nation should help ethnic students develop clarified, reflective, and positive ethnic identifications. This does not mean that the school should encourage or force ethnic minority students who have identifications with the Anglo-American ethnic group or who have identifications with several ethnic groups to give up these identifications. However, it does mean that the school will help all students develop an understanding of their ethnic group identifications, objectively examine their ethnic groups, better understand the relationship between their ethnic groups and other ethnic groups, and learn the personal and public implications of their ethnic group identifications and attachments.

A positive and clarified ethnic identification is of primary importance to students beginning in their first years of life. However, rather than help students develop positive and reflective ethnic identifications, historically the school and other social institutions have taught non-Anglo ethnic groups to be ashamed of their ethnic affiliations and characteristics. Social and public institutions have forced many individuals who are Polish Americans, Italian Americans, and Jewish Americans to experience self-alienation, desocialization, and to reject family heritages and cultures. Many members of these ethnic groups have denied important aspects of their ethnic cultures and changed their names in order to attain full participation within the school and other American institutions. However, we should not deny the fact that many ethnic individuals consciously denied their family heritages in order to attain social, economic, and educational mobility. However, within a pluralistic democratic society individuals should not have to give up all of their meaningful ethnic traits and attachments in order to attain structural inclusion into society.

National Identification

The school should also help each student acquire a clarified, reflective, and positive national or American identification and related cross-cultural competencies. Each American student should develop a commitment to American democratic ideals, such as human dignity, justice, and equality. The school should also help students to acquire the attitudes, beliefs and skills they need to become effective participants in the nation's republic. Thus, the development of social participation skills and activities should be major goals of the school curriculum within a democratic pluralistic nation such as the United States.[7] Students should be provided opportunities for social participation activities whereby they can take action on issues and problems that are consistent with American democratic values. Citizenship education and social participation activities are integral parts of a sound school curriculum.

The American national identification and related citizenship competencies are important for all American citizens, regardless of their ethnic group membership and ethnic affiliations. The national American identification should be acknowledged and promoted in all educational programs related to ethnicity and education. However, we should not equate an American identification and the American culture with an Anglo-American culture and an Anglo-American identification. Individuals can have a wide range of cultural and linguistic traits and characteristics and still be reflective and effective American citizens.

Individuals can have ethnic allegiances and characteristics and yet endorse overarching and shared American values and ideals as long as their ethnic values and behaviors do not violate or contradict American democratic values and ideals. Educational programs should recognize and reflect the multiple identifications that students are developing. In fact, and I will discuss this in more detail later, I believe that students can develop a reflective and positive national identification only after they have attained reflective, clarified, and positive ethnic identifications. This is as true for Anglo-American students as it is for Jewish American, Black, or Italian American students. Often Anglo-Americans do not view themselves as an ethnic group. However, sociologically they have many of the same traits and characteristics of other American ethnic groups, such as a sense of peoplehood, unique behavioral values and norms, and unique ways of perceiving the world.[8]

Anglo-American students who believe that their ethnic group is superior to other ethnic groups and who have highly ethnocentric and racist attitudes do not have clarified, reflective, and positive ethnic identifications. Their ethnic identifications are based on the negative characteristics of other ethnic groups and have not been reflectively and objectively examined. Many Anglo-American and other ethnic individuals have ethnic identifications that are nonreflective and unclarified. It is not possible for students with unreflective and totally subjective ethnic identifications to develop positive and reflective national American identifications because ethnic enthnocentrism is inconsistent with American creed values such as human dignity, freedom, equality, and justice.

It is important for ethnic group individuals who have historically been victims of discrimination to develop positive and reflective ethnic identifications before they will be able to develop clarified national identifications. It is difficult for Polish-American, Jewish-American or Mexican-American students to support the rights of other ethnic groups or the ideals of the nation state when they are ashamed of their ethnicity or feel that their ethnic group is denied basic civil rights and opportunities.

Many educators assume that in order to be loyal American citizens, students must acquire the Anglo-Saxon Protestant culture and an Anglo-American identification. These educators assume that American means the same as Anglo-American. This popular but inaccurate notion of American culture and identity is perpetuated by the popular media and by many school textbooks.

This is a widespread misinterpretation of American life and society. While Anglo-Saxon Protestants have profoundly influenced our society and culture (and in many ways very constructively—such as their influence on our political ideals and ideologies), other ethnic groups, such as Jewish Americans, Blacks and Mexican Americans have deeply affected American literature, music, arts, and values.

While the school should help students to clarify and examine their national identifications, we need new and more accurate conceptualizations of the nature of American society and culture.

Global Identifications

It is essential that we help students to develop clarified, reflective, and positive ethnic and national identifications. However, because we live in a global society in which the solution of the earth's problems requires the cooperation of all the nations of the world, it is also important for students to develop global identifications and the knowledge, attitudes, skills, and abilities needed to become effective and influential citizens in the world community. The President's Commission on Foreign Language and International Studies writes cogently about the need to help students develop global interests and perspectives and the lack of global education in American schools:

A nation's welfare depends in large measure on the intellectual and psychological strengths that are derived from the perceptive visions of the world beyond its own boundaries. On a planet shrunken by the technology of instant communications, there is little safety behind a Maginot Line of scientific and scholarly isolationism. In our schools and colleges as well as our public media of communications, and in the everyday dialogue within our communities, the situation cries out for a better comprehension of our place and our potential in a world that, though it still expects much from America, no longer takes American supremacy for granted. Nor, the Commission believes, do this country's children and youths, and it is for them, and their understanding of their own society, that an international perspective is indispensable. Such a perspective is lacking in most educational programs now.[9]

The Need for a Delicate Balance of Identifications

In a paper presented at an annual meeting of the National Council for the Social Studies, Professor Nagayo Homma of the University of Toyko points out that ethnic and national identifications may prevent the development of effective global commitments and the cooperation among nations that is needed to solve the world's global problems. He writes of this paradox:

> The starting point of our quest for a global perspective should be the realization that the world today is a world of paradox. On the one hand, we live in the age of increasing interdependence among nations and growing awareness of our common destiny as occupants of the "only one earth."
> ... But, at the same time, nationalism is as strong as ever, and within a nation we often witness a movement of tribalism, an assertion of ethnicity, a communitarian experiment, and, according to some critics and scholars, an ominous tendency toward narcissism. Apparently the force for integration and the force for fragmentation are working simultaneously in our world.[10]

Homma points out that nationalism and national identifications and attachments in most nations of the world are strong and tenacious. Strong nationalism that is nonreflective will prevent students from developing reflective and positive global identifications. Nonreflective and unexamined ethnic identifications and attachments may prevent the development of a cohesive nation and a unified national ideology. While we should help ethnic youths to develop reflective and positive ethnic identifications, students must also be helped to clarify and strengthen their identifications as American citizens—which means that they will develop and internalize American Creed values such as justice, human dignity, and equality.

Students need to develop a delicate balance of ethnic, national, and global identifications and attachments. However, in the past educators have often tried to develop strong national identifications by repressing ethnicity and making ethnic Americans, including many Euro-ethnic Americans, ashamed of their ethnic roots and families. Schools taught ethnic youths "shame," as William Greenbaum has compassionately written.[11] This is an unhealthy and dysfunctional approach to building national solidarity and reflective nationalism and to shaping a nation in which all of its citizens endorse its overarching values such as democracy and human dignity and yet maintain a sense of ethnic pride and identification.

I hypothesize that ethnic, national and global identifications are developmental in nature and that an individual can attain a healthy and reflective national identification only when he or she has acquired a healthy and reflective ethnic identification; and that individuals can develop a reflective and positive global identification only after they have a realistic, reflective, and positive national identification. (See Figure 14.1)

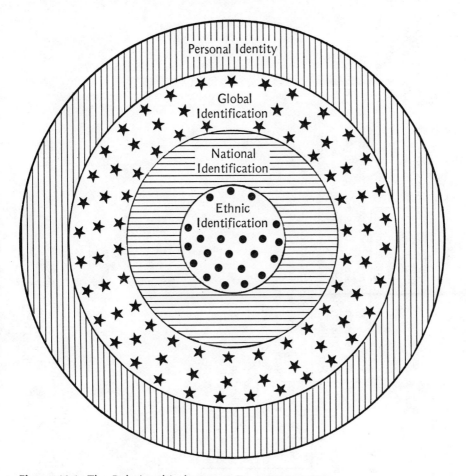

Figure 14.1. The Relationship between Personal Identity and Ethnic, National, and Global Identifications. Personal identity is the "I" that results from the life-long binding together of the many threads of a person's life. These threads include experience, culture, heredity, as well as identifications with significant others and many different groups, such as one's ethnic group, nation, and global community.

Individuals can develop a commitment to and an identification with a nation state and the national culture only when they believe that they are a meaningful and important part of that nation and that it acknowledges, reflects, and values their culture and them as individuals. A nation that alienates and does not meaningfully and structurally include an ethnic group into the national culture runs the risk of creating alienation within that ethnic group and of fostering separatism and separatist movements and ideologies.[12] Students will find it very difficult if not impossible to de-

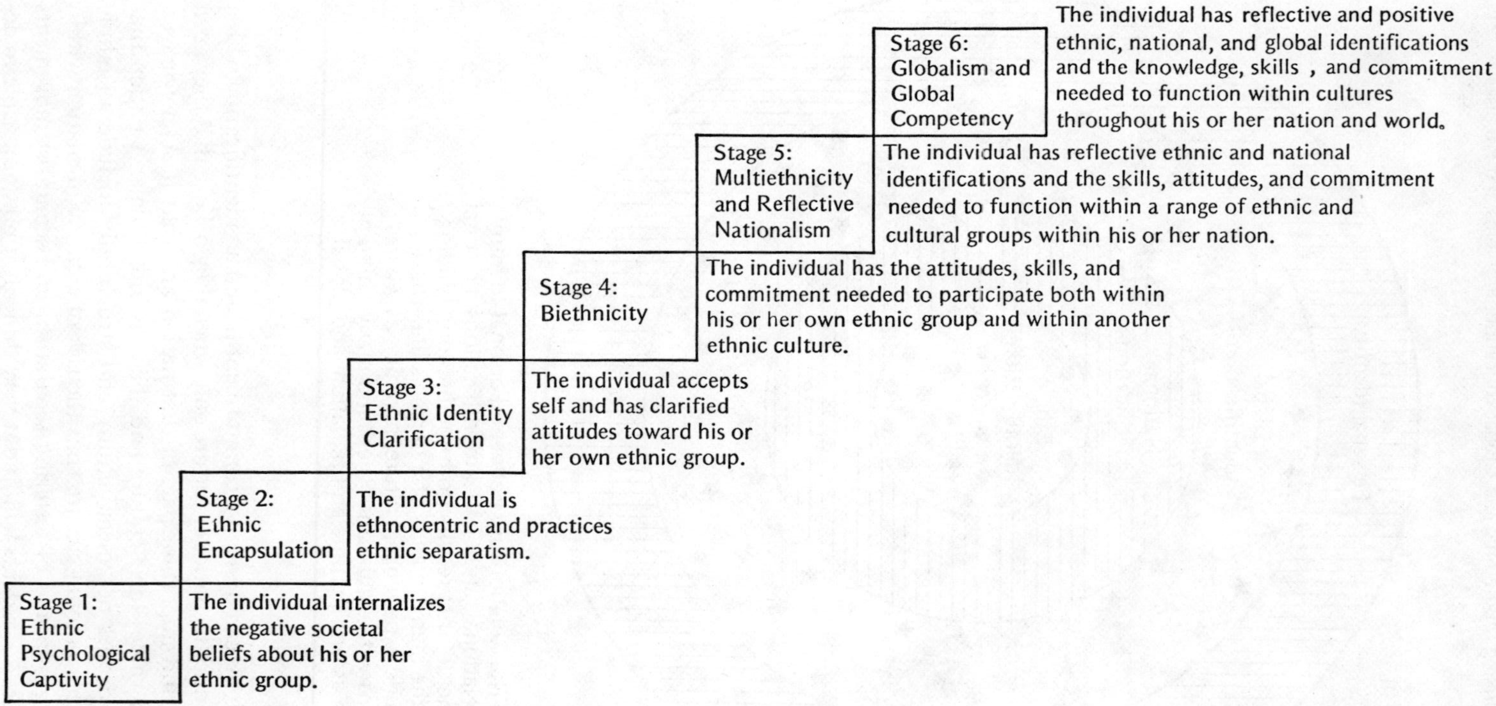

Stage 1:
Ethnic
Psychological
Captivity

The individual internalizes the negative societal beliefs about his or her ethnic group.

Stage 2:
Ethnic
Encapsulation

The individual is ethnocentric and practices ethnic separatism.

Stage 3:
Ethnic Identity
Clarification

The individual accepts self and has clarified attitudes toward his or her own ethnic group.

Stage 4:
Biethnicity

The individual has the attitudes, skills, and commitment needed to participate both within his or her own ethnic group and within another ethnic culture.

Stage 5:
Multiethnicity
and Reflective
Nationalism

The individual has reflective ethnic and national identifications and the skills, attitudes, and commitment needed to function within a range of ethnic and cultural groups within his or her nation.

Stage 6:
Globalism and
Global
Competency

The individual has reflective and positive ethnic, national, and global identifications and the knowledge, skills , and commitment needed to function within cultures throughout his or her nation and world.

Figure 14.2. The Expanding Identifications of Ethnic Youths: A Typology. This figure illustrates the author's hypothesis that students must have clarified and positive ethnic identifications (Stage 3) before they can attain reflective and positive national and global identifications (Stages 5 and 6).

velop reflective global identification within a nation state that perpetuates a nonreflective and blind nationalism.

The Expanding Identification of Ethnic Youths: A Typology

We should first help ethnic students develop healthy and positive ethnic identifications; they can then begin to develop reflective national and global identifications. A typology of the stages of ethnicity that describes the developmental nature of ethnic, national, and global identifications and clarification is presented in chapter 9. This typology assumes that individuals can be classified according to their ethnic identification and development. This typology, as summarized in Figure 14.2, illustrates the hypothesis that students must have clarified and positive ethnic identifications (Stage 3) before they can attain clarified and reflective national and global identifications (Stages 5 and 6). As pointed out in chapter 9, movement among the stages may be upward or downward. Some individuals, because of their socialization, may never experience a particular stage; some individuals may never experience Stage 1 or Stage 2. However, I am hypothesizing that the Stage 2 individual must experience Stage 3 in order to reach Stage 4. See chapter 9 for a detailed discussion of the complexity of this typology.

Summary

Educators should attempt to link and relate multiethnic and global education because of the common goals these two educational reform movements are trying to help students attain and because of the widespread fragmentation in the school curriculum. Since both multiethnic and global education have unique contributions to make to the general education of students and because they are in many ways distinct, efforts made to link multiethnic and global education should maintain the uniqueness of each reform movement. Educators should also take special precautions to assure that domestic ethnic cultures in the United States are not confused with the cultures of nations that are the original homelands of American ethnic groups.

During their socialization, students develop multiple group identifications. The school should help ethnic students develop three kinds of identifications that are of special concern to multiethnic educators: an *ethnic,* a *national,* and a *global* identification. To successfully help students to develop ethnic, national, and global identifications that are clarified, reflective and positive, the school must first recognize the importance of each of these identifications to students and to the nation state and acknowledge their developmental character. It is very difficult for students to develop clarified and positive national identifications and commitments until they have acquired positive and clarified ethnic identifications. Students will be able to develop clarified, reflective, and positive global identifications only after they have acquired thoughtful and clarified national identifications.

Most of the nation's schools are not giving students the kinds of experiences they need to develop clarified, reflective, and positive ethnic, national, and global identifications. Most of the nation's schools are Anglocentric in their cultures and orientations. American culture is frequently conceptualized as Anglo-American culture in the nation's schools. Students are often encouraged or forced to develop a commitment to Anglo-Saxon values and culture and identifications with Anglo-American culture and institutions. This Anglo-centric approach to education forces students who belong to non-Anglo-Saxon ethnic groups to deny their ethnic identifications and cultures and to experience self-alienation and shame. The Anglocentric approach to education also prevents students from developing reflective global awareness, skills, and identities.

Notes

1. Norman V. Overly, "A Perspective on Global Studies," in Norman V. Overly and Richard D. Kimpston, eds., *Global Studies: Problems and Promises for Elementary Teachers* (Washington, D.C.: Association for Supervision and Curriculum Development, 1976), pp. 1–8.
2. Seymour H. Fersh, "Studying Other Cultures: Looking Outward Is 'In,' " in James M. Becker and Howard D. Mehlinger, eds., *International Dimensions in the Social Studies* (Washington, D.C.: National Council for the Social Studies, 1968), pp. 122–144.
3. Lee F. Anderson, "Education and Social Science in the Context of an Emerging Global Society," in Becker and Mehlinger, *International Dimensions in the Social Studies*, pp. 78–97.
4. Carlos E. Cortés, "Multicultural Education and Global Education: Natural Partners in the Quest for a Better World," in *Curricular Dimensions of Global Education* (Philadelphia: Pennsylvania Department of Education and Citizen Education, Research for Better Schools, 1979), p. 84.
5. George A. Theodorson and Achilles G. Theodorson, *A Modern Dictionary of Sociology* (New York: Barnes and Noble Books, 1969), pp. 194–195.
6. Ibid., p. 195.
7. James A. Banks with Ambrose A. Clegg, Jr., *Teaching Strategies for the Social Studies: Inquiry, Valuing and Decision-Making*, 2nd ed. (Reading, Mass.: Addison-Wesley, 1977). See especially chapter 14, "Decision-Making and Social Action Strategies."

8. Milton M. Gordon, *Assimilation in American Life: The Role of Race, Religion and National Origins* (New York: Oxford University Press, 1964).

9. *Strength Through Wisdom: A Critique of U.S. Capability,* A Report to the President's Commission on Foreign Language and International Studies (Washington, D.C.: U.S. Government Printing Office, November 1979), p. 2.

10. Nagayo Homma, "The Quest for a Global Perspective: A Japanese View," a paper presented as a keynote address at the 59th Annual Meeting of the National Council for the Social Studies, November 23, 1979, Portland, Oregon, p. 1.

11. William Greenbaum, "America in Search of a New Ideal: An Essay on the Rise of Pluralism," *Harvard Educational Review* 44 (August 1974), p. 431.

12. An example of this phenomenon is the situation of the French Canadians. See Frank G. Vallee, Mildred Schwartz, and Frank Darkness, "Ethnic Assimilation and Differentiation in Canada," in Bernard R. Blishen, Frank E. Jones, Kaspar D. Naegele, and John Porter, eds., *Canadian Society: Sociological Perspectives,* 3rd ed. abridged (Toronto: Macmillan of Canada, 1971), pp. 390–400.

15

Ethnicity and Citizenship Education

Citizenship education should help students acquire the knowledge, skills, and values needed to make reflective public decisions consistent with American democratic ideals. The effective citizen within a democratic nation-state has a commitment to the overarching and shared national values and the skills, competencies, and commitment to act on them. The effective democratic citizen also takes actions to promote the shared and idealized values of the nation state. A major goal of civic education in a pluralistic, democratic nation is to help students acquire the values and the competencies needed to engage in successful and humane social and political action.[1]

Ethnic Groups and National Values

To develop *clarified, reflective,* and *positive* commitments and identifications with their nation state and its overarching values, the diverse ethnic groups within a culturally pluralistic nation such as the United States or Canada must perceive themselves as legitimate groups that are structurally included into the fabric of the social, economic, and political institutions in society. Individuals and groups who have clarified and reflective national attachments and identifications understand how these identifications and attachments developed; and are able to thoughtfully and objectively examine their nation, and understand both the personal and public implications of their national identifications. Individuals and groups who have *positive* national attachments and identifications evaluate their national identifications highly and are proud of their national attachments and affiliations.

Many members of ethnic groups within modernized Western nation states, while deeply loyal and patriotic citizens, have conflicting attachments to their nation states and often experience political alienation and anomie. Groups such as the Chamorros in Guam, the French and Indians in Canada, and Blacks and Puerto Ricans in the United States often feel alienated because their contributions to their national cultures have not been sufficiently recognized or legitimized and because they have not been given opportunities to fully participate in the institutions of their nation states, or to fully share in the benefits of modernization and high technology. These alienated ethnic groups often feel that they do not have a stake in the dominant societies of their nations or territories. Their shared sense of alienation and deprivation helps to maintain tight ethnic boundaries and ethnic communities.

Groups that are excluded from full participation in the nation state in which they are legal citizens and from the mainstream societies in which they live are likely to focus on particularistic concerns and goals rather than on the universalistic needs and problems of the nation state. Politically powerless and lower-status ethnic groups within a society, such as the Puerto Ricans and Indians in the United States, the North Africans in France, and the West Indians and Asians in Great Britain, are often so engrossed by their own problems of powerlessness, alienation, poverty, and institutionalized racism, that they devote little attention to the overarching problems of the nation state that are shared by all groups in their societies.

Ethnic groups that are structurally excluded, politically marginal, and that experience institutionalized discrimination within their nation-states, are likely to interpret both domestic and international events from particularistic perspectives, especially if the ethnic group has experienced a diaspora, still has attachments to its original homeland, perceives its members as marginal citizens, and has a distinctive ethnic culture and a cogent sense of peoplehood.

Jewish, Cuban, and Greek citizens of the United States often interpret world events that affect Israel, Cuba, and Greece from perspectives that are influenced by their ethnic affiliations and senses of kinship with their original homelands. Members of these groups often experience psychological conflicts when they believe that the interests of their original homelands and those of the United States are inconsistent. Jews are citizens of many nation-states throughout the world. Consequently, Jewish Americans are likely to be concerned about the human rights of Jews in nations as far apart as Brazil and the Soviet Union.

Ethnicity and Citizenship within a Democracy

I have stated that structural exclusion of ethnic groups within a nation-state is likely to promote and support ethnic group attachments, strong ethnic boundaries, and to foster particularistic and primordial concerns among ethnic group members.* What are the implications of primordial

---

* By primordial attachment is meant one that stems from the "givens"—or, more precisely, as culture is inevitably involved in such matters, the assumed "givens"—of social existence: immediate contiguity and kin connection mainly, but beyond them the giveness that stems from being born into a particular religious community, speaking a particular language, or even a dialect of a language, and following particular social practices. These congruities of blood, speech, custom, and so on, are seen to have an ineffable, and at times overpowering, coerciveness in and of themselves. One is bound to one's kinsman, one's neighbor, one's fellow believer, ipso facto; as the result not merely of personal affection, practical necessity, common interest, or incurred obligation, but at least in great part by virtue of some unaccountable absolute import attributed to the very tie itself.

Clifford Geertz, *The Interpretation of Cultures* (New York: Basic Books, 1973), p. 259.

and ethnic attachments for citizenship and citizenship education within a modernized, democratic nation such as the United States? Can and should ethnic attachments coexist with modernity in a pluralistic democratic nation such as the United States? Should the school curriculum within a modernized or a modernizing democratic nation-state recognize, acknowledge, and legitimize the ethnic attachments and identifications of ethnic youths? These complex questions are raised by the coexistence of ethnicity and modernity within Western democratic nation-states. I will explore these questions in this chapter. Within the last decade, the expressions of ethnic affiliations and primordial attachments increased significantly, thus making the question of the coexistence of ethnicity and modernity within society even more complex.[2]

The Assimilationist and Multiethnic Assumptions

The assimilationist assumes that the most effective way to reduce strong ethnic boundaries, primordial attachments, and ethnic affiliations with a nation-state, is to provide excluded ethnic and racial groups with opportunities to experience equality in the nation's social, economic, and political institutions.[3] As they begin to participate more fully in the universalistic or mainstream society and its institutions, argues the assimilationist, lower-status ethnic groups will focus less on particularistic concerns and more on national issues and priorities.

When ethnic groups experience equality, suggests the assimilationist, ethnicity and primordial attachments die of their own weight. Individuals who endorse a multiethnic or bicultural ideology believe that equality will not eliminate ethnicity from modernized democratic societies but that ethnicity will take new forms within an equal society and that ethnic traits will become part of the universal culture shared by all.[4] Ethnic characteristics within an equal society would become universalized. All ethnic groups, according to the multiethnic ideologist, share power and have equal-status interactions in an equal and just society. The assimilationist views the ideal society as one that has no traces of ethnicity. All groups would share a common Anglicized culture. The multiethnic ideologist believes that the ideal society is characterized by equal status among ethnic groups and a universal culture that consists of universalized ethnic characteristics.

The Assimilationist Fallacy

Apter, while acknowledging that he is an assimilationist and a pluralist,* calls the assimilationist position the "assimilationist fallacy."[5] This position

* When he calls himself a pluralist, Apter is using "pluralism" in the political science sense and not in the anthropological sense of "cultural pluralism."

Political pluralism is the name applied to those political doctrines, ranging from extreme to modest claims on behalf of group interests in society, which assert that holds that as modernization occurs, ethnic groups experience social, political, and economic equality, enlightenment eventuates, and commitments to ethnic and primordial atachments weaken and disappear. When modernization arises, ethnicity disappears and vice versa. Assimilationists see ethnicity and primordial attachments as fleeting and temporary within an increasingly modernized society. They view modernity and ethnicity as contradictory concepts. Ethnicity, argues the assimilationist, promotes divisions, exhumes ethnic conflicts, and leads to the Balkanization of society. Assimilationists such as Patterson also argue that ethnic groups promote group rights over individual rights and that individual rights are paramount in a democratic pluralistic nation. He writes:

> The defense of pluralism not only neglects individuality; much worse, an emphasis on group diversity and group tolerance works against a respect for individuality. This is what I call the *pluralist fallacy*, which originates in the failure to recognize a basic paradox in human interaction; the greater the diversity and cohesiveness of groups in a society, the smaller the diversity and personal autonomy of individuals in that society.[6] (Emphasis added.)

Assimilationists see the continuing expressions and existence of ethnicity within modernized democratic nation states as a "pathological condition."[7] Ethnic affiliations and cultures still exist in modernized societies, argues the assimilationist, because political and economic equality for ethnic groups such as Blacks, Indians, Mexican Americans, and Puerto Ricans, have been only partially attained. Thus, the assimilationist ideal is viable and possible but has yet to be completely realized. This will happen when inequality and structural exclusion of ethnic groups, such as Blacks and Mexican Americans, ends. Include ethnic groups into the structure of society and enable them to experience political and economic mobility, and ethnicity will, for all important purposes, disappear. Some symbolic forms of ethnicity might remain within the equal society, such as St. Patrick's Day and Chinese New Year, but ethnicity will not be an important social, cultural, or political force in society. This is the assimilationist's argument.

---

certain groups (e.g., family, church, union, local government) embody important social values prior to and independent of their authorization or approval by the state. The scope of pluralism is not usually interpreted as including anarchism or revolutionary syndicalism because, unlike such theories, most pluralists retain for government the functional responsibilities of compulsory citizenship and taxation, and admit the necessity for an inclusive governmental authority transcending group associations to regulate, direct, or coordinate, inter alia the domestic economy, personal liberties, national security, and foreign affairs.

Julius Gould and William L. Kolb, eds., *A Dictionary of the Social Sciences* (New York: Free Press, 1964), p. 507.

As Apter perceptively states, the assimilationist vision and ideal is not so much wrong as it is an incomplete and inadequate explanation of ethnic realities in modernized, pluralistic, and democratic nation states. Writes Apter:

> Clearly [modernizing] historical forces are at work. There is a widening of universalistic and pluralistic beliefs. However, primordialism is at work too. It pops up where we least expect it, in Scotland, Wales, and Quebec, and among the Basques, Catalans, and Bretons. Old primordialisms can fade away and yet revive. The reasons why are puzzling to pluralists and liberals, who have not expected it or have considered it to be of passing significance.[8]

A central fallacy of the assimilationist position is the assumption that when the "high culture" of modernization develops within a nation state, primordial and ethnic affiliations disappear into thin air and are no longer a "problem" for mainstream political leaders and modernizers. States Apter, "The enlightenment myth on which the assimilationist fallacy rests is that modern history is moving in a single direction away from provincial and local attachments and toward a greater common consciousness of the world."[9] However, as the ethnic revitalization movements of the 1960s and 1970s made dramatically and sometimes poignantly clear, ethnic attachments and identifications can become cogent forces within a modernized democratic society when particular political, social, and economic events develop.

The ethnic revitalization movements of the 1960s and 1970s caught mainstream social scientists almost completely by surprise and without the conceptual frameworks to either understand or adequately interpret these movements. When they emerged, most established social scientists still accepted some form of Robert E. Park's notions about ethnic groups in society. Park believed that race and ethnic relations proceeded through four inevitable stages: *contact, conflict, accommodation,* and *assimilation.*[10] When the Black civil rights movement of the 1960s and the consequent Black power movement emerged, it was clear that Park's conceptualization inadequately explained ethnic relations in modernized democratic nation states.

Ethnic Revitalization Movements Develop and Spread

Ethnic attachments and movements are more likely to develop among structurally and politically excluded ethnic groups than among ethnic groups who perceive themselves as included within the fabric of society and as beneficiaries of technology and modernization. Blacks led the ethnic revitalization movements in the United States because of their historic and profound discrimination in this nation and because of their rising expectations caused by social and political events in the 1950s and 1960s. However, shortly after the Black-led ethnic revitalization movement arose, ethnic groups such as Mexican Americans, American Indians, Puerto Ricans, and Asian Americans echoed concerns similar to those raised by Blacks and started their own ethnic movements.

Ethnic revitalization movements then spread like a chain reaction among White ethnic groups such as Italians, Poles, and other Slavic-American ethnic groups. The rise of White ethnic movements was signaled by the publication of Michael Novak's book, *The Rise of the Unmeltable Ethnics.*[11] This book was a sign that the time had come for ethnic expressions in modernized America. Some writers argue that the White ethnic movement is not genuine or legitimate and that it arose as a racist reaction to the civil rights movement led by Blacks. It is designed, some argue, to divert attention from the plight of non-White ethnic groups.[12] However, Judith Herman believes that the movement is both genuine and authentic.[13]

Many members of White ethnic groups who had in the past perceived themselves as full beneficiaries of modernization and high technology organized ethnic movements to fight for more political, economic, and cultural rights.[14] Ethnic expressions became strong in White ethnic communities in Boston when court-ordered desegregation took place there in the 1970s. The ethnic attachments and feelings of Anglo-Americans heightened as other ethnic groups attacked their values and behaviors and blamed them for the national mentality which resulted in the Vietnam war tragedy, the destruction of the nation's environment, and for perpetuating institutional and cultural racism which victimized other ethnic groups.[15] Jewish expressions of ethnicity became more cogent in the 1960s and 1970s when tensions developed between Jews and ethnic groups such as Blacks and Puerto Ricans over issues such as affirmative action and bilingual education, and as Israel's position in the world seemed to many Jews increasingly precarious.

These examples of ethnic movements and behaviors indicate that both ethnicity and modernity can and do coexist within society and that various political, social, and economic events influence whether members of particular ethnic groups act universal or primordial within particular times, settings, and cultural contexts. These examples also illustrate that ethnic attachments not only exist within ethnic groups that have been historic victims of institutionalized racism such as Blacks and American Indians, but that highly acculturated ethnic groups, such as Irish Americans and Anglo Americans, often act ethnic and express ethnic attachments and affiliations. *Ethnicity and assimilationism coexist in modernized democratic nation-states.* Writes Apter, "The two tendencies, toward and against primordialism, can go on at the same time. Indeed, the more development and growth that take place, the more some primordial groupings have to gain by their parochialism."[16]

Ethnicity and the Needs of Individuals and Groups

Ethnic attachments and assimilationism coexist within modernized and modernizing societies for a number of complex reasons, some of which social scientists do not understand. They coexist in part because of what the assimilationist calls the "pathological condition," i.e., ethnic groups such as Blacks and Mexican Americans maintain strong attachments to their ethnic groups and cultures in part because they have been excluded from full participation in the nation's social, economic, and political institutions.

However, members of these ethnic groups, as well as members of ethnic groups such as Poles, Italians, and Greeks, maintain ethnic affiliations and ethnic attachments for more fundamental psychological and sociological reasons. It helps them to fulfill some basic psychological and sociological needs which the "thin" culture of modernization leaves starving. Apter comments insightfully on this point: ". . .[P]rimordialism is a response to the thinning out of enlightenment culture, the deterioration of which is a part of the process of democratization and pluralization. . . . Assimilationism itself then vitiates the enlightenment culture. As it does, it leaves what might be called a primordial space, a space people try to fill when they believe they have lost something fundamental and try to recreate it."[17]

Ethnic individuals also hold onto their ethnic attachments because they help them to satisfy communal and personal needs. Ethnic group membership provides individuals with a bond that enables them to consider themselves a group that is distinct and unique from other groups.[18] Ethnic group members share a culture that binds them together. This shared culture equips individuals with a sense of belonging. Within a complex and impersonal modernized society, ethnic group identification, and membership provide individuals with a "familiar and reassuring anchor in a climate of turbulence and uncertainty."[19] Ethnic group membership also provides individuals with a foundation for self-definition, a sense of belonging, of shared traditions, and a sense of interdependence of fate.[20]

Schooling, Citizenship Education, and Ethnic Minorities

I have argued that ethnic groups that are structurally excluded from society often focus on particularistic issues and concerns rather than on the universal concerns of their nation-states. One implication of this observation is that schools, in order to support effective civic education for all youths, should promote equality and should itself become a democratic institution which promotes social class, economic, and cultural democracy.

However, my analysis also suggests that structural inclusion and equity will not eliminate ethnic affiliations and primordial attachments. Ethnicity and modernity coexist in pluralistic democratic nation-states. Apter uses the analogy of the pendulum to describe the relationship between assimilationism and primordialism in modernized democratic nation-states. The pendulum between universalism and ethnicity continues to swing back and forth.[21]

My analysis of the nature of ethnicity within modernized democratic nation-states suggests that the school, in order to foster effective civic education for all youths, should recognize, legitimize, and respect the ethnic attachments of students and practice cultural democracy. Ethnic affiliations and attachments help students to satisfy important psychological and sociological needs caused by the thin culture of modernization. Civic education should also help students to attain the commitments and skills needed to participate in reflective and humane political action designed to reform our nation so that all groups in the United States will experience justice and equality.

Anglo-conformity and Citizenship Education

Historically, our nation, using the schools and other public institutions as its agents, have tried to shape its diverse racial and ethnic groups into one nation with shared characteristics, values, and goals by a policy of *Anglo-conformity*.[22] The goal of this policy is to eradicate the ethnic attachments and characteristics of individuals and groups and to force them to endorse Anglo-Saxon values, charcteristics, and behaviors. Within Anglo-conformity, ethnic youths experience the desocialization of their ethnic characteristics and the assimilation of Anglo-cultural characteristics. This process of Anglicization became known as "Americanization," since "American" was perceived by those in power and by those who controlled the public schools as the same as "Anglo-American."

Anglicization was perceived as consistent with modernization, whereas the ethnicity of non-Anglo ethnic youths was viewed as inconsistent with modernization and dysfunctional within a modernized democratic nation-state. *Assimilation into Anglo-Saxon Protestant culture became viewed as a necessary and essential condition for effective civic participation in the United States.* "American" became defined as "Anglo-American." Groups with non-Anglo-Saxon languages and cultural characteristics were viewed as un-American and often as unpatriotic and disloyal. Nativistic sentiments became especially pervasive and cogent when the nation faced a real or imagined threat—such as during the turn of the century when masses of Southern, Central, and Eastern European immigrants were entering the United States, and during the two great world wars.[23] A suspicion and distrust of all foreigners became rampant and widespread near the turn of the century. Occasionally, extreme events took place. In 1891, eleven Italian Americans were lynched in New Orleans during the height of American nativism, after being accused of murdering a police superintendent.[24] Immigrant groups were not only suspected of being disloyal and un-American, but of being radicals and communists.

The outbreak of World War I in Europe in 1914 increased the suspicion and distrust of immigrant groups in the United States and further stimulated nativistic feelings and groups. After the United States entered the war against Germany in 1917, the loyalty of German Americans to the United States was seriously questioned. German Americans became the victims of verbal and other forms of public and private abuse.

During World War II, the Japanese citizens of the United States were victimized by nativistic sentiments after Japan attacked the United States naval forces on Pearl Habor in 1941.[25] Historical scholarship now reveals that most Japanese Americans were loyal and patriotic citizens during the war and that none were found guilty of engaging in fifth column activities.[26] However, the Japanese were interned because they had physical and cultural characteristics inconsistent with the image of the "One Model American" held by the nation's military and political leaders and because they were perceived as stiff competitors by agribusinessmen on the West Coast. To the powerful military and political leaders, the Japanese Americans did not "look" like Americans but like "foreign enemies." Most American citizens remained conspicuously silent as 110,000 Japanese Americans were sent off to internment camps.

The attempt by the nation and the schools to shape a unified nation with shared values and characteristics by a policy of Anglo-conformity has to a large extent succeeded in the United States. Most European Americans, who constitute the largest immigrant-descendant group in the United States, consciously see themselves *first* as Americans and not as Irish, Welsh, German, or Swedes and then as Americans. Individual members of these ethnic groups tend to have weak ethnic identifications and strong national identifications.

Because of the cogency of Anglicization in American life, most members of European heritage groups in the United States are culturally Anglo-Saxons. They are members of the Anglo-American ethnic group, even though they may have a German or Swedish biological heritage or surname. Ethnicity, in its most important forms in a modernized society, consists of behavioral characteristics and psychological identifications, and not of biological traits and physical characteristics. Groups with the same or highly similar physical traits are members of both the same and very different ethnic groups. Individuals that most people in the United States would regard as Black, White, and racially mixed are all part of the Puerto Rican ethnic group in cities such as New York City and Chicago.[27]

However, the Anglo-conformity approach to shaping a nation with shared values and characteristics has been only partially successful. Some ethnic groups in the United States, for a variety of historical, cultural, economic, and biological reasons, have been unable and/or unwilling to become identical to Anglo-Americans in their values, behaviors, and cultural characteristics.

The experiences of some ethnic groups, such as Blacks, Indians, and Mexican Americans, have been and are characterized by societal contradictions. Anglo-Saxon cultural characteristics and values are presented to them as ideals to attain, yet they have been denied, sometimes through legal means and caste-like institutions and practices, the opportunities to acquire the behaviors and characteristics needed to become culturally like Anglo-Americans.[28] The cultures of these ethnic groups have often been harshly condemned in the nation's history, yet they have been and still are frequently denied opportunities to acquire alternative cultural characteristics and values. Throughout most of the nation's history, groups such as Blacks, Indians, and Mexican Americans, have tried to acquire Anglo-Saxon cultural characteristics and to become effective citizens in ways defined by the Anglo-conformity conceptualization of American citizenship.[29]

However, when the ethnic revitalization movements of the 1960s emerged, many members of structurally excluded ethnic groups such as Blacks, Indians, and Puerto Ricans, lost faith in the assimilationist ideal and advocated cultural pluralism.[30] Many ethnic individuals began to perceive the Anglo-conformity idea as a racist concept which required them to strive to attain the impossible—to become totally like White Anglo-Saxon Protestants in their values, behaviors, and physical characteristics. They realized that their skin color prevented them from becoming identical to White Anglo-Saxon Protestants. They also realized that they needed to hold onto important aspects of their cultural heritages and identities in order to satisfy many of their sociological and psychological needs. These ethnic groups began quests for ethnic pride and ethnic cultural components. They highlighted the positive and substantial contributions that cultural diversity makes to a pluralistic democratic nation such as the United States.

The Need for a Broader Conceptualization of "American"

We need a conception of *American* in our nation that is consistent with the ethnic and cultural diversity within our nation and world. The Anglo-Saxon Protestant culture is only one of the cultures in American society (albeit it is politically and economically the most powerful ethnic group in the United States). Other ethnic groups, such as Blacks and Mexican Americans, are just as American as Anglos, even though these groups have a wide range of cultures, dialects, languages, values, and behaviors. Jack Forbes, the noted student of American Indian cultures, argues compellingly that American Indians are in some ways the most *American* of the groups that make up the United States.[31] One can challenge Forbes's claim. However, ethnic groups such as Indians, Blacks, and Puerto Ricans are American because they are legal citizens of the United States and because they share the overarching values and ideals of the nation-state. This is true even though these ethnic groups often focus on particularistic concerns and issues and sometimes experience conflicting allegiances when they believe that their ethnic group interests and what are described as the universalistic interests of the nation state are in conflict.

Many Afro-Americans, for example, could not enthusiastsically support President Carter's campaign for human rights in other nations because they feel that they do not have full human rights in the United States. Many Blacks see human rights at home as a priority to human rights in other nations. Thus, many perceived President Carter's call for human rights in other nations as a political charade. Other ethnic groups in the United States, who feel that they are experiencing a high level of human rights in the United States or who are concerned about the human rights of their ethnic kin in other lands, such as Jewish Americans and Polish Americans, were probably more enthusiastic about Carter's human rights campaign.

The School as a Democratic Institution: Traditional Interpretations

To help ethnic youths attain structural inclusion and to develop clarified, reflective, and positive identifications and commitments to the nation-state, the school itself should promote cultural, ethnic, and social class democracy. The school should be a micro-democratic community that is just and that promotes social change consistent with American Creed values such as equality, justice, and human rights. Educational historians have traditionally described the American public school as a citadel of democracy that promotes democratic ideals, values, and social justice. This statement by Arthur Lean reflects the traditional view of democracy and public education:

> Like the democracy of which they are a manifestation, public schools have justified the faith of the American people, like other institutions, they are not perfect; like any institution, they have shortcomings. But their contributions have been significant and lasting. The United States would not be

so democratic, so prosperous, so satisfying to the individual, and so strong in mind and spirit as it is today were it not for the nation's record in developing and supporting public schools.[32]

Educational historians near the turn of the century, such as Cubberley and Monroe, saw the American school as a democratic institution that helped mold immigrant children into responsible adults who had democratic political attitudes, and the knowledge, skills, and abilities needed to experience upward social class mobility.[33] They viewed the school as the major institution within society that enabled immigrant and other poor youths to experience social class mobility and to become effective democratic citizens of the nation-state.

The Revisionists' Critiques of Schooling

In recent years, a number of revisionist educational historians and economists, such as Michael B. Katz, Colin Greer, Martin Carnoy, Samuel Bowles, and Herbert Gintis, have strongly attacked traditional interpretations of American schools, such as those written by Cubberley and Monroe.[34] These writers argue that rather than promoting social class mobility and cultural and political democracy, the schools reflect the social class stratifications of society and teach students political apathy and to fit into the class structure of society. The schools, they argue, educate for political apathy and not for political and social reform.

The revisionists argue that the public school was designed primarily to reinforce the status quo, to legitimize the positions of those in power, to perpetuate and reinforce the social class stratification that exists within society, to make students politically passive, and to perpetuate myths about lower class and minority groups in order to make them content with their social and economic conditions in society. Writes Carnoy:

> Rather than building independence and self-reliance among the poor in America, schools are used to ensure, as much as possible and apparently with some success, that those in the worst economic positions do not rebel against the system which represses them and identifies with leaders who would work within the framework of action set by the dominant ruling class. . . . Schooling as a colonial institution attempts to make children fit certain molds, to shape them to perform predetermined roles and tasks based on their social class.[35]

Bowles and Gintis also argue that the schools teach political apathy and reinforce the social class stratification in society.

> . . . [E]ducation helps defuse and depoliticize the potentially explosive class relations of the production process, and thus serves to perpetuate the social, political, and economic conditions through which a portion of the

product of labor is expropriated in the form of profits. .... Schools legitimate inequality through the ostensibly meritocratic manner by which they
reward and promote students, and allocate them to distinct positions in the
occupational hierarchy.[36]

Greer calls the belief that the schools promote social justice for poor and
minority youths "the great school legend" that has harmful consequences
for today's minority students. If the schools helped European immigrants
to experience upward social class mobility and is not helping groups such
as Blacks and Mexican Americans today, then groups such as Blacks and
Mexican Americans must have genetic deficiencies. This is how, according
to Greer, the great legend results in reasoning that harms today's ethnic minority youths.

How Valid Are the Revisionists' Critiques of Schooling?

The interpretations of schools set forth by writers such as Carnoy, Greer,
Bowles and Gintis, and Katz contrast sharply with traditional educational
literature about the nature and purpose of schooling and with popular
conventional wisdom about the public schools. Katz, for example, argues
that the schools of a century ago, and that schools today, were and are
"universal, tax-supported, free, compulsory, bureaucratic, racist, and class-
biased."[37] Traditional educational literature and popular beliefs about
schools suggest that they are democratic institutions that help poor and minority youths to experience social class mobility and equality.

The revisionist historians and economists have stimulated thoughtful
and creative dialogue about traditional assumptions about schools and
about the power and willingness of the school to promote social class and
political democracy. However, the revisionists have not escaped criticism
and rigorous analyses. Diane Ravitch has written a book-length critique of
their arguments and positions.[38] She argues that the revisionists have over-
simplified history, have been too purist and ideological in their interpretations, and have not ackowledged the extent to which the public schools
have helped poor and minority youths to experience economic mobility.
She writes, "Because the demands of them are simultaneously liberal and
conservative. ... The continuing strength of the schools is due to the fact
that they have at least *partially fulfilled* the expectations of their differing
constituencies."[39] (Italics added)

How accurate and valid are the revisionist critiques of schooling? Because the school is only one of the educational institutions within society,
and because of the complex variables which influence student learning, occupational mobility, and political participation, it is very difficult for social
scientists and historians to resolve complex questions such as the extent to

which the school helps to bring about social and economic equality for minority youths. Because schools are social institutions that reflect the values, attitudes, and beliefs of the culture and society of which they are a part, the arguments and analyses of the revisionist historians and economists have much validity. Public schools are usually controlled by leaders in the business and professional communities. They are also tax supported. It is logical to assume that the schools reflect the values and attitudes of the peoples and groups who control them. Thus, in a society that is capitalistic, class stratified, and racist, it is reasonable to assume that its public schools will, at least to some extent, also be capitalistic, class stratified, and racist. Schools do not exist in a vacuum. They are social institutions which reflect the values and goals of the social systems of which they are a part.

However, the important question is not whether American public schools are capitalistic, bureaucratic, class stratified, and racist, but to what extent can American public schools be so characterized. The influences upon the public schools within a democratic society are complex, diverse, and conflicting. Our nation consists of realities such as racism and class stratification. However, as Myrdal points out in his landmark study of race relations in the United States, the "American Creed" and the values inherent within it, such as liberty, equality, justice, and fair opportunity, is a cogent ideal that is articulated by most institutions within the United States.[40]

Because the "American Creed" is institutionalized within our society, it is reasonable to assume that the ideals of the Creed are, to some extent, perpetuated in the nation's public schools. They are reflected, at the very least, to the extent that they are often taught in textbooks, with patriotic songs, legendary stories about national heroes, and with national symbols and myths. Thus, the revisionists are not wrong when they say that American schools are class stratified, capitalistic, and racist. However, they are misleading when they state or imply that the schools can be totally or completely so characterized.

The schools are racist and class stratified, but they, at least to some extent, also teach students American Creed values and ideals, such as equality, justice, and human rights. Consequently, the influences upon the schools are multiple and conflicting rather than singular and consistent as the revisionists sometimes imply. *The values which public schools teach or try to teach are contradictory and conflicting.* Children are often asked to read stories and sing songs that reflect American Creed values within a classroom setting that is racist and economically stratified. One could argue that the nondemocratic environment in which students are taught about American Creed values makes it impossible for them to inculcate democratic values and ideologies. However, my hunch is that some students learn both democratic and antidemocratic values in the public schools. This may sometimes result in the phenomenon which Myrdal calls the "American dilemma," i.e., with some students inculcating conflicting values related to justice and equality. Myrdal writes:

The "American dilemma" ... is the ever-raging conflict between, on the one hand, the valuations preserved on the general plane which we shall call the "American Creed," where the American thinks, talks, and acts under the influence of high national and Christian precepts, and, on the other hand, the valuations on specific planes of individual and group living, where personal and local interests; economic, social, and sexual jealousies; considerations of community prestige and conformity; group prejudice against particular persons or types of people; and all sorts of miscellaneous wants, impulses, and habits dominate his outlook.[41]

The Problems with the Grand Theories Used by the Revisionists

The revisionists, such as Bowles and Gintis and Carnoy and Katz, use *grand theories* to explain and interpret the American public school. Grand theories are all-embracing, unified explanations of events and phenomena.[42] Bowles and Gintis use a neo-Marxist theory to interpret American schools; Carnoy uses a "colonial domination" theory. He writes, "The domination of one people by another has taken place throughout history. This domination has been exercised for its own ends by a powerful group or class in a particular society."[43] One of the problems with social science grand theories is that researchers usually feel obligated to interpret their findings in ways that will support their theories.

The theory must remain intact. Observed phenomena and behavior must be interpreted in ways consistent with the theoretical framework used by the researcher. While grand theories are useful because they help the social scientists to order the universe and to explain and interpret relationships, they are also limiting because they often force researchers to depict extremes in order to make their observations and theoretical frameworks consistent.

Merton discusses the problems of social science grand theories and the advantages of middle range theories. Middle range "theories consist of limited sets of assumptions from which specific hypotheses are logically derived and confirmed by empirical investigation."[44] Merton believes that sociologists are not ready to develop grand theories because not enough preparatory work has been done. He states that grand theories cannot be developed until "a great mass of basic observations have been accumulated."[45]

When they are guided by grand theories, social scientists often formulate theories or use existing ones and then make their empirical observations. Consequently, their findings are described in ways that will fit the theory. This often results in descriptions of events and institutions that are extreme, and that are characterized by an inattention to details that the grand theory does not explain and by explanations that are incomplete and/or misleading.

The revisionist interpretations of public schools by historians and economists are not so much wrong as they are overdrawn and incomplete. Schools are racist, bureaucratic, social class stratified, and capitalistic. However, as Sowell, Ravitch, and Clark have pointed out, the public school can and does help many minority youths to escape poverty and to experience social class and economic mobility.[46] Most minority parents retain an unshaken faith in the power of the public schools to help their children attain upward social class mobility. While their faith in the public school may be overly optimistic, perceptions are enormously important in influencing behavior. Blacks and many other ethnic groups perceive the public school and formal education as one of the few means by which they can escape poverty and attain the benefits of a highly technological society. The important question before us is how can we reform the American public school so that it will become socially, culturally, and economically democratic and will help all youths to experience social class mobility and consequently become more effective and productive citizens of the nation-state.

Cultural Democracy and Citizenship Education

The most effective way for the schools to help students to develop the attitudes, values, and commitments needed to function effectively within a democratic nation-state is for the school to structure a total educational environment that enables students to experience democracy. Civic education involves the total school, as Mehlinger states: "Civic education is a process permeating the entire school. It exists in many planned and unplanned ways through extracurricular activities, the pattern of school governance, and the informal school culture."[47]

A public-issues curriculum and social action and participation activities can help students to develop the knowledge, skills, and commitments needed to function within a democracy.[48] However, because many ethnic youths have unclarified and conflicting national commitments and allegiances, the school should also help these students to develop clarified commitments to the nation-state. However, this can happen only when structurally and economically excluded ethnic and racial groups feel included into society and view themselves as legitimate citizens of the nation-state. The school can help this occur.

As the works by Jencks and Coleman indicate, the schools are probably limited in what they can do to help ethnic minority youths to attain structural inclusion into society and upward social mobility.[49] However, the school is a very important institution from which students learn many values, attitudes, and views of their ethnic groups and their cultures. *The school can play a significant role in legitimizing the cultures, values, and life-styles of minority groups and in helping them to gain a sense of inclusion into the fabric of society.* If the school accepts and legitimizes the cultures of ethnic minority youths, this will also affect the knowledge and attitudes of majority group children, many of whom will be policy makers and opinion makers in the future society. Consequently, the school's legitimization of the cultures of ethnic youths may very well have an impact on the norms and values of future institutions.

To legitimize, accept, and respect the cultures of ethnic minority youths, the school will need to practice what Julius Drachsler called "cultural democracy."[50] Cultural democracy "posits the right of ethnic groups in a democratic society to maintain their communal identity and their own subcultural values. . . . [D]emocratic values prescribe free choice not only for groups but also for individuals."[51] However, much evidence indicates that the school usually practices Anglo-conformity and cultural imperialism rather than cultural democracy. It usually forces non-Anglo ethnic youths to become alienated from their ethnic groups and to assimilate Anglo-Saxon cultural characteristics and values. Writes Castañeda:

> American public education has seriously jeopardized one of the three major features of American democracy. While American public education has continually attempted to keep alive the principles of political and economic democracy, it has been antagonistic to the principle of *cultural democracy,* the right of every American child to remain identified with his own ethnic, racial, or social group while at the same time exploring mainstream American cultural forms with regard to language, heritage, values, cognition, and motivation.[52]

Summary

Citizenship education should help students to develop the knowledge, skills, and values needed to participate in political action that will promote the nation's democratic ideals. To develop clarified, reflective, and positive commitments and identifications with their nation-state, the ethnic groups within a nation must perceive themselves as legitimate groups that are structurally included into the national society. Ethnic groups that are excluded from full participation in their nation-state have conflicting national identifications and often focus on particularistic concerns and problems rather than on the universal goals and problems of the nation-state.

The assimilationist assumes that ethnicity and particularistic concerns of ethnic groups can be eliminated by creating a just society in which ethnic groups will gain inclusion and equality. An analysis of the assimilationist position indicates that it does not adequately explain the nature of ethnicity in complex, modernized, and democratic nation-states. Ethnicity persists in modernized nation-states not only because of the exclusion of ethnic groups but because it helps individuals and groups to satisfy important psychological and sociological needs that are left unfilled by the "thin" culture of modernization.

To foster effective civic education, the school should promote social class and cultural democracy and legitimize the cultures of ethnic groups. Historically, the American public school has practiced cultural imperialism and fostered an Anglo-conformity conception of citizenship. Assimilation into Anglo-Saxon culture became viewed as an essential requisite for civic participation. A broader conception of "American" is needed to guide civic education. This conception should recognize that individuals who are members of diverse ethnic and cultural groups are *American* because they endorse the overarching values of the nation state.

Traditional educational literature and conventional wisdom have fostered the idea that the school has promoted democracy and enabled ethnic and poor youths to experience social class mobility and equality. In recent years, revisionist historians and economists have rejected these views and argued that the schools perpetuate and reflect the social class and racial stratifications in society. An analysis of the revisionists arguments and grand theories indicate that their positions are not so much wrong as they are incomplete, overdrawn, and sometimes misleading.

Ethnic minorities retain an unshaken faith in the school's ability to help them attain equality and social class mobility. The school remains a cogent factor in the lives of many youths who are members of excluded ethnic and social class groups. Consequently, the total school environment should be reformed so that it will help students to attain clarified, positive, and reflective ethnic, national, and global identifications, and the skills and commitments needed to help close the gap between the nation's realities and ideals.

Notes

1. James A. Banks with Ambrose A. Clegg, Jr., *Teaching Strategies for the Social Studies,* 2nd ed. (Reading, Mass.: Addison-Wesley, 1977); Fred M. Newmann, *Education for Citizen Action: Challenge for Secondary Curriculum* (Berkeley: McCutchan Publishing Corporation, 1975).
2. Nathan Glazer and Daniel P. Moynihan, eds. *Ethnicity: Theory and Experience* (Cambridge: Harvard University Press, 1975).
3. Orlando Patterson, *Ethnic Chauvinism: The Reactionary Impulse* (New York: Stein and Day, 1977).
4. James A. Banks, "Shaping the Future of Multicultural Education," *Journal of Negro Education* 45 (Summer 1979): 237–252.
5. David E. Apter, "Political Life and Cultural Pluralism," in Melvin M.

Tumin and Walter Plotch, eds. *Pluralism in a Democratic Society* (New York: Praeger, 1977) pp. 58–91.

6. Orlando Patterson, "Ethnicity and the Pluralist Fallacy," *Change* (March 1975): 11.

7. Apter, "Political Life and Cultural Pluralism."

8. Ibid., p. 60.

9. Ibid., p. 61.

10. "Robert Ezra Park 1864–1944," in Lewis A. Coser, ed., *Masters of Sociological Thought,* 2nd ed. (New York: Harcourt, 1977), pp. 357–384.

11. Michael Novak, *The Rise of the Unmeltable Ethnics* (New York: Macmillan, 1971).

12. Patterson, *Ethnic Chauvinism,* pp. 158–159.

13. Judith Herman, ed., *The Schools and Group Identity: Educating for a New Pluralism* (New York: Institute on Pluralism and Group Identity of the American Jewish Community, 1974), p. 15.

14. Andrew M. Greeley, *Why Can't They Be Like Us? America's White Ethnic Groups* (New York: Dutton, 1975).

15. Peter Schrag, *The Decline of Wasp* (New York: Simon and Schuster, 1973).

16. Apter, "Political Life and Cultural Pluralism," p. 65.

17. Ibid., p. 75.

18. Cynthia H. Enloe, *Ethnic Conflict and Political Development* (Boston: Little Brown, 1973). p. 15.

19. Ibid., p. 15.

20. James A. Banks et al., *Curriculum Guidelines for Multiethnic Education* (Washington, D.C.: National Council for the Social Studies, 1976), p. 20.

21. Apter, "Political Life and Cultural Pluralism," p. 89.

22. Milton M. Gordon, *Assimilation in American Life* (New York: Oxford University Press, 1964), pp. 84–114.

23. John Higham, *Strangers in the Land: Patterns of American Nativisim 1860–1925* (New York: Atheneum, 1972).

24. James A. Banks, *Teaching Strategies for Ethnic Studies,* 2nd ed. (Boston: Allyn and Bacon, 1979), p. 171.

25. Harry H. L. Kitano, *Japanese Americans: The Evolution of a Subculture,* 2nd ed. (Englewood Cliffs, N.J.: Prentice-Hall, 1976).

26. Roger Daniels, *Concentration Camps U.S.A.: Japanese Americans and World War II* (New York: Holt, 1971).

27. Stan Steiner, *The Islands: The Worlds of the Puerto Ricans* (New York: Harper Colophon Books, 1974).

28. John Dollard, *Caste and Class in a Southern Town,* 3rd ed. (Garden City, N.Y.: Doubleday Anchor Books, 1949); Oliver C. Cox, *Caste, Class, and Race* (New York: Monthly Review Press, 1959).

29. Meyer Weinberg, *A Chance to Learn: A History of Race and Education in the United States* (New York: Cambridge University Press, 1977).

30. Stokley Carmichael and Charles V. Hamilton, *Black Power: The Politics of Liberation in America* (New York: Vintage Books, 1967).
31. Jack D. Forbes, "Teaching Native American Values and Cultures," in James A. Banks, ed. *Teaching Ethnic Studies: Concepts and Strategies* (Washington, D.C.: National Council for the Social Studies), pp. 201–225.
32. Arthur Lean, "Review of Public Education of the Future," *History of Education Journal* 6 (Fall 1954): 167.
33. Diane Ravitch, *The Revisionists Revised: A Critique of the Radical Attack on the Schools* (New York: Basic Books, 1978), pp. 22–23.
34. Michael B. Katz, *Class, Bureaucracy, and Schools: The Illusion of Educational Change in America,* expanded ed. (New York: Praeger, 1975); Colin Greer, *The Great School Legend: A Revisionist Interpretation of American Public Education* (New York: The Viking Press, 1973); Martin Carnoy, *Education as Cultural Imperialism* (New York: David McKay, 1974); Samuel Bowles and Herbert Gintis, *Schooling in Capitalist America: Educational Reform and the Contradictions of Economic Life* (New York: Basic Books, 1976).
35. Carnoy, *Education as Cultural Imperialism,* p. 18.
36. Bowles and Gintis, *Schooling in Capitalist America,* p. 11.
37. Katz, *Class, Bureaucracy, and Schools,* p. xviii.
38. Ravitch, *The Revisionists Revised.*
39. Ibid., pp. 16–17.
40. Gunnar Myrdal, *An American Dilemma: The Negro Problem and Modern Democracy,* vols. 1 and 2 (New York: Harper Torchbooks, 1963).
41. Ibid., vol. 1, p. lxxi.
42. Robert K. Merton, *Social Theory and Social Structure,* enlarged ed. (New York: The Free Press, 1968), p. 45.
43. Carnoy, *Education as Cultural Imperialism,* pp. 33–34.
44. Merton, *Social Theory and Social Structure,* p. 68.
45. Ibid., p. 46.
46. Thomas Sowell, "Patterns of Black Excellence," *The Public Interest* 45 (Spring 1976): 26–58; Ravitch, *The Revisionists Revised*; Kenneth B. Clark, "Social Policy, Power, and Social Science Research," *Harvard Educational Review* 43 (February 1973): 113–121.
47. Howard D. Mehlinger, "The Crisis in Civic Education," in *Education for Responsible Citizenship: The Report of the National Task Force on Citizenship Education,* edited by B. Frank Brown, Director (New York: McGraw-Hill, 1977), p. 69.
48. Donald W. Oliver and James P. Shaver, *Teaching Public Issues in the High School* (Boston: Houghton Mifflin, 1966).
49. Christopher Jencks et al., *Inequality: A Reassessment of the Effect of Family and Schooling in America* (New York: Basic Books, 1972); James S. Coleman et al., *Equality of Educational Opportunity* (Washington, D.C.: U.S. Government Printing Office, 1966).

50. Julius Drachsler, *Democracy and Assimilation* (New York: The Macmillan Company, 1920).
51. Gordon, *Assimilation in American Life,* p. 263.
52. Alfredo Castañeda, "The Educational Needs of Mexican Americans," in *The Educational Needs of Minority Groups,* edited by Alfredo Castañeda, Ricard L. James, and Webster Robbins (Lincoln, Neb.: Professional Educators Publications, Inc., 1974), p. 15.

PART VI

Guidelines
for Multiethnic Education

Introduction

The first chapter in this part presents a rationale for ethnic pluralism in American society. The second chapter consists of twenty-three guidelines that educations can use to determine the extent to which their educational environments are multiethnic and to plan and implement reforms in multiethnic education. The guidelines presented in chapter 16 summarize and highlight the major points and issues discussed in this book.

I coauthored the two chapters in this part with Carlos E. Cortés, Geneva Gay, Ricardo L. Garcia, and Anna S. Ochoa. They were originally published as a position statement of the National Council for the Social Studies, *Curriculum Guidelines for Multiethnic Education.* Washington, D.C.: National Council for the Social Studies, 1976. Reprinted with permission of the National Council for the Social Studies.

16

A Rationale
for Ethnic Pluralism

Three major factors make multiethnic education a necessity: (1) ethnic pluralism is a societal reality that influences the lives of young people; (2) in
one way or another, individuals do acquire knowledge or beliefs, sometimes
invalid, about ethnic groups and ethnicity; (3) beliefs and knowledge about
ethnic groups limit the perspectives of many and make a difference, often a
negative difference, in the opportunities and options of members of ethnic
groups. Because ethnicity is important in the lives of many Americans, it is
important that all members of our society develop "ethnic literacy," a so-
lidly based understanding of ethnicity and ethnic groups. School cannot
afford to ignore their responsibility to contribute to the development of
ethnic literacy and understanding. Only a well-conceived, sensitive, thor-
ough, and continuous program of multiethnic education can create the
broadly based ethnic literacy so necessary for the future of our nation and
world society.

In the United States, ethnic diversity has remained visible despite the
assimilation process that takes place in any society made up of many different ethnic groups. Although ethnic affiliations are weak for many Americans, a large number still demonstrate at least some attachments to their
ethnic cultures and to the symbols of their ancestral traditions. The values
and behavior of many Americans are heavily influenced by their ethnicity.
Ethnic identification may also be increased by the discrimination experienced by many because of their racial characteristics, language, or culture.

In recent years, emerging ethnic revitalization movements have
greatly intensified ethnic attachments among the members of many groups
in American society. These movements have resulted in what some observ-
ers have called a "new pluralism." Clearly, ethnicity is a potent force in
contemporary American society. The challenge our nation faces is whether
ethnicity will function as a positive force rather than as a factor that limits
equality of opportunity for many groups in the United States.

The Guidelines presented in chapter 17 are predicated on a democratic ideology in which ethnic diversity is viewed as a positive, integral in-
gredient. A democratic society protects and provides opportunities for ethnic pluralism. Ethnic pluralism is based on the following four premises:

1. Ethnic diversity should be recognized and respected at individual,
   group, and societal levels.

2. Ethnic diversity provides a basis for societal cohesiveness and survival.

3. Equality of opportunity should be afforded to members of all ethnic
groups.

4. Ethnic identification should be optional for individuals.

Principles of Ethnic Pluralism

1. Ethnic Diversity Should Be
Recognized and Respected at the
Individual, Group, and Societal
Levels

Ethnic diversity is a social reality all too frequently ignored by educational institutions, yet it deserves open recognition. Ethnic groups often
have different world views, values, traditions, and practices.

Even in the midst of a marked degree of assimilation and in spite of
efforts to ignore, belittle, or eliminate some ethnic differences, many
Americans continue to demonstrate strong feelings of ethnic identity. In
the last two decades, some ethnic groups have, indeed, heightened their visibility and increased their demands for equal opportunity. Ethnicity continues to permeate American life. Its persistence suggests that it will characterize the future.

Simply admitting the existence of ethnic diversity is not enough. Acceptance of and respect for differences in ethnic values, traditions, and behavior are called for. The call for acceptance and respect is based on the
belief that the existence and expression of differences can improve the quality of life for individuals, for ethnic groups, and for society as a whole.

For individuals, ethnic groups can provide a foundation for self-definition. Ethnic group membership can provide a sense of belonging, of shared
traditions, of interdependence of fate—especially for members of groups
who have all too often been barred from entry into the larger society. When
society views ethnic differences with respect, individuals can define themselves ethnically without conflict or shame.

The psychic cost of assimilation was and is high for many Americans.
It too often demanded and demands self-denial, self-hatred, and rejection
of family ties. Social demands for conformity that have such exaggerated
effects are neither democratic nor humane. Such practices deny dignity by
refusing to accept individuals as persons in themselves and by limiting the
realization of human potential. Such demands run counter to the democratic values of freedom of association and equality of opportunity.

A society that respects ethnic group differences aims to protect them
from discriminatory practices and prejudicial attitudes. Such respect sup-

ports the survival of these groups and augments their opportunities to shape their lives in ways of their choice.

For society as a whole, ethnic groups can serve as sources of innovation. By respecting differences, society is provided a wider base of ideas, values, and behavior. Society increases its potential power for creative change.

Coping with change is fundamental to the survival of culture. Adaptation to new conditions is critical. Without constructive reaction to change, culture weakens and deteriorates. In the face of rapidly changing conditions, the United States, as a nation, has to be concerned with ensuring mechanisms for coping with change. The insights of anthropologists are useful here. One way cultures change is by the process of innovation: a person or persons introduce new ways of thinking or behaving that are accepted by society or challenge cultural views. By respecting the plurality of ethnic life styles, and by permitting them to flourish, our culture may expand the base of alternatives from which it can draw in responding to new conditions and new problems.

Conversely, to the extent that a culture is homogeneous, its capability for creative change is limited. When the range of tolerated differences in values and behavior is minimal, rigidity inhibits innovation. Too much conformity and convergence is characteristic of mass culture; there have been those who have so described American society. On the other hand, too little acceptance of common culture values and practices produces social disorganization. The balance is a delicate one in a culture that must face up to the challenge of changing conditions; but modern America cannot be left without access to competing, unique, and creative ideas.

Recognition and respect for ethnic differences enable society to enhance the potentialities of individuals and the integrity and contributions of ethnic groups, and so to invigorate the culture.

2. Ethnic Diversity Provides a Basis for Societal Cohesiveness and Survival

The "new pluralism" on which the Guidelines in Chapter 17 are based seeks not only to recognize and respect ethnic diversity but to establish, across ethnic lines, social bonds that will contribute to the strength and vitality of society.

This position maintains the right of ethnic groups to socialize their young into their cultural patterns as long as such practices are consistent with human dignity and democratic ideals. Therefore, the individual's primary group association—family relations, friendship groups, religious affiliations—may be heavily influenced by ethnic traditions. At the same time, the members of ethnic groups have both the right and the responsibility to help shape the significant institutions of the larger society. Legal and educational institutions must have commitment to affecting the conditions that will permit members of ethnic groups to become fully participating members of the larger society. Ethnic groups must feel that they have a stake in this society; to the extent that ethnic group members feel a sense of ownership in societal institutions, their cultural practices will also reflect the inherent values of society as a whole. What is needed is a cohesive society, characterized by ethnic pluralism, wherein the self-identities of individuals allow them to say: "I am an Afro-American, a Polish American, or a Mexican American—AND I am an American."

Respect for ethnic differences should promote, not destroy, societal cohesion. Research has shown that separatism is not the desire of most members of ethnic groups.[1] Rather, they are demanding that their ethnic traditions be respected as an integral part of the society. To the extent that society creates an environment in which all ethnic groups can flourish, and one in which such groups can contribute constructively to the shaping of public institutions, hostilities will be defused and the society will benefit from its rich base of ethnic traditions and cultures. In effect, unity thrives in an atmosphere where varieties of human potential are neither socially censored nor ignored, but valued.

An additional pedagogical advantage is inherent in the study of ethnic groups. Such study provides the learner with conceptual tools that permit him or her to advance from the simple to the complex and from direct to vicarious learning. For example, each ethnic group is a microcosm of the larger society. It has its own pattern of behavior with respect to such social institutions as religion, education, the economic system, and political action. In learning about this pattern of behavior as it relates to one ethnic group, one is acquiring concepts that can be used as a basis for more sophisticated inferences and generalizations about the role of such social institutions in society as a whole.

3. Equality of Opportunity Must Be Afforded to All Members of Ethnic Groups

Recognition and respect for ethnic groups need legal enforcement of equal economic, political and educational opportunity by the larger society. Anything less relegates ethnic groups and their members to the inferior status that has too often limited the quality of their lives.

Ethnic groups themselves are now demanding equal participation in society as a whole. If society is to benefit from ethnic differences, it must provide for significant interactions with social institutions. To reach this goal, ethnic groups must have access to the full range of occupational, educational, economic, and political opportunities. What is endorsed here is the structural integration of society, the mutual involvement of all sorts of people in political, educational and economic life.

4. Ethnic Identification for Individuals Should Be Optional in a Democracy

Although the assimilationist ideology has dominated our national thought for two centuries, ethnicity has proven to be a resilient factor in American life. The Anglo-American tradition notwithstanding, many individuals continue to derive their primary identity from their ethnic group membership. At the same time, it must be recognized that widespread cultural assimilation has taken place in American society. There are many individuals who have only a vague sense of their ethnic identities or have lost track of or have denied their ethnic origins.

Individuals vary greatly in the degree of their ethnic attachments. The beliefs and behavior of some individuals are heavily influenced by their ethnic culture; others maintain only some ethnic beliefs and behavioral characteristics; still others try to reject or lose, or are simply unaware of, their ethnic origins. There are also individuals of mixed ethnic origin, for whom ethnic-identification may be difficult or impossible.

For many persons, then, ethnic criteria may be irrelevant for purposes of self-identification. Their identities stem primarily from sources such as family, social class, occupational groups, and/or social associations.

Moreover, ethnic origins ought not to be romanticized. Many, though not all, who left their homelands did so because opportunities were closed to them there. However good were "the good old days," they are gone. The "old countries" too have been changing. Ethnicity should not be maintained artificially.

It is inconsistent with a democratic ideology to mandate ethnic affiliation. In an idealized democratic society, the individual is free to choose his or her group allegiances. Association should be voluntary, a matter of personal choice. However, in our society, members of some ethnic groups have this option while many others do not. One of our societal goals should be to maximize the opportunity for ethnic individuals to choose their group identifications.

While a democratic society can and should protect the right to ethnic identification, it should not insist on it. To do so would violate individual freedom of choice. To confine individuals to any given form of affiliation violates the principle of liberty guaranteed by the basic documents of this nation.

The Role of the School

The societal goals posited in this chapter are future-oriented. In effect, they present a vision of our society as one that recognizes and respects ethnic diversity rather than one which seeks to reduce ethnic differences. Further movement in that direction is consistent with our national democratic ideals—such as freedom, equality, justice, and human dignity—embodied in our basic national documents. By respecting ethnic differences, we can help to close the gap between our democratic ideals and societal practices. Such practices are too often discriminatory toward members of some ethnic groups.

It follows, therefore, that the school, as an agent of society, should assume a new responsibility. Its socialization practices should be predicated on a respect for the ethnic diversity which is an integral part of the American commitment to human dignity. However, at the same time, the school must help to socialize youth in ways that will commit them to the basic democratic ideals that serve as overarching goals for all American citizens. As schools embark on educational programs that reflect ethnic pluralism, they must demonstrate a commitment to do the following:

1. recognize and respect ethnic diversity
2. promote societal cohesiveness based on the shared participation of ethnically diverse peoples
3. maximize equality of opportunity for all individuals and groups
4. facilitate constructive societal change that enhances human dignity and democratic ideals.

The study of ethnic heritage should not be taken to be the narrow promotion of ethnocentrism or nationalism. Personal ethnic identity and/or knowledge of the ethnic identities of others is essential to the senses of understanding and the feeling of personal well-being that promote intergroup and international understanding. Multiethnic education should stress the process of self-identification as an essential aspect of the understanding that underlies commitment to the dignity of humankind throughout the world community.

The Nature of the Learner

As a result of socialization practices of ethnic groups, some students will demonstrate social behaviors and learning styles that are different from those of other students. Recent research indicates that individual learning styles vary. All people do not learn in the same way. Of particular interest to multiethnic education is emerging research that suggests that learning styles may in some ways be related to ethnicity.[2] Although such research is not sufficiently definitive to be prescriptive, it is of crucial importance that schools reject the notion that all children learn in precisely the same way. For too long, educational practices have reflected such universal views of learning and have expected all students to conform to them. Schools should recognize that they cannot treat all students alike. If they try to, they run the risk of denying equal educational opportunity to all persons. Educators should be aware of behavior that is normative and acceptable in the ethnic group. The practices of multiethnic schools must be both responsive and adaptive to ethnic differences.

Goals for School Reform

Two major goals for school reform follow. Both are based on what has preceded: the principles of ethnic pluralism, the role of the school, and ethnic differences among individual learners.

1. A Major Goal of Schools Should Be to Create Total School Environments That Are Consistent with Democratic Ideals and Ethnic Pluralism

Schools reflect their values not only in their curricula and materials, but in policies, hiring practices, procedures for governance, and the school climate. These latter are sometimes referred to as the informal or "hidden" curriculum. It can be argued that students often learn as much about the society from these nonformal areas as from the planned curriculum. Education for ethnic pluralism, therefore, requires more than a change in curricula and textbooks. It requires system-wide changes that permeate all aspects of school life.

2. A Major Goal of Schools Should Be to Define and Implement Curricular Policies That Are Consistent with Democratic Ideals and Ethnic Pluralism

The school should not promote the ideologies and political goals of any specific group, including those of dominant groups, but should promote a democratic ideology. Too often, the curriculum has promoted the interests of dominant groups and has been detrimental to the interests of some ethnic groups. Promoting the interests of any group over those of others increases the possibility of ethnic and racial conflict. When groups and individuals feel victimized by the school and the larger society because of ethnicity, conflict and tension result, and struggles to gain rights will occur.

School practices and programs must not emphasize the sins and virtues of any groups, but should teach accurate, valid accounts of our past and present form the perspectives of different ethnic and racial groups.

The young in our schools, the next generation, must recognize and respect ethnic pluralism. The understandings they develop, the skills they master, the values they learn, will influence not only their lives, but the whole fabric of society.

Notes

1. *Gallup Opinion Index Report 113* (Princeton, N.J.: The American Institute of Public Opinion, November 1974).
2. See Manuel Ramirez III and Alfredo Castañeda, *Cultural Democracy, Bicognitive Development and Education* (New York: Academic Press, 1974); and Susan S. Stodolsky and Gerald Lesser, "Learning Patterns in the Disadvantaged," *Harvard Educational Reviews* 37 (Fall 1967), pp. 546–593.

17

Curriculum Guidelines
for Multiethnic Education

1. Ethnic Pluralism Should Permeate the Total
School Environment

Effective teaching about American ethnic groups can best take place within an educational setting that accepts, encourages, and respects the expression of ethnic and racial diversity. To attain this kind of educational atmosphere, the total school environment must be reformed, not merely courses and programs. The school's informal or "hidden" curriculum is just as important as, and perhaps in some ways more important than, the formalized course of study.

Teaching about different ethnic groups in a few specialized courses is obviously not enough. Ethnic content about a variety of ethnic groups should be incorporated into all subject areas, preschool through grade twelve and beyond. Concern with ethnicity is as appropriate for the fine arts, the domestic arts, the natural sciences, mathematics, vocational education, and the consumer arts as it is for the language arts and the social studies. Ethnic diversity should also be a part of all other school activities and projects.

To permeate the total school environment with ethnic pluralism, it is necessary that students have resource materials readily available that provide accurate information on the diverse aspects of the histories and cultures of different ethnic groups. Learning centers, libraries, and resource centers should include a multitude of resources on the history, literature, music, folklore, views of life, and the arts of different ethnic groups.

Ethnic diversity in the school's informal programs should be reflected in assembly programs, classroom, hallway and entrance decorations, cafeteria menus, counseling interactions, and extracurricular programs. School-sponsored dances, for example, that consistently provide only one kind of ethnic music and/or performers are as contrary to the spirit and the principles of ethnic pluralism as are curricula that teach only about Anglo-American ideals, values, and contributions.

Participation in activities—such as cheerleading, booster clubs, honor societies, and athletic teams—should be open to all students; in fact, the participation of students from different ethnic backgrounds should be solicited. Such activities can provide invaluable opportunities not only for the development of self-esteem, but for students from different ethnic backgrounds to learn to work and play together, and to recognize that all individuals, whatever their ethnic identities, have worth and are capable of achieving.

2. School Policies and Procedures Should Foster Positive Multiethnic Interactions and Understandings among Students, Teachers, and the Supportive Staff

School governance should protect the individual's right to: (1) retain esteem for his or her home environment, (2) develop a positive self-concept, (3) develop empathy and insight into and respect for the ethnicity of others, and (4) receive an equal educational opportunity.

Each institution needs rules and regulations to guide behavior so as to attain institutional goals and objectives. School rules and regulations should enhance multiethnic harmony and understanding among students, as well as staff and teachers. In the past, school harmony was often sought through efforts to "treat everyone the same"; however, experience in multiethnic settings indicates that the same treatment for everyone is unfair to many students. Instead of insisting on one ideal model of behavior that is unfair to many students, school policies should recognize and accommodate individual and ethnic group differences. This does not mean that some students should obey school rules while others should not; it means that different ethnic groups may have different behaviors that should be honored so long as they are not inconsistent with major school goals. It also means that school policies may have to make allowances for different ethnic traditions. For example, Jewish customs that affect Jewish students' eating habits and school attendance on certain religious days should be respected.

Equal educational opportunity should be increased by rules that protect linguistically and culturally different students from procedures and practices that relegate them to low ability or special education classes simply because of their low scores on standardized English reading and achievement tests.

Guidance and other student services personnel should not respond to students in stereotyped ways regarding their academic abilities and occupational aspirations, and students must be protected from such responses. Counselors should be cautioned to counsel students on the basis of their individual potentials and interests as well as on the basis of their ethnic needs and concerns. Counselors will need to be particularly aware of their biases in the counseling of students whose ethnicity differs from theirs.

Schools should recognize the holidays and festivities of major importance to different ethnic groups in the school. Provisions should be made to see that traditional holidays and festivities reflect multiethnic modes of celebration. For example, the ways in which some Indian tribes celebrate Thanksgiving, Orthodox Greek celebrate Easter, and Jews celebrate Chanukah can be appropriately included in school programs.

3. The School Staff Should Reflect the Ethnic Pluralism within American Society

Members of different ethnic groups must be part of the school's instructional, administrative, and supportive staffs if the school is truly multiethnic. School personnel—teachers, principals, cooks, custodians, secretaries, students, and counselors—make as important contributions to multiethnic environments as do courses of study and instructional materials. Students learn important lessons about ethnicity and ethnic diversity by observing interactions among different racial and ethnic groups in their school, observing and experiencing the verbal behavior of the professional and supportive staffs, and observing the extent to which the staff is ethnically and racially mixed. Therefore, school policies should be established and aggressively implemented to recruit and maintain a multiethnic total school staff, sensitive to the needs of multiethnicity.

Students also can benefit greatly from positive interactions with students from various racial and ethnic groups. When plans are made to mix students from diverse groups—whether through school desegregation or exchange programs and visits—extreme care must be taken to make sure that the environment in which the students interact is a positive and enhancing one. When students from different ethnic and racial groups interact within a hostile environment, their racial antipathies are more likely to increase than decrease.

4. Schools Should Have Systematic, Comprehensive, Mandatory, and Continuing Staff Development Programs

The teacher is the most important variable in the student's formal learning environment. Major attention should be devoted to the training and retraining of teachers and other members of the professional and supportive school staff in order to create the kind of multiethnic school environment recommended in these Guidelines. Sound materials and other components of the instructional program are ineffective in the hands of teachers who lack the skills, attitudes, perceptions, and content background essential for a positive multiethnic school environment. An effective staff development program must involve administrators, librarians, counselors, and members of the supportive school staff, such as cooks, secretaries, and bus drivers. This is necessary because any well-trained and sensitive teacher must work within a supportive institutional environment in order to succeed. Key administrators, such as principals, must set by example the school norms of ethnic and cultural differences. The need to involve administrators, especially building principals, in comprehensive and systematic staff development programs cannot be overemphasized.

Effective professional staff development should begin at the preservice level and continue as inservice when educators are employed by schools. The focus should be on helping the staff members to: (a) clarify and analyze their feelings, attitudes, and perceptions toward their own and other ethnic groups, ((b) acquire content about and understanding of the historical experiences and sociological characteristics of American ethnic groups, (c) increase their instructional skills within multiethnic school environments, (d) improve their skill in curriculum development as it relates to ethnic pluralism, and (e) increase their skill in creating, selecting, evaluating, and revising instructional materials.

Staff development for effective multiethnic schools must be undertaken jointly by school districts, local colleges and universities, and local community agencies. Each bears a responsibility for training school personnel, at both the preservice and inservice levels, to function successfully within multiethnic instructional settings.

Effective staff development programs must be carefully conceptualized and implemented. Short workshops, selected courses, and other short-term experiences may be essential components of such programs, but these alone cannot be characterized as total staff development programs. Sound staff development programs should consist of a wide variety of program components, such as need assessments, curriculum development, laboratory teaching, and materials selection and evaluation. Lectures alone are insufficient. Ongoing changes should be made to make staff development programs more responsive to the needs of practicing professionals.

5. The Curriculum Should Reflect the Ethnic Learning Styles of the Students within the School Community

All students in a multiethnic school cannot be treated identically and still be afforded equal educational opportunities. Some students have unique ethnic characteristics to which the school should respond deliberately and sensitively.

Research and observations indicate that students who are members of minority groups, especially those who are poor, often have values, behavioral patterns, cognitive styles, expectations, and other cultural components that differ from those of the school's culture.[1] These often lead to conflicts between students and teachers. By comparison, most Anglo-American youths find the school culture to be consistent with their home culture, and they are much more comfortable in school. However, many students, regardless of their ethnic or racial identity, find the school culture alien, hostile, and self-defeating.

The school's culture and its instructional programs should be modified, where necessary, to reflect the cultures and learning styles of children from diverse ethnic and social class groups. Some recent research indicates that the instructional strategies and learning styles that are most often favored in American schools are inconsistent with the cognitive styles and cultural characteristics of some groups of minority students.[2] Other research indicates that ethnicity influences students' cognitive patterns of processing information, and that such patterns have instructional implications.[3] It is not feasible to base major educational policy on this research, because it is sparse and inconclusive. However, such findings should alert educators to the need to become more sensitive to student differences based on ethnicity, and to the implications of these findings for planning and organizing the school environment. Educators should not be blind to racial and ethnic differences when planning instruction; nor should they dismiss the question of racial and ethnic differences with the all-too-easy cliché, "I don't see racial differences in students and I treat them all alike." Emerging research on ethnicity and cognitive styles suggests that if all students are treated alike, they are probably being denied access to equal educational opportunities.[4]

Although differences among students are accepted in an effective multiethnic school, major goals must also be to teach the students how to function effectively in social settings different from the ones in which they were socialized, and to help them to master new cognitive styles and learning patterns. The successful multiethnic school helps students be aware of and able to acquire cultural and cognitive alternatives, thus enabling them to function successfully within other cultural environments as well as their own.

6. The Multiethnic Curriculum Should Provide Students with Continuous Opportunities to Develop a Better Sense of Self

The multiethnic curriculum should help students to develop a better sense of self. The development should be an ongoing process, beginning when the child first enters school and continuing throughout the child's school career. This development should include at least three areas:

1. Students should be helped to develop accurate self-identities. Who am I? What am I? These are questions with which students must deal in order to come to grips with their own identities.
2. The multiethnic curriculum should help students to develop improved self-concepts. Beyond coming to grips with who they are and

what they are, students should learn to feel positively about their identities, particularly their ethnic identities. Positive self-concepts may be expressed in several ways. The multiethnic curriculum, for example, should recognize the varying talents of students and capitalize on them in the academic curriculum. Students need to feel that academic success is possible. The multiethnic curriculum should also help students to develop a high regard for their home languages and cultures.

3. The mulltiethnic curriculum should help students to develop greater self-understanding. Students should develop more sophisticated understandings of why they are as they are, why their ethnic groups are as they are, and what ethnicity may mean in their daily lives. Such self-understanding will help students to deal more effectively with future situations in which ethnicity may have an impact.

Students cannnot fully understand why they are as they are and why certain things may occur in their future until they have a solid knowledge of the groups to which they belong and the effect of group membership on their lives. Multiethnic education should enable students to come to grips with these individual/group relationships in general and the effect of ethnicity on their own lives in particular.

Looking at group membership ought not undermine a student's individuality. Rather, it should add a dimension to the understanding of one's own unique individuality by learning how belonging to groups affects it.

Neither are students to be assigned and locked into one group. Instead, students should be aware of the many groups to which they belong in voluntary or involuntary memberships, and recognize that at various moments one or more of these groups may have significant effects on their lives.

The multiethnic curriculum should also help students to understand and appreciate their personal backgrounds and family heritages. Family studies in the school can contribute to increased self-understanding and a personal sense of heritage, as contrasted with the generalized experiences presented in books. They can also contribute to family and personal pride. If parents and other relatives come to school to share their stories and life experiences, students will become increasingly aware that ethnic groups are a meaningful part of our nation's heritage, meriting study and recording.

7. The Curriculum Should Help Students to Understand the Totality of the Experiences of American Ethnic Groups

The social problems that ethnic group members experience are often regarded as part of their cultural characteristics. Alcohol, crime, and illiteracy, for example, are considered by many people to be cultural characteristics of particular ethnic groups. Ethnicity is often assumed to mean something negative and divisive, and the study of ethnic groups and ethnicity becomes only the examination of problems such as prejudice, racism, discrimination, and exploitation. To concentrate exclusively on these problems when studying ethnicity creates serious distortions in perceptions of ethnic groups. Among other things, it stereotypes ethnic groups as essentially passive recipients of dominant society discrimination and exploitation. While these are legitimate issues to be included in a comprehensive, effective multiethnic curriculum, they should not constitute the entire curriculum.

Many ethnic group members face staggering sociopolitical problems, but these do not comprise the whole of their lives. Nor are all ethnic groups affected to the same degree or in the same ways by these problems. Moreover, many ethnic groups have developed and maintained viable life styles and have made notable contributions to American culture. Moreover, the experiences of each ethnic group are part of a composite of human activities. Although it is true that each ethnic group has significant unifying historical experiences and cultural traits, no ethnic group has a single, homogeneous, historical-cultural pattern. Members of an ethnic group do not conform to a single cultural norm or mode of behavior, nor are ethnic cultures uniform and static.

Consequently, the many dimensions of ethnic experiences and cultures should be studied. The curriculum should help students to understand the essential historical experiences and basic cultural patterns of ethnic groups, and the critical contemporary issues and social problems confronting each of them, as well as the dynamic diversity of the experiences, cultures, and individuals within each ethnic group.

A consistently multifaceted approach to teaching should benefit students in several major ways. It should help them to become aware of the commonalities within and among ethnic groups. It should help counteract stereotyping by making students aware of the rich diversity within each American ethnic group. It should also help students to develop more comprehensive and more realistic understandings of the broad range of ethnic group heritages and experiences.

8. The Multiethnic Curriculum Should Help Students Understand That There Is Always a Conflict between Ideals and Realities in Human Societies

Traditionally, students in the American common schools have been taught a great deal about the ideals of our society. Conflicts between ideals are often glossed over. Often values, such as freedom in the American democracy, are treated as ideals that can be attained, and the realities of American society have been distorted to make it appear that they have indeed been achieved. Courses in American history and citizenship especially have been characterized by this kind of unquestioning approach to the socialization of youth. Many writers have described this approach to citizenship education in terms such as "passing down the myths and legends of our national heritage." This approach to citizenship education tends to inculcate parochial national attitudes, promote serious misconceptions about the nature of American society and culture, and develop cynicism in youth who are aware of the gaps betweens the ideal and the real.

When ethnic studies emerged from the civil rights movement of the 1960s, there was a strong reaction to the traditional approach to citizenship education. A widely expressed goal of many curriculum reformers was to "tell it like it is and was" in the classroom. In many of the reformed courses, however, American history and society were taught and viewed primarily from the viewpoints of specific ethnic groups. Little attention was given to basic American values, except to highlight gross discrepancies between ideals and the harsh realities of American society. Emphasis was often on how minority groups had been oppressed by Anglo-Americans.

The unquestioning approach and the "tell it like it is" approach both result in distortions. In a sound multiethnic curriculum, emphasis should be neither on the ways in which the United States has "fulfilled its noble ideals" nor on the "sins committed by the Anglo-Americans" or any other groups of Americans. Rather, students should be encouraged to examine the democratic values that emerged in America, why they emerged, how they were defined in various periods, and to whom they referred in different eras. Students should also examine the extent to which these values as ideals have or have not been fulfilled, and the continuing conflict between values such as freedom and equality, as well as between ideals in other human societies.

Students should also be encouraged to examine various interpretations of the discrepancies between ideals and realities in American life and history. From the perspectives of some individuals and groups, there has been a continuing expansion of human rights in the United States. Others see a continuing process of weighing rights against rights as the optimum mix of values, none of which can be fully realized as ideals. Many argue that basic human rights are still too much limited to Americans with certain class, racial, ethnic, and cultural characteristics. Students should consider why these various interpretations arose and why different Americans view differently the conflicts between the ideals and between the ideals and realities of American society.

9. The Multiethnic Curriculum Should Explore
and Clarify Ethnic Alternatives and Options
within American Society

Educational questions regarding the ethnic alternatives and options of students are complex and difficult. Some individuals, for a variety of complex reasons, are uncomfortable with their ethnic identities and wish to deny them. Some individuals are uncomfortable when their own ethnic groups are discussed in the classroom. This discomfort means that the teacher must be careful about assuming, without adequate evidence, that students want to discuss and study their own ethnic heritages.

The degree of resistance when the class is studying their ethnic groups is influenced by the teacher's approach to the study of ethnicity. Students can sense when both the teacher and other students in the class are intolerant of their ethnic group or some of its characteristics. Students often receive such messages from nonverbal responses. The teacher can minimize student resistance to studying their ethnic heritage by creating a classroom atmosphere that reflects acceptance and respect for ethnic differences.

Moreover, teachers should help students understand the options related to their own ethnicity as well as the nature of ethnic alternatives and options within American society. Students should be helped to understand that, ideally, all individuals should have the right to select the manner and degree of identifying or not identifying with their ethnic groups. However, they should also learn that some individuals, such as members of many White ethnic groups, have the privilege; while others, such as most Afro-Americans, have more limited options. Most persons of White ethnic ancestry can become assimilated into the dominant Anglo-American society. When they become highly assimilated, they can usually participate completely in most American economic, social, and political institutions. However, no matter how culturally assimilated members of some ethnic groups become—Black Americans, for example—they are still perceived and stigmatized by the larger society on the basis of their ethnicity.

Students should also be helped to understand that while individualism is strong in American society, in reality many Americans, such as Native Americans and Chinese Americans, are often judged not as individuals but on the basis of the racial and/or ethnic group to which they belong. While teachers may give Native-American or Chinese-American students the option of examining or not examining their ethnic heritage and identity, such students need to be helped to understand how they are perceived and identified by the larger society. Educators must respect the individual rights of students, but at the same time they have a professional responsibility to help students learn basic facts and generalizations about the nature of race and ethnicity within American society.

10. The Multiethnic Curriculum Should
Promote Values, Attitudes, and Behaviors
That Support Ethnic Pluralism

Ethnicity is a salient factor in the lives of many Americans. It helps individuals answer the question, "Who am I?" by providing them with a sense of peoplehood, identity, and cultural and spiritual roots. It provides a filter through which events, life-styles, norms, and values are processed and screened. It provides a means through which identity is affirmed, heritages are validated, and some preferred associates are selected. Therefore, ethnicity serves necessary functions in many persons' lives. Ethnicity is neither always positive and reinforcing, nor always negative and debilitating, although it has the potential for both. The effective multiethnic curriculum should examine all of these dismensions of ethnicity.

The curriculum should help students understand that diversity is an integral part of American life. Because ethnic diversity permeates American history and society, schools should teach about ethnic diversity to help students acquire more accurate assessments of American history and culture. Major goals of ethnic pluralism include improving respect for human dignity, maximizing cultural options, understanding what makes people alike and different, and accepting diversity as valuable to human life.

Students should learn that to be different does not necessarily mean to be inferior or superior, and that the study of ethnic group differences need not lead to ethnic polarization. They should also learn that while some conflict is unavoidable in ethnically and racially pluralistic societies, it does not necessarily have to be destructive or divisive. Conflict is an intrinsic part of the human condition, especialy so in a pluralistic society where values rub against each other. Conflict is often a catalyst for social progress. Multiethnic education programs which explore ethnic puralism in positive, realistic ways will present ethnic conflict in proper perspective. They will help students to understand that there is strength in diversity, and that social cooperation among ethnic groups is not necessarily predicated upon their having identical beliefs, behaviors, and values.

The multiethnic curriculum should help students understand and respect ethnic diversity and to broaden their cultural options. Too many Americans now learn only the values, behavioral patterns, and beliefs of their own ethnic groups, cultural groups, and/or communities. Socialization is, in effect, encapsulating, providing few opportunities for most individuals to acquire more than stereotypes about ethnic groups other than their own. Therefore, many people tend to view other ethnic groups and life-styles as "abnormal" and/or "deviant." The multiethnic curriculum can help students correct these misconceptions by teaching them that there are other ways of living that are as valid and viable as their own.

The multiethnic curriculum should also promote the basic values expressed in our major historical documents. Each ethnic group should have the right to practice its own religious, social, and cultural beliefs, but within the limits of due regard for the rights of others. For there is a set of values which all groups within a society or nation must endorse to maintain societal cohesions. In our nation, these core values stem from our commitment to human dignity, and include justice, equality, freedom, and due process of law. Although the school should value and reflect ethnic pluralism, it should not promote the practices and beliefs of any ethnic group that contradict the core values of our nation. Rather, the school should foster ethnic differences that maximize opportunities for deomcratic living.

Ethnicity and/or ethnic group membership should not restrict one's opportunity and ability to achieve and to participate, but it is sometimes used by groups in power to the detriment of less powerful groups. Individuals who do not understand the role of ethnicity often find it a troublesome reality, one extremely difficult to handle. Multiethnic curricula should help students examine the dilemmas surrounding ethnicity as a step toward realizing its full potential as an enabling force in the lives of individuals and groups.

11. The Multiethnic Curriculum Should Help Students Develop Their Decision-making Abilities, Social-participation Skills, and Sense of Political Efficacy as Necessary Bases for Effective Citizenship in an Ethnically Pluralistic Nation

The demands on people to make intelligent decisions on ethnic issues are constantly increasing. When people are unable to process the masses of conflicting information—including facts, opinions, interpretations, and theories about ethnic groups—they are often overwhelmed.

The multiethnic curriculum must enable students to gain knowledge and apply it. Students need a rich fund of sound knowledge. Facts, concepts, generalizations, and theories differ in their capability for organizing particulars and in predictive capacity; concepts and generalizations have more usefulness than mere collections of miscellaneous facts. Young people need practice in the steps of scholarly methods for arriving at knowledge: identifying problems; formulating hypotheses; locating and evaluating source materials; organizing information as evidence; analyzing, interpreting, and reworking what was found; and coming to some conclusion. Students also need ample opportunities to learn to use knowledge in making sense out of the situations they encounter.

When curricular programs are inappropriate, teaching inept, and/or expectations low for students of some ethnic groups and especially for those who are poor, the emphasis in class is likely to be on discrete facts, memorization of empty generalizations, and low-level skills. Though the names and dates and exercises in using an index may be drawn from ethnic context, such an emphasis is still discriminatory and inconsistent with the basic purpose of multiethnic education. All young people need opportunities to develop powerful concepts and generalizations and intellectual abilities in their ethnic studies.

Students must also learn how to identify values and relate them to knowledge. Young people should be taught methods for clarifying their own values relating to ethnicity. Such processes should include identifying value problems, their own and others'; describing evaluative behaviors; recognizing value conflicts within themselves and in social situations; recognizing and proposing alternatives based on values; and making choices between values in the light of their consequences.

Determining basic ideas, discovering, and verifying facts, and valuing are interrelated aspects of decision making. Ample opportunity to practice is necessary—as often as possible—in real-life situations; such practice frequently requires interdisciplinary as well as multiethnic perspectives. Decision-making skills help people to assess social situations objectively and perceptively, identify feasible courses of action and project their consequences, decide thoughtfully, and then act.

The multiethnic curriculum must also help students develop effective social and political action skills because many students from ethnic groups are overwhelmed by a sense of a lack of control over their destinies. These feelings often stem from their belief that, as in the past, they and other ethnic minorities have little influence over political policies and institutions. The multiethnic curriculum should help students develop a greater sense of political efficacy and become politically more active and effective. With a basis in strong commitments to such basic American values as justice, freedom, and equality, students can learn to exercise political and social influence responsibly to influence societal decisions related to ethnicity in ways consistent with human dignity.

The school, in many ways, is a microcosm of society, including the changing dynamics of ethnic group situations. The school can provide limitless opportunities for students to practice social participation skills and to test their political efficacy as they address themselves to resolving some of the school's ethnic problems. Issues such as the participation of ethnic individuals in school government, discriminatory disciplinary rules, and preferential treatment of certain students because of their ethnic backgrounds are examples of problems that students can help to resolve. Students are applying social action skills effectively when they combine knowledge, valuing, and thought gained from multiethnic perspectives and experiences to the resolution of problems affecting ethnic groups.

By providing students with opportunities to use decision-making abilities and social-action skills in the resolution of problems affecting ethnic groups, schools can contribute to more effective education for citizenship.

12. The Multiethnic Curriculum Should Help Students Develop the Skills Necessary for Effective Interpersonal and Interethnic Group Interactions

Effective interpersonal interaction across ethnic group lines is difficult to achieve. The problem is complicated by the fact that individuals bring to cross-ethnic interaction situations sets and expectations that influence their own behavior, including their responses to the behavior of others. These expectations are formed on the basis of what their own groups deems to be appropriate behavior and what each individual believes he or she knows about other ethnic groups. Much knowledge about ethnic groups is stereotyped, distorted, and based on distant observations, scattered, superficial contacts, and incomplete factual information. The result is that attempts at cross-ethnic interpersonal interactions are often stymied by ethnocentrism.

The problems created by ethnocentrism can be at least partially resolved by helping students recognize consciously the forces operating in interpersonal interactions, and how these forces affect behavior. Students should develop skills and concepts to overcome factors that prevent successful interactions. These include identifying ethnic stereotypes, clarifying ethnic attitudes and values, developing cross-ethnic communication skills, recognizing how attitudes and values are projected in verbal and nonverbal behaviors, and viewing the dynamics of interpersonal interactions from others' perspectives.

One of the goals of multiethnic education should be to help individuals function easily and effectively with members of both their own and other ethnic groups. The multiethnic curriculum should provide opportunities for students to explore lines of cross-ethnic communication and to experiment with cross-ethnic functioning. Actual experiences can be effective teaching devices, for students can test stereotypes and idealized behavioral constructs against real-life situations, and they can make the necessary adjustments in their frames of reference and behaviors, especially when asked to reflect on their own experiences. In the process, they should learn that ethnic group members, in the final analysis, are individuals, with all of the variations that characterize all individuals, and that ethnicity is only one of many variables that shape their personalities. Students will be forced to confront their values and make moral choices when their experiences in cross-ethnic interactions produce information contrary to previously held notions. Thus, students should broaden their ethnic options, increase their frames of reference, develop greater appreciation for individual and ethnic differences, and deepen their own capacities as human beings.

13. The Multiethnic Curriculum Should Be Comprehensive in Scope and Sequence, Should Present Holistic Views of Ethnic Groups, and Should Be an Integral Part of the Total School Curriculum

Students learn best from well-planned, comprehensive, continuous, and interrelated experiences. In an effective multiethnic curriculum, the study of ethnicity should be integrated into all courses and subject matter areas from preschool through twelfth grade and beyond. This study should be carefully planned to encourage the development of progressively more complex concepts and generalizations. It should also involve students in the study of a variety of ethnic groups.

A comprehensive multiethnic curriculum should also include a broad range of experiences within the study of any group: present culture, historical experiences, sociopolitical realities, contributions to American development, problems faced in everyday living, and conditions of existence in society.

Students should also be introduced to the experiences of persons of widely varying backgrounds. The curriculum should include study of ethnic peoples in general, not just ethnic heroes and success stories. However, the study of ethnic heroes and success stories can help students of an ethnic group develop greater pride in their own group. In addition, those outside of an ethnic group can develop greater respect to that group by learning about these heroes and successes. Moreover, in establishing heroes and labeling people as successes, teachers should move beyond the standards of the dominant society and consider the values of each ethnic group and the worth of each individual life. An active contributor to an ethnic neighborhood may be more of a hero to the local community than a famous ethnic athlete. A good parent may be more of a "success" than a famous ethnic politician.

For optimum effectiveness, the study of ethnicity and ethnic group experiences must be interwoven into the total curriculum. It should not be reserved for special occasions, units, or courses, nor should it be considered supplementary to the existing curriculum. Such observances as Afro-American History or Brotherhood Week, Chanukah, Cinco de Mayo, St. Patrick's Day, and Martin Luther King, Jr.'s birthday are important and necessary, but insufficient in themselves. To rely entirely on these kinds of occasions and events, or to relegate ethnic content to a marginal position in the curriculum, is to guarantee the minimal impact of ethnic studies.

The basic premises and organizational structures of American education must be revised to reflect ethnic pluralism. The curriculum must be reorganized so that ethnic diversity is an integral, natural, and normal component of educational experiences for *all* students, with ethnic content accepted and used in everyday instruction, and with different ethnic perspectives introduced when various concepts, events, and problems are being studied. Ethnic content is as appropriate and important in teaching such fundamental skills and abilities as reading, thinking, and decision making as it is in teaching about social issues raised by racism, dehumanization, racial conflict, and alternative ethnic life styles.

14. The Multiethnic Curriculum Should Include the Continuous Study of the Cultures, Historical Experiences, Social Realities, and Existential Conditions of Ethnic Groups, Including a Variety of Racial Compositions

The multiethnic curriculum should involve students in the continuous study of ethnic groups of different racial compositions. A curriculum that concentrates on one ethnic group is not multiethnic. Nor is a curriculum multiethnic if it focuses exclusively on White ethnics or exclusively on multiracial and non-White ethnic groups, such as Blacks, Latinos, Asian Americans, and Native Americans. Every ethnic group cannot be included in the curriculum of a particular school or school district. The number is too large to be manageable. However, the inclusion of groups of different racial compositions is a necessary characteristic of effective multiethnic education.

Moreover, the multiethnic curriculum should include the consistent examination of significant aspects of ethnic experiences influenced by or related to race. These include such subjects as racism, racial prejudice, racial discrimination, and exploitation based on race. The sensitive and continuous development of such concepts should help students develop an understanding of the racial factor in the past and present of our nation.

15. Interdisciplinary and Multidisciplinary Approaches Should Be Used in Designing and Implementing the Multiethnic Curriculum

No single discipline can adequately explain all of the components of the life-styles, cultural experiences, and social problems of ethnic groups. Knowledge from any one discipline is insufficient to help individuals make adequate decisions on the complex issues raised by poverty, oppression, powerlessness and alienation. Concepts such as racism and anti-Semitism have multiple dimensions. To delineate these requires the concepts and perspectives of such disciplines as the various social sciences, history, literature, music, art, and philosophy.

Single-discipline or monoperspective analyses of complex ethnic issues can produce skewed, distorted interpretations, and evaluations. A promising way to avoid these pitfalls is to employ consistently multidisciplinary approaches in studying experiences and events related to ethnic groups. For example, ethnic protest is not singularly a political, economic, artistic, or sociological activity; yet, it is all of these. Therefore, a curriculum that purports to be multiethnic and is realistic in its treatment of ethnic protest must focus on its broader ramifications. Such study must address the scientific, political, artistic, and sociological dimensions of protest.

America's accomplishments are due neither to the ingenuity and creativity of a single ethnic group, nor to accomplishments in a single area, but rather to the efforts and contributions of many different ethnic groups and individuals in many areas. Black, Latino, Native American, Asian American, and European immigrant group members have all contributed to the fields of science and industry, politics, literature, economics, and the arts. Multidisciplinary analyses will best help students to understand them.

16. The Curriculum Should Use Comparative Approaches in the Study of Ethnic Groups and Ethnicity

The study of ethnic group experiences should not be a process of "one-upmanship." It should not promote the idea that any one ethnic group has a monopoly on talent and worth, or incapacity and weakness, but, instead, the ideas that each individual and each ethnic group has worth and dignity. Students should be taught that persons from all ethnic groups have common characteristics and needs, although they are affected differently by certain social situations and may use different means to respond to their needs and to achieve their objectives. Furthermore, school personnel should remember that realistic comparative approaches to the study of different ethnic group experiences are descriptive and analytical, not normative or judgmental. Teachers should also be aware of their own biases and prejudices as they help students to use comparative approaches.

Social situations and events included in the curriculum should be analyzed from the perspectives of several ethnic groups instead of using a monoperspective analysis. This approach allows students to see the subtle ways in which the lives of different ethnic group members are similar and interrelated, to study the concept of universality as it relates to ethnic groups, and to see how all ethnic groups are active participants in all aspects of society. Studying such issues as power and politics, ethnicity, and culture from comparative, multiethnic perspectives will help students develop more realistic, accurate understandings of how these issues affect everyone, and how the effects are both alike and different.

17. The Curriculum Should Help Students to View and Interpret Events, Situations, and Conflict from Diverse Ethnic Perspectives and Points of View

Historically, students have been taught to view events, situations, and our national history primarily from the perspectives of Anglo-American historians and social scientists sympathetic to the dominant groups within our society. The perspectives of other groups, such as Afro-Americans and American Indians, have been largely omitted in the school curriculum. When the World War II Japanese American internment and the Indian Removal Act of 1830, for example, are studied in school, they are rarely viewed from the points of view of the Japanese Americans interned or the Indians forced to leave their homes and move to the West.

To gain a more complete understanding of both our past and present, students should look at events and situations from the perspectives of Anglo-Americans and from the perspectives of people who are Jewish American, Polish American, Filipino American, and Puerto Rican. This approach to teaching is more likely to make our students less ethnocentric and more able to accept the fact that almost any event or situation can be legitimately looked at from many perspectives. When using this approach in the classroom, the teacher should avoid, as much as possible, labeling any perspective as "right" or "wrong." Rather, the teacher should try to help students to understand how each group may view a situation differently and why. The emphasis should be on understanding and explanation and not on simplistic moralizing. For example, the perceptions of many Jewish Americans of political events in the United States have been shaped by memories of the Nazi Holocaust—the attempt at extermination of European Jews—and the recurring anti-Semitism in the United States.

Ethnicity has strongly influenced the nature of intergroup relations in American society. The way that individuals perceive events and situations in our nation is often influenced by their ethnic experiences, and especially so when the events and situations are directly related to ethnic conflict and discrimination, or to issues such as affirmative action and busing for school desegregation. When students view a historical or contemporary situation from the perspectives of one ethnic group only—whether it is a majority group or a minority group—they can acquire, at best, an incomplete understanding.

18. The Curriculum Should Conceptualize and Describe the Development of the United States as a Multidirectional Society

A basic structural concept in the study and teaching of American society is the view that the United States has developed mainly in an east-to-west direction. According to this concept, the United States is the product of the spread of civilization from Western Europe across the Atlantic Ocean to the east coast of what is today the United States and then west to the Pacific. Within this approach, ethnic groups appear almost always in two forms: as *obstacles* to the advance of westward-moving Anglo civilization or as *problems* that must be corrected or at least kept under control.

The underlying rationale for this frame of reference is that the study of American history is for the most part an account of processes within the national boundaries of the United States. However, in applying this frame of reference, educators have been inconsistent, including as part of the study of the United States such themes as pre-United States geography, the pre-United States British colonies, the Texas revolution, and the Lone Star Republic. In short, the traditional study of the United States has generally included phenomena outside the boundaries of the political United States as part of the American experience.

Yet, while including some non-United States themes as part of the traditional study of the United States, American education has not adequately included study of the Native American, Hispanic, and Mexican societies that developed on the land which ultimately became part of the United States. Nor has sufficient attention been devoted to the northwesterly flow of cultures from Africa to America, the northerly flow of Hispanic and Mexican society, the easterly flow of cultures from Asia, and the westerly flow of latter-day immigrants from Eastern, Central, and Southern Europe.

Multiethnic education, from the early years of school and on, must redress these intellectually invalid and distorting imbalances by illuminating the variety of cultural experiences that have composed the total American experience. Multiethnic education must deal consistently with the development of the entire geocultural United States—that area which, in time, was to become the United States and the peoples encompassed by that area. Moreover, the flow of cultures into the United States must be viewed multidirectionally, with the richness that resulted in our nation.

19. The School Should Provide Opportunities for Students to Participate in the Aesthetic Experiences of Various Ethnic Groups

Ethnic groups should not be studied only at a distance. Although there is considerable value to incorporating statistical and analytical social science methodologies and concepts in the study of ethnic groups, an over-reliance on intellectualism will miss an important part of the multiethnic experience—the participation in the experiences of ethnic groups.

A number of teaching materials can be used. Students should read and hear the past and contemporary writings of members of different ethnic groups. Poetry, short stories, folklore, essays, plays, and novels should be used. Ethnic autobiographies offer special insight into the experience of what it means to be ethnic in the United States.

Ethnic music, art, architecture, and dance—past and contemporary—provide other avenues for experiential participation, as they interpret the emotions and feelings of ethnic groups. The arts and humanities can serve as excellent vehicles for studying group experiences by focusing on the question: What aspects of the experience of a particular ethnic group helped create these kinds of musical and artistic expressions?

In studying multiethnic literature and arts, students should become acquainted with what has been created in local ethnic communities. In addition, members of local ethnic communities can provide dramatic "living autobiographies" for students. Local people should be invited to discuss their viewpoints and experiences with students. Students should also have opportunities for developing their own artistic, musical, and literary abilities, even to make them available to the local community.

Role-playing of various ethnic experiences should be interspersed throughout the curriculum to encourage understanding of what it means to belong to various ethnic groups. The immersion of students in multiethnic experiences is an effective means for developing understanding both of self and others.

20. Schools Should Foster the Study of Ethnic Group Languages as Legitimate Communication Systems

A multiethnic curriculum recognizes the reality of language diversity and promotes the attitude that all languages and dialects are valid communicating systems among some groups and for some purposes. The program requires a multidisciplinary focus on language and dialect.

Concepts about language and dialect derived from disciplines such as anthropology, sociology, and political science expand the students' perceptions of language and dialect as something more than correct grammar. For example, the nature and intent of language policies and laws in the United States can be compared to those in nations officially bilingual. Students can also be taught sociolinguistic concepts that provide a framework for understanding the verbal and nonverbal behavior of others as well as themselves. Critical listening, speaking, and reading habits should be nurtured with special attention to the uses of language.

Recent research indicates that school rejection of the student's home language affects the student's self-esteem, academic achievement, and social and occupational mobility.[5] Research also indicates that school acceptance and use of the student's home language improves self-esteem, academic achievement, and relationships among students in a school.[6] In a multiethnic curriculum, students are provided opportunities to study their known dialects as well as others. They become more receptive to the languages and dialects of fellow students. Such an approach helps students to develop concepts in their own vernaculars whenever necessary while it promotes appreciation for home language environments.

The multiethnic program should provide for literacy in at least two dialects, develop respect for language and dialect diversity, and diminish language ethnocentrism.

21. The Curriculum Should Make Maximum Use of Local Community Resources

An effective multiethnic curriculum should include a study of ethnicity and ethnic groups not only nationally, but also in the local community. An effective multiethnic curriculum must expand beyond classroom walls. Teachers should use the local community as a "laboratory" where students can develop and use intellectual, social, and political action skills in the local ethnic communities. Planned field trips and individual or group research projects are helpful. Continuous investigation of the local community can provide insights into the actual dynamics of ethnic groups. It can create greater respect for what has been accomplished. It can promote awareness of and commitment to what still needs to be done to improve the lives and opportunities for all local residents.

Every member of the local community, including the student's family, is a valuable source of knowledge. There are no class, educational, or linguistic qualifications for participating in the American experience, for having a culture or society, for having family or neighborhood traditions, for perceiving the surrounding community, or for relating one's experiences. Teachers should invite local residents of various ethnic backgrounds to the classroom. In this setting, community people can share their experiences and views with students, relate their oral traditions, answer questions, give new outlooks on society and history, and open doors of investigation for students. Special efforts should be made to involve senior citizens in school multiethnic programs both to help them develop a higher sense of self-worth and to benefit the students and the school community.

It is important that students develop a sensitivity to ethnic differences and a conceptual framework for viewing ethnic differences before interacting with ethnic classroom guests or studying the local ethnic communities. Otherwise, these promising opportunities may reinforce rather than reduce ethnic stereotypes and prejudices.

In sound study projects, students can consider such topics as local population distribution, housing, school assignments, political representation, and ethnic community activities. Older students can take advantage of accessible public documents, such as city council and school board minutes, minutes of local organizations, and church records for insight into the community.

To separate the local community from the school is to ignore the everyday world in which students live.

22. The Assessment Procedures Used with Students Should Reflect Their Ethnic Cultures

To make the school a truly multiethnic institution, major changes must be made in the ways in which we test and ascertain student abilities. Most of the intelligence tests that are administered in the public schools are based on an Anglo-conformity, monoethnic model. Since many students socialized within other ethnic cultures find the tests and other aspects of the school alien and intimidating, they perform poorly and are placed in low academic tracks, special education classes, or low ability reading groups.[7] Research indicates that teachers in these kinds of situations tend to have low expectations for their students and often fail to create the kinds of learning environments that promote mastery of the skills and abilities needed to function effectively in society.[8]

Standardized intelligence testing frequently serves, in the final analysis, to deny some ethnic youths equal educational opportunities. The results of these tests are often used to justify the noneducation of ethnic youths and to relieve teachers and other school personnel from accountability. Novel assessment devices that reflect the cultures of ethnic youths need to be developed and used. Moreover, teacher-made tests and other routine classroom assessment techniques should reflect the cultures of ethnic youths. It will, however, do little good for educators to create improved assessment procedures for ethnic youths unless, at the same time, they implement curricular and instructional practices that are also multiethnic and multiracial.

23. Schools Should Conduct Ongoing, Systematic Evaluations of the Goals, Methods, and Instructional Materials Used in Teaching about Ethnicity

Schools must set up attainable goals and objectives for multiethnic education. To evaluate the extent to which these goals and objectives are accomplished, school personnel must judge—and with evidence—what ocurs in their own school in three broad areas: (1) school policies and governance procedures; (2) everyday practices of staff and teachers; and (3) curricular programs and offerings, academic and nonacademic, preschool through grade twelve. These guidelines will help schools in their evaluation programs.

Many sources of evidence should be used. Teachers, administrators, supportive staff, parents, students, and others in the school community ought to participate in providing and evaluating evidence.

Evaluation should be construed as a means by which a school, its staff, and students can improve multiethnic relations, experiences, and understandings within the school. Evaluation should be oriented toward analyzing and improving, neither castigating nor applauding multiethnic programs. (See Appendixes B and C.)

Notes

1. Manual Ramirez III and Alfredo Castañeda, *Cultural Democracy, Bicognitive Development and Education* (New York: Academic Press, 1974); Vernon L. Allen, ed., *Psychological Factors in Poverty* (Chicago: Markham Publishing Co., 1970); Roger D. Abrahams and Rudolph C. Troike, eds., *Language and Cultural Diversity in American Education* (Englewood Cliffs, N.J.: Prentice-Hall, 1972); Stephen S. Baratz and Joan C. Baratz, "Early Childhood Intervention: The Social Science Base of Institutional Racism," *Harvard Educational Review* 40 (Winter 1970), pp. 29–50; Frederick Williams, ed., *Language and Poverty: Perspectives on a Theme* (Chicago: Markham Publishing Co., 1970).
2. Ramirez and Castañeda, *Cultural Democracy;* Judith Kleinfeld, "Effective Teachers of Eskimo and Indian Students," *School Review* 83 (February 1975), pp. 301–344.
3. Susan S. Stodolsky and Gerald Lesser, "Learning Patterns in the Disadvantaged," *Harvard Educational Review* 37 (Fall 1967), pp. 546–593. G. S. Lesser, G. Fifer, and D. H. Clark, "Mental Abilities of Children from Different Social-Class and Cultural Groups," *Monographs for Research in Child Development* 30 (1965).
4. Ramirez and Castañeda, *Cultural Democracy*; Kleinfeld, "Effective Teachers"; Stodolsky and Lesser, "Learning Patterns."
5. United States Commission on Civil Rights, *A Better Chance To Learn: Bilingual-Bicultural Education* (Washington, D.C.: U.S. Government Printing Office, 1975), pp. 33–36.
6. Ibid., pp. 38–40.
7. Jane R. Mercer, "Latent Functions of Intelligence Testing in the Public Schools," in Lamar P. Miller, ed., *The Testing of Black Students* (Englewood Cliffs, N.J.: Prentice-Hall, 1974).

8. Ray C. Rist, "Student Social Class and Teacher Expectations: The Self-Fulfilling Prophecy in Ghetto Education," *Harvard Educational Review* 40 (August 1970), pp. 411–451; Eleanor B. Leacock, *Teaching and Learning in City Schools* (New York: Basic Books, 1969); United States Commission on Civil Rights, *Teachers and Students: Differences in Teacher Interaction with Mexican American and Anglo Students* (Washington, D.C.: U.S. Government Printing Office, 1973).

APPENDIX A

Race, Culture, Ethnicity, and Education: An Annotated Bibliography

Introduction

This bibliography is designed to help the reader locate additional resources related to the issues, topics, problems, and proposals discussed in this book. It is divided into four parts. Part One consists of social science references that can serve as informative background readings for educators. Effective educational policy related to ethnic groups must be based on accurate social science knowledge. Too often, educational policy related to ethnic groups is based on inaccurate information and knowledge that emanates from questionable or racist assumptions and research methodologies. The references in Part One are designed to help educators locate well researched informational sources that will help them to accurately interpret the experiences of ethnic groups in the United States.

Part Two consists of a comprehensive category of references that deal with a range of problems and issues related to the education of ethnic groups in the United States. References related to the history of ethnic education in the United States, the teaching of ethnic studies, the purposes and problems in minority education, the learning styles of specific ethnic groups, the testing of minority students, and the medical education of minorities are some of the topics in Part Two.

Part Three contains references that discuss and analyze issues and problems related to the complex question of ways to bring about equal educational opportunities for minority students. Some of these references discuss the problems of equal educational opportunity for minority populations from a broad policy perspective. Others analyze school desegregation from its myriad perspectives. Since the 1950s, educators and social scientists have debated and studied the effects of school desegregation on the academic achievement and personality growth of minority students. Some educators argue that school desegregation is the only feasible way to bring about equal educational opportunity for ethnic groups such as Blacks and Mexican Americans. However, school desegregation continues to be a hotly debated and discussed topic, as the references in this part indicate.

The final part of this bibliography, Part Four, includes references related to another important and yet controversial educational issue: language policies for language minorities. Language minorities in this bibliography are conceptualized broadly. Entries in this part deal with language minorities that speak a language different from English, such as Spanish, as well as with students who speak a variety of English that differs from standard Anglo-English, such as Black English.

Part One: Social Science References

Achor, Shirley. *Mexican Americans in a Dallas Barrio.* Tucson, Arizona: University of Arizona Press, 1978.
This book is an anthropological study of a low-income Mexican-American community in West Dallas.

Allen, Vernon L., ed. *Psychological Factors in Poverty.* Chicago: Markham Publishing Company, 1970.
This collection of essays discusses the theoretical and empirical developments in behavioral science that are related to poverty. Lee Rainwater, J. McVicker Hunt, Robert D. Hess, and Edmund W. Gordon are among the distinguished contributors.

Allport, Gordon W. *The Nature of Prejudice,* 25th Anniversary Edition. Reading, Mass.: Addison-Wesley, 1979.
This classic book on race relations was first published in 1950. It is an essential reference for individuals working in race relations because of the theoretical framework it provides for studying race relations.

Aswad, Barbara C., ed. *Arabic Speaking Communities in American Cities.* New York: Center for Migration Studies, 1974.
This is an informative collection of essays on Arabic speaking communities in the United States. Mary C. Sengstock, Louise E. Sweet, Philip M. Kayal, May Ahdab-Yehia, and Laurel D. Wigle are among the contributors.

Bahr, Howard, Bruce A. Chadwick, and Joseph H. Stauss. *American Ethnicity.* Lexington, Mass.: D. C. Heath, 1979.
A comprehensive volume that deals with issues such as prejudice, discrimination, intergroup contact, and racism. The book has chapters on Black Americans, Native Americans, Mexican Americans, Asian Americans, and White ethnics.

Billingsley, Andrew and Jeanne M. Giovannoni. *Children of the Storm: Black Children and American Child Welfare.* New York, N.Y.: Harcourt Brace, 1972.
An important book for those working in child welfare agencies. It reviews the history of welfare services for Black children, the effect of racism on Black children, and discusses areas where reform is needed.

Blauner, Robert. *Racial Oppression in America.* New York: Harper and Row, 1972.
The central thesis of this thought provoking book is that ethnic minor-

ities within the United States are colonized and share many characteristics with other groups that have been victimized by colonization.

Branch, Marie Foster and Phyllis Perry Paxton, eds. *Providing Safe Nursing
Care for Ethnic People of Color*. New York: Appleton-Century-Crofts,
1976.
The essays in this book discuss cultural health traditions and their implications for nursing care, guidelines for safe nursing care, and curricula models for training nurses to work effectively with ethnic pa-
tients.

Brown, Corinne Ina. *Understanding Other Cultures*. Englewood Cliffs, N.J.:
Prentice-Hall, 1963.
This is an easy-to-read and interesting introduction to the concept of
culture. It is an informative "first book" to read on culture by a veteran teacher of anthropology.

Clark, Kenneth B. *Dark Ghetto: Dilemmas of Social Power*. New York: Harper
Torchbooks, 1965.
This compassionately written and perceptive book, which has attained
the status of a classic, discusses diverse dimensions of the urban communities in which many Black youths are socialized. It is a sensitively
written and informative book.

Cortés, Carlos E., Arlin I. Ginsburg, Alan W. F. Green, and James A. Joseph, eds. *Three Perspectives on Ethnicity: Blacks, Chicanos and Native
Americans*. New York, N.Y.: G. P. Putnam, 1976.
An illuminating anthology covering six significant historical periods in
the history of three American ethnic minority groups. The letters,
essays, and other primary documents included in this book can be
used to supplement a basic American history text.

Cox, Oliver C. *Caste, Class, and Race: A Study in Social Dynamics*. New York:
Modern Reader Paperbacks, 1970.
This classic study of American race relations was first published in
1948.

Dinnerstein, Leonard and Frederic Cople Jaher, ed. *Uncertain Americans:
Readings in Ethnic History*. New York: Oxford University Press, 1977.
This book consists of a limited number of comprehensive essays that
deal with diverse aspects of the history of ethnic groups in the United
States.

Engel, Madeline H. *Inequality in America: A Sociological Perspective*. New York,
N.Y.: Thomas Y. Crowell, 1971.
Madeline Engel examines racial, ethnic, religious, social class, and age
inequality in America. She also provides strategies for change and
supplemental readings by writers such as James Baldwin and Piri
Thomas.

Enloe, Cynthia H. *Ethnic Conflict and Political Development*. Boston: Little
Brown, 1973.

This excellently written and well researched book presents some re-freshing interpretations on the complex relationship between ethnicity and modernization. The author challenges traditional interpretations about modernization and ethnicity.

Epps, Edgar G., ed. *Race Relations: Current Perspectives.* Cambridge, Mass.: Winthrop Publishers, 1973.

A comprehensive book of readings that covers some of the historical experiences of minorities in America, theoretical perspectives on race, and the effects of institutional racism on Black Americans.

Faderman, Lillian and Barbara Bradshaw, eds. *Speaking for Ourselves,* 2nd ed. Glenview, Ill.: Scott, Foresman, 1975.

This anthology consists of an excellent sample of literary writings by Native-American, Black-American, Asian-American, Hispanic-American, Jewish-American, and European-American writers.

Feagin, Joe R. *Racial and Ethnic Relations.* Englewood Cliffs, N.J.: Prentice-Hall, 1978.

This basic textbook on racial and ethnic relations includes theoretical chapters as well as chapters that focus on specific ethnic groups, such as the English Americans, Irish Americans, Jewish Americans, Native Americans, and Black Americans.

Geertz, Clifford. *The Interpretation of Cultures.* New York: Basic Books, 1973.

This book consists of a collection of thoughtful and well-crafted essays on culture by an eminent American anthropologist. "Thick Description: Toward an Interpretive Theory of Culture," "The Impact of Culture on the Concept of Man," and "The Growth of Culture and the Evolution of Mind" are among the essays included in the book.

Glock, Charles Y., Robert Wuthnow, Jane A. Piliavin, and Metta Spencer. *Adolescent Prejudice.* New York: Harper and Row, 1975.

This book, which focuses on anti-Semitism among adolescents, con-cludes that prejudice is "rampant in school populations."

Greeley, Andrew M. *Why Can't They Be Like Us? America's White Ethnic Groups.* New York: Dutton, 1975.

A witty and highly readable book that discusses various aspects of White ethnic group life in the United States.

Green, Robert L. *The Urban Challenge: Poverty and Race.* Chicago: Follett Publishing Co., 1977.

This well-written and well-researched book by a veteran in the field of race relations deals with the major areas of urban life: poverty, unem-ployment, welfare, law enforcement, urban finance, housing, educa-tion, and health care. The final chapter discusses the "Prospect for Change."

Goldschmid, Marcel L., ed. *Black Americans and White Racism: Theory and Re-search.* New York, N.Y.: Holt, 1970.

This collection of reprinted articles provides a general discussion of seven topics including IQ, racism, and the Black family. Each general topic has an introduction written by the editor. The articles are short and written at the introductory level. The article by Dr. Martin Luther King, Jr. will be of particular interest to the reader interested in the role of the social scientist in a changing society.

Goodman, Mary Ellen. *Race Awareness in Young Children.* New York: Collier Books, 1952.
This is a detailed and comprehensive study of the development of children's racial attitudes.

Gordon, Milton, M. *Assimilation in American Life: The Role of Race, Religion and National Origins.* New York: Oxford University Press, 1964.
This seminal and well-crafted theoretical book has deeply influenced teaching and research in ethnic studies in the United States. It is essential reading for the serious student of ethnic cultures in America.

Gordon, Milton M. *Human Nature, Class, and Ethnicity.* New York: Oxford University Press, 1978.
This collection of essays is divided into five parts: human nature and social action; subsocieties, subcultures and ethnicity; assimilation and pluralism; social class; and marginality. The essays are informative and thoughtful.

Hannerz, Ulf. *Soulside: Inquiries into Ghetto Culture and Community.* New York: Columbia University Press. 1969.
This anthropological study of a Black urban community in Washington, D.C., describes important aspects of the socialization of Black males.

Haveman, Robert H., ed. *A Decade of Federal Antipoverty Programs: Achievements, Failures, and Lessons.* New York, N.Y.: Academic Press, 1977.
This book was begun in 1974, ten years after the start of federal Antipoverty Programs. Nine scholars from diverse disciplines were called together at a conference sponsored by the Institute for Research on Poverty to access various antipoverty programs. This book contains the papers presented at that conference and two conference discussants for each paper.

Henderson, George, *To Live in Freedom: Human Relations Today and Tomorrow.* Norman, Okla.: University of Oklahoma Press, 1972.
Henderson examines the barriers to freedom faced by some members of our society. He looks at the questions of race and social conditions in the United States. The book also includes a glossary of human relation terms and a bibliography.

Higham, John, ed. *Ethnic Leadership in America.* Baltimore: The Johns Hopkins University Press, 1978.
This well-researched collection of essays discusses ethnic leadership among Jews, the Japanese, the Germans, Afro-Americans, Native Americans, Eastern and Southern Europeans, and the Irish. The introductory and concluding chapters discuss the nature of ethnic leadership.

Holli, Melvin G. and Peter d'A. Jones, eds. *The Ethnic Frontier: Essays in the History of Group Survival in Chicago and the Midwest.* Grand Rapids, Michigan: William B. Eerdmans Publishing Co., 1977.
This collection of original and well-researched essays deals with ethnic group communities in selected midwestern cities.

Jones, James M. *Prejudice and Racism.* Reading, Mass.: Addison-Wesley, 1972.
This is an excellent and comprehensive treatment of racism from the perspectives of psychology, sociology, and history. It is a very useful introductory book on racism in American life.

Kinloch, Graham C. *The Sociology of Minority Group Relations.* Englewood Cliffs, N.J.: Prentice-Hall, 1979.
This book includes a discussion of key concepts and theories in minority group relations and descriptions of physically defined, cultural, economic, and behavioral minorities in the United States.

Kurokawa, Minako, ed. *Minority Responses.* New York: Random House, 1970.
This book consists of an excellent collection of theoretical articles and case studies related to race relations in the United States.

Leacock, Eleanor Burke, ed. *The Culture of Poverty: A Critique.* New York, N.Y.: Simon and Schuster, 1971.
An excellent collection of original papers examining the concept of the culture of poverty, community control, language, and other related issues.

Light, Ivan H. *Ethnic Enterprise in America: Business and Welfare Among Chinese, Japanese, and Blacks.* Berkeley: University of California Press, 1972.
This highly acclaimed study of the development of business among several ethnic groups is formative and well-researched.

Maehr, Martin L., and William M. Stalling, eds. *Culture, Child and School: Sociocultural Influences on Learning.* Monterey, California, Brooks/Cole, 1975.
This book contains original and reprinted articles that focus on the many ways cultural differences affect learning. The articles are divided into three categories: the cultural mileu of the child, the child's cognitive development, and the child's educational environment.

Memmi, Albert. *The Colonizer and the Colonized.* New York, N.Y.: Orion Press, 1965.
Memmi's book has attained the status of a classic. In it he reveals the relationship between the oppressor and the oppressed. While written about colonial Algeria, it can help the reader to understand the situation of ethnic minorities in the United States.

Miller, Kent S. and Ralph Mason Dreger, eds. *Comparative Studies of Black and Whites in the United States.* New York, N.Y.: Seminar Press, 1973.
An excellent collection of papers summarizing, analyzing, and interpreting the research on seventeen important topics. The article on be-

havior-genetic analysis will be of particular help in understanding the
Black IQ question.

Milner, David. *Children and Race.* Baltimore, Md.: Penguin Books, Ltd.,
1975.

Milner, a British psychologist, draws upon research done both in the
United States and England to present a comprehensive picture of the
development of children's racial attitudes and identities.

Montagu, Ashley. *Man's Most Dangerous Myth: The Fallacy of Race.* 5th ed.
New York: Oxford University Press, 1974.

An excellently written and comprehensive book by the famed anthropologist. This book can help to shatter many destructive myths about
race.

Myrdal, Gunnar with the assistance of Richard Sterner and Arnold Rose.
An American Dilemma: The Negro Problem and Modern Democracy. Volumes
1 and 2. New York: Harper Torchbooks, 1944. Reissued in 1962.

This book is a classic and landmark study of race relations in the
United States by a Swedish social economist.

Rose, Peter I., ed. *Nation of Immigrants: The Ethnic Experience and the Racial
Crisis.* New York: Random House, 1972.

This anthology consists of a comprehensive collection of essays that
deal with a wide range of issues and ethnic groups. Richard Wright,
Piri Thomas, Nathan Glazer, Gunnar Myrdal, and Robert Blauner
are among the contributors. The selections are from previously published sources.

Rose, Peter I. *They and We: Racial and Ethnic Relations in the United States.* New
York: Random House, 1974.

This is an excellent and extremely well-written introduction to the
major concepts in the field of race relations. Concepts such as race,
ethnicity, prejudice, and discrimination are defined and illustrated.

Schermerhorn, R. A. *Comparative Ethnic Relations: A Framework for Theory and
Research.* New York: Random House, 1970.

This is a sophisticated and thoughtful theoretical work on the nature
of ethnic relations. Topics discussed include dual perspectives on society and ethnic relations, intergroup sequences and racism, intergroup sequences and pluralism, and societies as contexts.

Silverstein, Barry and Ronald Krate. *Children of the Dark Ghetto: A Developmental Psychology.* New York, N.Y.: Praeger, 1975.

Two psychologists write about their formal and informal observations
of their students during their tenure as Harlem elementary school
teachers. Their book integrates their observations with a review of literature related to the develoment of Black children. The book is written in a conversational style.

Sowell, Thomas, ed., with the assistance of Lynn D. Collins, *American Ethnic
Groups.* Washington, D.C.: The Urban Institute, 1978. This book consists of a well-researched collection of essays that discusses Blacks, Chi-

nese and Japanese Americans, European immigrant groups, ethnic income variations, discrimination in the academic marketplace, and the question of race, ethnicity and IQ.

Sowell, Thomas. *Race and Economics.* New York: David McKay, 1975.
This is an informative and well-crafted book by an economist who has written extensively on problems in education and race relations. In a highly readable style, Sowell discusses the relationship between race, ethnicity, and economic achievement.

Spicer, Edward H., ed. *Ethnic Medicine in the Southwest.* Tucson, Ariz.: The University of Arizona Press, 1977.
The essays in this book discuss popular medicine, health, and illness in a Black neighborhood, a Mexican-American barrio, a Yaqui community, and among lower-income Anglos in the Southwest. This book will help teachers of science and health to integrate their curricula with ethnic content.

Stewart, Edward C. *American Culture Patterns: A Cross-Cultural Perspective.* LaGrange Park, Ill.: Intercultural Network, Inc., 1972.
This book contains an interesting and informative discussion of American assumptions, values, and patterns of thinking.

U.S. Commission on Civil Rights, *Mexican Americans and the Administration of Justice in the Southwest.* Washington, D.C.: U.S. Government Printing Office, 1970.
This report by the Commission discusses various problems related to Mexican Americans and law enforcement in the Southwest.

Wilson, William J. *Power, Racism and Privilege: Race Relations in Theoretical and Sociohistorical Perspectives.* New York: The Free Press, 1973.
This book includes a theoretical discussion of race, power, and racial conflict and analyses and comparisons of race relations in the United States and South Africa.

Wilson, William Julius. *The Declining Significance of Race: Blacks and Changing American Institutions.* Chicago: University of Chicago Press, 1978.
Wilson presents his controversial thesis that increasingly in American society social class status rather than race is becoming the most important variable in explaining the situation of Blacks in the United States.

Yetman, Norman R. and C. Hoy Steele, eds. *Majority and Minority: The Dynamics of Racial and Ethnic Relations,* 2nd ed. Boston: Allyn and Bacon, 1975.
This comprehensive collection of essays includes both theoretical articles and essays dealing with problems such as education, testing, employment, and the courts.

Part Two: The Education of Ethnic Groups

Banks, James A. and Jean D. Grambs, eds. *Black Self-Concept: Implications for Education and Social Science*. New York: McGraw-Hill, 1972.
This original collection of essays discusses issues and problems related to the self-image of Black youths. Racial prejudice and the Black Self-concept, Black youth and motivation, and the political socialization of Black youths are among the topics discussed by the authors.

Banks, James A., ed. *Teaching Ethnic Studies: Concepts and Strategies*. Washington, D.C.: National Council for the Social Studies, 1973.
This collection of essays focuses on the histories and cultures of American ethnic groups and women. Issues related to racism and cultural pluralism are also examined.

Banks, James A. *Teaching Strategies for Ethnic Studies*, 2nd ed. Boston: Allyn and Bacon, 1979.
This is a comprehensive sourcebook for teaching ethnic studies. Part I discusses the problems of goals in ethnic studies and key concepts for ethnic studies units and lessons. Part II consists of a chapter on each major American ethnic group with related teaching strategies and bibliographies. The final part of the book illustrates how the teacher can use the information in Parts I and II to develop multiethnic units and curricula.

Bowles, Samuel and Herbert Gintis. *Schooling in Capitalist America: Educational Reform and the Contradictions of Economic Life*. New York: Basic Books, 1976.
A copiously researched and well-argued book. It is perhaps the best treatment of the thesis that the major role of the schools in American society is to perpetuate class stratification and to socialize students for functioning in a capitalist economy.

Brookover, Wilbur B. and Edsel L. Erickson. *Society, Schools and Learning*. Boston: Allyn and Bacon, 1969.
Brookover has done seminal work on the self-concept of academic ability and its effects on academic achievement. In this book, Brookover and Erickson summarize their work on self-concept of ability and discuss the relationship between social class, race, and education.

Bullock, Henry Allen. *A History of Negro Education in the South: From 1619 to the Present*. Cambridge: Harvard University Press, 1967.
This comprehensive and well-written history of Black southern education was awarded a Bancroft Prize in American history in 1968.

Carnoy, Martin. *Education as Cultural Imperialism*. New York: David McKay Company, 1974.
A major thesis of this book is that education has been used by Western nations to support the colonization of Third World peoples not only in India, West Africa, and in Latin America but in the United States as

well. This provocative book will stimulate a spirited dialogue about the relationship between education and colonization.

Carter, Thomas P. and Roberto D. Segura. *Mexican Americans in School: A Decade of Change.* New York: College Entrance Examination Board, 1979.

This book replaces Carter's *Mexican Americans in School: A History of Educational Neglect,* published in 1970. It includes a comprehensive treatment of Mexican-American education and updates the earlier book and yet retains its strengths.

Castañeda, Alfredo, Richard L. James, and Webster Robbins. *The Educational Needs of Minority Groups.* Lincoln, Neb.: Professional Educators Publications, 1974.

Three educators examine the educational problems of Mexican Americans, Black Americans, and Native Americans in this book. The book is divided into three parts. Each part covers one ethnic group and includes a bibliography. The three essays are independently conceptualized and represent individual approaches to the problem of minority education.

Challenging the Myths: The Schools, the Blacks, and the Poor. Harvard Educational Review Reprint Series Number 5, 1975.

This is an excellent collection of essays that were previously published in the *Harvard Educational Review.* The topics covered include models for studying Black culture, the learning patterns of minorities, teacher expectations, and early childhood intervention as an expression of racism.

Clark, Kenneth B., ed. *Racism and American Education: A Dialogue and Agenda for Action.* New York, N.Y.: Harper and Row, 1970.

A distinguished group of Americans discuss important educational issues such as integration, Black identity, and inequality. The book also contains specific recommendations for actions needed to improve the nation's educational system.

Cook, Lloyd Allen, ed. *College Programs in Intergroup Relations.* Washington, D.C.: American Council on Education, 1950.

This is the first of two volumes in a series that describes the College Study in Intergroup Relations. The College Study was a project designed to infuse teacher education curricula with intergroup experiences and content. Twenty-four colleges participated in a total of more than 200 projects in the College Study.

Cook, Allen Lloyd. *Intergroup Relations in Teacher Education.* Washington, D.C.: American Council on Education, 1951.

This book describes a comprehensive project designed to infuse the teacher education curricula with intergroup relations content and experiences. It is divided into four parts: A General Orientation; Prejudice and Its Re-education; Improving Teacher-Leader Training; and In Point of Emphasis.

Cordasco, Francesco and Eugene Bucchioni, eds. *Puerto Rican Children in Mainland Schools: A Source Book for Teachers.* Metachen, N.M.: Scarecrow Press, 1968.

An interesting collection of articles about Puerto-Rican culture, family life, and experiences on the United States mainland. This book includes recommendations for improving the school experiences of Puerto-Rican students on the mainland.

Covello, Leonard. *The Social Background of the Italo-American School Child: A Study of the Southern Italian Family Mores and Their Effect on the School Situation in Italy and America,* edited with an introduction by Francesco Cordasco. Totowa, N.J.: Rowman and Littlefield, 1972.

This classic book on the school experiences of the Italian-American child, originally published in 1944, has been reissued with an introduction by Francesco Cordasco.

Cross, Dolores E., Gwendolyn C. Baker, Lindley J. Stiles, eds. *Teaching In A Multicultural Society: Perspectives and Professional Strategies.* New York, N.Y.: The Free Press, 1977.

This book of readings provides general information on multicultural education and specific teaching strategies in areas such as history and the language arts.

Della-Dora, Delmo and James E. House, ed. *Education for an Open Society.* Washington, D.C.: Association for Supervision and Curriculum Development, 1974.

Published on the twentieth anniversary of the historic *Brown* decision, this book of original essays discusses the curricular, political, and other factors related to using the school as a vehicle to help create a society that is open to minorities, women, and other excluded groups.

Epps, Edgar G., ed. *Cultural Pluralism.* Berkeley: McCutchan Publishing Corporation, 1974.

This collection of essays discusses such topics as assimilation and the schools, persisting ideological issues of assimilation in America, and making the schools a vehicle for cultural pluralism. The contributors include Alfredo Castañeda, Barbara A. Sizemore, Thomas F. Pettigrew, and Andrew T. Kopan.

Fuchs, Estelle and Robert J. Havighurst. *To Live on This Earth: American Indian Education.* Garden City: Doubleday, 1973.

This book includes a comprehensive discussion of various aspects of Indian Education. It is based largely on the National Study of American Indian Education that the authors directed and completed in 1971.

Grant, Carl A., ed. *Community Participation in Education.* Boston: Allyn and Bacon, 1979.

This book consists of a series of thoughtful and well-researched essays that discuss the problems and promises of involving the community in the educational process. Several of the essays focus on the role of the ethnic minority community in education.

Grant, Carl A., ed. "Multicultural Education in the International Year of the Child." *The Journal of Negro Education* 48 (Summer 1979).

This comprehensive collection of essays deals with diverse aspects of the emerging concept of multicultural education. Contributors include James A. Banks, Gwendolyn C. Baker, Geneva Gay, Barbara A. Sizemore, and Carl A. Grant.

Green, Robert L., ed. *Racial Crisis in American Education*. Chicago: Follett, 1969.

This is one of the earlier but still valuable collection of essays that deal with issues related to minority and urban education. The essays which constitute this book are informed and well-researched. Donald H. Smith, Mark A. Chesler, Kenneth R. Johnson, and Barbara A. Sizemore are among the contributors.

Hansen-Krening, Nancy. *Competency and Creativity in the Language Arts: A Multiethnic Focus*. Reading, Mass.: Addison-Wesley, 1979.

This book is designed to help teachers develop the skills to teach basic language arts skills while helping students to increase their knowledge and appreciation of American ethnic cultures.

Henderson, George, ed. *Human Relations: From Theory to Practice,* Norman, Okla.: University of Oklahoma Press, 1974.

This book consists of a collection of articles on human relations. It includes articles on encounter groups, T-groups, transactional analysis, and simulation games.

Herriott, Robert E. and Nancy Hoyt St. John. *Social Class and the Urban School: The Impact of Pupil Background on Teachers and Principals*. New York: John Wiley and Sons, 1966.

In this interesting study, the authors conclude, "Quite clearly, the role of teachers and principals, as defined by their views of the needs of pupils, is very different in schools of different socioeconomic composition."

Hummel, Raymond C. and John M. Nagle. *Urban Education in America: Problems and Prospects*. New York: Oxford University Press, 1973.

This is a comprehensive and well-written book that focuses on the school systems of the nation's fifty largest central cities. The problems, people, and organization of urban schools are some of the topics treated by the authors. The final chapter discusses strategies for reform in urban schools.

Johnson, Henry Sioux and William J. Hernandez-M., eds. *Educating The Mexican American*. Valley Forge, Pa.: Judson Press, 1976.

This introductory book of readings discusses many issues related to educating the Mexican-American child.

Katz, Judy H. *White Awareness: Handbook for Anti-Racism Training*. Norman, Okla.: University of Oklahoma, 1978.

Katz sees racism as a White problem. She feels that racism has a profound effect on White people. Katz uses the first three chapters of this book to outline and defend her position. The rest of the book is used to present her six stage program designed to change racist attitudes and behaviors. The book contains bibliographies and other helpful resources.

Katz, Michael B. *Class, Bureaucracy, and Schools: The Illusion of Educational Change in America.* Expanded edition. New York: Praeger, 1975.

This thoughtful and cogently written revisionist history of American schools maintains that schools are designed to perpetuate the social class and ethnic stratifications of the society. It has evoked considerable discussion and debate about the role of the school in bringing about equality and social justice.

Leacock, Eleanor Burke. *Teaching and Learning in City Schools.* New York: Basic Books, 1969.

This book reports a study of elementary classrooms by an interdisciplinary team headed by anthropologists. It provides some useful insights about education in urban schools.

Lightfoot, Sara Lawrence. *Worlds Apart: Relationship between Families and Schools.* New York: Basic Books, 1978.

In five skillful and sensitively written essays, the author discusses how teachers and parents must jointly participate in the education of Black children in order to bring about equal educational opportunities of Black students.

Longstreet, Wilma S. *Aspects of Ethnicity: Understanding Differences in Pluralistic Classrooms.* New York: Teachers College Press, 1978.

Designed to help teachers to become more sensitive to ethnic differences and to use them constructively in the classroom, the author presents a system designed to help teachers learn how to observe the ethnic behaviors of their students and to systematically record and interpret them. She calls this the "ethnic profile."

Mercer, Jane R. *Labeling the Mentally Retarded: Clinical and Social System Perspectives on Mental Retardation.* Berkeley: University of California Press, 1973.

Mercer's chapter on the labeling process in the public schools documents the extent to which Mexican Americans and Black students are victims of labeling procedures that result in their disproportionate ratio in classes for the mentally retarded.

Miller, Harry L. and Roger R. Woock. *Social Foundations of Urban Education.* 2nd ed. Hinsdale, Ill.: The Dryden Press, 1973.

This is an informative and well-conceptualized text on urban education. Many of the discussions in the text are based on data-based research.

Miller, LaMar P., ed. *The Testing of Black Students: A Symposium.* Englewood Cliffs, N.J.: Prentice-Hall, 1974.

The importance of this book has increased because of the mass media attention given to Arthur R. Jensen's *Bias in Mental Testing* (1980). Thoughtful and careful scholars, such as Robert L. Williams, Edgar G. Epps, and Jane R. Mercer discuss, in a series of essays, how Black and other minority youths are victimized by standardized tests normed on other cultural and ethnic groups.

Morris, Lee with Greg Sather and Susan Scull, eds. *Extracting Learning Styles from Social/Cultural Diversity: A Study of Five American Minorities*. Southwest Teacher Corp. Network, 1978.

This book contains original papers on the learning styles of Chicanos, Native Americans, poor Whites, Chinese Americans, and Afro-Americans. It also contains a general paper on learning styles and one on how to develop an instructional unit that reflects cultural diversity.

Multicultural Education and the American Indian. Los Angeles: American Indian Studies Center, University of California, 1979

This book consists of a collection of papers that discusses a variety of issues related to American Indian education. Multicultural education policies, Indian student performance, teacher training, and curriculum development are among the topics discussed. Jack Forbes, Frederic R. Gunsky, and Willard E. Bill are among the contributors.

Odegaard, Charles E. *Minorities in Medicine: From Receptive Passivity to Positive Action*. New York: The Josia Macy, Jr. Foundation, 1977.

This thoughtful and compassionately written report examines the problems of increasing the numbers of minorities in medical schools, pilot programs that have been developed, and the resistence to these programs. The author focuses on American Indians, Blacks, Mexican Americans, and Mainland Puerto Ricans.

Ogbu, John U. *Minority Education and Caste: The American System in Cross-Cultural Perspective*. New York: Academic Press, 1978.

This is an insightful and well researched book that compares minority education in the United States to a caste system. The education of ethnic groups in Britain, New Zealand, India, Japan, and Israel are discussed and compared with minority education in the United States.

Ogbu, John U. *The Next Generation: An Ethnography of Education in an Urban Neighborhood*. New York: Academic Press, 1974.

This is a sensitive and thoughtful ethnographic study of the educational experiences of students in a low-income neighborhood in Stockton, California. Most of the students in the neighborhood are Black or Mexican American. The author discusses the implications of his findings for bringing about equal educational opportunities for American minorities.

Pedersen, Paul, Walter J. Lonner, and Juris G. Draguns, eds. *Counseling Across Cultures*. Honolulu: The University Press of Hawaii, 1976.

This volume contains an excellent and thoughtful collection of essays that deal with issues and problems involved in counseling across cultures. Both domestic and international cultures are considered by authors.

Rist, Ray C. *The Urban School: A Factory for Failure, A Study of Education in American Society.* Cambridge, Mass.: the M.I.T. Press, 1973.

In this sensitive and cogent ethnographic study of an urban classroom, the author documents how the school perpetuates social class discrimination and denies lower-class students educational equity.

Roberts, Joan I. and Sherrie K. Akinsanya, eds. *Schooling in the Cultural Context: Anthropological Studies on Education.* New York: David McKay, 1971.

Anthropological perspectives and insights can help educators work with culturally diverse students more effectively. This excellent collection of previously published essays include essays on anthropological analyses of classrooms; culture, education, and the individual; and language and cultural learning.

Rosenthal, Robert and Lenore Jacobson. *Pygmalion in the Classroom: Teacher Expectation and Pupils' Intellectual Development.* New York: Holt, 1968.

An interesting study of the effects of teacher attitudes and expectations on student achievement. Although this study has evoked much controversy, many teachers still believe in the cogency of its message.

Samuda, Ronald J. *Psychological Testing of American Minorities: Issues and Consequences.* New York: Dodd, Mead, 1975.

The author summarizes and synthesizes over four hundred selected studies related to the testing of ethnic minorities. He also discusses "important ways in which psychological testing can and does impede the party of American minorities and deny them access to and participation in the goods of society." The final chapter of the book discusses "Alternatives to Traditional Standardized Tests."

Smith, Louis M. and William Geoffry. *The Complexities of An Urban Classroom: An Analysis Toward A General Theory of Teaching.* New York: Holt, 1968.

This book is an ethnography of an urban classroom. The authors add their analyses and interpretations to the data they collected. They also provide a glossary of psychological concepts.

Stent, Madelon, William R. Hazard, and Harry N. Rivlin, eds. *Cultural Pluralism in Education: A Mandate for Change.* New York: Appleton-Century-Crofts, 1973.

The papers that comprise this book were presented at a Conference on Education and Teacher Education for Cultural Pluralism held in Chicago in 1971. Manuel H. Guerra, John Aragon, Vincent Harding, Vine Deloria, Jr., William L. Smith, and Malcolm P. Douglass are among the contributors.

Szasz, Margaret. *Education and the American Indian: The Road to Self-Determination, 1928–1973.* Albuquerque, N.M.: University of New Mexico Press, 1974.

This book is a historical review of Indian education in the United

States. The author tries to identify the conditions that significantly affected Indian education from 1928 to the 1970s. She discusses issues such as teacher training, the Meriam Report, and cross-cultural education.

Taba, Hilda, Elizabeth Hall Brady, and John T. Robinson. *Intergroup Education in Public Schools.* Washington, D.C.: American Council on Education, 1952.

This book describes the theory and practice of an experimental project in intergroup education in a group of cooperating schools. Fundamentals of intergroup education, curriculum development, and group life in school are some of the chapter topics.

Thompson, Thomas, ed. *The Schooling of Native America.* Washington, D.C.: American Association of Colleges for Teacher Education, 1978. This series of essays by Native-American educators grew out of the first Native-American Teacher Corps Conference held in 1973. The essays discuss a wide range of topics related to Indian education such as politics, college students, compensatory education, and teachers for Indian children.

Tyack, David B. *The One Best System: A History of American Urban Education.* Cambridge: Harvard University Press, 1974.

This is a brillant and highly acclaimed history of urban education in the United States.

United States Commission on Civil Rights. *Mexican American Education Study* 6 volumes. Washington, D.C.: United States Government Printing Office, 1971–1974.

The reports in this comprehensive study of Mexican-American education deal with 1-*Ethnic Isolation of Mexican Americans in the Public Schools of the Southwest;* 2-*The Unfinished Education;* 3-*The Excluded Student;* 4-*Mexican American Education in Texas: A Function of Wealth;* 5-*Teachers and Students;* and 6-*Toward Quality Education for Mexican Americans.*

Verma, Gajendra K. and Christopher Bagley, eds. *Race and Education Across Cultures.* London: Heinemann, 1975.

This collection of well-conceptualized and well-researched essays examines and reports research findings related to race and education in the United States, Australia, and England.

Verma, Gajendra K. and Christopher Bagley, eds. *Race, Education and Identity.* London: The Macmillan Press Ltd., 1979.

This book consists of a number of studies that focus on racism and race relations in education. Cognitive studies, curriculum and evaluation studies, and studies related to identity are included.

Weinberg, Meyer. *A Chance to Learn: A History of Race and Education in the United States.* New York: Cambridge University Press, 1977. A well-researched and well-written history of the educational experiences of

Blacks. Mexican Americans, Indians, and Puerto Ricans in the United States.

West, Earle H., ed. *The Black American and Education.* Columbus, Ohio: Charles E. Merrill, 1972.

Documents related to Black education from colonial times to the present are contained in this well-conceptualized book. The documents are divided into three major historical periods: Before Emancipation; Emancipation to World War I; and World War I to 1970. Each section is preceded by a brief essay by the editor.

Woodson, Carter G. *Mis-Education of the Negro.* Washington, D.C.: The Associated Publishers, Inc., 1933. Reissued in 1969.

This classic in Black education was penned by the "Father of Negro History." It has cogent implications for Black education today.

Part Three: Equal Educational Opportunity and Desegregation

"The Courts, Social Science and School Desegretation." *Law and Contemporary Problems* 39 (Winter 1975), School of Law, Duke University, Parts 1 and 2.

An excellent collection of papers that discuss the legal, theoretical, and empirical issues and problems related to school desegregation. Meyer Weinberg, Elizabeth G. Cohen, Edgar G. Epps, and Derrick A. Bell, Jr. are among the contributors.

Equal Education Opportunity. Cambridge, Mass.: Harvard University Press, 1969.

This collection of essays is an expansion of the Winter, 1968 special issue of the *Harvard Educational Review.* These essays are largely related to the controversial "Coleman Report" that documents the limited effectivness of schooling. The contributors include James S. Coleman, Daniel P. Moynihan, Thomas F. Pettigrew, and Samuel Bowles. This book contains an excellent summary of the Coleman Report and thoughtful examinations of it.

Friedman, Murray, Roger Meltzer, and Charles Miller, eds. *New Perspectives on School Integration.* Philadelphia: Fortress Press, 1979.

A collection of original and previously published essays make up this anthology that deals with a variety of topics related to school integration. Irving M. Levine, Derrick A. Bell, Jr., James A. Banks, and James S. Coleman are among the contributors.

Harris, Norene, Nathaniel Jackson, Carl E. Rydingsword, eds. *The Integration of American Schools: Problems, Experiences, Solutions.* Boston, Mass.: Allyn and Bacon, 1975.

A collection of articles presenting diverse views on school integration.

This book contains several interviews with civil rights leaders, politicians, judges, and educators.

Jencks, Christopher et al. *Inequality: A Reassessment of the Effect of Family and Schooling in America.* New York: Basic Books, 1972.

This controversial and widely discussed book by Jencks and his colleagues emphasizes the limitations of formal schooling in bringing about equality for America's structurally excluded groups.

Levinsohn, Florence and Benjamin D. Wright, eds. *School Desegregation: Shadow and Substance.* Chicago: The University of Chicago Press, 1976.

This collection of essays was originally published as the May, 1976 issue of *School Review.* This book contains a well-written and thoughtful collection of essays that explore the myriad issues related to school desegregation. Charles V. Willie, Alvin F. Poussaint, and Ray C. Rist are among the contributors.

"A Look at Anti-Egalitarian Research: Symposium Papers," *Journal of Negro Education* 42 (Fall 1973), pp. 528–569.

These four papers critically analyze various aspects and dimensons of the controversial Jencks et al study about the ineffectiveness of schooling. The authors of the papers are Charles A. Asbury, Faustine C. Jones, Lois Powell, and Charles A. Martin.

Mosteller, Frederick and Daniel P. Moynihan, eds. *On Equality of Educational Opportunity.* New York: Vintage Books, 1972.

The papers that constitute this book grew out of a Harvard University Faculty Seminar designed to reanalyze and reconceptualize the data collected in the massive Coleman Report. Christopher S. Jencks, James S. Coleman, David J. Armor, as well as others, contributed to this thoughtful and informative volume.

Noar, Gertrude. *The Teacher and Integration.* Washington, D.C.: National Education Association, 1966.

This book provides teachers with basic information about the desegregated classroom and attempts to help them understand and be sensitive to the needs of children of different races. It contains specific strategies for achieving a fully functioning integrated classroom. The author addresses questions related to materials, discipline, student needs, learning, and other issues facing the teacher in an integrated classroom.

Persell, Caroline Hodges. *Education and Inequality: The Roots and Results of Stratification in America's Schools.* New York: The Free Press, 1977.

This refreshing and thoughtful study of inequality in the schools of the United States challenges traditional interpretations of the causes of inequality and offers a systematic theory that emphasizes the relationship of the school to other social and economic institutions in society.

Rist, Ray C. *The Invisible Children: School Integration in American Society.* Cambridge, Mass.: Harvard University press, 1978.

This book is an insightful and sensitive anthropological study of a newly desegregated school in Portland, Oregon. It has cogent implications for designing desegregated educational environments that have pluralistic norms and values.

Tesconi, Charles A., Jr. and Emanuel Hurwitz, Jr. *Education for Whom? The Question of Educational Opportunity.* New York: Dodd, Mead and Company, 1974.

This book includes a text by the authors as well as articles reprinted from other sources. It is a thought-provoking volume.

United States Commission on Civil Rights. *Fulfilling the Letter and Spirit of the Law: Desegregation of the Nation's Public Schools.* Washington, D.C.: U.S. Government Printing Office, 1976.

In this book, the Commission provides a comprehensive report on the status of desegregation in a number of school districts. This report also addresses such issues as community preparation, student attitudes, and minority staff.

Part Four: Linguistic Pluralism and Education

Abrahams, Roger D. and Rudolph C. Troike, eds. *Language and Cultural Diversity in American Education.* Englewood Cliffs, N.J.: Prentice-Hall, 1972.

This is a useful collection of previously published essays that deal with a variety of topics related to linguistic pluralism in American education. The final section of the book focuses on guidelines for educational practice.

Andersson, Theodore and Mildred Boyer. *Bilingual Schooling in the United States.* 2 volumes. Austin, Tex.: Southwest Educational Development Laboratory, 1970.

The first volume of this publication deals with issues such as definitions, the history of bilingual schooling, a rationale for bilingual education, planning a bilingual program, and the implications of bilingual schooling for education and society. The second volume deals with a number of issues and problems in bilingual education and includes chapters that focus on bilingual education for specific language groups such as Spanish, German, Polish, and French speakers in the United States.

Bilingual Education: Current Perspectives. Volumes 1 through 5. Arlington, Va.: Center for Applied Linguistics, 1977–1978.

The five volumes that constitute this comprehensive series of books on bilingual education deal with these topics respectively: *Social Science, Linguistics, Law, Education,* and *Synthesis.* Each volume consists of a series of essays prepared by authorities in the various social science disciplines. The volumes constitute a useful resource on bilingual education.

Burling, Robbins. *English in Black and White.* New York: Holt, 1973.
The author provides an interesting, well-written, and informed discussion of Black English.

Casasola, Constance. *Bilingual-Bicultural Education: A Manual for Teachers Trainers and Trainees.* Berkeley, Calif.: Editorial Justa Publications, Inc., 1978.
A useful guide for teacher educators responsible for training teachers to teach English as a second language. Topics include lesson plan development, first and second language acquisition, methods for teaching a second language, principles of language learning, and the features of language.

Cordasco, Francesco, ed. *Bilingual Schooling in the United States: A Sourcebook for Education Personnel.* New York: Webster Division, McGraw-Hill, 1976.
This book consists of an interesting collection of articles divided into four sections: Historical Backgrounds; Typology and Definitions; Linguistic Perspectives; and Programs, Practices, and Staff Development. The two appendixes consist of an overview of court decisions related to bilingual education and a list of programs and projects in bilingual education. A comprehensive but nonannotated bibliography is included.

Dillard, J. L. *Black English: Its History and Usage in the United States.* New York: Vintage Books, 1972.
This book is a well-researched, readable and comprehensive treatment of Black English. Chapters include "On the Structure of Black English," "A Sketch of the History of Black English," and "Black English and Education."

Epstein, Noel. *Language, Ethnicity and the Schools: Policy Alternatives for Bilingual-Bicultural Education.* Washington, D.C.: Institute for Educational Leadership, 1977.
In this book, which has evoked considerable controversy, Epstein raises serious questions about the role of the federal government in bilingual-bicultural education. Jose A. Cardenas and Gary Orfield respond to Epstein.

Feitelson, Dina, ed. *Mother Tongue or Second Language? On the Teaching of Reading in Multilingual Societies.* Newark, Del.: International Reading Association, 1979.
The papers in this volume, except one, was prepared for the Sixth World Congress on Reading held by the International Reading Association that was held in Singapore in 1976. Reading programs are discussed in such nations as Malaysia, Indonesia, Afghanistan, and Korea.

Gingras, Rosario, ed. *Second-Language Acquisition and Foreign Language Teaching.* Arlington, Va.: Center for Applied Linguistics, 1978.
This book consists of an excellent collection of articles that deal with

topics such as the monitor model for second-language acquisition, the acculturation model for second-language acquisition, the monitor model and monitoring in foreign language speech communication, and the implications of research on adult second-language acquisition for teaching foreign languages to children. The book also contains a comprehensive bibliography.

Hatch, Evelyn Marcussen, ed. *Second Language Acquisition: A Book of Readings.* Rowley, Mass.: Newbury House Publishers, 1978.

This book consists of a collection of readings organized around these four major topics: Case studies; Experimental studies; Discourse analysis, and Abstracts. Topics treated in the book include simultaneous acquisition of two languages; adding a second language; second language acquisition of older learners; multiple measures; age comparisons; and natural sequence order of morphemes.

McLaughlin, Barry. *Second-Language Acquisition in Childhood.* Hillsdale N.J.: Lawrence Erlbaum Associates Publishers, 1978.

This well-researched publication deals with questions such as bilingualism in society, first-language acquisition, language acquisition and learning in childhood and adulthood, simultaneous acquisition of two languages in childhood, successive acquisition of two languages in childhood, second-language programs in the elementary school, and the effects of bilingualism.

Mackay, Ronald, Bruce Barkman, and R. R. Jordan, eds. *Reading in a Second Language: Hypotheses, Organization, and Practice.* Rowley, Mass.: Newbury House Publishers, Inc., 1979.

This book consists of a series of essays organized around three major topics: hypotheses, organization, and practice. James Coady, Muriel Saville-Troike, David E. Eskey, Sheila Been, and Salwa Ibrahim are among the contributors.

National Advisory Council on Bilingual Education. *The Fourth Annual Report.* Rosslyn, Va.: InterAmerica Research Associates, 1979.

This annual report discusses the status of bilingual education in the United States, the administration of the bilingual education program, other federal programs addressing aspects of bilingual education, current federal research in bilingual education, and state legislation on bilingual education. The reader should consult more recent annual reports from the National Advisory Council on Bilingual Education for more current overviews of developments in this field.

Poblano, Ralph, ed. *Ghosts in the Barrio: Issues in Bilingual-Bicultural Education.* San Rafael, Calif: Leswing Press, 1973.

A group of Mexican-American educators who have worked in different levels of education discuss a variety of issues related to the schooling of Mexican-American students in this book. Employment, the political process, and bilingual-bicultural education are some of the topics discussed.

Ritchie, William C. ed. *Second Language Acquisition Research: Issues and Implications.* New York: Academic Press, 1978.

This collection of papers explores such topics as theory and practice in second language research and teaching, bilingualism: a neuro-linguistic perspective; the right roof constraint in an adult-acquired language; order of difficulty in adult second language acquisition; beyond statistics in second language acquisition research; and the strategy of avoidance in adult second language acquisition.

Simoes, Antonio, Jr., ed. *The Bilingual Child: Research and Analysis of Existing Educational Themes.* New York: Academic Press, 1976.

This collection of papers discusses bilingual-bicultural education in both the United States and Canada. The topics discussed include developing cultural attitudes scales, research in cognitive mapping, a bilingual interaction analysis model, social and psychological implications of bilingual literacy, immersion programs, and the socioeconomic implications of bilingual education on a Navajo reservation.

Smith, Arthur L., ed. *Language, Communication, and Rhetoric in Black America.* New York: Harper and Row, 1972.

This book consists of a comprehensive collection of articles that deal with diverse issues related to Black English and Black communication styles. The function of Black oratory within Black society is examined at considerable length.

Trueba, Henry T. and Carol Barnett-Mizrahi, eds. *Bilingual Multicultural Education and the Professional: From Theory to Practice.* Rowley, Mass.: Newbury House Publishers. 1979.

A comprehensive book of readings covering theoretical questions as well as practical issues in bilingual education. Most of the articles focus on bilingual topics, however several articles address the more general topic of culture. This book contains several articles that are useful when introducing, defining, and justifying bilingual programs.

United States Commission on Civil Rights. *A Better Chance to Learn: Bilingual-Bicultural Education.* Washington, D.C.: U.S. Government Printing Office, 1975.

This book presents an overview of the history of bilingual-bicultural education and its current status. It examines English as a second language (ESL) programs, reviews the research on bilingualism, and discusses its legal status.

Von Malfitz, Frances Willard. *Living and Learning in Two Languages: Bilingual-Bicultural Education.* New York, N.Y.: McGraw-Hill, 1975.

An introductory book on bilingual-bicultural education. It reviews the history of bilingualism, discusses how other countries deal with language minorities, and presents questions raised in opposition to bilingual education. Bilingual education for Native Americans and Puerto Ricans are among the topics discussed.

Williams, Frederick, ed. *Language and Poverty: Perspectives on a Theme.* Chicago: Markham Publishing Company, 1970.
This excellent collection of papers deals with language issues affecting both dialect and language minorities in the United States. The contributors include Joan C. Baratz, Basil Bernstein, Courtney B. Cazden, Vera P. John, William Labov, and Roger W. Shuy.

APPENDIX **B***

A Course Inventory
for Multiethnic/multicultural Education

Course————

Instructor's Name————

Course Objectives

List the current course objectives in your course that are related to multiethnic/multicultural education. For example: "The students will be able to distinguish the cultural pluralist from the cultural assimilationist ideology." If your course has no objectives in this area, write "NONE" in the space provided.

List Current Objectives

New Course Objectives

Identify course objectives related to multiethnic/multicultural education that you can add to your course.

305

List New Course Objectives

Concepts

Identify the major concepts in your course that are related to multiethnic/multicultural education. Examples: racism, cultural diversity, cultural assimilation, structural assimilation, ethnicity, race, intercultural communication, multicultural education, multiethnic education. If your course has no concepts in this area, write "NONE" in the space provided.

List Current Concepts

New Concepts

Identify key concepts related to multiethnic/multicultural education that you can add to your courses.

List New Concepts

Content

List the major content or topics in your course that relate to multiethnic/multicultural education. For example:

1. the learning styles of minority students
2. teacher attitudes toward minority youths
3. scientific explanations of the concept of race
4. the linguistic characteristics of Black and Mexican-American youths
5. the values of ethnic minority youths

(If your course has no content in this area, write "NONE" in the space provided.)

List Current Content

New Content

Identify content related to multiethnic/multicultural education that you can add to your course.

List New Content

Current Strategies

Identify strategies used in your course that are related to multiethnic/multicultural education. Examples:

1. doing an ethnography of a multiethnic school
2. role-playing stories related to ethnic and racial problems
3. viewing films on racial and ethnic minorities
4. a clinical experience in a multiethnic school

(If your course has no strategies related to multiethnic/multicultural education, write "NONE" in the appropriate space.)

List Current Strategies

New Strategies

Identify strategies related to multiethnic/multicultural education that you can add to your course.

List New Strategies

Current Materials

List the print and nonprint materials you currently use in your course that are related to multiethnic/multicultural education. Examples:

James A. Banks. *Teaching Strategies for Ethnic Studies.* 2nd ed. Boston: Allyn and Bacon, 1979.

Geneva Gay. "Viewing the Pluralistic Classroom as a Cultural Microcosm." *Educational Research Quarterly* (Winter 1978), pp. 45–59.

Wilma S. Longstreet. "Learning and Diversity: The Ethnic Factor." *Educational Research Quarterly* (Winter 1978).

Alfredo Castañeda and Tracy Gray. "Bicognitive Processes in Multicultural Education." *Educational Leadership* 32 (December 1974), pp. 203–207.

List Current Materials

New Materials

Identify the print and nonprint materials related to multiethnic/multicultural education that you can add to your course in order to develop your current and/or new course objectives identified above.

List New Materials

APPENDIX C

Evaluation Guidelines for Multicultural-multiracial Education*

School Structure Relating to Multicultural-multiracial Education

A. Racial-ethnic Balance of the Total Staff

1. List below percentages for the various racial and ethnic groups.

	American Indian %	Black %	Asian American %	Spanish speaking %	European American %	Others specify %
Administrators						
Classroom Teachers						
Guidance Counselors						
Media Personnel						
Health Services Personnel						
Specialists and Consultants						
Food Services Personnel						
Secretaries and Clerks						
Custodial and Maintenance Personnel						
Paraprofessionals						
Others						

* Reprinted from *Evaluation Guidelines for Multicultural-Multiracial Education.* Arlington, Virginia: National Study of School Evaluation, 1973, pp. 25–33. Used with permission of the National Study of School Evaluation. Not to be reproduced without permission.

a. How many of the non-White professional personnel in the school are under tenure?

b. What percentage is this of all tenured personnel in the school?

c. How many of the administrators are women?

Checklist*

1. Minority* personnel on the staff are more numerous now than five years ago.   na   1   2   3   4

2. The racial composition of the professional staff is in keeping with the racial makeup of the student body.   na   1   2   3   4

3. Minority* staff members have been given professional assignments other than that of classroom teachers.   na   1   2   3   4

4. The racial-ethnic composition of the professional staff fairly reflects the racial-ethnic balance of the community.   na   1   2   3   4

Evaluations

a) Are minority* personnel sufficiently represented on the school's teaching staff so as to provide a favorable setting for multiracial education?   na   1   2   3   4

b) Are minority* personnel sufficiently represented on the school's administrative and other non-teaching professional staff so as to provide a favorable setting for multicultural-multiracial education?   na   1   2   3   4

c) Are minority* personnel on the school's professional staff represented to a degree that reflects the broad pluralistic society of the United States rather than the immediate community?   na   1   2   3   4

d) Are women sufficiently represented on the school's administrative staff so as to indicate the absence of sexual bias?   na   1   2   3   4

e) In the general school structure, is there an effort to reduce sex stereotyping?   na   1   2   3   4

Comments

* 4 = Excellent;   3 = Good;   2 = Fair;   1 = Poor, Missing;   na = Not applicable. Whereever the word minority is asterisked, it refers to racial or ethnic groups that are the numerical minority within this particular school or district.

B. The Teaching Staff

Checklist

1. The staff is receptive to minority* colleagues.   . na 1 2 3 4
2. Teachers attend in-service workshops or institutes on multicultural-multiracial education.   . . . na 1 2 3 4
3. Teachers recognize the need for multicultural-multiracial education in this school.   . . . . na 1 2 3 4
4. Teachers search for ways to overcome the reluctance of students to recognize and discuss racial and ethnic questions.   . . . . na 1 2 3 4
5. Teachers are relatively consistent in expecting adequate classroom behavior of all students.   . na 1 2 3 4
6. Teachers establish legitimate standards for classwork, but also make special efforts to see that all students, despite any initial learning deficiencies, can reach those standards.   . . . . na 1 2 3 4
7. Teachers openly recognize racial and cultural biases in themselves and in students and attempt to overcome these.   . . . . na 1 2 3 4
8. Teachers respect the cultural, racial, and ethnic differences of their students.   . . . . na 1 2 3 4

Evaluations

a) To what extent is the staff committed to multicultural-multiracial education in this school?   . na 1 2 3 4
b) To what extent does the teaching staff make a consistent effort to promote sound multicultural-multiracial relationships in all their contacts with students in this school?   . . . . na 1 2 3 4
c) To what extent do the teachers practice sound interpersonal and intergroup relationships among themselves?   . . . . na 1 2 3 4
d) To what extent are all staff members required to have training in multicultural-multiracial education?   . . . . na 1 2 3 4

Comments

C. The Principal and His or Her Administrative Staff

Checklist

1. Members of the administrative staff have participated in workshops, seminars, institutes, etc., in human relations and minority issues.   . .   na 1 2 3 4
2. The principal actively seeks and welcomes minority* group teachers.   . . . .   na 1 2 3 4
3. The principal promotes better relations between faculty members from minority and majority groups.   . . . .   na 1 2 3 4
4. The principal is accessible to minority* parents wishing to discuss racial, ethnic, and school issues.   . . . .   na 1 2 3 4
5. The principal is accessible to minority* students wishing to discuss racial, ethnic, and school issues.   . . . .   na 1 2 3 4
6. The principal regularly reports to the parents about the progress of the multicultural-multiracial education program in the school.   . . .   na 1 2 3 4
7. The principal makes program and other recommendations to the superintendent for improving multicultural-multiracial education.   . . .   na 1 2 3 4
8. The principal deals directly and openly with minority* groups.   . . . .   na 1 2 3 4
9. The principal regularly works with the teaching staff to help them improve the quality of their efforts in multicultural-multiracial education.   na 1 2 3 4
10. The principal is committed to the need for multicultural-multiracial education in this school.   na 1 2 3 4
11. The administrative staff is committed to the need for multicultural-multiracial education in this school.   . . . .   na 1 2 3 4

Evaluations

a) How effectively does the principal perform his or her duties in relation to multicultural-multiracial education?   . . . .   na 1 2 3 4
b) To what degree do the assistants to the principal support his or her policies and program relating to multicultural-multiracial education?   . . . .   na 1 2 3 4

Comments

D. School Organization and Grouping

Checklist

1. In organizing the school, consideration has been given to the subtle and overt effects of the schedule, grade placement, course requirements, and the like, on minority group students.   . . . .   na   1   2   3   4

2. Rules and regulations of the school relate strictly to the need for general control and not to nonessential culture differences and mores.   . . .   na   1   2   3   4

3. The school recognizes the need among its students for self-segregation at times in the classrooms, in their leisure moments, and in their extracurricular activities.   . . . .   na   1   2   3   4

4. The school is aware of the specific learning conditions in those schools previously attended by its students.   . . . .   na   1   2   3   4

5. The school has attempted to eliminate the negative effects on pluralistic education of formal tracking in student placement.   . . . . . .   na   1   2   3   4

6. The school has sought to reduce the negative effects on pluralistic education of informal tracking.
   . . . .   na   1   2   3   4

7. The only courses in the school for which prerequisites have been established are those of a strictly sequential nature, such as French I and II.   . .   na   1   2   3   4

8. Concern is given to having classes fully representative of the racial-ethnic, cultural diversity of the student body.   . . . .   na   1   2   3   4

9. Lunchroom facilities are organized so as to promote the free association of all students.   . .   na   1   2   3   4

Evaluations

a) To what degree does the organization of the school provide a total experience promotive of multicultural-multiracial education?   . . . .   na   1   2   3   4

b) To what extent do the grouping, class scheduling, and student assignment policies and procedures in the school promote multicultural-multiracial interaction? . . . . na 1 2 3 4

c) To what extent are the published policies of the board relating to multicultural-multiracial education observed in this school? . . . . na 1 2 3 4

Comments

The Educational Program

A. The Formal Curriculum

Checklist

1. The English curriculum includes the writings and works of a wide range of ethnic groups.   . . . na 1 2 3 4
2. The social studies curriculum purposely has been revised to include the historic, cultural, and intellectual contributions of American Indians, Blacks, Asians, Spanish-speaking people, etc.   . . . na 1 2 3 4
3. Special courses are provided in a broad spectrum of ethnic studies.   . . . . na 1 2 3 4
4. All students are encouraged to take special courses in ethnic studies.   . . . . na 1 2 3 4
5. Special help in basic skills is provided so that all students may succeed in all curriculum areas.   . na 1 2 3 4
6. All courses are readily available to students from all ethnic groups.   . . . . na 1 2 3 4
7. The school's curriculum provides genuine options for nonwhite students to pursue education beyond high school.   . . . . na 1 2 3 4
8. The school's curriculum provides worthwhile options for those non-White students who will enter the work force upon graduation from high school.
   . . . . na 1 2 3 4
9. Where pertinent, the content in all courses includes a focus on multicultural-multiracial education.   . . . . na 1 2 3 4

Supplementary Data

1. Describe the formal curriculum for the study of multiethnic and multiracial history and culture.

2. Explain in what other ways the curriculum facilitates multicultural understandings.

3. Describe how the curriculum supports equal power, prestige, and access to a full life in a pluralistic society for non-White students.

4. Describe the efforts made within the last two years to make the curriculum more pertinent to the needs and requirements of non-White students.

Evaluations

a) To what degree does the school's formal curriculum promote multicultural-multiracial education? . . . . na 1 2 3 4

b) To what extent is the school preparing every one of its students for a productive life in the pluralistic society of America? . . . . na 1 2 3 4

c) To what extent does concern for multicultural-multiracial education permeate the entire school program? . . . . na 1 2 3 4

d) To what extent are appropriate programs and teaching materials being developed for ethnic studies? . . . . na 1 2 3 4

Comments

B. Learning Materials

Checklist

1. There is in the school's professional library a good collection of multicultural-multiracial materials. . . . .   na 1 2 3 4
2. There are in the media center current and pertinent books and other printed materials written by members of non-White groups. . . . .   na 1 2 3 4
3. There are in the media center nonprinted materials on nonwhite groups and diverse cultures.   na 1 2 3 4
4. The materials on multicultural-multiracial matters in the media center are readily accessible to all students. . . . .   na 1 2 3 4
5. Factual materials in the library have been evaluated for accuracy and authenticity as far as multicultural-multiracial concepts are concerned.   na 1 2 3 4
6. Textbooks are carefully selected for their equitable treatment of non-White and ethnic minority groups. . . . .   na 1 2 3 4
7. Teaching materials for multicultural-multiracial education are available in a range of interest levels for students. . . . .   na 1 2 3 4
8. Multicultural-multiracial teaching materials are provided at varying levels of difficulty. . .   na 1 2 3 4
9. Curriculum materials are judged on their coverage and treatment of nonwhite group contributions, as well as on other criteria. . . . .   na 1 2 3 4
10. Curriculum materials are continually being reviewed in relation to their impact on multicultural-multiracial relationships. . . . . .   na 1 2 3 4
11. No student is denied the learning materials he or she needs because of his or her inability to pay fees or charges. . . . .   na 1 2 3 4

Evaluations

a) To what extent do the learning materials available to students contribute to support the school's efforts towards multicultural-multiracial education? . . . .   na 1 2 3 4
b) To what extent do the teaching materials available to teachers contribute to and support the school's efforts towards multicultural-multiracial education? . . . .   na 1 2 3 4

Comments

C. Special Education

NOTE: Special education is generally accepted to mean education designed for and avaiable to handicapped children and youth whose educational needs are different in part from those of most of their peers.

Checklist

1. The special education program is an integral part of the instructional program and operates on a nondiscriminatory basis. . . . . na 1 2 3 4
2. Students are placed in programs for the mentally handicapped or for the mentally disturbed on the basis of learning or behavioral defficiencies alone, and not because of racially, socially, or culturally conditioned factors. . . . . na 1 2 3 4
3. The special education staff is integrated racially and ethnically. . . . . na 1 2 3 4
4. Students are provided special supportive services on an integrated basis, in accordance with individual needs. . . . . na 1 2 3 4
5. In referring its handicapped students to supporting lay and professional groups, the school insists that all its students be treated equally. . . . na 1 2 3 4
6. Multicultural multiracial programs are fully available to special education students. . . . na 1 2 3 4
7. Handicapped students, regardless of race or ethnic background, are encouraged to seek the highest levels of education and or employment for which they are suited. . . . . na 1 2 3 4

Index